U0948240

亞洲與世界

ASIA AND THE WORLD

第2辑

主编 李雪涛 〔日〕沈国威

社会科学文献出版社
SOCIAL SCIENCES ACADEMIC PRESS (CHINA)

主办单位： 北京外国语大学

目　录

东方与世界的互动研究

亚洲宗教研究

东西语言接触史研究

东方与世界的互动研究 >>>

承德历史的全球史解读*

李雪涛**

摘　要

作为一个重要政治中心，承德在清代历史上有着举足轻重的地位。本文作者认为，承德史的研究应当在充分利用汉、满、蒙、藏等语言史料的基础之上，同时运用近代以来世界语境下对承德历史、人文的记载和研究成就，用这些外在观察的记录来补充内部史料的不足，只有这样才能呈现承德在清帝国中多面、立体、丰满的历史面貌。本文提出用一种中心—边缘的研究视角，在广阔的相互关系情境中来考察参与清代历史建构的几方之间的互动关系，并确定承德在其中所扮演的角色。

关键词

承德/热河　全球史　清史

一

自晚明以降，中国历史的写作就不再局限于中文的范围之内了。语言是一种手段，唯有多语言的史料，才可能支持多种历史世界、多种秩序的存在。传统的清史研究，由于史料语言的单一性导致过分依赖汉语史料。完全使用汉语的史料来建构清朝的历史，所揭示的只是汉人眼中的清朝。在充分利用满蒙藏等语言史料的基础之上，同时注意近代以来世界语境下

* 本文系作者为“热河/承德历史文集译丛”撰写的“总序”，收入本书时做了部分修改。该丛书中的部分图书已由社会科学文献出版社（北京）于2019年出版。

** 李雪涛，北京外国语大学历史学院教授。

对承德历史、人文的记载，通过这些外在观察的记录来补充内部史料的不足，只有这样才能呈现出承德在清帝国中多面、立体、丰满的历史面貌。多语言的史料和研究成果，是理解承德作为一个多民族帝国政治中心的前提。

1492年哥伦布（Christopher Columbus, 1451－1506）发现美洲大陆，六年后的1498年，达·伽马（Vasco da Gama, 1469－1524）绕过好望角进入印度洋和太平洋水域，标志着世界发生了根本性的改变，世界历史从此进入了一个崭新的时代。一个半世纪后的1644年清军入关，此时全球历史的帷幕已经拉开，继葡萄牙、西班牙之后，荷兰也逐渐开始称霸世界。清朝从一开始就与世界建立了联系：顺治皇帝一直尊称耶稣会士汤若望（Johann Adam Schall von Bell, 1592－1666）为"玛法"。顺治帝临终议立嗣皇，也曾征求汤若望的意见，可见他们之间的亲密程度。[①] 康熙与白晋（Joachim Bouvet, 1656－1730）、张诚（Jean－François Gerbillon, 1654－1707）等国王数学家之间的关系更是密切，除了跟他们学习西学之外，也让王致诚（Jean Attiret, 1702－1768）、郎世宁（Giuseppe Castiglione, 1688－1766）等到避暑山庄作画。清朝的皇帝从一开始就乐于与世界接触。

18世纪初康熙在热河修建热河行宫，标志着承德进入了一个新的发展时期。雍正元年（1723）设热河厅，十年后，雍正取"承受先祖德泽"之义，罢热河厅设承德直隶州，这是"承德"名称的来源。乾隆六年（1741），乾隆开始临幸避暑山庄，承德开始进入繁荣期。三百年来，承德是中国统一的多民族国家发展的历史见证，也是清代第二政治中心，特别是与边疆民族相关的很多事务都是在承德的避暑山庄处理的。乾隆年间诸如安置达什达瓦部（1744，1759），平阿睦尔撒纳（1755），接见率领本部17万人东迁的渥巴锡（1771），会见率领甘丹、哲蚌、色拉三大寺堪布喇嘛前来祝寿的六世班禅喇嘛（1780），接受朝鲜的贺寿使团的朝觐（1780），接见马戛尔尼使团（1793）等等盛大的事件都发生在避暑山庄。第二次鸦片战争后，《北京条约》和《天津条约》都是在避暑山庄获得咸丰皇帝的批准而签订的，咸丰后来也因企图重新扭转内外交困的被动局面而开启洋务

① 〔法〕费赖之：《在华耶稣会士列传及书目》，冯承钧译，中华书局，1995，第174、177－178页。

运动。可惜的是，1861 年 31 岁的咸丰皇帝病死在避暑山庄。晚清至民国，无数国外的探险家、外交人士、传教士到过承德和热河地区。1933 年日本关东军占领承德，从而使得这一地区成为伪满洲国的一部分。这一阶段涌现了大量的有关承德的记录，除了文字方面的描述外，很多建筑学家、艺术史家、摄影爱好者也留下了数量众多的照片。

1793 年，马戛尔尼使团（The Macartney Mission）在承德觐见乾隆，之后提出了开埠、占地、减税、驻使等要求，特别是要求准许英国商人像俄国商人一样在北京设立货栈。乾隆认为，“天朝物产丰盈，无所不有，原不籍外夷货物，以通有无”。[①] 按照西方的传统，《罗马法》根据“万民法”的原则规定贸易是开放的（Commercium iure gentium commune esse debet.，*Dig.* 1，1，5）。因此，马戛尔尼理所当然地认为，没有谁可以垄断贸易，这也不是个别人的特权。实际上，按照贡德·弗兰克（Andre Gunder Frank，1929－2005）的观点，18 世纪美洲白银的产量约为 7.4 万吨，其中的 5.2 万吨（占产量的 70%）运往了欧洲，而这 70% 中的 40%，约 2 万吨运往了亚洲。另外留在美洲本土的白银约有 3000 吨经马尼拉运抵中国。按照他的计算，如果加上日本和其他地区零星生产的白银，全球白银产量的一半最终抵达亚洲，尤其是中国和印度。[②] 也就是说，当时乾隆皇帝完全看不见的全球化经济之手，已经在推动世界经济与中国经济的融合了。

二

多年前北京外国语大学提出：如果说北外以往几十年的使命是将世界介绍给中国的话，那么从现在开始北外的新使命是将中国介绍给世界。我们认为，这两者并非对立，而理应是同步进行的，所谓“全球化”，既包括“世界走向中国”，也包括“中国走向世界”。中国应当不断地从世界文明中汲取养分，即便是有关中国的学术研究，也应当不断引进国外的最新研究

① 见魏源《海国图志》（光绪平庆泾固道署重刊）卷七十七“乾隆五十八年敕谕后一道”。另见，另见《上谕档》，转译自秦国经、高换婷《乾隆皇帝与马戛尔尼——英国首次遣使访华实录》，紫禁城出版社，1998，第 148 页。

② 〔德〕贡德·弗兰克：《北银资本：重视经济全球化中的东方》，刘北成译，中央编译出版社，2008，第 6 页。

成就。

面对20世纪90年代以来不断引进海外汉学的各种理论的现状，有学者不无担忧地提出：

> 一旦大规模地引进作为完整系统的汉学……它有可能直接触及和瓦解原有文明共同体的自我理解，使国人在一系列悖反的影响中丧失自我认同的最后基础……一旦丧失阅读和思考的主动性，陷入别人的话语场中而无力自拔，就有可能被别人特有的问题意识所覆盖，乃至从此难以名状自己的切身体验，暴露出文化分析的失语和学术洞察的失明。①

实际上大可不必有这样的担心。即便你不知道，这些研究和理论依然存在。面对天主教和西洋历可能会对中国传统伦理道德造成的巨大影响，杨光先（1597－1669）在涉及儒家名教方面的问题时，决不妥协，其言辞之激烈，在当时是绝无仅有的。按照杨光先的逻辑，作为技术层面的中国历法如果失去地位的话，那么随之而来的将是“道”层面的天崩地裂。从杨光先所处历史时代的角度，我们当然可以设身处地地体会到知识分子在面对中国传统可能瓦解时痛苦而复杂的心态。但这并不意味着，传教士所传来的西方天文学知识就不存在，天圆地方的理论可以在中国一直传下去。

在德语中“宗教批判”（Religionskritik）是康德的弟子蒂夫特伦克（Johann Heinrich Tieftrunk，1760－1837）在康德思想的影响下，于1790年在《试论对宗教及所有宗教教义的批判》中提出的概念。② 蒂夫特伦克主张通过“宗教批判”来建立一个“符合理性的宗教”，反对宗教的“错误与狂热”。对于宗教而言，宗教批判是其赖以存在和发展的动力，这一点在宗教史中一再被证明。任何一种宗教一旦成为唯我独尊者，就标志着其式微的开始。大部分有关宗教的重要理论建构都是面对攻击时的回应。明末的际明禅师在论述当时天主教对佛教的冲击时写道：

① 刘东：《阅读中国序》，见〔美〕何伟亚《怀柔远人：马嘎尔尼使华的中英礼仪冲突》，邓常春译，社会科学文献出版社，2002，第2页。

② Johann Heinrich Tieftrunk, *Versuch einer Kritik der Religion und aller religiösen Dogmatik*, 1790.

若谓彼攻佛教，佛教实非彼所能破。且今时释子，有名无义者多，藉此外难以警悚之，未必非佛法之幸也。刀不磨不利，钟不击不鸣，三武灭僧而佛法益盛，山衲且拭目俟之矣！（《复钟振之居士书》）

际明是在收到钟始声（字振之，1599－1665）的《天学初征》一书后，在回信中提出自己的观点的。钟始声后来从憨山德清的弟子雪岭剃度，法号智旭，时人称之为“蕅益智旭”，编有批判天主教的《辟邪集》（1643）。现代比较宗教学研究指出：任何一种宗教都不是真理大全本身，只有各宗教间相互论战、批判，才能使宗教自身得以不断完善。实际上，此类的批判绝不仅限于宗教。一个缺乏正常的批判的社会，也不可能健康地发展。

尽管海外人士对承德的记载和研究的对象与中国学者相同，但透过他们的视角和方法，使得不论是作为传统资源的中国园林建筑，还是作为多民族帝国的史实，都得到了新的理论化阐释，从而产生了新观念、新思想。

对于有关中国的著作的译介，我们既要关注他者的视角、他者的理论，更要关注自我与他者的互动，以及由这种互动所产生的新成果。从另外一个方面来讲，自我身份的确定，一定是通过了解他者对自我的解读，才能得以实现。以《怀柔远人》（*Cherishing Men From Afar*, 1995）而名声大噪的美国历史学家何伟亚（James L. Hevia）对于所谓的“局内”和“局外”的划分也有自己的看法。他认为“生在某一国并说那一国的语言并不意味着对当地之过去有着特许的（先天）接近能力”。生于斯长于斯的人要理解当地之过去“仍需转译和诠释，而两者都要求心通意会（empathy）与想象力”。[①] 也就是说，所谓局内人与传统的天然联系，以及局外人与传统的“断裂”实际上只不过是一种以往的想象而已。实际上，就文化的范围来看，他者是一种理想视角，因为只有在他者文化的眼中，异域文化才能更全面和彻底地予以展现，并且在他者与自我的对话基础之上更好地理解他者和自身。

海外承德研究使我们能够真正摆脱所谓的华夷之辨，超越汉族中心视

① 罗志田：《译序》，见〔美〕何伟亚《怀柔远人：马嘎尔尼使华的中英礼仪冲突》，邓常春译，社会科学文献出版社，2002，第12页。

角，即认为“先进”的汉文化同化了其他满蒙藏等“落后”族群的观点，从而用一种中心－边缘的比较视角，在广阔的相互关系情境中考察参与清代历史建构的几方之间的互动关系。只有这样，我们才能真正理解清代以来所形成的中国历史特殊性的一面。

三

据不完全统计，有关热河（承德）的记述和研究著作，仅日文的就有百余种，文章更是数不胜数。在西方世界，随着新清史的一些观点不断受到更多学者的关注，以承德为中心的清史研究的最新成果也不断涌现。早期的传教士、外交人士、探险家、记者纷纷来到承德，他们回去之后写了大量的东西，到目前为止翻译成中文的仅是很少的一部分。这些记载固然有一定的时代性、局限性，但无论如何这些有关承德不同时期的描述都是特别珍贵的历史文献。如果说清朝与之前的朝代有什么最大不同的话，可以说，清朝自始至终都与世界保持着联系。而承德在当时的中外关系中扮演着非常重要的角色。正因如此，如果我们不了解世界的大背景，就很难解释清楚很多清代的问题，当然就更不会明白发生在承德的一些历史事件的前因后果了。

本套译丛选择了以往没有翻译的八部重要外文著作。

承德，在清代作为北京之外的第二政治中心，从异域的视角来看待和研究又是怎样的？作为译丛的第一部，我们选编了《海外承德历史读本》，以期以他者的视角对承德历史有一个概览。

德国汉学家福兰阁（Otto Franke，1863－1946）的《热河纪述》[①]（《对直隶省热河地区的描述》）是一部研究承德历史的著作，也描述了作者1890年的热河之行以及1896年他对整个东蒙古地区的实地考察。德国建筑师鲍希曼（Ersnt Boerschmann，1873－1949）可以说是最早且最为全面系统地研究中国建筑的西方学者。在1907年5月至6月的三周时间里，鲍希曼对承

① 1933年王光祈在翻译海尼士（Erich Haenisch，1880－1966）的文章中就介绍过这部专著：“对于地理一学，工作尚嫌太少……迄至今日止，计有两种模范工作，可以称述：一为佛郎克所著之《热河纪述》……”见海尼士著，王光祈译《近五十年来德国之汉学》，载李雪涛编《民国时期的德国汉学：文献与研究》，外语教学与研究出版社，2013，第28页。

德地区的建筑进行了极其细致的考察，拍摄图片图像近240张，绘制了一些建筑测绘图，并且制作、搜集了大量寺庙的碑石拓片。正是由于其在自己有关中国建筑的著作中所使用的照片、测绘图的专业性，使西方世界的读者渐渐以科学的方式来认知中国建筑。《图像与历史：鲍希曼与承德建筑的考察和研究》以鲍希曼的照片和测绘图为主，对照当时一些其他的照片，对鲍希曼的承德建筑研究做了总结。

1933年日本侵占承德后，承德成为伪满洲国的一部分。之后东京大学教授、日本著名建筑史学者关野贞（1868－1935）率考察团队进入该地区，在关东军、驻“满”使领馆和满铁的支持下，对热河行宫进行了大规模的调查，共拍摄了2000余幅照片。关野贞当时具体负责摄影和资料的搜集，他的助手竹岛卓一（1901－1992）和荒木清三（1884－1933）负责测绘，荒木曾经设计过北京的日本大使馆正门。之后出版了署名为关野贞和竹岛卓一的四卷本《热河》图集。[①] 由于作者是研究中国建筑史的著名学者，这部四卷本的图集对20世纪30年代的承德建筑进行了非常细致的学术梳理。有些当时还存在的建筑，如清音阁、碧峰寺、珠源寺、罗汉堂等今已无存，因此这些照片弥足珍贵。自1936年开始，五十岚牧太（1898－?）用了四年的时间在热河调查古建筑，同时也特别关注藏传佛教艺术，他于1942年出版了《热河古迹与西藏艺术》一书。[②] 这本书收录照片279幅，测绘图18幅。本书中的大部分照片由毕业于米泽工业专科学校的高橋正拍摄。

日本有关承德的文献非常丰富，我们委托国际日本文化研究中心的刘建辉教授和宋琦女士为我们编译了包括关野贞、五十岚牧太著作在内的五种图书，从建筑史、艺术史、历史地理、旅行以及图像五个方面全面展示日本对承德的记载和研究。其中既包括日本学者有关承德的比较严肃的学术著作，也有一般性的介绍承德名胜古迹的图书和观光导游书，还有从政治角度宣传日军侵占承德的战争宣传品。这一切都需要我们以一种批判的眼光予以对待。翻译这些著作并非目的，我们真正希望看到的是有关承德与清史研究的蓬勃开展。即便是日占时期有关承德一般性的介绍文字，对于今天的研究者了解当时的时代状况，依然是至关重要的历史文献。

---

① 《熱河》図版4冊本，文末刊，座右宝刊行会，1934（昭和九年）。

② 《熱河古蹟と西藏藝術》，洪洋社，1942（昭和十七年）。

以往有关海外承德历史著作的翻译，都是分散式进行的，或者是单本的图书，或者收录在其他的丛书之中。此次，我们尝试编辑“热河/承德历史文集译丛”，希望以此作为契机系统译介迄今依然不为国内学术界所知的海外有关热河/承德的重要历史文献。第一辑我们将陆续推出。虽然我们在挑选书稿时力求做到统筹兼顾，但受制于视野和学识的局限，难免会有疏漏之处，尚祈读者不吝指正。

附：“热河/承德历史文集译丛”第一辑出版书目

1. 李雪涛编《海外承德历史读本》
2. 福兰阁著，罗颖男译《热河纪述》
3. 赵娟编《图像与历史：鲍希曼与承德建筑的考察和研究》
4. 刘建辉、宋琦编《热河遗迹的建筑史意义——日本对承德建筑史的考察》
5. 刘建辉、宋琦编《热河古迹与西藏艺术——日本对承德艺术的查考》
6. 刘建辉、宋琦编《日本对热河事件的报道》
7. 刘建辉、宋琦编《热河之旅——日本对承德的旅游开发》
8. 刘建辉、宋琦编《日本图像中热河》

An Interpretation of the History of Chengde/Jehol from the Perspective of Global History

Li Xuetao

Abstract

As an important political center, Chengde/Jehol played a vital role in the history of Qing Dynasty. This paper suggests that the study of Chengde's history should not only make full use of the historical material recorded in Chinese, Manchu, Mongolian, Tibetan languages, but it should also exploit the accounts and research findings of Chengde's historical and cultural activities in the global context since the beginning of the modern time. The latter resources, as reports of outer observations, can in certain aspects make up for the insufficiency of the inner records. Only in this way can a diversified, solid and full image of Chengde in the map of Qing Empire become possible. This paper provides a comparative center - periphery perspective, in which the interactive relations of the relevant powers in the construction of the history of Qing dynasty are explored in a wide correlative context, so that the role of Chengde can be more precisely located.

Keywords

Chengde/Jehol　Global history　History of Qing Dynasty

Heraldry and "Material Culture" * During the Mamlūk Period in Egypt and Syria

Nur Güne**

Abstract

The goal of this project is to produce a critical work on Mamlūk heraldic devices in their social setting: the deliberate visual forms of self-representation of the Mamlūk elite, their role in the creation of a Mamlūk "popular" visual culture, the institutions behind their production and distribution, and their changing of meanings over time. In addition to critical analysis, a catalog, which includes representative examples of published and available non-published heraldic symbols from different media, produced throughout the Mamlūk era will also be included.

With the categorization, cataloging and analysis presented in this manner, it will be possible to make an initial classification of the coat of arms on the basis of art-historical principles, followed by a comparison of it with the designs and styles of other regions.

Keywords

Mamlūk Heraldry　Coats of Arms　Material Culture　Islamic Art History / Archaeology

---

* For a working definition of "material culture", see Hans Peter Hahn, *Materielle Kultur. Eine Einführung*, Berlin: Reimer (Ethnologische Paperbacks), 2005.

** Nur Güne, Ph. D., student at The University of Bonn, email: noezl@uni-bonn.de.

This is a very short abstract of a current written dissertation at the University of Bonn, which is funded by the DFG (German Research Foundation) .

This project explores the changing visual vocabulary of Mamlūk public art, and those elements that have came to epitomize the ways Mamlūks represented themselves: heraldic devices. The combination of blazons and titular inscriptions (used in a heraldic fashion) in decorative registers was the most immediately recognizable element on public buildings-defining the cityscape-and on objects used for official and public display and ceremony. The visual world thus created by Mamlūk inspired artists was saturated with such images. The Mamlūk sultans and their amirs took this imagery of political legitimacy beyond the cities to villages and the frontiers of their territories. Thus these symbols were the means of expressing the projection of state power in deeper levels of local society. ①

The primary method of analysis used in this study will be art history, but at the same time, we will also look at the archaeological (spatial) context and its reference to contemporary Arabic and Turkish literature.

Who are the Mamlūks, and What is Heraldry?

In simple terms, the Mamlūks were a dynasty of former military slaves who became a military aristocracy, and ruled much of the eastern Mediterranean from their capital in Cairo from 1250 – 1516. Their most notable military achievements were their ultimate victory over Crusader forces and the eventual dissolution of the Crusader states in the Holy Land, as well as bringing an end to the Mongol (Il Khanid) expansion to the west. These victories lent the regime political and religious clout in the Islamic world until the Ottoman conquests of the early 16th century.

The long reign of the Mamlūks (two and a half centuries) makes its conducive for studying the long-term changes in the devices that appeared on nearly every genre of portable object and building. The project, then, has a relevance that goes beyond that of Mamlūk studies, allowing a comparison to be done between it

① This was accomplished through the public display of such objects as parade gear, serving vessels used for public banquets (*simāṭ*), and ceremonial robes (*khilaᶜ*) given as gifts to local elite.

and the European heraldry of the medieval era. Through stylistic study, archaeological research, and textual analysis, this study determined whether the heraldic devices of Mamlūk art functioned as heraldry in a technical sense, began as such but developed into something else, or carried an entirely different meaning from that of their European counterparts. In addition to this, such a comparison has the potential to raise important questions about the differing natures of medieval society in both worlds.

Instead of heraldry, the following words are also commonly used in different contexts: coat of arms, blazon, emblem, embroidery, design, motif, symbol and others.

According to the Encyclopaedia Britannica Online, heraldry is defined as follows:

> "Heraldry [is] the science and the art that deal with the use, display, and regulation of hereditary symbols employed to distinguish individuals, armies, institutions, and corporations. Those symbols, which originated as identification devices on flags and shields, are called armorial bearings. "①

If you look for a translation of heraldry in the Encyclopedia of Islam you will find that itis commonly translated as "hilāl", "shiʿār" and "rank". All three words have several meanings and were used in several contexts. But as Mayer put it, "In the strict sense of the word, the technical term in Arabic is the word 'rank'"②

Nasser Rabbat said the word "rank" (plural "runuk") comes from the Persian word "reng" meaning "color" or "tincture" and he continues explaining that the "emblems were stylized representations of objects and were most of the time displayed in a circle, which like its European counterpart seems to have been de-

① Frederick Hogarth and Leslie Gilbert Pine, "Heraldry", in Encyclopædia Britannica, <https://www.britannica.com/topic/heraldry> Date published online: 28 September 2018. Consulted online on 16 October 2018.

② Leo Ary Mayer, *Saracenic Heraldry, A Survey*, Oxford: Clarendon Press, 1933, p. 26.

rived from a shield of a soldier. "[1]

I prefer also to use "rank" (plural "runuk"), European sources sometimes use the plural form of the word, i. e. "ranks", but often it needs to use the German or Norman/English or French heraldic terms.

Runuk appear on buildings like mosques, madrasas, mausoleums, doorways, cenotaphs, as well as portable glass objects (mosque lamps, flasks, rose water sprinklers, bottles and vases, and others.), metal objects (candlesticks, bowls, basins, pen boxes, ink-pots, helmets and swords, coins, and others), textiles (horse blankets, saddlecloths and other horse trappings, tents, embroideries, flags and banners, and others), books covers, portraits, playing cards, and many other "everday" items. Depending on the material, they were either carved, painted, engraved, embossed, embroidered or dyed. But the abundance of material evidence is not confirmed by contemporary textual evidence. [2]

State of Research

Because of the active production of the kilns of Fustat and the vast quantities of emblazoned pottery found in Cairo as a result, the earliest scholarly work conducted on Mamlūk blazons focused on ceramics, namely sgraffitos and slip-painted wares. The first of these studies was done by Daniel Fouquet's Contribution á l'étude de la céramique orientale (Cairo, 1900)[3], now well over a century old. The stylistic analysis of heraldry on Egyptian earthen wares continued with the American Research Center in Egypt's excavations of Fustat (Scanlon, 1980)[4]. This was followed by two important studies by Leo Ary Mayer, namely *Saracenic*

① Nasser Rabbat, "Rank", in *Encyclopaedia of Islam*, *Second Edition*, Edited by P. Bearman, T. Bianquis, C. E. Bosworth, E. van Donzel, and W. P. Heinrichs, <http://dx. doi. org/10. 1163/1573 -3912_islam_SIM_6221> First published online: 2012. Consulted online on 16 October, 2018.

② Nasser Rabbat, "Rank", 2012.

③ Daniel Fouquet, 1900.

④ Georg T. Scanlon, 1980.

Heraldry: *A Survey*, originally published in 1933①, and his *Mamlūk Costume* (1952)②, which documents the appearance of blazons on textiles of that period. These studies remain today as key reference works for Mamlūk heraldic designs, though they are far from comprehensive in their coverage of blazon forms.

Attention then quickly turns to architecture. The central work in this field is Michael Meinecke's 1972 monography *Zur Mamlūkischen Heraldik*. Of the more than 220 registered Mamlūk-era buildings in Cairo, he recorded more than 90 coats of arms and emblems, 30 of which were published for the first time. He suggested that originally all Mamlūk buildings were marked by coats of arms. ③ Most recent studies of Mamlūk architecture include some discussion of heraldic devices, as they appear on building façades; notable in this sense is the work of Doris Behrens-Abouseif④ and Nasser Rabbat. ⑤

There are few scholarly studies of blazons in other media. *Outside of Mayer's Mamlūk Costume*, emblazoned textiles have not been a subject of study (Bethany J. Walker's Mamlūk Studies Review article on silks and embroideries is a notable exception⑥). As for metalwork, there is a handful of articles on well-known works of art in public collections ("Wade Cup in the Cleveland Art Museum" in 1957,⑦ or alternatively, Whelan's⑧ important study of a corpus of inlaid vessels in 1988) which include subsidiary discussions of blazons as part of the surface decoration. Because of their wide circulation and strictly controlled production, coinage is an important category of emblazoned objects for exploring the ways heraldic images of authority were created (in conjunction with inscriptions) and penetrated local society. Their potential for research results, however, has not been fully realized. In a series of articles (Balog 1964 and 1977), the numismatist Balog has

① Leo Ary Mayer, 1933.

② Leo Ary Mayer, 1952.

③ Michael Meinecke, 1972.

④ Doris Behrens-Abouseif, 2012.

⑤ Nasser Rabbat, 2010.

⑥ Bethany J. Walker, 2000.

⑦ Richard Ettinghausen, 1957.

⑧ Estelle Whelan, 1988.

discussed in detail the single elements of heraldic devices on coins, such as the bar (fesse), napkin (buqja), lion (lion passant), cup (hanab), fleurs-de-lis, and some amiral blazons. ① Stefan Heidemann's studies on this topic from the field of numismatics (namely 1993)② and Warren Schulz discourses in Bonn have been important contributions in this regard.

These art historical works are largely descriptive and rely on stylistic analysis of surface decorations. They do not address meaning, intention, or reception, and do not aim at social-historical interpretation. Mamlūk blazons, however, have recently attracted the attention of archaeologists working in Greater Syria, whose scholarship focuses on the organization of production and distributional patterns of emblazoned pottery recovered from systematic excavations (Walker③ 1998, 2004, 2010 and 2013; Walker and LaBianca 2003④; Milwright 1997/98⑤). Walker's work has made inroads into a cultural interpretation of such pottery, in combination with critical readings of contemporary Arabic texts (administrative manuals, chronicles, and geographical treatises).

Arabic and Turkish primary sources will be consulted in this study, in an effort to reconstruct meaning (intention of the patron and visual and cultural reception by the viewer/consumer) from the heraldic patterns.

In Qalqashandī's Ṣubḥ al-aᶜshā, we read that every amir owned a coat-of-arms possessed by their own preferences in different colors and field divisions. These could adorn his buildings, such as palaces, but also the sugar factories, grain chambers, and other such industrial buildings under amiral control, as well as the covers (qumaš) of his horses and camels. The 14th century Egyptian secretary also noted that these devices were found in combination with the gold-embroidered monogram (laqab) of the Sultan on his robes. ⑥

① Paul Balog, 1964; Paul Balog, 1977.

② Stefan Heidemann, 1993.

③ Bethany J. Walker, 1998, 2004, 2010, 2013.

④ Bethany J. Walker and Øystein S. Labianca, 2003.

⑤ Marcus Milwright, 1997, 1998.

⑥ Cited after Leo Ary Mayer, 1933, Heraldry, p. 3; from him: Kitāb ṣubḥ al-aᶜshā fī sināᶜ at al-insha'li -l Qalqashandī, Ed. Cairo IV, p. 61: pp. 21 – 62: 5; cf. the translation of M. Gaudefroy-Demombynes: La Syrie a l'Époque de Mamlouqs, Paris, 1923.

Two and half centuries later, the Ottoman scholar Evliyā Çelebi, in his famous travelogue, describes for us the flags, inscriptions and some coats-of-arms on the architecture, some remains of which were quite old. Such texts give an impression of how the designs on buildings constructed in a much earlier era were interpreted and received by a public that no longer remembered the social or political context of these symbols.

From the Ayyūbid period there are a number of references to ranks given by Ibn Taghrībirdī①, Ibn al-Dawādārī②and Abu 'l-Fidā'③.

What is missing collectively from the art historical and archaeological literature to date are catalogues and cross-media analysis.

The System of Mamlūk Heraldic Designs

Weapons of Europeans were unique coats of arms. They served as an identifying feature in combat and tournaments and showed an individual's family origins. They mark the household, the family, and particularly the children, so that someone recognizes who they belong to.

The Mamlūks had a system of heraldry, which was almost unique in the Islamic world. But it was not used in the same way that the Europeans used it. At the beginning, only Sultans, amirs and high ranking people had heraldic devices.

These emblems which marked the bearer even after his death were not only reserved for the rulers. The ruler lent them, for example, to Mamlūks at their retirement from active military service or upon their promotion to officer's rank. Wives and daughters of the sultans were also able to inherit the blazons. ④ Over the course of the fourteenth century-during a period of intense changes in the political and economic spheres-these very symbols of Mamlūk authority and the exclusive privileges of Mamlūk rank were popularized and spread to objects of local production and consumption, such as household-produced embroideries and mass-produced earth-

① IBN TAGHRĪBIRDĪ, al-Manhal al-ṣāfī, Cairo, 1988, v, p. 296.

② IBN AL-DAWĀDĀRĪ, al-Durra al-dhakiyya fī akhbār al-dawla al-turkiyya, Cairo, 1971, pp. 56-57.

③ ABU 'L-FIDĀ', Kitāb al-Mukhtaṣar fī akhbār al-bashar, Beirut, 1979, vi, p. 49.

④ Michael Meinecke, 1972, p. 214.

en wares. Heraldic designs, which were formerly restricted to the officials and public spheres, were thus transferred to private and non-elite use. Heraldic inscriptions were broken into smaller elements and reconstituted in new and creative ways in "popular art" . By the term "popular art" I mean here objects produced for mass consumption, produced and distributed free from state control.

The adaptation of the motifs on everyday objects and household products (urban as well as rural) is an important starting point to consider the traditional categories of "elite art" "andpopular art" . The popularization of "militarized art" in this way parallels the development of vernacular literature and "popular" religion in the 14th century.

This is where the collection of Professor Bethany J. Walker in the labor in Bonn comes into play, namely ceramics, as the most immediate reflections of daily use, mass consumption, and changes in production.

The study, then, begins with a creation and stylistic analysis of a database for the most poignant representatives of this pottery on the popular level: the so-called Egyptian "barracks" sgraffito ware usually associated with Fustat productions and Syrian glazed relief ware. This work will consist largely of physical inspection and analysis of key archaeological and study collections. As a reference, it needs to compare the ceramics with well-known as well as unknown pieces in the museums and on architecture.

But because of spatial context (locations of the object used, and its association with other objects in those spaces) and patterns of distribution are critical to understanding the function and social value of portable and emblazoned objects, this project heavily references archaeological material, namely emblazed and inscribed pottery from the Citadel and village of Tall Hisban①, as well as field reports from archaeological projects throughout Egypt and Syria.

Understanding the archaeological contexts of "Mamlūk" and "popular" objects is critical in understanding the processes of physical, functional, and spatial transfer of these symbols. I will also examine Mamlūk-era texts, as appropriate,

① Project websites can be found at: http://www.mamluk.uni-bonn.de/islamic-archaeology and www.madabaplains.org/hisban.

for information on the administrative function of blazons and heraldic inscriptions, the institutions that produced objects with these designs, the socio-economic relations between garrisons and villages, and the local reception of public ceremonial.

On the level of art historical analysis, a systematic study of the designs themselves, their relationship with other decorative devices, and the kinds of vessels and buildings on which they appear suggests the following aspects about that the system of Mamlūk heraldic designs:

- It is closely connected with the history of rulers and offices
- It has a strong relation to the military
- It represents the striving for power and acquisition of prestige
- It physically projects power and makes visual claims to territory
- It is influenced by the charisma of the foreigner
- It is popular with the so-called elite, but eventually has influence on the popular level, acquiring new meaning in the process
- It can, on some level, be compared with European and Asian Heraldry
- It is subject to culturally bound notions of aesthetics and transfer processes
- It urges stylistic comparison with contemporary motifs and styles of other regions and previous dynasties
- It is also present in the form of portable coats-of-arms and flags, and is present beyond the territories under the sultan's control.

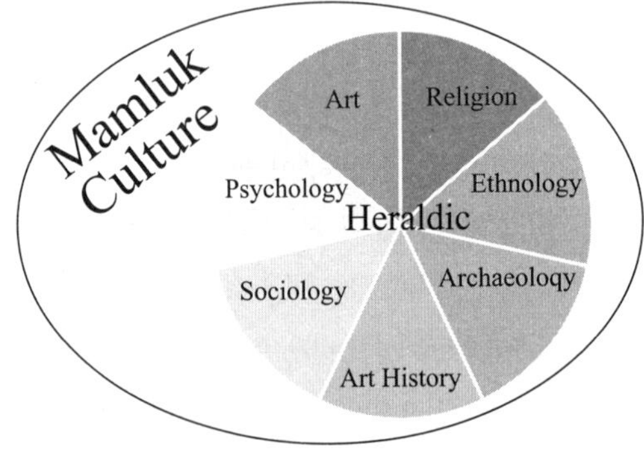

Figure 1 Disciplines①

① Figure 1: Drawing Nur Özdilmaç, 2018.

So far we can see heraldry is more than just a small picture on great media, and it touches subjects as art history, archaeology, religion, sociology, psychology and ethnology.

It also shows in a cultural way how visual symbols and decorative devices in art and architecture were understood by the public.

Characteristics of Mamlūk heraldry

Shapes and forms:

Mamlūk runuk come in varied shapes and forms. That said, the single most common form by far was *al-Da'ira*, the "Circle" or roundel, based on the round shields carried by so many Islamic men-at-arms. They are solid-colour or multi-coloured, freestanding or enclosed in round, pointed, or polygonal shields. ①

Muslim runuk usually consisted of the *ard* (field, or "ground"). They first appeared as single-element emblems. From the 14th century the emblazons developed into composite shields which were divided into three parts, called *shatfas* or *shatabs*, that means horizontal strips. The division of "checkly", "barry" and "bendy" are also presented, but they are rare.

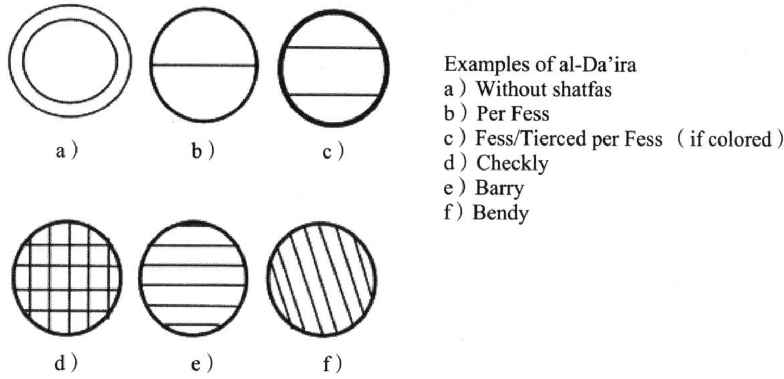

Figure 2 Given only some, but not the final examples of *al-Da'ira* ②

The representation of the rank was not limited to one shatfa, nor to a certain class of persons. In fact, it is possible to find the rank of a single person appearing

① Nasser Rabbat, "Rank", 2012.

② Figure 2: Drawing Nur Özdilma, 2018.

on different field shapes adorning the same building. ①

Tinctures (colours)

Colours dominate everything in the world. Everything in nature has its colour and seems to harmonize well with each other. Colours do not only affect the eyes of people but also their thoughts, feelings, senses and actions. It should also be noted that the word "rank" also means colour. The most used colours in Mamlūk heraldry are the following seven tinctures: The two metal colours gold/yellow and (or) white/silver (argent), plus the five colours of green (vert), blue (azur), red (gules), brown (brunâtre), black (sable), as well as self-coloured. That means the colour of the material on which the emblazon was placed has the colour of the material, i. e. runuk on stone are "stone-coloured", on metal are metal-coloured, etc.

Table 1 Tinktures②

Tinktures / Language							
German	Gelb / Gold	Weiß / Silber	Grün	Blau	Rot	Braun	Schwarz
Arabic	صفر/ ذهبي	ابيض / فضي	اخضر	أزرق	احمر	اللون البني	اسود
Türkish	Altın / Sarı	Beyaz / Gümüş	Yeşil	Mavi	Kırmızı	Kahve	Siyah
French	Or	Argent	Sinople	Azure	Gueules	Brunâtre	Sable
English	Or	Argent	Vert	Azur	Gules	Brunâtre	Sable

① David B. Appleton, "Islamic Heraldry: An Introduction", < http://www.appletonstudios.com/MamlukHeraldry2001.pdf. >, Consulted online on 16 October, 2018.

② Figure 3: Drawing Nur Özdilmaç, 2018.

Categories

unuk may be classified into several categories. ①

(1) Familia to European and / or Asian heralds

(2) Symbols of office / Symbols of Islamic use

(3) Tamghas / Tribal marks / Ornaments

(4) Inscriptions②

Those runuk which can be seen that are similar to European or Asian heralds are: the lion, the eagle (or the falcon), fleur-de-lis, the crescent, and rarely, the bend.

Although animal motifs were unusual, and the only animals that appear in heraldry are the lion (or the panther), the eagle (or the falcon), and occasionally the horse passant, we have many well-preserved examples for the first two motifs with different versions. According to Nasser Rabbat is the "earliest firmly established rank", the so-called lion or panther of Sultan alẒāhir Baybars (reg. 658 – 76 /1260 – 77); or the eagle as a heraldic symbol of Ṣalāḥ al-Dīn (Saladin). ③ But the attributes are disputed by archaeologists, who also do not count the horse as a rank, believing it is only the bearer of another charge.

Some controversy exists regarding the fleur-de-lis and the crescent and their meaning. The Islamic fleur-de-lis is what we think of as a "true" fleur-de-lis, but no one seems to be sure how it came into Muslim heraldry or what it means. ④

The category of the symbols of the office is the largest category of runuk. These runuk are purely Islamic charges, and often relate directly to the office which the bearer held when elevated to the rank of amir.

That category of runuk are charges which have only Islamic use and meaning, but according some researchers, they are not symbols of the office. The most com-

---

① This category is currently the subject of my research and not yet completed.

② This project would not work on inscriptions.

③ Nasser Rabbat, "Rank", 2012.

④ I was tempted to say it was adopted from the Europeans, but there is also no evidence to indicate that.

mon of this category are the *sarawil al-futuwwa*, the "trousers of nobility". No clear consensus has been (nor perhaps can be) achieved as to just what exactly these represent, either literally or figuratively. An argument has been made recently that they are actually drinking horns. However, much of the argument is based upon little more than speculation, and it has not been widely accepted. In any case, the "trousers of nobility" are a very common charge, and always appear in pairs, frequently "framing" another charge as in the example shown here. ①

(Here I have my own view, which I hope to publish soon in my thesis.)

Writing in the early 14th century, Abu 'l-Fidāʾ records that the Secretary's emblem is the pen-box, the Armor-bearer's the bow, the Superintendent of Stores'the ewer, the Master of the Robes'the napkin, the Marshal's the horseshoe, and the Jawish a golden saddle. ②

Figure 3 Some Examples of Runuk of the Offices③

① David Appleton, 2001.

② ABU 'L-FIDĀʾ, Kitāb al-Mukhtaṣar fī akhbār al-bashar, Beirut, 1979; Ian HEATH, < http://www.warfare.meximas.com/WRG/Crusades-64-Saracen_Heraldry.htm >, Consulted online on 16 October, 2018.

③ Figure 4: Drawing Nur Özdilmaç, 2018.

Some other motifs represented Tamghas, the tribal symbols, were used as brands by many Asiatic peoples and introduced into the Near East by Turkish Mamlūks. Small ornaments, arabesques, scrolls and flowers appear profusely scattered among almost all the media. ①Beside the true ornaments, inscriptions are also common and often used.

Conclusion

The goal of this project is to produce a critical work on Mamlūk heraldic devices in their social setting: as deliberate visual forms of self-representation of the Mamlūk elite, their role in the creation of a Mamlūk "popular" visual culture, the institutions behind their production and distribution, and their change of meaning over time. It will be accompanied by a (nearly ready) catalogue, which includes representative examples of published and available non-published heraldic symbols from different media, produced throughout the Mamlūk era.

It is my hope that this Islamic Art History work can serve as a bridge between Islamic Archeology, Mamlūk studies and the larger fields of Islamic Studies, and Central Asian Studies. ②

References

ABU 'L-FIDā᾽, Kitāb al-Mukhtaṣar fī akhbār al-bashar, Beirut, 1979.

Paul Balog, *The Coinage of the Mamlūk Sultans of Egypt and Syria*, New York: The American Numismatic Society, 1964.

Paul Balog, *New Considerations on Mamlūk Heraldry*, The American Numismatic Society Museum Notes, 1977.

Doris Behrens-Abouseif, *The Arts of the Mamlūks in Egypt and Syria - Evolution and Impact*, Göttingen: V&R unipress, 2012.

Richard Ettinghausen, *The "Wade Cup" in the Cleveland Museum of Art, Its Origin and Decorations*, Ars Orientalis 2, 1957.

① Paul Balog, <http://numismatics.org/digitallibrary/ark: /53695/nnan55713>, Consulted online on 16 October, 2018.

② This work is in progress and therefore changes are reserved.

Daniel Fouquet, *Contribution à l'étude de la céramique orientale*, Cairo: Institut Égyptien, 1900.

Hans Peter Hahn, *Materielle Kultur. Eine Einführung*, Berlin: Reimer (Ethnologische Paperbacks), 2005.

Stefan Heidemann, *Coins as Works of Art: in Oriental Splendour*, Islamic Art from German Private Collections, ed. , C. -P. Haase, J. Kröger, and U. Lienert. Edition Temmen, 1993.

IBN AL-DAWĀDĀRĪ, al-Durra al-dhakiyya fi akhbār al-dawla al-turkiyya, Cairo, 1971.

IBN TAGHRĪBIRDĪ, al-Manhal alṣāfī, Cairo, 1988.

Leo Ary Mayer, *Saracenic Heraldry, A survey*, Oxford: Clarendon Press, 1933.

Leo Ary Mayer, *Mamlūk Costume. A Survey*, Genève: A. Kundig, 1952.

Michael Meinecke, *Zur Mamlūkischen Heraldik*, Mainz/Rhein: Philipp von Zabern, 1972.

Michael Meinecke, *Patterns of Stylistic Changes in Islamic Architecture: Local traditions versus migrating artists*, New York University Press, 1996.

Marcus Milwright, *The Cup of the Sāqī: Origins of an Emblem of the Mamlūk Khāṣṣakiyya*, ARAM, 1997/1998.

Nasser Rabbat, *Mamlūk History through Architecture. Monuments, culture and politics in medieval Egypt and Syria*, Tauris, 2010.

George T. Scanlon, *Fustat Expedition: Preliminary Report 1971*, 1980.

Bethany J. Walker, *The Ceramic Correlates of Decline in the Mamlūk Sultanate: An Analysis of Late Medieval Sgraffito Wares*, University of Toronto, 1998.

Bethany J. Walker, "The Social Implications of Textile Development in Fourteenth-Century Egypt", *Mamlūk Studies Review*, 2000.

Bethany J. Walker and Øystein S. Labianca, "The Islamic Qusur of Tall Hisban: Preliminary Report on the 1998 and 2001 Seasons", *Annual of the Department of Antiquities of Jordan*, 2003.

Bethany J. Walker, " Ceramic Evidence for Political Transformations in Early Mamlūk Egypt", *Mamlūk Studies Review*, 2004.

Bethany J. Walker, "From Ceramics to Social Theory: Reflections on Mamlūk Archaeology Today", *Mamlūk Studies Review*, 2010.

Bethany J. Walker, *What Can Archaeology Contribute to the New Mamlukology? Where Culture Studies and Social Theory Meet*, in Stephan Conermann (ed.); *Ubi sumus? Quo vademus: Mamlūk Studies-State of the Art*, Bonn University Press, 2013.

Estelle Whelan, *Representations of the Khāṣṣakiyya and the Origins of Mamlūk Emblems*,

Pennsylvania State University, 1988.

David Appleton, (B. Da'ud ibn Auda): "ISLAMIC HERALDRY, An Introduction", http://www.appletonstudios.com/MamlukHeraldry2001.pdf.

Frederick Hogarth and Leslie Gilbert Pine, "Heraldry" in Encyclopædia Britannica, inc. https://www.britannica.com/topic/heraldry. Date published online: 28 September 2018, Consulted online on 16 Oct. 16, 2018.

Nasser Rabbat, "Rank" in Encyclopaedia of Islam, Second Edition, Edited by: P. Bearman, Th. Bianquis, C. E. Bosworth, E. van Donzel, W. P. Heinrichs., http://dx.doi.org/10.1163/1573-3912_islam_SIM_6221. First published online: 2012. Consulted online on 16 Oct. 16, 2018.

Paul Balog: http://numismatics.org/digitallibrary/ark:/53695/nnan55713.

Ian Heath: http://www.warfare.meximas.com/WRG/Crusades-64-Saracen_Heraldry.htm.

Tell Hisban-Project websites can be found at: http://www.mamluk.uni-bonn.de/islamic-archaeology and www.madabaplains.org/hisban.

埃及和叙利亚马穆鲁克时期的纹章学和“物质文化”

努尔·兹迪尔玛

摘　要

本课题的目标是将马穆鲁克的纹章图案置于当时的社会背景进行研究，其中包括马穆鲁克精英有意表现自身形象的需要，纹章图案在创建马穆鲁克“流行”视觉文化中的作用，纹章图案产生和分配背后的体系，以及纹章随时代而变化的意义。课题研究将制作一份目录，包括整个马穆鲁克时代不同媒介上纹章符号的代表性示例，其中包括已公布及未公布的研究。

通过这样的分类、编目和分析，我们可以基于艺术史原则对族徽进行初步分类，并与其他地区（族徽）的设计和风格进行比较研究。

关键词

马穆鲁克　纹章学　物质文化　伊斯兰艺术史/考古学

The Study of Illustrations of *Robinson Crusoe* in Early Modern East Asia

Li Yun*

Abstract

The purpose of this study is to discover the features of the illustrations in *Robinson Crusoe* in early modern East Asia. A descriptive survey methodology was adopted to collect all the Japanese and Chinese versions that were printed in early modern Asian history. The results revealed a relationship between the Japanese and the Chinese versions. Based on the Japanese and Chinese versions of *Robinson Crusoe*, the survey shows: (a) the original of each Japanese or Chinese version, and (b) how the original *Robinson Crusoe* was rewritten as the other versions. The study findings may serve as a base for research on *Robinson Crusoe* in early modern East Asia.

Keywords

Illustrations *Robinson Crusoe* Cultural Interaction Translation

The Oldest Version of *Robinson Crusoe* Translated in East Asia

Since the 19th century, *Robinson Crusoe* has been translated into mainly two

* Li Yun, Ph. D. , student at Graduate School of East Asian Cultures Department, Kansai University, email: yunkinkle-lee@ hotmail. com.

East Asian's languages: Japanese and Chinese. According to my statistics, there are 26 Japanese versions and 7 Chinese versions which were completed before 1912[①]. The first translation of *Robinson Crusoe* in early modern East Asia was not published immediately at that time; it was initially translated by Kuroda Kikuro (黒田麴盧[②]) under the title, *Hyōkō kiji* (漂荒紀事), we can see that it was a handwritten work (Fig. 1: from left to right are the cover of *Hyōkō kiji*, the translator's note and first page of the text) . From that information, we can deduce that this version was translated from Dutch into a Japanese kanji and Katakana syllabary that differs somewhat from the modern writing system.

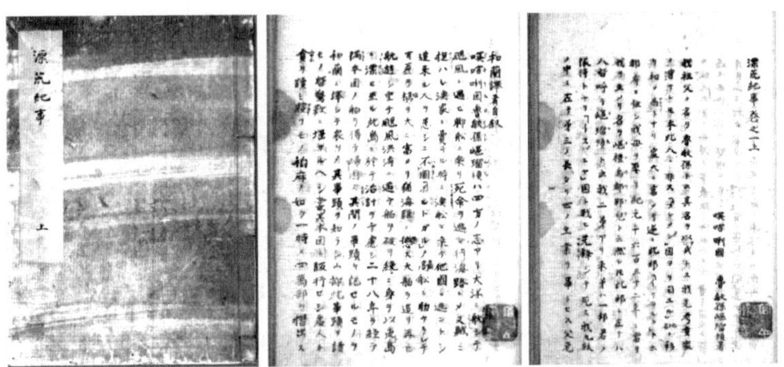

Figure 1 *Hyōkō kiji* (漂荒紀事)

In addition, this version was first published by the translator, Saitō Ryōan (斎藤了庵) as *ĒkokuRobinson zenden* (英國魯敏孫全伝) in 1872 (Fig. 2).

Comparing it with *Hyōkō kiji*, the title was changed, and the names of the translator and proofreader were added, but the content remained unchanged. In fact, this version was simply a copy of Kuroda's work. According to the research of Sugimoto[③]

① The year 1912 ushered in a new era for both China and Japan. In China, Chunghwa Minkuo (Republic of China, 1912 – 1949) replaced the Qing Dynasty, and in Japan, the Meiji period was replaced by Taishō, so in this paper, I have chosen 1912 as the final year of analysis.

② Kuroda Kikuro had the alternative first names of 行 and 行元. For more information on this topic, see: Kameda Jiro, 'Kuroda Kikuro no gyōseki oyobi sono chosho' (The Achievements of Kuroda Kikuro and His Works) in *Geibun* (芸文), Vol. 17, 1926.

③ Sugimoto Tsutomu, *Hyōkō Kiji* (shahon) no kentō-shoshiteki na ten o shu soshite (Study on the *Hyōkō Kiji*-centering Mainly on the Bibliographical Points) (Manuscript), *Waseda Paigaku Thoshokan Kiyo*, 1983, p. 26.

(1983), although details about Saitō Ryōan are unclear, this case is evidence that translation in the Meiji period was influenced by that in the Edo. This version was republished in 1883 under the title, *Ēkoku Robinson shima monogatari* (英國魯敏孫嶋物語, Fig. 3). This version survived for at least 30 years. It was influenced by Dutch Studies (Rangaku, 蘭学). Because it was handwritten, and there are no illustrations.

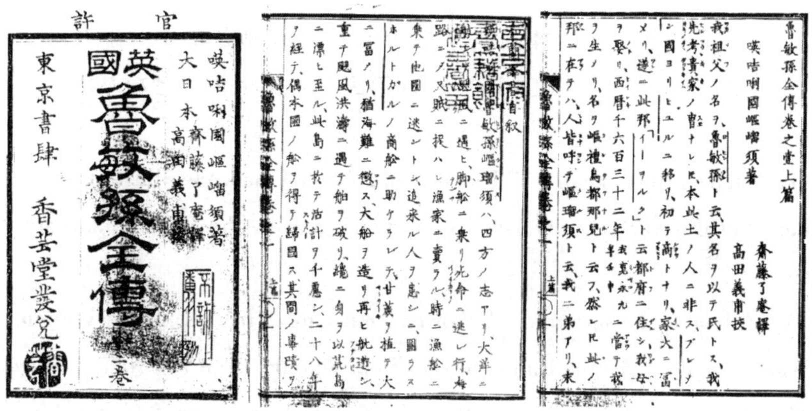

Figure 2 ***Ēkoku Robinson zenden*** **(英國魯敏孫全伝)**

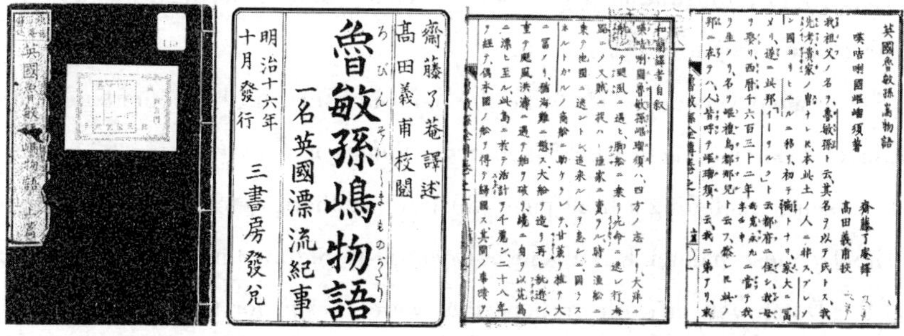

Figure 3 ***Ēkoku Robinson shima monogatari*** **(英國魯敏孫嶋物語)**

The Oldest Published Version of *Robinson Crusoe* Translated in East Asia

Another version was also translated from Dutch. It was translated by a Japanese named Yokoyama Yoshikiyo（横山由清）in 1857 with the title, *Robinsonhyōkō kiryaku*（魯敏遜漂行紀略, Fig. 4）. It was also the first published version of *Robinson Crusoe* in East Asia. In this version, Robinson Crusoe started to have an official image in East Asia through the illustrations, which were drawn by Kawakami Tōgai[①]（川上冬崖, Fig. 5）. On the right side of the page, it says:

> 原本一章ごとに挿画ありて所謂出像の稗史なり、今その一、二をここに出して、其他を略す、即第五章と第七章のとなり。

Translated, this means: "The original version has one illustration in each chapter, but this version only uses two of them, namely the fifth and seventh illustrations."

According to the foreword, Yokoyama must have read Kuroda's version. But Yokoyama used a different Dutch version from Kuroda. The research of Maeda Ai (1975) shows that Yokoyama got the job of translator in the Bansho Shirabesho（藩所調所）by way of introduction from the painter Kawakami (Ezu shirabeyaku, 絵図調役, illustration researcher). That is how Yokoyama was able to obtain the Dutch version to translate it.

The original version seems to be the one published in the Netherlands, under the title of *Beknopte Levensgeschiedenis van Robinson Crusoe* (Fig. 6). In this Dutch version, including a front page illustration, there were 26 illustrations in total. The Japanese painter Kawakami only chose to redraw three of them. Figure 7 shows the Dutch version's illustrations that were chosen for the Japanese version. Through a comparison of the two versions, it is clear that there are hardly any differences between them except for the color.

---

① For more information on Kawakami Tōgai, see Kumamoto Kenjirō, 'Kawakami Tōgai to yōfūga' (Kawakami Tōgai's Western-style Paintings), Bijutsu Kenkyū, 1938, p. 303 – 319.

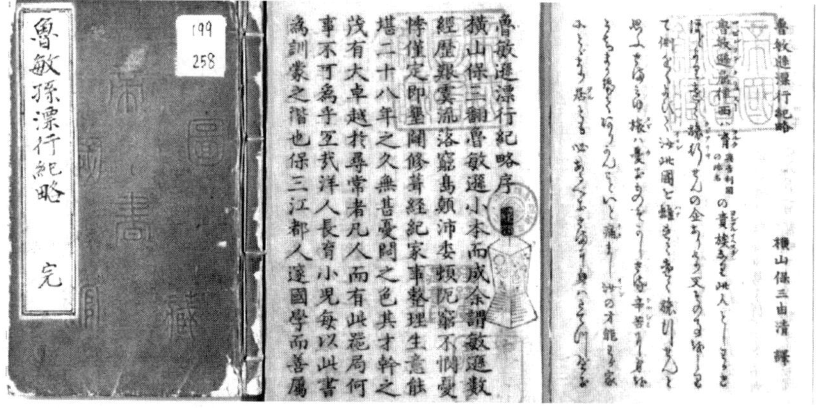

Figure 4 ***Robinson hyōkō kiryaku*** **(魯敏遜漂行紀略)**

Figure 5 Drawnby Kawakami Tōgai (川上冬崖)

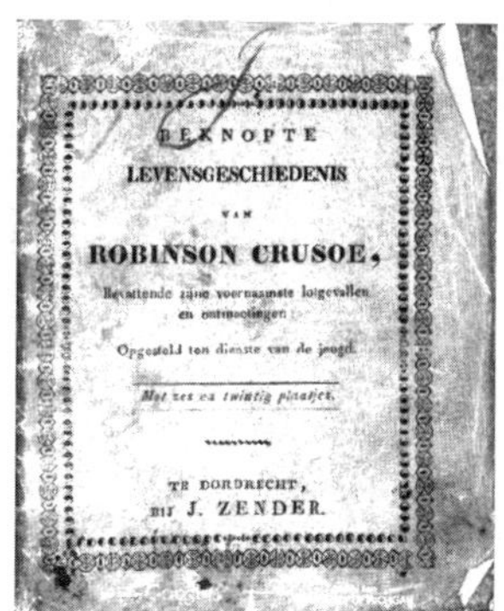
BEKNOPTE
LEVENSGESCHIEDENIS
VAN
ROBINSON CRUSOE,
Bevattende zijne voornaamste lotgevallen en ontmoetingen.
Opgesteld ten dienste van de jeugd.
Met zes en twintig plaatjes.
TE DORDRECHT,
BIJ J. ZENDER.

Figure 6 Dutch version

Figure 7 Dutch version

Western Illustrations of *Robinson Crusoe* in East Asia

Beside the frontispiece introduced in Part II, there are also many versions with illustrations both in Japanese and in Chinese, but most were copies of the Western version.

The most popular version in this period may be the one translated by Inoue Tsutomu (井上勤), under the title, *Zessē kidan Robinson hyōryū ki* (絶世奇談魯敏孫漂流記), published by Hakubunsha (博聞社) in 1883 (Fig. 8). This version was sold to three publishers in Japan at that time. It was reprinted nine times. Most Japanese learned of Robinson Crusoe through Inoue's version. The illustrations in this version were all copies of Grandville's work (Fig. 9). On the cover of this version, a large statue of Robinson Crusoe was represented in which he accompanied by a parrot and dog. He is holding a rifle and sitting on a stand decorated with the image of Friday's face. This statue is surrounded by many children. Robinson Crusoe was admired as a super hero. The difficulties he faced only made him stronger and more successful. This point is evidence that Robinson Crusoe was an ideal character in the Japanese mind.

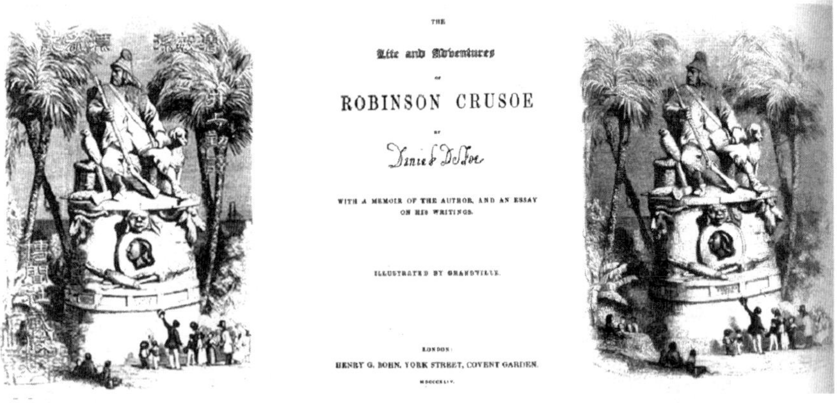

THE

Life and Adventures

OF

ROBINSON CRUSOE

BY

Daniel De Foe

WITH A MEMOIR OF THE AUTHOR, AND AN ESSAY ON HIS WRITINGS.

ILLUSTRATED BY GRANDVILLE.

LONDON:

HENRY G. BOHN, YORK STREET, COVENT GARDEN.

MDCCCLIV.

Figure 8 ***Zessē kidan Robinson hyōryū ki***　　**Figure 9 Grandville's work**

Another version that used the Western illustrations was published in 1887, under the title, *Shinyaku Robinson hyōryūki*（新譯魯敏遜漂流記）, the translator was Ushiyama Ryōsuke（牛山良助）. This version was a copy of John Dawson Watson（1832 – 1892）.

John Dawson Watson's illustrations were also used in the later Chinese dialect version, which was published under the title of *Gusulicheng*（辜蘇歷程）. The Chinese version was a Cantonese version. It was translated by an English missionary with the Chinese name of Yingweilin（英為霖）, published in Guangzhou province in 1902. According to my findings, Yingweilin was a Wesleyan Methodist missionary who once worked in Fatshan hospital, named William Bridie. We can see the connection between the two names by the note on the cover of *Gusulicheng* in The National Library of Australia. There is a note: "J. H. Revd Esq. with translator Comfit（W. Bridie）Hong Kong March 1903 Robinson Crusoe in a new docere"（Fig. 10）. In addition, *Catalogue of Chinese Books and Manuscripts in the Library of the Wellcome Institute for the History of Medicine*① also mentioned this translation. The explanation states, "Ms. Note on cover: The Revd. Dr [C.] Wenyon with W. Bridie's kind regards." And also says: "Bridie joined the English Wesleyan Mission in 1882." In a book titled *Wesley's World Parish: A Sketch of the Hundred Years' Work of the Wesleyan Methodist Missionary Society*, I found more evidence. "Whitehead and Selby have been invalided home; George Piercy has been compelled to retire, after thirty-two years of toil and struggle. Grainger Hargreaves（from 1878 onwards）figures on the Stations, Charles Bone（1880）, William Bridie and Samuel G. Tope（1882）-each of whom has done notable work; and the beloved Roderick J. J. Macdonald is by Dr. Wenyon's side at Fatshan."②

There are two versions of Robinson Crusoe with illustrations painted by J. D. Watson. One was published in 1864, and the other was published in 1879. Part I

① Hartmut Walravens, *Catalogue of Chinese Books and Manuscripts in the Library of the Wellcome Institute for the History of Medicine*, The Wellcome Institute for the History of Medicine, 1994, p. 68.

② George G. Findlay, D. D. and Mary Grace Findlay, M. Sc. *Wesley's World Parish: A Sketch of the Hundred Years' Work of the Wesleyan Methodist Missionary Society*, Hodder and Stoughton Charles H. Kelly, 1913, p. 156.

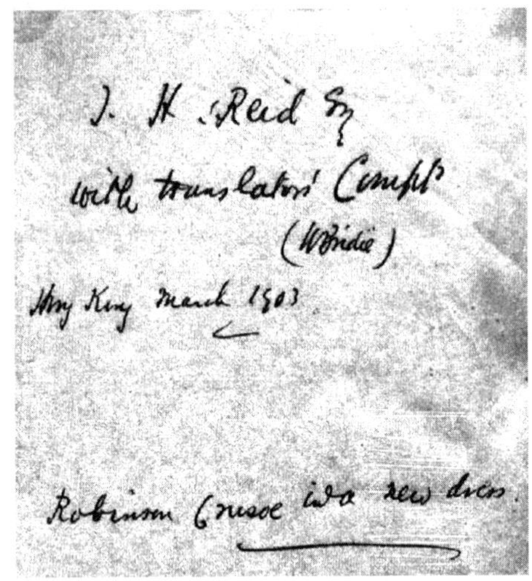

Figure 10　Cover of *Gusulicheng*

of the 1864 version has 70 illustrations; the 1879 version has 32. By checking the illustrations in these four versions, I found that the 32 illustrations in *Gusulicheng* are all included in the 1864 English version, but not in the 1879 version.

The distinctive features of each version became clear when I compared the 1864 English version with the1887 Japanese version (*Shinyaku Robinson hyōryūki*) and the 1902 Chinese version (*Gusulicheng*).

1864	1887	1902
1	1	None
2	None	None
3	2	None

续表

1864	1887	1902
4 	None	None
5 	None	None
6 	None	None
7 	None	None
8 	 5	None
9 	None	None
10 	None	None
11 	None	None
12 	None	None

续表

1864	1887	1902
13 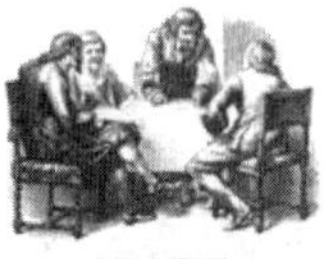	None	None
14 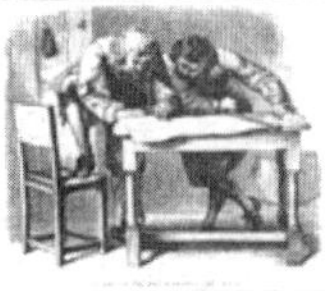	None	None
15 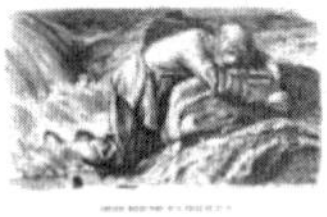	None	2 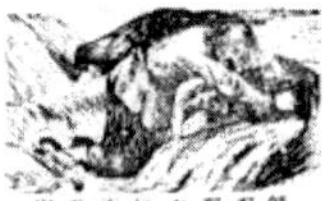
16 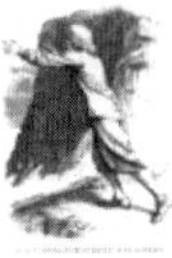	None	None
17 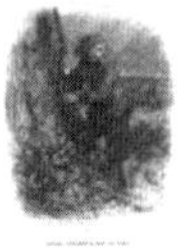	None	None
18 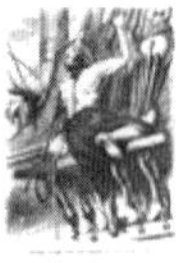	None	None
19 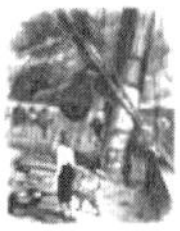	None	None
20 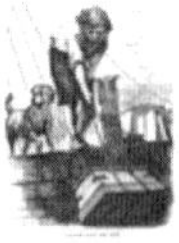	None	None
21 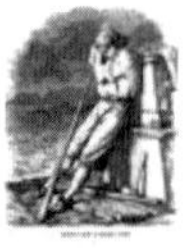	None	3 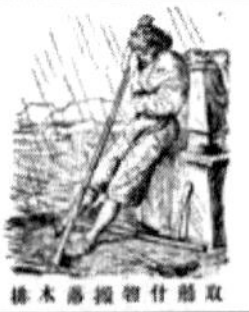

续表

1864	1887	1902
22 	None	5 
23 	None	None
24 	None	4 
25 	None	None
26 	 3	6 
27 	None	None
28 	None	None
29 	None	8 
30 	None	9 

续表

1864	1887	1902
31 	None	11 
32 	None	10 
33 	None	None
34 	None	None
35 	None	17 
36 	None	None
37 	None	12 
38 	None	14 
39 	None	None

续表

1864	1887	1902
40 	None	15 
41 	None	None
42 	None	1 
43 	None	None
44 	None	16 
45 	None	7 
46 	None	18 
47 	None	21 
48 	None	19 

续表

1864	1887	1902
49 	None	None
50 	None	None
51 	None	20 
52 	 4	22 
53 	None	None
54 	None	13 
55 	None	23 
56 	None	24 
57 	None	25 

续表

1864	1887	1902
58 	None	26 
59 	None	27 
60 	 6	28 
61 	None	30 
62 	None	31 
63 	None	32 
64 	None	29 
65 	None	None
66 	None	None

续表

1864	1887	1902
67 	None	None
68 	None	None
69 	None	None
70 	None	None
Part 2 	 7	None
	 8	None

Table 1　The 1864 English version, the1887 Japanese version (*Shinyaku Robinson hyōryūki*) and the 1902 Chinese version (*Gusulicheng*)

From Table 1, it is evident that the 1887 Japanese version includes not only the first volume of *Robinson Crusoe*, but also the second. Although the Japanese version does not include many of the original book's illustrations, the order of the pictures is nearly the same. In contrast, the1902 Chinese version focuses on Crusoe's life on the uninhabited island, while his life before and after is omitted. As the translator was a missionary, he may have made the revision to bolster the religious aspect of the narrative.

One more point regarding the Chinese version is of interest: the order of the illustrations is changed. For example, numbers 10 and 11 in the 1864 English version are in reverse order in the Chinese version, but the explanations under the illustrations are not included (Fig. 11 and 12). Why did these changes happen?

Figure 11　1864 English version

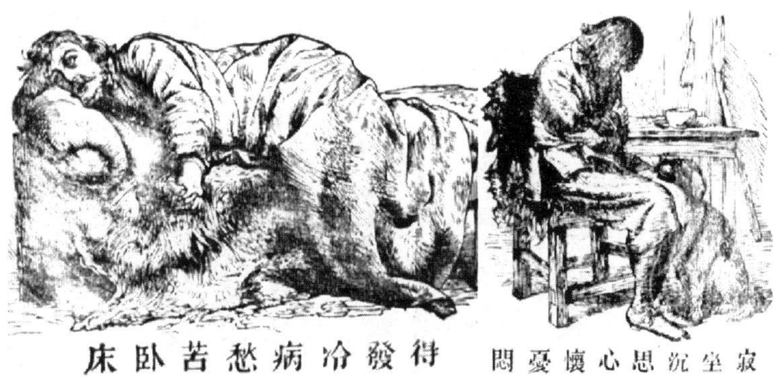

Figure 12　1902 Chinese version (*Gusulicheng*)

It is possible that the reason for this may be derived from cultural difference between Great Britain and China. When Chinese are sick, they do not sit, but lie in bed. The translator adapted the Chinese version to suit Chinese readers, so Chinese from the Canton area could understand the story. Another example is the death of Crusoe's dog. In the original version, it says "Crusoe buried his dog" followed by "Crusoe feels contented with his lot" (Fig. 13). In the Chinese version, the dog is still alive but is not depicted. The title "與猫鳥狗大家安樂 (Fig. 14)" which means "living a happy life with cats, dogs and a parrot." The translator omitted the death of the dog so as not to disturb Chinese sensibilities.

Figure 13　1864 English Version

Figure 14　1902 Chinese Version (*Gusulicheng*)

In 1894, a new version was published by a translator named Takahashi Yūhō (高橋雄峯), under the title, *Robinson Kurūsō zettō hyōryūki* (ロビンソンクルーソー絶島漂流記). A Chinese translator named Shen Zufen (沈祖芬) used the title of *Juedao Piaoliuji* (絶島漂流記) in imitation of Takahashi's Japanese title when he translated the book into Chinese and published it in China in 1902.

The illustrations used in Takahashi's version were copies of Walter Paget's work. These illustrations were also used in the versions published by Gakuso Yodansha（學窓餘談社）. One addition was published in 1909 with the title, *Robinson Kurusōbōkenkidan funtō no shōgai*（ろびんそんくるそう 冒険奇談奮闘の生涯）; the other addition was published in 1911 under the title, *Funtōbidan Robinson Kurusō*（奮闘美談ろびんそんくるそう）. The illustrations were not copies but original drawings done by the Japanese artist Oda Tōu（織田東禹）based on the work of Walter Paget. The illustrations in these versions are evidence of the Japanese painters' efforts to upgrade from simple imitation to original creative works. Fig. 15 is a scene of Crusoe talking with a friend on a ship. On the left side is Paget's work; on the right is Tōu's. Based on this illustration, it appears that Oda deliberately changed the depiction of the character's actions. The pen and ink drawing is not particularly detailed, but shows Oda's growth as a painter and his potential. The same phenomena can also be seen in the work of *Munintō daiō Robinson hyōryūki*（無人島大王ロビンソン漂流記, 1899）by the painter Watanabe Shinya（渡部審也）. Shinya's version is also based on a drawing by Walter Paget. Shinya's drawing takes more liberties than does Oda's to express the scene in a new way.（Fig. 16, left: Walter Paget's work; right: Watanabe Shinya's work）

Figure 15　Paget's work and Tōu's work

Figure 16　Walter Paget's work and Watanabe Shinya's work

Translations for Children

The first version for children was published by a person named Yamada Masataka (山田正隆) in 1878 with the title *Kaiyobidan* (回世美談, Fig. 17). In this version, 'Crusoe' was translated as '狗児僧'. It is different from the other versions in Japan or China. The title gives the story an air of fantasy because in Japanese folktales, the main character is often an acolyte, and the kanji for dog in the name makes the title character sound humorous. This version of *Robinson Crusoe* is short and easy to understand but there are no illustrations in the book.

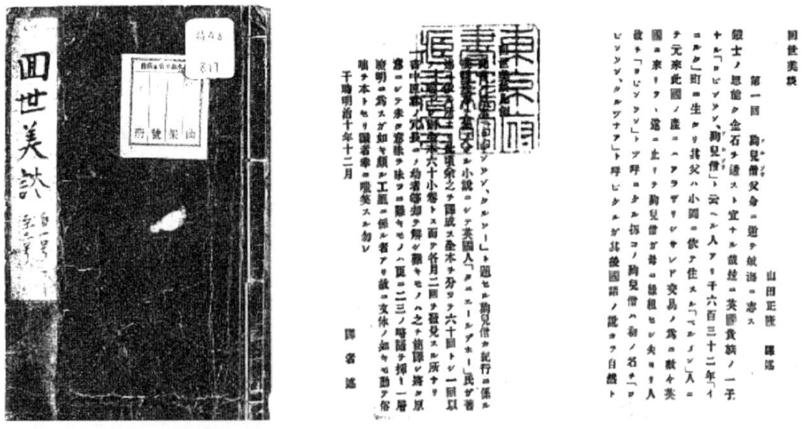

Figure 17　*Kaiyobidan* (回世美談)

Two years later in 1879, Yokosuka Tachibanasono（横須賀橘園）'s translation was published in the weekly magazine *Kibidango*（驥尾團子）under the title, *Robinson Monogatari*（魯敏孫物語）. The story was divided into seven chapters and serialized in 13 issues.① The first chapter has an illustration (Fig. 18) portraying the Robinson family talking. In the scene, Crusoe's parents are trying to dissuade the boy from sailing abroad. There is no information about the illustrator, and the drawings are unsigned. As no similar illustrations were published before 1879, it is conceivable that the drawings in *Kibidango* are original. In Thomas Stothard's illustration (Fig. 19), Crusoe is in the center of the picture and is hemmed in by his parents. Unlike the Stothard illustration, the depiction in *Kibidango* uses triangle symmetry and Crusoe is physically independent of his parents. Other illustrations in *Kibidango* show Crusoe as heroic and seeming to be never fearful or able of losing his ambition (Fig. 20). This point can also be seen in other Japanese versions during this period.

In 1892, another version entitled *Robinson Kurusō*（ロビンソン、クルソウ）was published in the magazine *Shōkokumin*（小国民）. It was a synopsis of Crusoe's life on the uninhabited island. The three illustrations in it were chosen from Sir John Gilbert's work.

Another important version was published in 1899. This version has already been mentioned in Part III of this paper. Iwaya Sazanami（巌谷小波）rewrote the story under the title, *Munintō daiō Robinson hyōryūki*（無人島大王ロビンソン漂流記）. In this translation, *Robinson Crusoe* turned into a modern children's story book. The words used in the text are much easier to understand than the other versions published. The written language reflects the vernacular understood by children. Illustrations in this version are more simple and are the work of Watanabe Shinya（渡部審也）. This version also influenced Chinese. A woman writer and

① The first chapter was published in the No. 27 issue, April 30, 1879. The sequel of the first chapter was published in the No. 28 issue, May 7, 1879. The second chapter and the sequel were published in issue No. 29 and 31; the third chapter and the sequel were published in issue No. 33 and 34; the fourth chapter and the sequel were published in issue No. 37 and 38; the fifth chapter and the sequel were published in issue No. 39 and 41; the sixth chapter and the sequel were published in issue No. 43 and 44; the seventh chapter was published in issue No. 46, September 10, 1879.

painter named Tang Hongfu (湯紅绂) translated it and published it in installments in the newspaper *Minhu Daily Newspaper* (民呼日報) using the same Chinese characters in the title as the Japanese version. She redrew the work of Watanabe. Hongfu changed the plot and combined some of Watanabe's illustrations. There is only one final sentence in Iwaya's version, but Hongfu expanded it over an entire chapter (Fig. 21). She used illustrations in other locations in the book to portray the part she added (Fig. 22). In order to make the work more understandable to a Chinese audience, Hongfu made the revisions both in the passages and the illustrations.

Figure 18 *Robinson monogatari* (魯敏孫物語)

Figure 19 Thomas Stothard's illustration

Figure 20 illustrations in *Kibidango*

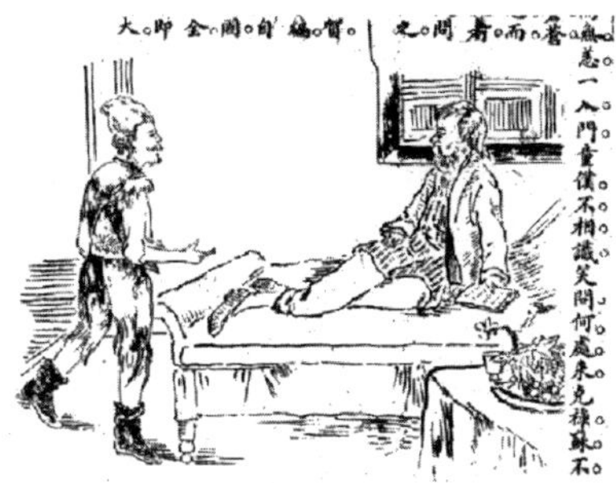

Figure 21 Hongfu's version

Figure 22 Iwaya's version

Conclusion

The illustrations included in *Robinson Crusoe* in early modern East Asia, show the relationship between the Japanese and Chinese versions. The illustrations also underwent a process from merely copying Western works to making drawings based on them, and finally, transforming them into new creations. This process showed the growth of East Asian painters, as well as the culture interaction. Translators made various revisions, including adapting the work to the cultures they lived in and making changes to complete the image they sought. The study findings may serve as a base for research on *Robinson Crusoe* in early modern East Asia.

References

Yokoyama Yoshikiyo, *Robinsonhyōkō kiryaku*, 瓊華書屋, 1857.

Saitō Ryōan, *ĒkokuRobinson zenden*, 香芸堂, 1872.

Yamada Masataka, *Kaiyobidan*, 嚴〻堂, 1878.

Yokosuka Tachibanasono, *Robinson monogatari*, 驥尾團子, 1879.

Saitō Ryōan, *Ēkoku Robinson shima monogatari* , 三書房, 1883.

Inoue Tsutomu, *Zessē kidan Robinson hyōryū ki* , 長尾景弼, 1883.

Ushiyama Ryōsuke, *Shinyaku Robinson hyōryūki*, 和田篤太郎, 1887.

Robinson Kurusō, 小国民, 1892.

Takahashi Yūhō, *Robinson Kurūsō zettō hyōryūki*, 博文館, 1894.

Iwaya Sazanami, *Munintō daiō Robinson hyōryūki*, 博文館, 1899.

Gakuso Yodansha, *Robinson Kurusōbōkenkidan funtō no shōgai* , 春陽堂, 1909.

Gakuso Yodansha, *Funtōbidan Robinson Kurusō*, 春陽堂, 1911.

Shen Zufen, *Juedao piaoliuji*, 上海開明書店, 1902

Yingweilin, *Gusulicheng* , 羊城眞寶堂書局, 1902.

Tang Hongfu, *Wurendao dawang*, 民呼日報, 1909.

George G. Findlay, D. D. and Mary Grace Findlay, M. Sc. , *Wesley's World Parish: A Sketch of the Hundred Years' Work of the Wesleyan Methodist Missionary Society*, Hodder and Stoughton Charles H. Kelly, 1913.

Hartmut Walravens, *Catalogue of Chinese Books and Manuscripts in the Library of the Wellcome Institute for the History of Medicine*, The Wellcome Institute for the History of Medicine, 1994.

Kameda Jiro, 'Kuroda Kikuro no gyōseki oyobi sono chosho' (The Achievements of Kuroda Kikuro and His Works) in *Geibun*, 1926.

Kumamoto Kenjirō, 'Kawakami Tōgai to yōfūga' (Kawakami Tōgai's Western-style Paintings), Bijutsu Kenkyū, 1938.

Sugimoto Tsutomu, "*Hyōkō Kiji* (shahon) no kentō-shoshiteki na ten o shu soshite", *Waseda University Library Journal*, *Nos. 22 - 23*, 1983.

近代早期东亚《鲁宾孙漂流记》(*Robinson Crusoe*)中的插图研究

李　云

摘　要

本文的目的是研究近代早期东亚地区《鲁宾孙漂流记》中的插图。本文采用描述性的研究方法，收集了近代早期东亚地区该书所有的中、日文版本。研究结果显示，中、日文版本的《鲁宾孙漂流记》中存在一定关联。基于对中、日文版本比较研究，可以发现（1）中、日文版本的原版形态；（2）原版的《鲁宾孙漂流记》如何被逐渐改写成了诸多新版本。本文为近代早期东亚《鲁宾孙漂流记》的研究奠定了基础。

关键词

插图　鲁宾孙漂流记　文化互动　翻译

Si Teh Ciao Bao (The Press of Overseas Chinese in West Germany) and the History of Chinese in West Germany (1973 –1990)

Dong Yue*

Abstract

The history of Chinese residence in Germany goes backabout 200 years. Untilthe eve of the Second World War, Chinese settlements in Hamburg and Berlin had begun to take shape. However, the war caused such severe damage to the Chinese society in Germany that Chinese started to return home in succession. After the Second World War, official and private contacts between Mainland China and West Germany began to revive in the 1970s. At the same time, with the rapid development of economy in Taiwan, Hong Kong and other places, a large number of Chinese wentto West Germany, and the Chinese society in West Germany became active again. The Press of Overseas Chinese in West Germany was born against this background. In 1973, the West German Overseas Chinese Association began publishing their journal called *Si Teh Ciao Bao*. The purpose was to unite the West German Overseas Chinese community on the one hand, and to publicize the political views of the association on the other hand. It has recorded the living conditions of overseas Chinese from all over the world in West Germany, their integration with the West German society and their compli-

* Dong Yue, Heilongjiang Unirersity, Beijing Foreign Studies University, email: goodluckdongyue @ hotmail. com.

cated internal relationship.

Keywords

Chinese in Germany *Si Teh Ciao Bao*

The Beginning of the Publication *Si Teh Ciao Bao* (《西德侨报》)

In 1750, the Marine Trade Company was established in Emden, in the Kingdom of Prussia. The company specialized in importing lacquerware, silk, and tea from China. Although merchant ships often traveled from Prussia to China, the question remains whether any Chinese actually made the journey along with the goods. ①According to existing records, two young Cantonese men, Assing Feng and HahoFeng, were the first Chinese to livein Germany. Assing Feng was born in 1792 and became a businessman. Haho was five years younger than Assing, and workedfor a period of timeas a secretary for his uncle, who was a customs tariff officer. ②After arriving in Britain by ship in 1816, the two men traveled to Germany with a Dutchman named Lusthausen. Their main motivation of going to Europe was the hope of getting to know the continent and making a fortune. ③After reaching Berlin, they made a living by playing erhu (a traditional Chinese two stringed instrament) dressed up in Chinese garments. Later, the two were entrusted by Frederick William I, the King of Prussia, with the task of assisting Sinologist Wilhelm Schott with his Chinese studies in Halle. In 1829, Assing returned to China but Haho stayed in Germany for the ramaing years of his life. ④

---

① Gütinger Erich, *Die Geschichte der Chinesen in Deutschland*: *Ein Überblick über die ersten* 100 *Jahre seit* 1822, München: Waxmann, 2005, p. 56.

② Benton George/ Pieke N. Frank, *The Chinese in Europe*, London: Houndmills, Basingstoke, Hampshire, 1998, p. 197.

③ Benton George/ Pieke N. Frank, *The Chinese in Europe*, London: Houndmills, Basingstoke, Hampshire, 1998, p. 197.

④ Yü - Dembski Dagmar, *Chinesen in Berlin*, Berlin: be. bra Verlag, 2007, p. 9.

At the turn of the 20th century, sailors and peddlers came to Berlin, Hamburg, and other German cities. After the outbreak of World War I, however, many Chinese returned to Germany and opened restaurants or other businesses, mostly in Hamburg. Some of the sailors opened restaurants or started their own business in Germany. Furthermore, the Qing government began to send many Chinese students to Europe to study, primarily in Britain, France, and Germany. After World War II, Germany was left in ruins which prompted many Chinese to return home. By the end of 1945, only about 500 Chinese remained in Germany, and half of them lived in Berlin. The majority worked as merchants, while 40 were students. By then, Germany was divided into two parts: the Federal Republic of Germany (West Germany) and the German Democratic Republic (East Germany). In West Germany in 1970, the number of Chinese from Taiwan was about three times the number of Chinese from mainland China. As the number of economic and cultural exchanges between Taiwan and West Germany increased, more and more Taiwanese came to West Germany, mostly to study and run restaurants. According to the inaugural issue of *Si Teh Ciao Bao*, the number of students coming from Taiwan had reached 400 by 1973. Since the late 1960s, Taiwanese nurses had been coming to work in hospitals in West Germany to fill the need for such workers. By 1975, the number of Chinese from Taiwan reached 2, 612 and that from mainland China totaled 730. As they gradually spread throughout West Germany, they had more and more trouble communicating with each other. Thus, some Taiwanese restaurant owners decided to publish a newspaper, which led to the birth of *Si Teh Ciao Bao*.

The Characteristics of *Si Teh Ciao Bao*

Si Teh Ciao Bao followed the principles of "serving, bridging and uniting overseas Chinese" and the guideline of "being communicative, practical and amicable." The paper positioned itself as a non – political publication. Articles that were considered constructive, or reasonably advisory were published, whereas those that tended to be fiercely offensive or biased werenot published.

Si Teh Ciao Bao offered columns for Chinese students as well as Chinese doing business in West Germany. The editing committee entrusted specialized students to write articles that addressed the recent concerns of the community, such as "The Insurance System of the Federal Republic of Germany," "The Sanit-aryStandards for Restaurants in Germany," and "How can you invite your relatives to Germany?" The earliest edition of *The Guidelines of Studying in Germany*was published in this paper. An irregular column named "*Qiao-Fu-Shi-Pu*" (Recipes of a Good Wife) was a platform for housewives to discuss how to make tasty Chinese dishes using local ingredients. Most Chinese living in Germany benefited from *Si Teh Ciao Bao*. The editors of the paper insisted that the entire paper be handwritten, and readers appreciated the intense effort that was made. The stories were usually about major events and festivals, such as the Dragon Boat Festival and the Mid-Autumn Festival, or folk tales, such as Chang'e Flies to the Moon. From its first issue to its last, the paper mostly adhered to the traditional Chinese book layout, in that it was written from right to left instead of from leftto right, the characters were written vertically instead of horizontally, and the date was indicated according to the Republic of China instead of according to the Gregorian calendar. *Si Teh Ciao Bao* was able to capture the hearts of its readers easily thanks to both its contents and details. Therefore, by the time the 100th issue was published, circulation had grown from roughly 100 to nearly 2, 000. The paper covered news not only in West Germany but also in some neighboring countries, becoming, in essence, spiritual food for the Chinese living in the region.

The nationalistic ideologies that the paper promoted appealed to the community of overseas Chinese. For example, news of the Diaoyu-islands-defending Movement set off nationalistic enthusiasm on the part of students and patriotic Chinese living overseas. It became an important topic in all overseas Chinese communities at that time.

*Si Teh Ciao Bao*also supported the *Three Principles of the People* developed by Sun Yat-sen and the government of the Republic of China, a practice that greatly united the local overseas Chinese and strongly opposed Taiwanese independence and secession. At the same time, the paper strove to have the community recognize theirmotherland, promote Chinese culture, and increase national cohesion. *Si Teh Ciao Bao* belonged to the Association of Overseas Chinese in West Germany, whose members were mainly merchants from Taiwan, so it supported the policies of the Republic of China. Reading the paper, one can clearly see the relationship between the Chinese mainland und Taiwan.

Si Teh Ciao Bao was characterized by an excellent style of writing and was therefore well worth reading. When Ms. Zhao Shuxia, a Chinese writer living in Switzerland, recalled her past years as a writer for *Si Teh Ciao Bao*, she said, "The literary and artistic writings tookup most of the paper. And the quality of articles were as good as newspaper supplements and were very well written. "① The main authors of the paper were Yu Ligong, Gong Huizhen, Mai Shengmei, Wang Shuangxiu (Shi Xian), Mosuoer, Zhu Wenhui (Yu Xinle), Yang Ling, Xie Shengyou (Hua Hua), Chi Yuanlian, Zhao Man, Qiu Yu, Tan Lvping, and Huang Hesheng, all of whom were members of the Association of Chinese Language Writers in Europe, which was established in 1990. *Si Teh Ciao Bao* was an important instrument for them to use to practice their writing. One of the chief editors, Miss Zheng Meizhi (Zheng Qing/Zheng Ruqing) worked as chief editor of the supplement of the *Mandarin Daily News*and as deputy editor-in-chief of *Zhong Guo Wen Hua* (*Chinese Culture*). The last editor of *Si Teh Ciao Bao*, Zhang Xiaoyun, was also the vice chairman of the Association of Chinese Language Writers in Europe. Thanks to her efforts, many new columns were added, such as *Di-Fang-Dong-Tai* (Local News), *Lun-Tan* (Forum), *Wen-Hua-Yu-Zi-Xun* (Culture and News), *Cai-Jing-Zi-Xun* (Financial News) and *Bao-Jian-Chang-Shi* (Healthy Tips). The number of literary articles increased as well. For example, essays were published about *Wan-Xiang* (The World) and novels were published about *Xiao-Shuo-Lian-Zai* (Serial Stories). For each issue, Zhang Xiaoyun wrote an editorialdiary as an introduction. With her influence, more and more writers in the Association of Chinese Language Writers in Europe began to write for *Si Teh Ciao Bao*. The paper had always maintained a high level of literary writing in the style of contemporary Chinese literature.

① Zhao Shuxia, "Working Hard from Nothing—on the Literature Development of the Overseas Chinese in Europe over the Past Half Century", *Chinese Literature*, No. 2, 2001, p. 8.

The History of Chinese in West Germany Reflected in *Si Teh Ciao Bao*

From 1973 to 1990, the paper covered the life of Chinese in West Germany, including how they adapted to German society as well as the difficulties that they faced.

1. Life in and Adaptation to West Germany

Most Chinese that went to West Germany from 1973 to 1990 traveledthere for the first time, so one of the first problems they faced was the language. To study in Germany, students had to pass language tests that were administered at the Goethe Institute. Students who were sponsored by the Chinese government received language training at Tongji University before they went abroad, but those who never had language training were not able to speak German at all, especially those who ran restaurants. In order to help them learn German, the Chinese Association of West Germany and the Chinese Association of Hamburg provided German courses. ①

Another problem that these immigrants had to face while trying to adapt to German society was, naturally, culture shock. One reader wrote to *Si Teh Ciao Bao* suggesting that a new column be introduced that discusses social etiquette in Germany, such as table manners, preparations for going to a dinner, and gift giving. Not long thereafter, a new column entitled "De-Guo-Ren-De-Sheng-Huo" (Daily Life of Germans) dealing with different aspects of German life was published in seven consecutive issues.

The publication also provided a great deal of other useful information, such as explanations aboutthe Divorce Law and Labor Law, procedures for Chinese relatives visiting Germany, and how to avoid being overcharged when havingone'scar repaired.

2. Interacting with Germans

Interacting with Germans was what the Chinese people living in Germanyhad to do every day, so that was a major topic covered in *Si Teh Ciao Bao*. In some ar-

---

① Qiao-Qing-Bao-Dao (Stories of Overseas Chinese), *Si Teh Ciao Bao*, vol. 91, p. 4/ No. 123, p. 4.

ticles, writers used first-person narration to describe how they mingled with Germans and other foreigners. Other writers created short stories about interactions between Chinese and Germans, all of which were reflections of real life.

Most of the writers believed that, although Chinese and Germans originatedfrom different races and China and Germany were located tens of thousands of miles away from each other, these immigrants had had a good impression of Germany before they arrived, because the Chinese were just as hardworking as the Germans were and China and Germany had not had conflicts of any major significance in the past. In one of thearticlesa Chinese studentrecalled the following, "The traffic order was so well maintained that no police were needed. I couldn't help but feel respect for this country. "①

The Federal Republic of Germany is not an immigrant country. In the 1970s and the 1980s, only 5% - 8% of the population was made up of foreigners. ②Compared to the 60 million Germans, the number of Chinese representeda tiny percentage, amounting to around 30, 000 at its peak. During those years, Germans were rather curious about the Chinese people and their culture because China was such a remote country to them. Based on what *Si Teh Ciao Bao* published, most Germans were very friendly, especially towards Chinese students who were hardworking and fluent in German and the intellectuals who stayed there after finishing school. According to Professor Li Changshan, when he first arrived in Bonn locals offered him a great deal of help:

"One day I was looking for the Chinese Embassy in Germany. I was trudging downthe street, carrying a large suitcase in my hand, and was sweating profusely. A taxi driver saw me, stopped his car and asked me if I needed help and where I was going. At that time, the Chinese Embassy was not located in the city proper. Although it was very far away, the driver took me to the Embassy. Before leaving, he gave me a name card and told me, 'Now you have my phone number and address. If you have difficulty like this in the future, I can help you.' While I was

① Yu Taixin, "My First Impressions of Germany", *Si Teh Ciao Bao*, vol. 52, p. 79.

② Song Quancheng, "Sociological Analysis on Foreign People in Germany", *Germany Studies*, No. 3, 2014, p. 96.

in the taxi, I asked him, ‘Does the Chinese Embassy happen to be on the way to where you wanted to go?’ He replied, ‘No. I'm going home and my home is in another direction.’”

However, Chinese students were unsure about how far friendship could go when interacting with Germans. *Si Teh Ciao Bao* published four stories about boys from Germany or other countries accostingChinese girls. One of the stories was about a girl who, after having told a German classmate of hers that she was married, was puzzled by the fact that he still saved a seat for her in class. “Is this how Germans treat regular friends or does he have a crush on me?”①

Stories about Chinese interacting with German senior citizens were also published in *Si Teh Ciao Bao*. The senior citizens were the writers' landlords, neighbors, relatives, and customers, etc. From these stories, we can see that German senior citizens led different lives from their Chinese counterparts. For instance, they were quite independent and strove to maintain a decent appearance, even if they were sick or near the end of their lives. One author wrote about some disagreements that she had with her German mother-in-law. In one case she offered to take care of her when she was sick, but her kindness was not appreciated and she was even accused of being a disturbance. Cultural differences with regard to the concepts of family distressed Chinese immigrants. ②Cooking also led to some disharmony. Because the Chinese burned quite a bit of oil, it created smoke, which often upset landlords and neighbors. Fortunately, such problems could almost always be quickly ironed out. Typical characteristics could also be seen inGerman senior citizens, who were generally stubborn and principled, but in a reasonable way. Some Chinese students even forged close bonds with them. For example, a girl who worked in a Chinese restaurant became such good friends with an elderly German couple who often ate there that the couple called her their “Chinese daughter.” Even after the girl left her job at the restaurant, she still kept in touch with the couple by letter and often visited them.

---

① Zi dan, “A Dream of Swan”, *Si Teh Ciao Bao*, vol. 82, p. 69.

② Manqing, “A Cat Catching its Tail”, *Si Teh Ciao Bao*, vol. 89, p. 48.

Although they did their best to interact with Germans, Chinese immigrants in West Germany continued to feel a sense of distance between them and their host country.

3. The Internal Relationship of the Overseas Chinese Communities

Due to the fact that *Si Teh Ciao Bao* was affiliated with the Association of O-verseas Chinese in West Germany, a Chinese group that was pro-Taiwan, the pa-per often talked about mainland Chinese students in a negative light. Some were described as "rigid in thought, but fluent in speaking political slogans"① and one was said to have "never returned the dictionary he borrowed from us."② Because of such articles, one student wrote a letterof protest, asserting that the paper was "twisting, attacking and defaming the socialist new China."③ In the following is-sue, the editing committee published the following reply to his letter: "Due to va-rious subjective and objective constraints, our articles cannot always be perfect. (We did not) maliciously twist, attack or defame any individual or group."④

Due to the increasing number of mainland Chinese living in West Germany, Taiwanese authorities maintained that they "should try to absorb these personnel and students sent by the Communist Party of China. Surely they will make rational choices once they get to know Taiwan as a free and democratic society and the a-chievements of the Three Principles of the People here."⑤ Because there was only a very small number of Chinese from mainland China, Taiwan, Hong Kong, and Southeast Asia studying in West Germany, many of them formed close ties with-each other. Mainland Chinese students did not have their own student organiza-tion, however, out of curiosity and national brotherhood, they sometimes attended events organized by groups such as the Association of Overseas Chinese in West Germany and the Association of Overseas Chinese in Rhineland.

Starting with the 94th issue of *Si Teh Ciao Bao*, there were sometimes stories

① Yang Guoguo, "Another Short Passage", *Si Teh Ciao Bao*. vol. 93, p. 18 – 19.

② Lai-Han-Zhao-Deng (Letters form Readers), *Si Teh Ciao Bao*, vol. 92, p. 34.

③ Lai-Han-Zhao-Deng (Letters form Readers), *Si Teh Ciao Bao*, vol. 75, p. 14.

④ Bian-Zhe-De-Hua (What the Editors Say), *Si Teh Ciao Bao*, vol. 76, p. 6.

⑤ Mei-Yue-Xin-Wen-Jian-Ji (Monthly News Selection), *Si Teh Ciao Bao*, vol. 65, p. 29.

about mainland Chinese students joining the "Chinese Alumni Association", which was dominated by Taiwanese students, and attending events held by local overseas Chinese groups. In 1982, in Issue 104, an article was published in the You-Xue-Zou-Lang (Student Life) column about mainland Chinese students hosting Taiwanese students and inviting them to dinner at a New Year's party in Zurich, Switzerland. ① At another New Year's party in West Berlin, mainland Chinese students watched the Taiwanese film *Good Morning, Taipei* and two documentaries about mainland China with their Taiwanese schoolmates. ②From 1973 to 1990, no news was reported about any disagreements between students from mainland China and Taiwan, because they had a good, albeit delicate, relationship characterized by kindness and competitiveness.

Conclusion

Si Teh Ciao Bao provides insight into the lives and struggles of Chinese in West Germany from the 1970s to the 1990s. Because there were Chinese from both mainland Chinaand Taiwan, however, there were constant conflicts and struggles within the community. Nevertheless, their kinship and common ancestry allowed them to cooperate with each other.

《西德侨报》与西德地区华侨华人史(1973 - 1990)

董　悦

摘　要

华人在德国的定居历史只有200年左右，第二次世界大战摧毁了汉堡初

① You-Xue-Zou-Lang (Student life), *Si Teh Ciao Bao*, vol. 104, p. 14.

② Ibid.

具雏形的唐人街，华人纷纷逃离德国，第二次世界大战之后，经济迅速发展的联邦德国再次吸引了华人的目光。自 1970 年开始，中德间官方和民间交流日益增多，同一时期，来自中国台湾、中国香港以及东南亚等地的华人陆续到西德经商、学习。西德侨界逐渐活跃起来。《西德侨报》诞生于这样的背景之下，这份报纸是西德华侨协会的会刊，其办报目的一方面是为了团结侨界，另一方面是为了向侨界灌输其政治理念。这份报纸记录了西德地区华侨华人的发展脉络，他们在德国社会的融入情况以及他们的内部关系。

关键词

德国华侨华人　《西德侨报》

《小孩月报》载动物学文章研究

于晓琳*

摘　要

中国第一份儿童启蒙杂志《小孩月报》中刊载的科普类文章占总篇幅的一半，主要涉及天文地理、物理化学、生理学和动物学、植物学的文章。19 世纪，西方传教士的译著、报刊主要侧重于动物学理论的介绍。1875 年《小孩月报》用对具体动物的描述介绍代替了理论知识的说明，种类之多，前所未有。精美的图画配合浅显易懂的文字，即使没见过的动物也能够让儿童快速认识，很多动物借由《小孩月报》第一次出现在中国读者的视野。

关键词

《小孩月报》　动物学　海马

清代来华传教士翻译的关于动物学、植物学方面的专门译著并不多，多数被划归博物学研究范畴。专门性的关于动物学方面的译著最早应数康熙年间意大利传教士利类思（Ludovic Bugli，1606－1682）所撰写的《狮子说》和《进呈鹰论》。根据邹振环的考察，《狮子说》的成书年份应为 1678 年。[①] 1855 年由上海墨海书馆出版的英国传教士合信（Benjamin Hobson，1816－1873）所编的《博物新编》第三卷，以及 1877 年出版的由英国傅兰雅口译，国人赵元益笔述而成的《西药大成》的第九卷“论动物类”都是

* 于晓琳，关西大学东亚文化研究科在读博士生。

① 邹振环：《康熙朝贡狮与利类思的〈狮子说〉》，《安徽大学学报（哲学社会科学版）》2013 年第 6 期，第 1 页。

有关动物学方面的知识。

目前，在西学东渐晚清文化交流的范围内，国内研究动物学的学者更偏重植物学方面的研究。关于《博物新编》的研究，可参见多个版本。此外，除了传教士的译著外，19 世纪起，近代报刊成为传播西学的另一途径。从 1815 年《察世俗每月统记传》创刊，到 1875 年《小孩月报》出版，这 60 年，由传教士创办的中文报刊主要有《遐迩贯珍》《中外新报》《六合丛谈》《中西闻见录》《教会新报》等。这些杂志在出版技术、设备和资金上主要依托外国基督教会，因此传教自然成为办报的主要目的之一。这些报纸杂志刊载了很多关于西方科学的文章，其中部分文章融合了宗教与近代科学。《察世俗每月统记传》最早刊登天文、地理方面的文章，之后的杂志报纸慢慢开始出现介绍物理、化学、动物学的文章。在传教士所创办的杂志中，科学文章所涵盖的范围越来越广，分类越来越细致。

一 《小孩月报》中的动物学

被誉为中国“第一启蒙杂志”的《小孩月报》，由美国传教士范约翰（John Marshall Willoughby Farnham，1829 - 1917）创办于 1875 年 5 月。在《小孩月报 · 志异》的序言中，范约翰曾表达创办《小孩月报》的缘由，他说道：“报之类多也，或关于国家，或关于商贾，或平街谈巷议为奇闻，或据怪状奇形为创见，或借文藻为铺张，而要之皆无补于童年初基也”，[①] 以及宗旨“予以童年初基，首在器识，文艺次之，故以二者兼而行之”。[②]《小孩月报》中刊载的科普类文章占总篇幅的一半，主要可以分为以下几类：（1）天文学。《小孩月报》中的一篇科普文章《地球说略》就是介绍天文知识的，之后开设了“天文易知”栏目，不定期连载；（2）地理学。《小孩月报》在“游历笔记”栏目翻译连载了主编范约翰出版的 *Homeward; or, Travels in the Holy Land, China, India, Egypt, and Europe*。以前的杂志主要以国家地区为单位，刊登独立文章介绍世界地理方面的知识，而《小孩月报》连载的“游历笔记”则可以让儿童以主人公的视角，通过连续性的冒险故事

① 《小孩月报 · 志异》，清心书院，1875 年第 1 卷第 1 期，第 1 页。

② 同上，第 1 页。

学习感受不同国家的历史、人口、特产、建筑风格等地理知识；（3）生理学。内容转载自美国传教士博恒理的《省身指掌》，还补充了两篇儿童保健的文章；（4）动物和植物。本文主要考察《小孩月报》中介绍动物的科普文章的主要内容与特征，以及对汉语中动物名称的影响。

1858 年《六合丛谈》中刊载的《动植二物分界》是中文报刊上第一篇讲述动植物理论的文章。这篇文章的作者是英国传教士慕威廉。1871 年的《教会新报》也转载过这篇文章。这篇文章主要是以陆生、水生的分类基准介绍动物和植物的栖息地、生存环境以及不同种类之间的区别。中国报刊中刊载的介绍具体动物的文章最早可见于 1856 年的《遐迩贯珍》，有《象论》《虎论》两篇。1871 年的《教会新报》刊载了几篇介绍大象、老虎、狮子的文章，但更多的还是关于动物学理论的文章。

《小孩月报》是第一本详细介绍具体动物的杂志。从第一卷第 4 期到第五卷第 11 期共计 37 篇文章，分别介绍了犀牛、羊、鸵鸟、袋鼠、象、之猎猢、鹤、阿拉伯骆驼、松鼠、海马、鹿、蝗、奥客鸟、甲斯多儿、人熊、飞鱼、光颈鹤、猫头鹰、木勺鯆、脚鱼、虎、猫、河马、野牛、狮子、瑟尾鸟、鸵鸟、蝴蝶、海狗、大蛇、犬类、杀鲨、啄木鸟、鳗鱼 34 种动物。犀牛，古时称“兕”，猫头鹰则被古人称为“枭、鸮、鸱、鸱鸮、鵩”。羊、鹿、蝗虫、虎、猫、蝴蝶、犬类、松鼠、啄木鸟等动物在 19 世纪的中国人眼里也许并不陌生，但对儿童来说未必能熟知关于它们的具体知识。除了这些寻常动物外，还有很多动物从未被介绍过，中国也未曾有过。

图 1　瑟尾鸟

图 2　袋鼠

首先，《小孩月报》介绍了两种栖息在澳大利亚的动物：瑟尾鸟和袋鼠。瑟尾鸟是澳大利亚的特有鸟类（见图1），中文学名“琴鸟”，因求偶炫耀时尾羽展开的形状尤如一张竖琴而得名。这是琴鸟第一次被介绍给中国读者。关于袋鼠的文章最早见于《教会新报》1869年第34期，配有图画（见图2），这幅插画转载于《小孩月报》1875年第1卷第8期，然而文章语焉不详。文章写道：“鼠有各种，以上之鼠名袋鼠，见之西国，罕有腹下一袋可兜小鼠行走跳卧如常，亦惧猫比如松鼠，能逼家鼠克亦畏猫想猫能治鼠系相生相克也”。[①] 这篇文章把袋鼠与老鼠混为一谈，既没有介绍清楚栖息地，也没有描述其体貌特征与生存习性。《中西闻见录》1873年第11期刊登过一篇名为《袋鼠护子》的文章：“有母子游于园中，见巨鼠携小鼠数四，往来草际，子怪而问其母曰，这见一兽，腹下若更便便者，何也，母曰是名袋鼠，形若狐，鼠中最慈者，生即附一皮囊于腹下，设其子遇危，即走避其中，汝试鼓掌作惊，观之”。[②] 这是一篇拟人化的小故事，没有动物知识的说明讲解。《小孩月报》1875年第1卷第8期刊登了《袋鼠》一文：“奇兽一只出在澳大利亚，肚子下有一皮袋，形又像鼠，所以人叫他袋鼠，前脚短，后脚长，尾也长得很，顶会跳，肚子下的袋是保护小鼠的，跳动的时候，见他生下的小鼠，跟随不上，他就抱在袋裹，像繈褓的样儿，有一回，有母亲领了儿子，在园裹游逛，见一个大袋鼠，领几个小袋鼠，在草丛中跳跃往来，儿子问他母道，那个兽肚子下拖的是什么，母说道，这叫袋鼠，顶慈爱的，生来就有个皮袋，在他肚下，他生下的小鼠，一遇危难，就会逃至他皮袋裹去，你可以试试拍手吓他”。[③] 这篇文章既介绍了袋鼠来自澳大利亚，又写明了袋鼠肚子有皮袋，外形像鼠，因而得名，首次正确且详细地把袋鼠介绍给中国读者。这篇文章结合了之前《教会新报》中的图片，同时借用了《中西闻见录》中生动有趣的小故事。对比故事中的语言表达可以看出，《小孩月报》中的文章更接近口语白话，非常适合儿童读者阅读学习。

还有一些动物名称不仅当时的中国人闻所未闻，现在听起来好像也很陌生，比如奥客鸟、甲斯多儿、人熊。图3所示的鸟在杂志中被称为“奥客鸟”，中文名是巨嘴鸟科，又称鵎鵼，有6属41种，颜色也不尽相同，由于插画为黑白印刷，具体种类无法判断。“甲斯多儿”见于《小孩月报》

---

① 《教会新报》，林华书院，1869年第34期，第6－7页。

② 《中西闻见录》，1873年第11期，第99－100页。

③ 《小孩月报》，清心书院，1875年第1卷第8期，第4页。

图 3　奥客鸟

1877 年第 3 卷第 5 期，被描述为“出北亚美理驾。大如犬。毛最细如绒。可作帽。每巢于河中巢之门在水下。屈树枝作窝，外用泥。泥之以尾”。[①]通过外表以及栖息地的描述可以知道是指现在名为“水獭”的动物。最早刊登“人熊”相关文章的杂志是《教会新报》。在《教会新报》1872 年第 213 期中“人熊”被描述为“英国兵丁有驻扎印度者承平无事常于林木深处高山峻岭之间周游猎现今猎得熊五只四只已毙独一人熊存活其人熊本系人身儿时食熊乳以长成两腿生有厚皮手亦成爪并脚如四足以履地不能起立行走”,[②] 人熊似乎是由熊抚养的“野人”，而并非一种动物。《瀛寰琐纪》1874 年第 20 期中又有“世之鬼域其性者吾得而称之曰人面兽心世之人言兽行者吾得而称之曰猩猩今有一人焉居印度幼食熊乳腿生厚皮手亦成爪起立言语并皆未谙此其人谓如何人耶吾不得而称之矣”，用“人熊”指代“人面兽心之人”,[③] 与《教会新报》的描述一致。《小孩月报》1878 年第三卷第 9 期介绍了生存在美国的灰熊和栖息在北冰洋的北极熊,[④]“人熊”（见图 4）是对熊类的统称。最早对北极熊进行介绍的是《博物新编》中的《熊羆论》，文章写道：“羆為北極最大之獸，高約四尺，長七八尺，毛色純白，獨行不羣”。[⑤] 由此可见，19 世纪，熊类还没有具体名称，主要根据毛色来区分。此外，河马虽然首见于《东西洋考每月统记传》1838 年 5 月期，但

① 《小孩月报》，清心书院，1877 年第 3 卷第 5 期，第 4 页。

② 《教会新报》，林华书院，1872 年第 213 期，第 12 页。

③ 《瀛寰琐纪》，第 20 期，第 31 页。

④ 《小孩月报》，清新书院，1878 年第 3 卷第 9 期，第 5 页。

⑤ （英）合信：《博物新编》1865 年第 3 卷，富士川文庫，第 14 – 15 页。

《小孩月报》第一次为河马配上了图画。

图 4　人熊

二　近代报刊中的“海马”

《小孩月报》在介绍动物时，形态特征和分布范围是文章的最基本要素，多数文章还详细介绍了动物的生活习性、与人类的关系以及捕捉方式等。最有趣的是，19 世纪的中国，似乎有三种动物在争夺“海马”的名称。

图 5　海马《小孩月报》（1877）

图 6　海马《儿童世界》（1922）

图 5 中的动物是早已为中国人所熟知的海象，然而在《小孩月报》中，它被介绍为“海马”。杂志中这样描述了它的样貌：“身子比牛还大，很有力气，有两只牙齿，生在面前，这牙齿比象牙更有用头，他们的脚，短而

软，状如鸭爪，不便行路，便于划水，所以在水里很灵巧，到了岸上，就蠢笨得了不得，这样东西大概产在北冰洋"[①]。从图5中可以看到"海象"标志性的细长牙齿。根据《汉语大词典》[②]，海马有三个释义：（1）海里的小型鱼类。头似马头，故名。也称龙落子，是一种名贵的中药。明代李时珍《本草纲目·鳞二·海马》[集解]引陈藏器曰："海马出南海，形如马，长五六尺。"又引《圣济总录》："海马，雌者黄色，雄者青色。"明徐元《八义记·权作熊掌》："更有海虾海羓，海里出的海马。"（2）海象的别称。参见"海象"。（3）指青蛙。《中国谚语资料·农谚》："七九六十三，行人路上把衣袒；九九八十一，海马跳出清水泥。""海象"一词则指"哺乳动物。生活在海洋中，也能在陆地上行动。身体大，颜色深褐或灰黄，皮上没有毛，眼小，没有耳廓，上颌有两个特别长的牙齿，可做象牙的代用品。以小鲨鱼、乌贼和魟鱼等为食"。简单释义，没有词源出典。这样看来，"海马"一词的使用由来已久。1815年到1935年，"海马"与"海象"二词在中国报刊的使用情况统计如下（见表1）。

表1　1815－1935年中文报刊中"海马""海象"二词使用情况统计

海马（walrus）	海马（hippocampus）	海象（walrus）	海马（hippopotamus）
东西洋考每月统记传（1838）			
教会新报（1869）			
小孩月报（1877）			
画图新报（1880）			
格致新报（1898）			
启蒙画报（1903）			
万国商业月报（1909）			
画图日报（1910）			
			大共和画报（1913）
大共和画报（1915）		繁华杂志（1915）	
		小说大观（1915）	

① 《小孩月报》，清新书院，1877年第3卷第1期，第5页。

② 汉语大词典编辑委员会、汉语大词典编纂处编《汉语大词典》，上海辞书出版社，2008，第1225页。

续表

海马（walrus）	海马（hippocampus）	海象（walrus）	海马（hippopotamus）
	中华妇女界（1916）		
		新潮（1919）	
儿童教育画（1921）	东方杂志（1921）		
	儿童世界（1922）		
		儿童世界（1923）	
		东方杂志（1926）	
新闻报（1927）			
			津浦之声（1928）
	儿童世界（1929）	国闻周报（1929）	图画时报（1929）
		学衡（1930）	
		东方杂志（1931）	
		良友画报（1932）	
	南星杂志（1933）		
小世界：图画半月刊（1933）	小世界：图画半月刊（1933）		
新中华（1933）			
海王（1933）			
科学画报（1934）			
妇人画报（1935）			
现象漫画 1935）			
	良友（1936）		
	少年科学杂志（1936）		

通过表 1 可以看出，在 1910 年之前的杂志，海马专门指代“walrus”。“海马”第一次被使用是在《东西洋考每月统记传》（1838）刊载的一篇介绍北极熊的文章中，但仅仅被提及了一次，并没有做解释说明。《教会新报》（1869）刊登了一篇文章，专门介绍了海马的栖息地、形态特征以及它的价值，并配有一幅图片。这张图片被《小孩月报》转载使用。之前的两份杂志都没有说明使用“海马”一词指代“walrus”的原因，直到《小孩月报》中写道：“海里的活物不一，除鳞介以外，另有许多兽类，有的像狮，有的像虎，有的像熊，有的像马，各样的海兽，人依他们像什么形状，就叫他为什么名字，以上是海马图。”也就是说，“海马”一词是根据它的形

象而来，并且《小孩月报》明确给出了海马的英文是“walrus”。从 1916 年开始，传统意义上的海马，也就是“hippopocamus”开始重新被使用。之后，“海马”一词同时指代“walrus”和“hippopocamus”。1915 年左右，海象一词开始出现，并同时用于指代“walrus”。此外，曾有三个杂志用“海马”指代过“hippopotamus”，不过大多数杂志仍使用“河马”一词指代“hippopotamus”。也许因此，这个意思没有保留下来。

除了杂志之外，新中国成立前出版的很多英汉词典对“海马”的指代也不同，有些也用来指代“walrus”，例如《英华合解辞典》（1928）中的注解：“Walrus n.（动）A very large marine mammal of the Seal family，native of the Arctic Ocean，and hunted for ita oil，ivory，and skin，海马。”[①]由此可见，从 19 世纪初期到中期，“海马”一词的指代一直没有确定。

结　语

对于当时的中国人来说，西方科学的传入和学习不是一蹴而就的。对于动物的科普同样也不是短时间内就可以完成的。在 19 世纪后期，报纸杂志媒体的兴盛成为译著之外传播西学的另一助力。与专门介绍动物学的译著不同，报刊媒体的发行量和区域更广，变现形式更加灵活，内容更加丰富多样，因此更易于被更多的普通读者接受。19 世纪的中国，近代多本报刊杂志持续使用了“海马”一词指代“walrus”和“hippopocamus”。包括《小孩月报》在内，这些杂志在传播科学的同时，对于外来事物的介绍还有名称的确定发挥了一定作用。虽然现在我们更倾向用“海象”指代“walrus”，但“海马”一词表示“walrus”的意思仍然被收录在了词典中。

《小孩月报》的发行量最多达到每月 4000 份，读者遍及上海、浙江、江苏、广东、山东等地区。美国教会创办的学校几乎都有订阅。作为儿童启蒙读物，与之前的杂志不同，《小孩月报》用具体动物的描述介绍代替了理论知识的说明，被介绍的动物种类之多，前所未有。此外，很多动物都是第一次出现在中国读者面前，比如奥克鸟、飞鱼等。此外，河马的图片也是首次出现。精美的图画配合浅显易懂的文字，即使是没有见过的动物

① 翁良等编《英华合解辞典》，商务印书馆，1928，第 1390 页。

儿童也能快速认识，这大大拓宽了儿童读者的视野。

Articles on Zoology in *Child's Paper*

Yu Xiaolin

Abstract

From the publication of the *Chinese Monthly Magazine* in 1815 to the publication of *Child's Paper* in 1875, the magazines compiled by the missionaries mainly include *Chinese Serial*, *Chinese and Foreign Gazette*, *Shanghae Serial*, *The Peking Magazine*, *The Church News* and others. Basically these magazines rely on printing technology and equipment brought from the West. Although the main purpose of these magazines is to preach, there are also a large number of articles on science published from the West. Editors of every magazine have a determination to spread the knowledges of sciece and technology. In April 1875, *Child's Paper* began publication monthly in Shanghai, and the numbers of artides on science and technology are the majority. Since most of readers are children, unlike the previous magazines, *Child's Paper* introduces some of animals that rarely living in China, The publication, a compelling narrative that is both rich in detailed introduction and deep in analytical insights contributes to the spread of knowledge.

Keywords

Child's Paper　Walrus　Chinese Magazine

亚洲宗教研究 >>>

Representation of Early Islamic History in the Discourses of Egyptian Islamists (1924 – 1970)

Abbas Basiri *

Abstract

In the Islamic world during the 20th century, there was an important problematic that confronted Modern civilization, namely the conflict between tradition and modernity. This problematic surrounded many elements of Islamic societies and also effected the political thoughts of intellectuals and traditional thinkers. These groups in order to strengthen their attitude and legitimacy in reasoning referred to the early era of Islam, because this period was a utopia. Also, since Egypt was a center of Islamic thought in the 20th century, the thoughts, books, and magazines which were produced in Egypt affected muslims in other countries. This research tries to explain how thinkers in Islamic circles discuss their ideas, specifically how some of the Ikhwan Al Muslemin Ideologies from1924 to1970 represented the early era of Islamic history, and the aims they followed which distinguished that era.

As a result, these groups applied their understanding of early Islamic history for hegemony of their point of view. By applying their understanding of the early era of Islam, Islamists could demonstrate themselves against secular discourses and make themselves a model for Islamists in other Islamic countries.

* Abbas Basiri, Ph. D. , student at Tehran University.

Keywords

Early Islamic history Islamic discourse Egypt.

Problem Statement

Many intellectuals, modernists and Islamists in the Islamic world study subjects related to humanities and especially history, from different approaches. All of these groups have hypothesis and assumptions in their fields of study. Therefore, it is clear that there would be different discourses in Islamic studies. The central question of this article is to find out how Islamic thinkers in the 20th century looked at early Islamic history in their works. Also, this piece of research addresses an Islamic trend in Egypt (1924 to1970), displaying its representation of the early Islam history era in their attitudes.

Egyptian society by the revocation of *khilafa*① (1924) faced a new challenges. On one side, onegroup believed the historical continuity of the *khalifa* institution was necessary and insisted that it was necessary for Egyptian society. Other Muslim thinkers in other countries were of the same opinion as well. On the opposite, however, there was another group who believed it was important to dissolve this institution. They announced that this revocation was the prelude of new period in history. Here was the point of referring to the early era of Islamic history for making a decision about keeping or losing the Caliphate. Also, Islamists were accosted by the modern world and its requirements and the problems concerning it. Some Islamic thinkers endeavored to answer these questions through the study of early Islamic history.

This research looks into various approaches to Islamic political thought, consisting of applied social and political topics in these decades.

Concerning the political and historical changes of the 20th century, how can one refer to the Prophet's era and the caliphate? By studying the works of Egyptian Islamic thinkers during this period, we can perceive how they encountered current

① Khalifa or Khalifah is a name or title which means "successor", "ruler" or "leader". It most commonly refers to the leader of a Caliphate, but is also used as a title among various Islamic religious groups and orders.

societal issues and understood early Islamic history.

Research Methods and Timeframe

This research tried to study representations of the early era of Islamic history with a descriptive view, by examining typology of representations, discussion topics and aims of various authors.

The year 1924 was selected as the beginning period of this research because that year saw the downfall of the Ottoman *khilafah*, which was an important issue in the Islamic world. In every Islamic country, much discussion was conducted around this event, and during the discussions many references were made to the era of early Islam. Although the *khalifa* had lost its original position of magnitude over the past centuries, it was still a romantic element which could band Muslims together. Then from 1924 to1931, many attempts were made to renovate it, but none of them were successful. ①Finally, the Egyptian Islamic trend split into multiple approaches after the death of Jamal Abd Al-Naser in 1970, which is the last point of this research.

Preface

In this research, we study Egyptian Islamic trends and preeminent thinkers and their viewpoint regarding early Islamic era between 1924 to 1970. Since there were many Islamist thinkers in Egypt during this period, we analyzed the works of preeminent Islamists, especially Ikhwan Al- Muslemin. For a more comprehensive understanding of their ideas, we should observe the social and cultural circumstances in Egypt during that period. They were studying the era of early Islam to find solutions to their problems and questions and help them find a path that would lead them to progress and change. In this regards, it is necessary to pay attention to: 1) the social context in which texts have been produced, and 2) the text itself and the meanings which are linked to the author. We cannot analyze the thoughts of thinkers, while neglecting the social circumstances in which they lived.

---

① Ridwan As-Sayyid & Ahmad Barqawi, Ai-Masala al-saqafiah fi al-alam al-islami/Cultural problem in islamic world, preparation and editing by Abd Al-Wahid Alwani , Beirut: Dar al-Fikr Al-Muasir, 1998, p 35.

Typology of Thought Trends in Egypt

The first essential thing in the study about thought trends in a special geographic region and period is typology and assortment. In the absence of a suitable assortment, we may place together thinkers who are not convergent in viewpoints and attitudes.

Hassan Hanafi, an Egyptian thinker, breaks down intellectual trends in the contemporary Islamic world and in Egypt as well into three groups:

(1) "Reformist trend": those who have been stablized and follow Sayyed Jamaal al-Din Asadabadi, and are incipient disciples of his school, Muhammad Abduh, Rashid Rizah and Hassan Al- Banna. Sayyid Qutb, Muhammad Al Ghazali and some of the other current Islamic trends are classified in this category.

(2) "Liberal trend": founded by Rifa'a al- Tahtawi in Egypt, Hayreddin Pasha, Tunisian politician, in Tunisia, and Ahmed Lutfi el- sayed followers. Taha Hussein and new Vafdian members were in this category too.

(3) "Secular-Scientific trend": founded by Shibli Shumayyil, Farah Antun, Ya 'qub Sarruf, Salama Moussa and Ismail Mazhar.

It is obvious that thinkers attitudes change, even causing them to join other trends, thus making this study much harder. For example, some thinkers belonged to more than one trend: Qasim Amin, Muhammad Husayn Haykal, abbas Mahmud al-Aqqad and Khalid Muhammad Khalid belonged to a combinatory trend named "Liberal-Reformist" . Tantawi Gohary and a generation called "science and faith" were classified as "Secular-Reformist trend" . Zaki Naguib Mahmoud, Fouad Zakariyya and others were classified as scientist 'Secular- Liberal' trend. ①

All of the trends rely on two kinds of sources: internal sources with roots in Islamic heritage and external sources based on new rationalism of Western heritage. Each trend has different approaches to these two fields of rationalism. "Reformist" rationalism is closer to the roots of past tradition rationalism, while the rationalism of the "Liberal trend" tries to compile both sources and create a balance

① Hasilah al-aqlaniah wa Al-Tanwir fi al-fikr al-Arabi al-muasir /Rational result and enlightenment in contemporary Arabic thought, Beirut: Markaz Dirasat Al-Wahdah Al-Arabiah, 2005, pp. 24 – 25 between them. ①This research studies the representation of the early Islam era in Islamism trends, at the same time it must be noted that all the trends had their own representation.

Early Islam History asan Ideology

Iranian traditional thinker, Seyyed Hussein Nasr together with Muhammed Arkoun, believed that the ideological application of Islam as an opposition to the West is inappropriate, because failure of ideological watchword is a great challenge for Muslims. According to Nasr, the most important encounter with the West is not in political, military or religious aspects, but in the intellectual scope. The traditional rationality of Islam must be applied as a whole without any selective parts. In addition, it is inevitable to know the modern world and its challenges. ②

Ideology in the battlefield of factions is efficient, making it impossible to overlook it. The most important field in which every social group needs ideology is when they are facing an external threat or a new adversary. Ideology's function is directly connected with the degree of impasse in having conflicts with others. For example, among the Islamic reformism, whenever there was an increase of threats against the Islamic world from the West, the functional role ideology performed was to reinforce the 'Reformist' situation. Hisham Sharabi believes that the applied ideology on behalf of the Islamist 'Reformist' trend was due to the absence of a correct perception of social problems. They neglected changes and evolutions in facts and thoughts in Islamic societies. This issue led to a reduction in rationality of the ideological approach, causing social reality to be represented differently from what it actually was. The reason for this is because ideology does not merely seek to represent reality and facts, but also expresses necessities and un-necessities-, desires and ideals. Islamic reformism did not just rely on faith and beliefs when approaching parts of traditional viewpoints, but took into consideration secular attitudes as well. ③

① Ibid, p. 25.

② Hossein Nasr, *Traditional Islam in Modern World*, trans. Muhammad Salehi, Tehran: Office of research and publication of Sohrawardi, 2007, pp. 491 - 495

③ Hisham Sharabi, *Arab Intellectuals and West: The Formation Years, 1875 - 1914*, translated by Abdol Rahman Alam, Tehran: political and international studies office, 1989, p. 50.

Abdallah Laroui, a contemporary Arab intellectual, believes that contemporary Arab authors' concern of new ideas can be represented by their discussion on topics of prophet of Islam as a leader of a social revolution, Ali Ibn Abi-Talib as forerunner of socialism and victim of the Meccan bourgeoisie, democracy as part of Arab's intrinsic matter, Islam as a supporter of women's rights and a promoter of social benefits. Works of Muhammad Al-Ghazali, Sayyid Qutb, Khalid Mohammad Khalid and others are discuss these topics a lot but rely on weak accounts. Therefore, it is easy for orientalists to condemn them. The ideological representation can be seen as the erector of this approach. ①

One of the other ideological viewpoint factors is the reinforcing of heroism which marks mythical and ideal characters as a super hero. For instance, Muhammad Ahmed Jad Al-Mula's book entitled, *Muhammad Perfect Example* is a model of this viewpoint. In his book, he imagined the ideal model of an Islamic and humane society that collects all of the superior human specifications. ②

This ideologicalization of history and the early Islam era also has somehow affected the religion of Islam at that time. Ahmed Barghawi, as a critic, deprecates a shift in Islam from a religion to an ideology and identifies this as a sign of crisis. The ideology of Islam appears when society is too fatigued to obey Islamic dictation. When political Islam emerges, the ideal type of Islamic society gradually recedes and changes to an unknown society with elements of Western lifestyle. ③

Influence of Early Islam Era History on Radicalized Islamist Trends

The partition among the Islamic trend in Egypt and Islamic revival formed when the "Reformist" trend relied on Cultural Revolution to achieve their goals, while the Islamism trend on the other end was seeking a political revolution to get rid of the *Jahiliyyah*④ society. This disconnection caused each trend to form their

① Aballah Laroui, *Contemporary Arab Ideology*, Beirut: Markaz Al-saqafi al-arabi, 1999, p. 122.

② Muhammad Ahmad Jad Al-mula, *Prophet Muhammad Is the Ideal*, trans. Mahmud Shahabi, Tehran: n. p: n. d, pp. 7 - 55, pp. 280 - 294.

③ Ridwan As-Sayyid & Ahmad Barqawi, p. 98.

④ Jahiliyyah (Arabic: جاهلية *ǧāhiliyyah/jāhilīyah* "ignorance") is an Islamic concept referring to the period of time and state of affairs in Arabia before the advent of Islam.

own special approach. This dissociation took place entirely in the second generation of Ikhwan Al- Muslemin, specifically in discourse of Sayyid Qutb who was impressed by Maududi. In this new approach, educational and cultural functions in "Reformist" discourse have been replaced with Qutbism that was based on political revolutionary acts. ① The *Jahiiliah* concept that was rooted in the early era of Islam history and Quran as a text related to this era, strengthened this radicalism.

Critics state that, having a Salafi attitude proves to be an obstacle to a critical study of the early era of Islam history. To have a comprehensive view of Islam's history, we must carry out a study based on texts of this period, with an unbiased non-mythical view and no hero worshiping. Only in this way can we obtain an accurate knowledge of the past, which is a prelude to having an accurate comprehension of contemporary history. ②

Some cultural critics in the Islamic world believe that the roots of Arabic cultural problems of latter decades emerged in the 6th and 7th decade of the 20th century which led to a firm ideology. Besides, Arab society didn't have an alternative perspective. Involving in devastating pragmatism the culture began to crumble. Extreme historicism, systematic reconstruction and representation of history, trying of new hermeneutics approaches, and venerating and disapproving it then started in the 1960swith the studies of heritage of Islam. ③

Early Islam History and Arabism Consolidation

It is obvious that the beginning of Islam finds its roots in the region of the Arabian Peninsula, and the foundation of this religion was laid in an Arabic environment. But Islamists by in large do not seek to distinguish between Arabs and non-Arabs. On the contrary, Arabism is forced to accept the status of Islam and its survival and expansion in order to strengthen its own position. Even Ikhwan Al- Muslemin leader Hasan al-Banna refers to the overlap of Islam on the Arabic language

① Emad Abdul-Ghani, Al-Islamiun Bain Al-saurah wa Al-Daulah/Islamists between revolution and state, Beirut: Markaz Dirasat Al-Wahdah Al-Arabiah: 2013, p. 68, p. 70.

② Salih Al-Wardani, Al-saif wa Al-siasah fi Al-Islam/Sword and Politic in Islam, Beirut: Dar- Al-rai: 1999, pp. 5 - 6.

③ Ridwan As-Sayyid & Ahmad Barqawi, p. 111.

and culture, saying, "Islam would have never come to pass without the rise of Arabs, Arab society has the character and superiority. A unifying language, unifying land, common wishes and common history. It is imperative for every Muslim to admit the reproduction of Arab unity. "① This point of view is full of Arabism.

The Early History of Islam as an Opposition to the West

Since the 1930s Muslim writers began to criticize the concept of Westernization, meaning the Western ways of thinking and living. This was originally a social critique, then a cultural one, and in the 1960s the political issues were also included. These criticisms were directed toward social and cultural groups within Islamic countries who imitated Western thought and lifestyle. Through the Cold War, the West saw itself facing two types of Muslim writers: one in terms of evangelical approaches and its effects on Muslim culture, and secondly, the Orientalist approaches as a partner in evangelical politics and complicity with imperialism. This confrontation was obviously against political and cultural imperialism, and, moreover, the tradition was facing modernization. This confrontation served to somewhat transform the cultural struggle (al-ghzu al-Rahqafi) in which Islamists turned to the struggle against Western Marxist and capitalist culture. In this campaign, at times they even saw traditional and modern nationalists beside themselves. ②The Egyptian Islamists, based on the pattern of the early era of Islam, tried to prove that Islam had been seeking to satisfy the needs of people in society before socialism and communism tried to do that. In the Islamic model, racist tendencies were suppressed, and even the leadership of a black slave was admitted, which was in contrast to the colonial and exploitative views of Western empires and capitalism. ③

The most important factor influencing the methods and approaches of Islamic thinkers in revising holy texts and their past heritage was "modernity" . In this re-

① Mustafa Al-faqi, Tajdid Al-fikr Al-qaumi/Renovation of nationalistic thought, Cairo: Dar Al-shoruq, 1994, p. 14.

② Ridwan As-Sayyid & Ahmad Barqawi, pp. 14 – 15.

③ Muhammad Qutb, Shobahat Haul Al-Islam/Suspicions about Islam, translated by Abd Al-basit Isazadeh, Tehran: Ihsan, 2009, pp. 49 – 52.

gard, Muslim thinkers are divided into two traditional and modern categories. ①The traditional Muslim thinker is one who is not aware of modernity and still adheres to tradition or else understands modernity, but does not recognize it as an effective element. According to Nasr Hamed Abu Zayd, a part of this group, by giving prominence to the Islamic past tradition, was overwhelmingly ignoring the reality of contemporary times. In the same group there are some who consider the modern world and try to present a new interpretation of Islam in accordance with modern realities. On the other hand, a modern Muslim thinker takes modernity at least as an influential reality and respects modern world principles. ②

Until the late nineteenth and early twentieth century, traditional scholars had a very special dignity among the Arab people in Islamic countries. They did no intend to flourish their thoughts and innovations. They believed that knowledge is a treasure among old books, and that scientists should discover these treasures through serious searching and patient research. Mohammed Rashid Reza and Saleh al-Sharif al-Tunsi also believed this point of view, but took a little bit more innovative approach to it. ③

Ayesha Abdul Rahman refers to the abundance of resources over time and throughout the Muslim world, not just Egypt. He criticizes those who tend to follow Western modern thinking. He believes academic research is focused on the needs, problems and new issues, and has not had much to do with the past, and this rupture has dangers for today and tomorrow. Writers and critics do not pay much attention to the legacy, while our current situation is rooted in our past. ④

Conclusion

Since Egypt was the center of thought in the Muslim world, we examined the views of some of the Islamist thinkers during the period between 1924 and 1970

---

① Ali Akbar Alikhani & others, Methodology in Islamic Political Studies, Tehran: Imam Sadiq University Publication, 2009, p. 190.

② Ibid, pp. 190 - 191

③ Jacques Berque, Al-Arab, tarikh wa Al-mustaqbal/les Arab, Histoire et Future, trans. Khairi Hammad, Cairo: Al-Haiah Al-misriah, 1971, pp. 28 - 29.

④ Aisha Abd al-Rahman, Torasona Bain maz wa Hazir/Our Heritage among Past and Present, Cairo: Maahad al-Bohuth wa al-Dirasat al-Arabiah, 1968, pp. 7 - 8.

and showed why and how they represented the early history of Islam. It is clear that the confrontation of the Egyptian Muslims with the thought of modernity during this period and, on the other hand, the disappearance of the last religious site of the Sunni Caliphate, forced Muslim scholars to revive and reform the Muslim community. Islamists should draw on instances which were accepted by the majority of Muslims. Therefore, they tried to legitimize their reformist views based on the early period of Islam. They represented parts of the early history of Islam in order to gain a stronger base in Egyptian society. They tried to counter the socialist discourse in the Egyptian society by referring to the justice instructions in the early era of Islam. They also tried to reinforce Arabism among the Egyptians by relying on the role of the Arabs in the advent of Islam and its dissemination. However, critics considered it to be against Islamism. With this representation, Islamists also attempted to confront the Western discourse based on capitalism and colonial politics. They were even pessimistic about the Orientalists ' efforts in Islamic history, trying to diminish their efforts. It is certain that these are just a few examples of the Islamists' goals of representing the early history of Islam during the twentieth century. It should not be forgotten that the works of the thinkers of this period should be applied in order to understand the origins of contemporary Islamic fundamentalist trends.

早期伊斯兰历史在埃及伊斯兰话语中的呈现（1924－1970）

Abbas Basiri

摘　要

在 20 世纪的伊斯兰世界中，现代文明面临着一个重要问题，即传统和现代性之间的冲突。这一问题困扰着伊斯兰社会中的诸多成员，对知识分子和传统思想家的政治思想也产生了一定影响。为使其理论更加坚固且具有合法性，他们转向了早期伊斯兰历史，因为那是一段乌托邦一样的时光。埃及是20世纪伊斯兰思想的中心，在埃及产生的各种思想、书籍、杂志影响了其他国家的穆斯林。本文试图解释：（1）1924 - 1970年，早期伊斯兰历史是如何呈现在伊斯兰话语体系中的，特别是伊斯兰兄弟会的意识形态是如何被呈现的；（2）他们追求的目标使得这个时代与众不同，那这个目标又是什么呢？通过追溯早期伊斯兰历史，他们将自身与世俗话语对立起来，并成为其他伊斯兰国家的模范。

关键词

早期伊斯兰历史　伊斯兰话语　埃及

The Gospel of Matthew, the Missionary Gospel in Persia

Ali B. Langroudi*

Abstract

This article is addressing the particular position of *The Gospel of Matthew* among the other materials, used by the Catholic missionaries during the 16th to18th centuries in Persia. Why did the missionaries select *The Gospel of Matthew*? How did they use it? These questions are investigated in this article.

The present research is a very preliminary survey of a number of copies of *The Gospel of Matthew* in Persian. It is supposed to provide basic information about the application of these copies in Safavid Persia.

Keywords

The Gospel of Matthew　Persia　Persian language　Catholic missionary　Safavid Dynasty　Polyglot Bible

The missionaries, who during the end of the 16th and beginning of the 17th centuries traveled to China, India and Persia, madea considerable amount of effort to not only know the culture of their hosts and also adapt their own mission and strategy of evangelization to the local cultures. The missionaries, especially showeda diligence in learning local languages, which then enabled them to produce con-

* Ali B. Langroudi, Ph. D., student at The University of Göttingen, email: ali. balaeilangroudi@uni - goettingen. de.

siderable amounts of literature.

Historical accounts, extracted from existing correspondences and handwritings, depict the missionary activities of the Catholic Church taking place in Persia at the end of the 16th century. ① Among the missionaries from various orders, the Discalced Carmelites were one of the most committed. ② What they composed has significantly enriched the historiography of Persia concerning not just their missionary activities but also about many other aspects of Persian society. This paper investigates how missionaries understood their own Scripture and beliefs and how they shared these with the populace.

The Outline of the Research

Surviving manuscripts reflect the encounter of the missionaries with local people from various ranks of society. The missionaries found the Persians to be a curious people interested in learning and knowing more, and very eager to discuss all kinds of topics. ③ This differentiated Persians from other Muslims, who had hostile interactions with Catholic missionaries, and gave them hope in producing Persian converts.

The missionaries' impressions concerning the Persians and their openness was mostly true. Persians, whether Sunni or Shi'a, have been influenced by their diverse classical literature. A significant feature of Persian literature is that it offers a particular point of view regarding belief and religion, which does not match dogmatic religious orthodoxy. ④ Persian Sufis and thinkers applied classical Persian literature to promote their own type of spirituality. The poetic expression of religiosity was the most influential understanding of religious behavior among Persians, differentiating it from the orthodox perspective supported mainly by the clerics who

---

① Walter J. Fischel, THE BIBLE IN PERSIAN TRANSLATION, UNIVERSITY OF CALIFORNIA, BERKELEY, Volume 45, Issue 1, January 1952 , pp. 3 – 45.

② Manuchihr Sutudih, Remained documents of Carmilite padres since shah Abbas era, Tehran, 2004.

③ Mario Scipano, Viaggi di Pietro Della Valle, Vol. I, Torino, 1843.

④ J. R. LeMaster, Sabahat Jahan, *Walt Whitman and the Persian Poets*: *A Study in Literature and Religion*, Ibex Publishers, 2009.

were experts in the Quran and *Hadith*, the tradition of the Prophet. Thus, the Persian language became the language of popular religion in Persia rather than Arabic, the official language of doctrines and practices.

The Quranic stories narrated by Persian poets, reflected new mystical interpretations of the ancient holy script which were widely welcome by the populace. ① The best example of this genre is the story of Joseph, who was lifted out of a well in Canaan by God, and despite of the guile of his brothers, rose to the throne of Egypt. The story of Jesus and his miracles occupied a significant place in Persian literature as well. ② Jesus, as one born supernaturally, who performed miracles and was wondrously taken up to heaven, left a deep impression on the Persian mind.

Furthermore, political changes had their own influence on Persian literature. In a world of international conflicts, the expansion of the Ottoman Empire, which posed a threat to both the Papacy and Safavids alike, gave Persians and many European sovereigns a common interest to see to it that neither failed. The Safavids used this necessity as an occasion to develop the silk trade with Europe (specifically with Italy and Spain) and the Europeans regarded this as an ideal opportunity to promote Christianity among the Persians. ③ It is also important to note that Persia was in a transition period in terms of its religious outlook. Following the Sassanid Empire, the Safavid rulers unified territory in order to establish a new Iran. They designated Shiism as the official religion of the kingdom and imposed it on the Sunni majority and other minorities. ④

Europeans who came in contact with the Persian world noticed the appreciation Persians had for visual art and literary imagery. This not only included artistic paintings and illustrations but also visual narratives and visual figures of speech.

---

① As an example: Leonard Lewisohn, *Hafiz and the Religion of Love in Classical Persian Poetry*, London – New York, 2010.

② Andrew Phillip Smith, *The Lost Sayings of Jesus: Teachings from Ancient Christian, Jewish, Gnostic and Islamic Sources*, Woodstock, 2005, xv.

③ Willem Floor and Edmund Herzig, eds., *Iran and the World in the Safavid Age*, I. B. Tauris, New York, 2012.

④ Rula Jurdi Abisaab, *Converting Persia*, I. B. Tauris, New York, 2004.

An outstanding present that was carried from Europe to Persia reflects this fact. One of the most beautiful illustrated Bibles of all time was presented to Shah Abbas I (reign: 1588 – 1629) by the cardinal of Kraków. ①

Due to the limitation of oral communication between Europeans and Persians, the language of pictures and images played a key role as a mediator between both cultures. Despite this fact, it was obvious to the Europeans, especially to those who were inspired to promote Christianity in Persia that the Scripture should be preached to Muslims. ② Presumably, it was therefore important for the missionaries to discover to what extent Persians were already familiar with Christianity and its Scriptures.

The first New – Persian translation of the Gospels dates back to a 14th century composition of a harmony of the four Gospels, mistakenly known as "Persian Diatessaron". The Diatessaron was actually a harmonious combination of the four Gospels in the Syriac language compiled in the second century. The original Syriac book was lost but an Arabic translation survived. The author of the Persian harmony however, was probably inspired by the Arabic translation to compose his own version. ③ There is also a translation of *The Gospel of Matthew*, from the same century and highly influenced by the Persian harmony of the Gospels. ④

This translation has been saved at the Vatican Library. About two centuries later during the reign of Shah Abbas I, a new copy of *The Gospel of Matthew* was produced, not in Persia but in Rome. The colophon of this copy of the manuscript provides interesting information about the text. It was copied by Tomajan, an Armenian from Aleppo in 1598, who emphasized that he copied the Gospel during the papacy of Clement VIII. The colophon begs the following two questions: Why should an Armenian from Aleppo copy a Persian Gospel in Rome and why was only

① William Noel and Daniel Weiss, *The Book of Kings: Art, War, and the Morgan Library's Medieval Picture Bible*, Third Millennium Publishing, 2002.

② John Flannery, *The Mission of the Portuguese Augustinians to Persia and Beyond (1602 – 1747)*, Brill, Leiden, Boston, 2013.

③ Bruce Metzger, "Tatian's Diatessaron and a Persian Harmony of the Gospels", *Journal of Biblical Literature*, Vol. 69, No. 3, Sep., 1950, pp. 261 – 280.

④ It will be discussed in a future essay.

The Gospel of Matthew copied?

A probable answer to the first question is that Tomajan was called to Rome to copy the Gospel so that it could be used for missionary services and evangelismduring the reign of Shah Abbas in Persia and the papacy of Clement VIII in Rome, who both wished to maintain a strong relationship with each other. A considerable quantity of survived documents demonstrate that this alliance worked in arelatively effective way. ①

The reason why *The Gospel of Matthew* was used and saved by the Vatican shows how missionaries perceived the evangelization ofPersia. A variety of reasons related to both missionaries and their addressees isconsiderable. It depends also on some unique features of this specific book. Matthew's Gospel has features not found in the other Gospels or the rest of the books of the New Testament.

First, it includes a greater number of stories about the life of Jesus than any of the other three gospels. Its narrative style was likely one that appealed toPersian preferences, the kind they were keen to hear and eager to read. Second, compared withthe other books of the New Testament, Matthew's Gospel has many passages that are reminiscent of passages about Jesus in the Quran. In his study on the Quran and the Aramaic Gospel traditions, Emran Iqbal El – Badawi provides much well analyzed data that confirms the occurrence of several intertextual relationships between the passages of the Quran and that of the Gospel of Matthew. ② Third, the content of this gospel could be regarded as more in line with what Muslim scholars considered to be "true Christianity". Here the person of Jesus seemed more like a traditional prophetic figure rather than as a deity "that was from the beginning" or the "Word made flesh" as the Gospel of John states. Forth, the Gospel of Matthew "is" the gospel of mission. It contains the most famous "missionary verse" of the four Gospels, "Go therefore and make disciples of all nations …" (Matthew 28: 19). The specific ending of Matthew's Gospel makes the message of its conclusion different from the other gospels. These reasons designated the Gospel of

① Manuchihr Sutudih, Remained documents of Carmilite padres since shah Abbas era, Tehran, 2004.

② Emran Iqbal El – Badawi, The Qur'an and the Aramaic Gospel Traditions, Routledge, 2014, p. 218.

Matthew as the gospel of mission in Persia.

It is important to know that New Persian, which has been used since the 8th century, was not popularly used in liturgy and Christian literature until the arrival of the European missionaries in the late 16th and early 17th centuries. Local Christian communities, such as the Nestorians spoke Syriac while the Armenians had their own language. There are some evidences regarding the translation of the Christian texts into New Persian but the survived exemplars do not demonstrate widespread prevalence of the New Persian among the "native" Christians of the time. ① The use of Persian in the translation of Matthew's Gospel, was therefore a way to evangelize the non – Christians who knew only Persian.

This manuscript of the Gospel of Matthew also provided the impetus for the missionaries to learn Persian. In another manuscript, which is actually a copy of Tomajan's text, there is a word-by-word translation of the Persian terms of Matthew's Gospel into Latin. The work reflects the missionaries' tirelesseffort to deal with the Persian language in a professional way focusing on one text. Translation in different languages, indeed, occupied a considerable part of the missionaries' agenda. Furthermore, the Carmelites composed a quadilingual dictionary in Persian, Latin, Italian and French. ② They were determined to work on Persian Christian literature with a precise scholarship. The Gospel copied by Tomajan and the other copiesof that, which includes Latin translation, are saved at The Bibliothèque nationale de France in Paris.

Another Persian translation of *The Gospel of Matthew* from 1653 at the Vatican library confirms the reputation of this book in terms of its reception by those who were engaged in the process of evangelization. Still, an undated copy of Matthew's Gospel, saved in Berlin, seems to have been copied before the 18th century according to its style of writing. It is significant to note that until the middle of the 18th century therewas neither a single translation of the other gospels nor the books of the New Testament. The Gospel of Matthew is unique in this aspect thatthere were-

---

① Christopher Buck, "The Universality of the Church of the East: How Persian was Persian Christianity?", *Journal of the Assyrian Academic Society*, 10. 1, 1996, pp. 54 – 95.

② Angelo Tolosano, Gazophylacium Linguae Persarum, Amsterdam, 1684.

several copies from the 14th to the middle of the 18th century that survived.

Nevertheless, the 17th century was the time of the propagation and development of the phenomenon of polyglotism. The polyglot Bibles contained the Scripture in a variety of languages including Persian. ① The available Persian translations served to fill the column of Persian in the polyglot Bibles beside the other languages. The usage of the Persian versions raised a new question: To which extent werethe available Persian translations reliable? In the middle of the 18th century, in order to find the answer to this important question and to investigate the content of the Persian scripture, the European scholarship decided to translate one of the books of the Bible from Persian to Latin. The chosen book, maybe not surprisingly, was nothing but *The Gospel of Matthew.* It is, however, a particular example of the translation of the Christian Scripture from Persian to Latin. The existence of this translation, published in the middle of the 18th century, again demonstrates that *The Gospel of Matthew* was such a unique book among the other books of the Bible that its Persian translation had a widespread reputation. The results of this investigation with the above mentioned translation was published in 1750. The introduction of the work also informs us about some manuscripts, observed by the scholars, which are unknown to us, as well as shows the existence of some other translations of *The Gospel of Matthew*. ②

Through studying the Latin sources of the time, another aspect of the importance and priority of *The Gospel of Matthew* is revealed. This Gospel includes the Lord's Prayer. Even though there is a Lukan version of the Lord's Prayer, the Matthean version, which is the longer one, has been more popular especially in its liturgical function. ③ A variety of materials in Latin used by missionary during that time, which didactically deal with the Persian language, include the Persian translation of the Lord's Prayer as a par excellence example to berepeated, practiced

① Walter J. Fischel, THE BIBLE IN PERSIAN TRANSLATION, UNIVERSITY OF CALIFORNIA, BERKELEY, Volume 45, Issue 1, January 1952 , pp. 3 – 45.

② Christophorus Augustus Bodivs, Evangelium Secundum Matthaeum ex Versione Persici Interpretis, Hemstadii, 1750.

③ Nicholas Ayo, *The Lord's Prayer: A Survey Theological and Literary*, University of Notre Dame, 2003.

and memorized. ①

Furthermore, it is important to note that the missionaries quoted the verses of this Gospel in their correspondence with Persian authorities. Although the authorities were not familiar with the Scriptures, the missionaries justified their service according to the verses of the gospel. In an instance, when the vicegerent of the capital city of Isfahan objected "Padre" Juan, the head of Carmelites, on their missionary activities, the Padre remembered the teaching of Jesus, namely the Great Commission mentionedin Matthew 28: 16 – 20, in terms of promoting the message of the Gospel as an unneglectable principle. ② He, citing the Great Commission, implicitly stated the universality of Jesus' authority above all other ones.

Conclusion

This survey on survived Persian manuscripts and Latin sources of the Biblereflects the numerical superiority of the copies of *the Gospel of Matthew* compared with other biblical texts translated into the Persian language. It has been the unique book of the New Testament that not only was translated but also copied separately as a single book. Some of the existent copies are clearly associated with the missionary activities of the Catholic Church during the time of concordance between the Papacy and the Safavid Empire.

The Gospel of Matthew was considered an introduction to Christian faith for Persian Muslims; an introduction that was both helpful for people unaware of the gospel, andalso informative of what it meant to be Christian. The fascinating narration of Matthew about Jesus maybe could not convince clergymen of the renewing Shiism, who were playing a considerable role in the religio – politic life of the territory, but it could be interesting enough for other ranks of the Persian society.

While the Safavid Empire forced all religious majorities and minorities to convert to Shiism, the missionaries in Persia posed their own faith and concentration on one book: *The Gospel of Matthew*. They not only preached the Gospel but also

① Iohannes Christophorus Amadutius, Alphabetum Persicum cum Oratione Dominicali et Salutatione Angelica, Romae, 1783, pp. 23 – 24.

② Manuchihr Sutudih, Remained documents of Carmilite padres since shah Abbas era, Tehran, 2004, pp. 232 – 233.

saw it as the statement of a higher authority compared to the Safavid one.

However, the missionaries ultimately failed in their mission during the last decades of the Safavid dynasty. Nevertheless, they disseminated the Gospel through their use of Persian literature. What they left is a valuable source for scholars to carry out research onthe missionary activities of the time. Textual analysis of the surviving manuscripts reflect remarkable information about the preachers and the audience of the Gospel of St. Matthew in Persia.

《马太福音》

——在波斯使用的传教福音书

Ali B. Langroudi

摘　要

本文试图探讨16至18世纪，天主教传教士在波斯使用的诸多材料中，《马太福音》处于怎样的地位。为何传教士们选择了《马太福音》？他们如何运用《马太福音》？本文将对这些问题进行研究。

关键词

《马太福音》　波斯　波斯语　天主教传教士　萨菲王朝　多语圣经

Sarmatian-Celtic Cultural Contacts in Thrace and Beyond: Trade of Central Eurasian Beliefs, Religious Concepts and More

Attila Mátéffy *

Abstract

This paper focuses on the problem of whether certain Celtic cultural elements originate from the Sarmatians, e. g. the Sword Bridge of the Arthurian Legends vs. the "Bridge as Narrow as a Hair" of the Caucasian Nart epic and the Chinvat Bridge in the Zoroastrian Mythology. The common feature of these motifs is that the "perilous bridge" connects our world with the otherworld. This problem is also related to the origin of some iconographical motifs of the Gundestrup cauldron (between 150 BCE and 1 BCE), which motifs had most probably been adopted by the Celts of Thrace from the Sarmatian tribes.

Keywords

Sarmatians   Chinvat Bridge   Gundestrup Cauldron   ethno-cultural contacts   Celtic studies

Introduction

The research question of this paper is whether certain Celtic cultural elements

* Attila Mátéffy, Ph. D., student at the University of Bonn, Germany, email: atilla. mateffy@ gmail. com.

(narrative and material) originated from the Central Eurasian Sarmatians. Among other fundamental motif correspondences (the sword in the stone, the Holy Grail vs. Nartomongæ, Arthur's vs. Batraz's death, the knights of the round table, the lady of the lake, etc.), one can observe the extremely similar motif of the Sword Bridge of the Arthurian Legends (Malory's *Le Morte Darthur*, Chrétien's *Charrette*) and of the "Bridge as Narrow as a Hair" of the Caucasian heroic epics (the variants and fragments of the Nart epic) and traditional beliefs, of the Bridge of Welfare of the Vedic (Rigveda) as well as the Chinvat Bridge of the Zoroastrian Mythology ("Bridge of Judgement"; *Avesta*, *Bundahishn*). ①

The common feature of these episodes is that the "perilous bridge" connects our world with the otherworld. First, the possibility of a relation between the bridges cited in the Arthurian and the Alano-Sarmatian traditions shall be reviewed. Then the structural elements and the mythological background of the "narrow bridge" and the otherworld of the narratives in question shall be analyzed, looking closely at the relation from a logical and symbolic perspective. Another related narrative motif, the kiss of the fairest maiden in the Arthurian tradition② must be a late survival element of the original North Central Asian animistic, shamanic and totemic transformation of the doe that took a human form ("Prinzessin als Hirschkuh"; AaTh401/ATU 400) and the marriage between the hero (shaman, hunter) and the doe, which tradition was introduced to Britain most probably by the 5, 500 Sarmatian *cataphracti* in 175 CE and was adopted by the local population during the following centuries. The (antlered reindeer) doe is pursued across the bridge, because she (as a female tutelary spirit) is leading the main protagonist (originally antlered male shaman) to the otherworld. That is the reason why the shaman figure has deer antlers and is surrounded by deer figures on the interior plate A of the Gundestrup cauldron (between 150 BCE and 1 BCE). This icono-

① Or "Bridge of the Judge"; "This bridge leads across the aërial abyss to Heaven, and all souls must essay to traverse it; but the righteous alone can succeed, whilst the wicked fall from it into Hell beneath. It is the origin of the Muhammedan bridge Al Sirât, 'laid over the midst of hell, finer than a hair, and sharper than the edge of a sword,' whence the wicked will fall into the abyss." Brown 1879, pp. 21 – 22; "The Place of Judgment", Coomaraswamy, 1944, p. 203.

② Loomis, 1949, p. 68.

graphical motif most probably had been adopted by Celts of Thrace (or rather Thracian silversmiths; see: Bergquist and Taylor, 1987) from the Sarmatian tribes (Scythians, Kelto-Scythians; vide: Strabo: *Geographica*, 7.3.2; 11.6.2).

In this paper, we shall focus on the nature and forms of the above mentioned intensive Sarmatian/Iazyges-Celtic ethnic and cultural contacts. The research in this paper is interdisciplinary, which includes methods of historical-comparative folklore and mythology, semiotics, anthropology and archaeology.

The Text-Corpora for the Comparison

Chrétien de TROYES: *Lancelot, the Knight of the Cart* (*Lancelot, le Chevalier de la Charrette*; between 1175 and 1181)

Sir Thomas MALORY: *Le Morte Darthur* (*D'Arthur*; first published in 1485)

PENNINC and P. VOSTAERT: *The Romance of Gawain* (*Roman vanWalewein*; Middle Dutch Arthurian romance; 13th c.; the manuscript: U.B. Leiden, hs. Letterk. 195 - 2)①

Ulrich von ZATZIKHOVEN: *Lanzelet* (after 1194)②

Vedic Literature:

Rigveda (composed between c. 1500 and 1200 BCE);

Zoroastrian Literature:

Avesta (Sasanian Empire; 224 - 651 CE) -The oldest surviving manuscript (K1) of an Avestan language text is dated 1323 CE; *Gāthās* (old Avestan,

① Barber, 2001, pp. 225 - 314; Penninc and Vostaert, 2000.

② Kragl, 2006, pp. 378 - 379; pp. 402 - 403; 6730 den wîzen hirz si wolten vân, ‖ und daz der künic danne næme ‖ von rehte, als im gezæme, ‖ der schœnsten kus; daz was sîn lôn. ‖ sîn vater Urprandagôn, ‖ 6735 der het ez alsô ûf geleit. ‖ di selben gewonheit ‖ behielt der sun imer sît. (…); Kragl, 2006, pp. 378; 6730 Sie wollten den weißen Hirsch fangen, ‖ und damit der König dann rechtens, ‖ wie es ihm ziemte, den Kuss ‖ der Schönsten nehmen würde; das war sein Lohn. ‖ Sein Vater Urprandagon ‖ 6735 der hatte es so festgesetzt. ‖ Dieselbe Gewohnheit ‖ behielt der Sohn für immer (…), Kragl 2006, p. 379; 7145 zeiner brücke gein dem wege. ‖ diu hiez ze dem Stiebendem Stege, Kragl 2006, p. 402; 7145 zu einer Brücke, die am Weg lag. ‖ Die hieß Zum Stiebenden Steg, Kragl 2006, p. 403; Coomaraswamy, 1944, p. 207.

"hymns, psalms")①

Later (Younger) Avestan Texts:

Vendīdād XIII. 9 (6), (24) and XIX. 29 f.; (The Zend-Avesta, Part I)②

Pahlavi Texts (Sasanian period, 226 – 651 CE):

Bundahishn XII. 7; XXX. 1 (9 – 13) ("creation of the beginning" or "original creation")③

Dādistan-i-Dīnīk XX – XXII; *Dādestān ī Dēnīg* (*The Datistan-i-dinik* / Dâdistân-î dînîk; 'religious judgements'; 'religious opinions or decisions'), Pahlavi work by Manūš Čihr, high priest of the Persian Zoroastrian community in the 9th century CE ("several years before a. d. 881")④

Arda Virāt (*Ardā Wīrāz nāmag* /*Artāk Vīrāz Nāmak*) V. 1 (Middle Persian Pahlavi texts, 8th and 9th centuries CE; the oldest existing copy dates to the mid-16th century)⑤

Nart sagas (*Nartœ*; Abaza, Abkhaz, Chechen-Ingush, Circassian, Ossetian, Ubykh variants): syncretic oral epic cycle of ancient Scythian (600 BC to 300 CE), Sarmatian (Iazyg / Iazyx; 3rd c. BC to 4th c. CE) and Alanian (1st c. CE to 13th c. CE) oral epic tradition and Caucasian folk beliefs.⑥

Celtic and Arthurian Studies: A Short Critical Survey

The well-known British (Edward Davies, J. Gwenogvryn Evans, Sir Ifor

① Nyberg, 1938, pp. 182 – 187; Pavry, 1926, pp. 49 – 59.

② Translated by J. Darmesteter, 1890.

③ Pavry, 1926, pp. 91 – 92.

④ See: Anklesaria, 1976, pp. 44 – 45; Boyce, 1984, pp. 83 – 84; West, 1882: xxii – xxv, pp. 1 – 276; The word *Chinvat Bridge* had been transcribed by E. W. West as *Kinvad* bridge (see: West 1882, p. 469; under *K-* in his Index), by Darmesteter as *Kinvad* or *Kinvat* bridge (Darmesteter, 1880: lxxxviii, p. 152, p. 154). In the Subject Index (*Sachregister*) of Henrik Samuel Nyberg: *Činvat-Brücke* (*Činvatō pərətu*) (Nyberg, 1938, pp. 180 – 186; The Younger Avestan texts: *Vendidad* 18, pp. 5 – 6 (adjectival usage: *činvaṭ. uštāna*; *uštāna* 'die Lebensseele'), 19, pp. 28 – 32; Middle Persian Pahlavi texts: *Mēnōkē chrat* (*Mēnōkē χrat*), Chapter 2, *Bundahišn*, Chapter 30, 34, Book of *Arda Viraf* (*Ardā Wīrāz*), Chapter 3: 1 – 2, 4: 7, 5: 1 – 4, 53: 1 – 2; as well as the *Gāthās* 32: 13, 46: 10 – 11, 48: 8, 50: 2 – 4, 51: 13).

⑤ Coomaraswamy, 1944, p. 203; Pavry, 1926, p. 14, p. 23, p. 85, p. 91, pp. 107 – 109.

⑥ Colarusso and Salbiev, 2016.

Williams, and many others), German (e. g. Helmut Birkhan, Alfons Hilka, and Heinrich Zimmer) and North American (e. g. James Douglas BRUCE, Norris J. Lacy, and Roger Sherman Loomis) scholars of Celtic and Arthurian studies have compared exhaustively the Arthurian Legends and Romances with texts of Old Irish, Welsh,[①] or French folklore from various centuries, or with the so called "classical" motifs of mythology they had read during their university years. Their methodology is similar to this point of view as well: it has never occurred to any of them that the basic elements of the Arthurian tradition may have partially or wholly originated from a different source than the Celtic mythology itself.[②] The names of Scythians, Alans, Sarmatians or the Nart epic are never mentioned in their work or index at all, although the English translation of the notable historico-geographical opus of Strabo (64 or 63 BCE-c. 24 CE; *Geographica*) had been published already in 1856 in London, with the mentioning and detailed discussion of the Kelto-Scythians in Thrace.[③]

Scythian and Sarmatian Studies: An Overview

M. I. Rostovtzeff[④] was the first modern scholar to study the history of these

---

① "It is impossible to explain all these correspondences between *Perlesvaus*, *Sone*, *Historia Meriadoci*, *Le Chevalier de la Charrette*, and *Vita Gildae* as due to late literary borrowings. The relationships are too complex.", Loomis, 1941, p. 935).

② Completed with the Theory of Christian origin of the motif of Holy Grail (Bruce, 1928, I, pp. 219 – 269).

③ Hamilton and Falconer, 1856, I, pp. 453 – 454; II, p. 240; The first complete English translation of Cassius DIO (c. 155-c. 235 CE) is due to Herbert Baldwin Foster. It had been published under the title of *Dio's Rome* (...) in 1905 – 1906. C. Scott Littleton has used the translation of Earnest Cary, which is based on the translation of the former one (Cary 1927 (9), pp. 35 – 37; DIO, Book LXXII: 16): " [a. d. 175] (...) The Iazyges were defeated (...) Indeed, the emperor had wished to exterminate them utterly. For that they were still strong at this time and had done the Romans great harm was evident from the fact that they returned a hundred thousand captives that were still in their hands even after the many who had been sold, had died, or had escaped, and that they promptly furnished as their contribution to the alliance eight thousand cavalry, fifty-five hundred of whom he sent to Britain (…)"

④ Rostovtzeff, 1922, 1925.

peoples, and then Georges Dumézil[①] the first western scholar who dealt with their mythology; they were followed by János Harmatta[②] and Bernard S. Bachrach.[③] However, until C. Scott Littleton (with Anne C. Thomas),[④] and two minor publications on the similar circumstances of the death of Arthur and the Nart Batraz,[⑤] the possibility of a historical-mythological connection between the Sarmato-Alan Nart sagas and the Arthurian tradition never came up. Referring to the possible historical background of the close motivic correspondences, Tadeusz Sulimirski, the author who published an important book in English[⑥], mentioned firstly the relevant historical data (Cassius DIO 71: 11) about the sending of a number of Sarmatian *cataphracti* (auxiliary cavalry) to Britain by Marcus Aurelius in 175 CE. Much later another popularand unique publication was the book about the cultural influences of the Sarmatians among Germanic peoples in the Middle Ages, written by Urs Müller (University of Zurich) in German.[⑦] As a reviewer wrote about his work with good reason, "It is this conservative tradition of scholarship, a tradition that has treated barbarian groups as self-evident and ancient historians as conscientious observers of alien peoples that may dissatisfy many readers." The same scholar also mentioned the "sceptical readers" and the "ideologically charged ancient ethnography" on the occasion of the very first book in Europe about this almost totally neglected area of research.[⑧] The first entire English translation of the Nart epic was completed thanks to Walter May and edited with a preface by John Colarusso and Tamirlan Salbiev.[⑨] The volume includes the first English translation of an extremely informative introductory paper on the Ossetian epic tradition written by the renowned Ossetian linguist and scholar of mythology V. I.

① Dumézil, 1930, 1946, 1956, 1958, 1960, 1968, 1971, 1978.

② Harmatta, 1941, 1950, 1970.

③ Bachrach, 1967, 1969, 1973.

④ Littleton and Thomas, 1978.

⑤ Griswarl, 1969, 1973.

⑥ Sulimirski, 1970.

⑦ Müller, 1998.

⑧ Hummer, 2001.

⑨ Colarusso and Salbiev, 2016.

ABAEV. ① And last but not at least, I have to mention the name of John COLARUSSO, who has made an enormous contribution to the western scholarship of the Nart epic studies in the last four decades.

From Scythia to Camelot **(Littleton and Malcor 1994)**

The book named with this stitle appeared in 1994. Because it is well known these days, I shall only remark about its most important notes on the historical background of the motif-correlation of the Nart epic and the Arthurian legends.

> [...] at the end of the Marcomannian War in the year 175 of the Common Era (c. e.), the Roman emperor Marcus Aurelius sent a contingent of 5, 500 Sarmatian *cataphracti*, or heavily armed auxiliary cavalry, from Pannonia (modern Hungary) to Britain. [...] their descendants managed to survive as an identifiable ethnic enclave at least until the beginning of the fourth century, and perhaps longer. [···] the stories are so similar that the possibility of a chance parallelism is remote. [...] a passage in Dio Cassius's *Roman History*, written ca. 225 C. E., that describes how, at the end of the Marcomannian War, 8, 000 *cataphracti* from a Sarmatian tribe known as the Iazyges (or Jazyges) were impressed into the Roman legions. Of these Iazyges 5, 500 were sent to Britain. ②

There are many very close similarities between the characteristics and motives of Arthurian and Nart; the Lady of the Lake, the famous Sword in the Stone episode, the magical cup (or cauldron) called the *Nartamongæ*. Among many other close correspondences appears the hunt of the white animal, ③ or white hart, stag, deer or hind. ④ The authors wrote the followingin ashort passage describing the hunt:

---

① Ibid. XXIX-LXVIII.

② Littleton and Malcor 1994.

③ Ibid. pp. 102 - 103.

④ Ibid. pp. 121 - 122; Loomis, 1949, pp. 68 - 70.

The White Animal

Other Scythian elements appear in the Lancelot corpus as well. One of the most prominent is the motif of the hunt for the white animal. In Ulrich von Zatzikhoven's *Lanzelet*, Guinevere is abducted by Valerin as Lanzelet (Lancelot) and Walewein (Gawain) join Arthur on the hunt for a white stag. The custom that the successful hunter of the white stag would receive a kiss from the most beautiful woman was initiated, according to the text, by Uther Pendragon. The Middle Dutch verse romance *Lanceloet en het hert met de witte voet* (*Lancelot and the Deer with the White Foot*; 1200 – 1250; transmitted exclusively in the *Lancelot-Compilatie*), the Second Continuation of Chrétien's *Perceval*, the Didot-*Perceval*, the Welsh *Peredur*, and the late twelfth-century Old French *Tyolet* all use the white-footed animal. In *Tyolet* the hero cuts off the white foot of a stag, but a false knight claims to have accomplished the feat after Tyolet is attacked by lions who leave him for dead. In related tales, a hound (of unspecified color) leads Gawain over a bridge to the Waste Manor, where he finds a woman with a dead knight [···] The animal at the ford is a typical steppe motif and could have come from the Alans or Huns. ①

Since the authors did not notice the connection between the bridges leading to the Otherworld of Celtic tradition and Caucasian folklore, the motif of the bridge leading to the otherworldly castle is only casually mentioned in the part reviewing the hunt of a white animal:

In Malory's *Le Morte Darthur* Lancelot follows a black brachet, or female hound, which had been tracking a deer, over a bridge and eventually to a castle, where he finds a dead knight. ② At least on the surface these stories, combined with the Arthurian tales of the hunt for the white stag, resemble the Ossetic narrative in which a white stag leads Uryzmæg to an enchanted house where he meets a

① Ibid. pp. 102 – 103.

② In this place, Littleton and Malcor referred to the northern Central Eurasian origin narrative type of the chased doe (AaTh 401/ATU 400) in the antique literature (Gregory of Tours, Priscus, Jordanes), but not to the motif of the "bridge had been thrown, no wider than the sharp edge of a knife", Colarusso and Salbiev 2016, p. 166.

woman who involves him in an adventure. ①

The reason for this is that the two successive motifs, the deer hunt and the crossing of the bridge are directly related logically, as well as symbolically, although the bridge-motif disappeared from the corresponding place of the Nart epic until its first collections and editions, which happened at the beginning of the last third of the 19th century, ② it appears not much later in the events of the Land of the Dead, where the pursued doe leads the Nart hero Soslan.

Soslan in the Land of the Dead

[…]

That night Soslan could not sleep however he tried. In the early morning, when day divided from night, he threw his felt cloak round his shoulders, took his bow and quiver, hung his sword in his belt, and set off for the reeds and rushes where Uryzmag had seen the doe with its coat of gold. The sun had only just risen, and its first rays had penetrated the reeds. In their light, Soslan saw the golden doe that Uryzmag had met. It was coming slowly toward him, nibbling around at the grass. The sun's rays reflecting from her golden pelt seemed finer than the sharpest small needles, and pricked Soslan's eyes, which were already large with surprise.

'If that deer only fell into my hands, there would be none more famous than I among the Narts!' said Soslan beneath his breath.

Creeping up quietly, grass blade by grass blade, he approached the golden doe. Now he was within bow-shot. He placed an arrow in his bow, and was about to shoot, when it suddenly dropped and disappeared. Soslan seized his quiver, but not another single arrow was left in it. The deer was

① Ibid. pp. 102; Here, the authors referred to Dumézil, 1930, p. 27, but not the original text of Nart epic; most probably that is the reason why the continuation of the story slipped their notice: Soslan in the Land of the Dead Colarusso and Salbiev, 2016, pp. 160 – 181.

② The first documentary transcriptions of the Nart tales were made by teachers of the Tbilisi Spiritual Seminary: the Ossetian Vasily Tsoraev, and the Georgian writer , Daniel Chonkadze. They were translated into Russian with commentaries in *Ossetian Texts*, and published as "Papers of the Academy of Sciences" in 1868. The translation and notes were the work of the Russian academician Anton A. Schiefner. , Colarusso and Salbiev, 2016.

still there, and had not moved from its place.

'Is it just there to shame me?' thought he to himself, and drawing his sword, he sped on toward the deer, and came quite near in one great leap. But the golden doe saw him and bounded away, making off toward the Black Mountains.

'No, no! You won't get away from me!' thought Soslan, and flew off after her.

The golden doe flew to the Black Mountains, and hid herself in a deep cavern. ①

Soslan was quite unaware that he was pursuing the daughter of the sun, Atsirukh, who, though disguised as a deer, had seven giants to protect her. Still thinking that he was chasing a golden deer, he came to the cavern where she had hidden herself, and saw nearby a seven-storied tower fortress.

[…] Soslan […]: 'Let our ward, the daughter of the sun, Atsirukh, tell us what to do!'

So the giants went to the daughter of the sun, and said to her, 'An unusual guest has visited us. He calls himself Nart Soslan. We wanted to make an offering of him, but our knives could not touch him!'

The daughter of the sun listened, and hearing the name Soslan, cried, 'If that is really Soslan, then he is my predestined one!' ②

Somewhat later, when the hero is already in the Land of the Dead (still in the same episode):

Here was a river, and in the middle of it stood an island. From the bank to the island a bridge had been thrown, no wider than the sharp edge of a

① This is also a very close parallel of the Nart epic with the Turkic and Tibetan (Gesar) heroic epics, that the gateway to the underworld is through a rocky hole or cave on a mountain summit, Chadwick and Zhirmunsky, 1969, pp. 263 - 264.

② Colarusso and Salbiev, 2016, pp. 160 - 162.

knife. On the island, in an eggshell, sat a naked old man. ①

"Farther on I saw a bridge, as thin as the blade of a knife, thrown across to an island in a river. On the sharp edge of the bridge sat an old man in an eggshell. What was the reason for that?" [asked Soslan]

"That old man lived unsociably all his life. Neither on weekdays nor on holidays did he ever invite any guests in, so now he sits alone in the Land of the Dead, and passes his days in solitude." [answered Vedukha]②

[…] Soslan had paid the bride-price in full, and so they handed over to him their ward, the daughter of the sun Atsirukh, to be his wife. ③

There are some angry critics who speak against the research resultsdiscussed briefly above made by few Celticists during the last decades. Among others the German scholar Stefan Zimmer (former emeritus professor at the University of Bonn) who devoted roughly seven pages to the free and sloppy interpretation of the theory of Littleton and Malcor at the end of his book④ in which he published the German translation of the oldest completely preserved Arthur manuscript together with another version. However, his critics are neither careful nor emotionless, miss the serious arguments and include the following negligent assertions:

Natürlich gibt es keinerlei direkte Verbindung zwischen der ossetischen und der arthurischen Literatur (…) Viele seiner [i. e. C. Scott Littleton] *weitreichenden Schlüsse sind nicht hinreichend gesichert (s. u. Anhang* 4). ⑤*Soweit die historischen Fakten; alles andere ist Spekulation.* ⑥*Nun zu den Spekulationen: Die Möglichkeit ist daher nicht auszuschließen-allerdings auch in keiner Weise durch Argumente zu stützen! -daß sich gewisse iranische Traditionen, darunter auch Mythen und Sagen, in der lokalen provinzialrömischen*

① Ibid. p. 166.

② Ibid. 173.

③ Ibid. 181.

④ Zimmer, 2006, p. 181, pp. 183 – 190.

⑤ Ibid. 181.

⑥ Ibid. 185.

Bevölkerung jahrhundertelang gehalten haben könnten. Dies kann nicht mehr als eine bloße Vermutung sein, die ja nur angestellt wurde, um hypothetische Anhaltspunkte für iranische Einflüsse bei der Herausbildung der Artussage zu haben. [①]*Littleton & Malcor spekulieren aber noch weiter: Jeder weitere Kommentar erübrigt sich.* [②]

As one can see, the author is not really familiar with the scrutiny in the methods of comparative mythology and folklore, cultural anthropology, sociology and structural text analysis (bilingualism, inter-marriage, intercultural communication, stability and change, orality and cross-cultural oral transmission, intertextuality, cultural and/or religious syncretism, internal and external memory, motif and allomotif, variability, variant, invariant, affinity, creativity and innovation, survival, and many other important terms which seems to be unknown by the author)[③] and tends to follow much more a hypercritical skepticism instead of an elaborated professional argumentation. "Every further commentary is redundant."

The Sword Bridge and the Water Bridge in the Arthurian Literature

The well-known Arthurian scholar Roger Sherman Loomis summed up the Irish, Welsh and French renditions of the topic related tradition as follows:

THE WATER BRIDGE

Verses 651 - 71, 693 - 700, 5116 - 47

The damsel who informed Lancelot and Gauvain that Guenievre had been carried off to the land of Goirre went on to say that one could not enter that land except by two passages. One was called the "Pont Evage," and consisted of a bridge a foot and a half in width, which lay beneath the surface of the water so that there was as much water above it as below it. Gauvain chose to

① Ibid. 186.

② Ibid. 189.

③ Shils, 1981; Rubin, 1995, pp. 122 - 145; Ortutay, 1959, 1965, pp. 3 - 8; Bauman, 1972, 2004; Heissig and Klimkeit, 1987; Bloch, 1992, 1998; Dundes, 2007, pp. 319 - 324; and many other scholars.

follow the road which led to this bridge. Several days later, when nothing had been seen or heard of him, a search was made at the water bridge at the instance of Lancelot, and Gauvain was discovered, still wearing hauberk and helm and rising and sinking in the stream. In attempting to cross the bridge he had fallen off. By means of poles and hooks the half-drowned knight was dragged out and his body was emptied of water. As soon as he recovered consciousness, he asked for news of the Queen and learned of her deliverance by Lancelot.

Professor Hibbard's remarks regarding the Pont Evage deserve quotation, "This bridge seems directly reminiscent of the concept of an otherworld lying beneath the water. [...] ①

The following chapter is of the Sword Bridge:

THE SWORD BRIDGE

Verses 672 – 77, 3017 – 55

Of the two passages to the land of Goirre, the more dangerous was the Sword Bridge. Lancelot, after parting from Gauvain and encountering various adventures, came to a black and raging stream. The bridge which spanned it was a sword as long as two lances, fixed at each end in a tree trunk. At the farther side there appeared to be two lions tied to a great rock. Removing the mail from his hands and feet, Lancelot crept across the sword, which was sharper than a scythe and cut his hands, knees, and feet. When he reached the other bank of the stream, he looked for the lions, but he did not see so much as a lizard. ②

In the Irish *Training of Cuchulainn*, the Bridge of the Cliff by which the hero reaches the island of Scathach combines the features of the various Bridges just noted. "When one sprang upon it, it was narrowed till it was as nar-

---

① Loomis, 1949, p. 222.

② Ibid. p. 225.

row as a hair, and it was as sharp as a blade-edge and as slippery as an eel's tail. At another time it would rise so that it was as high as a mast." Here, then, is a bridge which combines the properties of sharpness, narrowness, and automatic elevation, and which well deserves to be called "le Pont de l'Anguille." This group of correspondences did not occur by chance. And since we have already seen that several characteristicsof the *Chárrette* are of Irish origin, it is natural to assume that the sword bridge is derived from *The Training of Cuchulainn*. In one version the bridge leading to Scathach's isle is a narrow rope; in another it rises. In these earlier stages of the tradition, therefore, the Bridge of the Cliff already possessed two of the four properties attributed to it in the fifteenth century. There is a balance of probability, therefore, that the author of *The Training of Cuchulainn* found the other two properties-blade-like sharpness and eel-like slipperiness-in earlier traditions concerning the Bridge of the Cliff-traditions as old perhaps as the tenth century [⋯]

Passed on by the Welsh, this concept of the perilous bridge was connected with the island abode of Bran, son of Llyr. ①

Two other features of the Sword Bridge may also be plausibly accounted for by Irish tradition. Professor Hibbard pointed out that one of the feats of the famous lover Diarmaid was to place two forked poles upright, fix a sword, edge upward, between them, and then thrice measure the sword by paces from the hilt to the point. This may well be the "blade feat," which Cuchulainn learned on the isle of Scathach, and which might very naturally coalesce with the crossing of the narrow bridge to the same island. Certainly, the fixing of the sword in the forked poles seems to correspond with Chrétien's assertion that the *Pont de l'Epée* was fixed in two tree trunks on opposite sides of the river. Another feature possibly derived from Irish saga is the two phantom lions, for in Version III of *The Wooing of Emer* the glen crossed by the rising bridge was filled with spectral monsters. ②

① Ibid. p. 226.

② Ibid. p. 227.

The following is a summary of the most significant attributes of the various motifs in the Arthurian tradition:

The hero (Lancelot or Gawain)

(1) Goes to hunt; (2) chases a white doe ("animal"); (3) goes across asword bridge, which was sharper than a scythe; (4) the bridge is guarded by two lions; and (5) aperilous bridge leads to a castle, where the hero finds; (6) a woman with (7) a dead knight.

From the text, it is obvious that the place beyond the bridge is the otherworld. Every significant motif of the motif-sequence can be found in extremely similar relation in the Nart epic, as well as in the traditional folk beliefs on the otherworld of the Caucasian peoples. The parallel of the two lions and the two four-eyed dogs, appear in Zoroastrian Mythology: the mythological beings are guarding the Chinvat Bridge① that leads to the otherworld. Mircea Eliade, partly quoting Georges Dumézil writes as follows:

> It is known that the Caucasian peoples, and especially the Osset, have preserved a number of the mythological and religious traditions of the Scythians. Now, the conceptions of the after life held by certain Caucasian peoples are close to those of the Iranians, particularly in regard to the deceased crossing a bridge as narrow as a hair, the myth of a Cosmic Tree whose top touches the sky and at whose root there is a miraculous spring, and so on. ②

Then he goes on:

> Among the Osset "the deceased, after taking leave of his family, mounts on horseback. On his road, he soon comes to various kinds of sentinels, to whom he must give some cakes, the same that have been placed in his grave. Then he comes to a river, over which, by way of bridge, there is only a beam

① In Islam, it is called *As-Sirāt*, the hair-narrow bridge. It occurs some forty-five times in *Qur'ān Sirāt*, Jeffery, 2007, pp. 195 – 196; see also: Coomaraswamy, 1944, p. 199, pp. 202 – 203.

② Eliade, [1951] 1964, p. 395.

> [...] Under the steps of the just, or rather, of the truthful, the beam widens, becomes stronger, turns into a magnificent bridge." (Dumézil, *Légendes sur les Nartes*, pp. 220 - 221). "There is no doubt that the 'bridge' of the beyond comes from Mazdaism, like the 'narrow bridge' of the Armenians, the 'hair bridge' of the Georgians. All these beams, hairs, etc. have the power to widen generously for the soul of the just man and to narrow to the width of a sword blade for the guilty soul" (p. 202). ①

The entire subject of the Chinvat/Perlilous Bridge in the Celtic-Alano-Sarmatian-Caucasian-Iranian/Zoroastrian-Indian/Vedic correlations deserves a wider analysis. However, concerning the connection of the Arthurian tradition with the Nart epic, a direct relation of the two seems undoubted.

The Chinvat Bridge in Zoroastrianism

The Chinvat Bridge (*Cinvatô Peretûm*; *Č invatō pərətu*)② is a razor-thin bridge, a passage to the beyond in the Zoroastrian mythological texts and religious beliefs as well as in the Indo-Iranian cosmological conceptions, which the soul of the deceased must cross in order to reach Paradise. It is mentioned several times in the *Avesta* and in the *Bundahishn*. The bridge is guarded by two four-eyed dogs, both in the Vedic and the Zoroastrian tradition. For the sake of concision, I quote an illustrative short paragraph from a Zoroastrian text:③

> This, the 'Religious Judgments', is a collection of answers given by Manushchihr, a Zoroastrian high priest in the ninth century AC, to questions put to him by members of his community.
>
> "(1) The [Chinvat] Bridge is like a sword [···] one of whose surfaces

① Ibid. pp. 395 - 396; footnote 91.

② See: Boyce, 1984, pp. 83 - 84; Nyberg, 1938, pp. 180 - 186; Pavry, 1926, pp. 49 - 59, pp. 72 - 98; West, 1882, pp. 46 - 49.

③ Anklesaria, 1976.

is broad, one narrow and sharp. With its broad side, it is so ample that it is twenty-seven poles wide; with its sharp side, it is so constructed that it is as narrow as a razor's edge. (2) When the souls of the just and the wicked arrive, it turns on that side which is required for them. (3) Through the great glory of the Creator, and at the command of him who is the true judge and protector of the Bridge, it becomes a broad crossing for the wicked it becomes a narrow crossing, just like a razor's edge. (4) The soul of a just person sets foot on the Bridge, because of the sharpness it falls from the middle of the Bridge and tumbles down."①

Jal Dastur Cursetji Pavry wrote the following substantive analysis regarding the role of the Chinvat Bridge in the Pahlavi literature (*Bundahishn* 30. I, 9 – 13):

The difficulties of the passage over this 'Brig o'Dread' are often alluded to and dilated upon in the Pahlavi books. Their teaching is that the Bridge becomes broad or narrow according to the nature of the soul that steps upon it, presenting to the righteous a pathway of nine spears (*nēzak*) or twenty-seven arrows (*nāδ*) or a league (*frasang*) in breadth; but it turns to the godless man a sharp edge (*tāy I tēž*), like that of a sword (*šapšēr*) or a razor (*ōstarak*), so that this soul, when half-way across, falls into the abyss of Hell.

The same notable chapter goes on to give another account of the crossing, namely, that the soul of the righteous is guided over the Bridge by its own Daēnā (conscience) in the form of a lovely damsel, and is led by three steps, which are its good thoughts (*humat*), good words (huxt), and good deeds (*hvaršt*), to the resplendent Garōtmān. But if the soul is wicked, it is met by the Conscience of its evil deeds, which commands it to walk over the sharp edge of the Bridge. The wicked soul cries out that it would rather be cut to pieces by a sharp knife (*kārt*) or be pierced by an arrow (*tiγr*) or be ut-

① Boyce, 1984, pp. 83 – 84.

terly annihilated, than be forced to walk over the keen edge. ①

There is no hunt into the otherworld in all of the Zoroastrian literature, but it is an essential element both in Siberian shamanic rituals and in Central Eurasian heroic epic tradition.

What do the Motifs Mean?

In the discussed motive sequence of the Arthurian tradition, there are several elements that are impossible to clarify without the text of the Nart epic and the Central Eurasian mythology or mythologies.

(1) Why do they hunt?

(2) Why is the hound which leads them on the games' traces a female (brachet)?

(3) Why is the deer (doe) white?

(4) Why does it have to be chased to the other side of the bridge?

(5) Why is the most successful hunter given a kiss by the most beautiful lady?

There are five important questions, for which the Arthurian Legends hold no answer. Briefly: there is a tight semantic relation between the dawn and the colour of the chased deer, as clearly shown by the Nart epic: the doe is a Sun-symbol in Central Eurasian cosmology, ② that is why it appears at dawn, and it is white in the Arthurian tradition③ and golden in the Nart epic for the very same reason.

---

① Pavry, 1926, pp. 91 - 93.

② Anisimov, [1959] 1991, p. 19; Berze nagy, 1927, pp. 66 - 68; Colarusso and Salbiev, 2016, pp. 160 - 161; Martynov, 191: 229; Pschmadt, 1911, pp. 22 - 27; Sebestyén, 1902.

③ The ancient mythological connection between the North Central Asian fertility and solar symbol white doe and a river or a lake (otherworld) has been documented by Chinese sources already in 860 C. E. from the Old Turks: „ The ancestor spirit of the Türks was called Shê-mo-shê-li, a lake spirit who lived to the west of the A-shih-tê cavern. A miraculous thing happened to Shê-mo. Every evening the daughter of the lake spirit sent a white deer to fetch him and take him into the lake. At dawn she sent him back. After several decades the tribe (of Shê-mo) set out for a great hunt. In the middle of the night the (daughter of the) lake spirit said to Shê-mo: ' Tomorrow during the hunt a white deer with golden horns will come out from the cavern where your ancestors were born. If your arrow hits the deer we will keep in touch as long as you live, but if you miss it our relationship will end. ' [...]", Sinor, 1982, p. 230.

It is a doe (Mother or Master of the Animals,① *Hauptgeist*, *einijä-kyl*, '*Mutter-Tier*'② leading female animal guardian or *Tiermutter* [animal mother]③; female-spirit,④ spirit of animals ⑤) because the hero⑥ is fated to marry her, after she receivesa human shape (totemic transformation); conclusively the hero is not to be given a kiss, which in this form is entirely senseless. This kiss of the fairest maiden⑦ in the Arthurian tradition must be a late survival element of the original North Central Asian animistic, shamanic and totemic transformation of the (antlered reindeer) doe into human form⑧ and marriage between the hero (shaman, hunter) and the doe, which tradition had been transmitted to Britain by the 5, 500 Sarmatian *cataphracti* in 175 CE and was adopted by the local population during the following centuries.

The doe was pursued across the bridge, because she (as a female tutelary spirit) leads the main protagonist (originally the shaman) to the otherworld:⑨ either into the celestial sphere, or into the underworld. This is the motif that does not appear in ancient Indo-Iranian religious and mythological texts, but it is a core characteristic of the world view and shamanic ritual practice of Neolithic, Bronze and early Iron Age (third-second millennium BCE-7th century BCE) Siberian hunter-gatherer societies and their descendants. ⑩This is why it was adopted into the North-Asian Scytho-Siberian (early Iron Age) as well as Scythian (Black Sea

---

① See Jacobson-Tepfer, 2015; Vitebsky, 1995, p. 32.

② Harva, 1938, p. 477.

③ Vajda, 1964, pp. 268 – 290; Hultkrantz, 1993, pp. 8 – 9.

④ Hamayon, 1993, p. 16.

⑤ Helskog, 1999, p. 77.

⑥ The ancient North and Inner Asian as well as Scytho-Sarmatian cosmology and astral mythology the chased (antlered) reindeer doe (or female moose) is the solar symbol, while in the Sanskrit (Ṛgveda) tradition the Solar Hero is male (see among others: Coomaraswamy 1944, p. 201). This is one of the main differences between the two characteristic mythological traditions.

⑦ Loomis, 1949, p. 68.

⑧ "Prinzessin als Hirschkuh" (AaTh 401/ATU 401; Rühle 2002: 1351 – 1355); Uther 2004, I, pp. 231 – 234.

⑨ See the next chapter of this paper "The Scythian Origin of the Antlered Figure on the Gundestrup Cauldron".

⑩ Jacobson, 1983.

nomads: Alan and Sarmatian, etc. ; for such a periodization and terminology,[①] mythology and folklore already existed in these ancient times. There are a number of Neolithic rock carvings from Siberia and Inner Asia which represent cosmological scenes with a solar deer or male figures (most probably shamans or hunters) copulating with female moose (Tom' and Angara rivers) .[②] These petroglyphs are situated mostly in riversides,[③] where the Neolithic shamanic séances took place: this is the venue for the rites of passage[④] and for the shamanic journey to the otherworld by the help of tutelary spirits, mostly the solar reindeer doe. This went unnoticed by Dumézil or Eliade: the celestial or solar doe leading the hero to the Otherworld is not Indo-Iranian origin, but arose from Siberian cosmology and they amalgamated it with Scytho-Siberian and Alano-Sarmatian mythology and folklore. The bridge leading to the otherworld must be an archaic Iranian (Zoroastrian) substratum in the Scytho-Sarmatian cosmology, consequently in the Nart epic. The Arthurian Legends are indirect proof of the theory that it had to already be a feature in the Alano-Sarmatian traditions of the 2nd century CE.

The Scythian Origin of the Antlered Figure on the Gundestrup Cauldron

As we mentioned above, the doe is pursued across the bridge, because she (as a female tutelary spirit) is leading the main protagonist (originally the shaman) to the otherworld: either into the celestial sphere, or into the underworld. That is the reason why the shaman figure bears deer antlers and is surrounded by deer figures on the interior plate A of the Gundestrup cauldron (between 150 BCE and 1 BCE), and he is not "Cernunnos", it is more than obvious. This iconographical motif most probably had been adopted by Celts of Thrace (or rather Thracian silversmiths)[⑤] from the Sarmatian tribes (Scythians).

The Greeks indeed considered the Getæ to be Thracians. They occupied either the bank of the Danube, as also did the Mysians, likewise a Thracian people, who

① Jacobson-Tepfer, 2015, p. 25.

② Martynov, 1991, 153.

③ Helskog, 1999.

④ Van Gennep, 1960.

⑤ Bergquist and Taylor, 1987.

are the Scythian Hamaxoeci and Sarmatians. Until this day, all these nations, as well as the Bastarnæ, are mixed with the Thracians, more especially with those beyond the Danube, and some even with the Thracians on this side the Danube; also amongst these are the Celtic tribes of the Boii, Scordisci, and Taurisci. The ancient Greek historians called all the nations towards the north by the common name of Scythians, and Kelto-Scythians (Strabo: *Geographica*, 7. 3. 2; 11. 6. 2). ①

Conclusion

Every source text reviewed here includes the motif of an arrow bridge leading to the otherworld that has to be passed with difficulties by the hero. The Arthurian tales and the Nart epic show significant affinity in a number of fundamental motifs and particular details, that may not be mere coincidence considering the long lasting historical as well as inter-ethnic connections between the Sarmatian and the Celtic tribes, not just in Britain but also in Thrace. The inherent logic of the motive sequence which has partially been lost in the Arthurian variants and the recent large geographical space (Britain and the Caucasus), and in between we do not know any other folklore narrative (fairy-tale, legend or other genre), which would include the motif of a peculiar sword or razor-thin bridge leading to the otherworld.

After the investigation of the Celtic Arthurian as well as the Scytho-Sarmatian Nart epic traditions and oral narratives, it is my personal conviction, that the motif of the Sword Bridge connected with the hunt of a (white or golden) deer was introduced into Britain by the members of the Sarmatian Iazyges in 175 CE. and through the long lasting inter-ethnic communications during the subsequent centuries, just as the other basic motifs and narrative elements of the Nart epic. The essential motive sequence of hunt for the white/golden [reindeer] doe into the Otherworld through a river/mountain pass/cavern, the transformation of the doe into a human, marriage with the shaman/hunter (who bears deer antlers both in the archaic Siberian shamanism and on the Gundestrup cauldron), and returns from the [shamanic] journey, had been adopted by the early Scythian tribes during their long lasting inter-ethnic contacts with the indigenous peoples in the Bronze

① Hamlton and Falconer, 1856, I, pp. 453 - 454; II, p. 240.

and Iron Age. This syncretic (Zoroastrian-Siberian) religious and narrative tradition was transmitted to the later generations of Central Eurasian Scythian tribes before their further waves of their westward migration to the Pontic Steppe region, the northern slopes of the Caucasus Mountain, Thrace and the Carpathian Basin ("Great Hungarian Plain"), among the other Alano-Sarmatian tribes, the Iazyges. The narrative and visual motives discussed in this paper were most probably transmitted into Britain as well as into Thrace by the latter.

References

T. D. Anklesaria, *The Datistan-i Dinik*: *Pahlavi Text Containing* 92 *questions Asked by Mitr-Khurshit Atur-Mahan and Others*, *to Manush-Chihar Goshn-Jam*, *Leader of the Zoroastrians in Persia*, *about* 881*a. d.* , *and Their Answers.* Pt. 1, *Pursishn* I-XL, Bombay: Fort Printing Press; reprint: Shiraz: Asia Institute of Pahlavi University, 1976.

Bernard S. Bachrach, "The Alans in Gaul", *Traditio* 23, 1967.

—— "Another look at the Barbarian settlements in southern Gaul", *Traditio* 25. 1969.

——*A history of the Alans in the West*, Minneapolis, MN: University of Minnesota Press, 1973.

Anders K. Bergquist, and Timothy F. Taylor, "The origin of the Gundestrup cauldron", *Antiquity* 61, 1987.

Mary Boyce, (ed. and trans.), *Textual Sources for the study of Zoroastrianism*, Textual sources for the study of religion, edited by John R. Hinnells, Manchester: Manchester University Press, 1984.

Robert Brown, *The Religion of Zoroaster*: *Considered in Connection with Archaic Monotheism*, London: D. Bogue; Edinburgh: J. Thin, Dublin: Galignani & Co. , 1879.

James Douglas Bruce, *The Evolution of Arthurian Romance*: *From the Beginnings Down to the Year* 1300. 2nd ed. , edited with a supplement by Alfons Hilka. Vol. I-II. Charles Village, Baltimore, MD: Johns Hopkins Press, 1928.

Earest Cary (trans.), *Dio's Roman History* with an English translation by Earnest Cary, Ph. D. on the basis of the version of Herbert Baldwin Foster, PhD. Vols I-IX. London: William Heinemann Ltd. And Cambridge, Massachusetts: Harvard University Press, 1927.

John Colarusso, "Parallels between the Circassian Nart Sagas, the Ṛg Veda and Germanic Mythology", *South Asian Horizons*, 1984.

John Colarusso and Tamirlan Salbiev (eds.), *Tales of the Narts: ancient myths and legends of the Ossetians*, Translated by Walter May, Princeton and Oxford: Princeton University Press, 2016.

Doña Luisa Coomaraswamy, "The Perilous Bridge of Welfare", *Harvard Journal of Asiatic Studies*, 1944.

James Darmesteter, *The Zend-Avesta.* Part I. *The Vendîdâd*, Oxford: Clarendon Press, 1880.

Georges Dumézil, *Légendes sur les Nartes*, Paris: Librairie ancienne Honoré Champion, 1930.

Mircea Eliade, *Shamanism: archaic techniques of extasy*, London: Routledge and Kegan Paul, 1964.

Joël Grisward, "Le motif de l'épée jetée au lac: la mort d' Artur et la mort de Batraz", *Romania*, 1969.

Roberte N. Hamayon, "Are "Trance," "Ecstasy" and Similar Concepts Appropriate in the Study of Shamanism?", *Shaman*, 1993.

H. C. Hamilton and William Falcomer (trans. with notes), *The Geography of Strabo.* Vol. I-III, London: Henry G. Bohn, 1856.

Jɑ́nos Harmatta, *Forrɑ́stanulmɑ́nyok Herodotos Skythikɑ́jɑ́hoz* (Study of primary sources for Herodotus's Skythika), Budapest: M. Kir. Pɑ́zmɑ́ny Péter Tudomɑ́nyegyetem, Görög Filológiai Intézet, 1941.

Knut Helskog, "The shore connection: cognitive landscape and communication with rock carvings in northernmost Europe", *Norwegian Archaeological Review*, 1999.

Åke Hultkrantz, Introductory Remarks on the Study of Shamanism, "*Shaman* 1, 1993.

Esther Jacobson, "Siberian Roots of Scythian Stag Image", *Journal of Asian History* 17, 1983.

Arthur Jeffery, *The foreign vocabulary of the Qurān*, Leiden and Boston: Brill, 2007.

Urs Müller, *Der Einfluss der Sarmaten auf die Germanen* (The influence of the Sarmatians on the Germanic peoples), Bern: Peter Lang, 1998.

H. S. Nyberg, *Die Religionen des alten Iran*, Leipzig: J. C. Hinrichs Verlag, 1938.

Jal Dastur Cursetji Pavry, *The Zoroastrian Doctrine of a future life. From Death to individual Judgment*, New York: Columbia University Press, 1926.

Carl Pschmadt, *Die Sage von der verfolgten Hinde. Ihre Heimat und Wanderung, Bedeutung und Entwicklung mit besonderer Berücksichtigung ihrer Verwendung in der Literatur des Mittelalters* (The legend of the chased doe: its homeland and migration, meaning and development, with particular regard to its application in the literature of Middle Ages), Greifswald: Druck von Julius Abel, 1911.

Mikhail Ivanovich Rostovtzeff, *Iranians and Greeks in South Russia*, Oxford: Clarendon Press, 1922.

Stefanie Rühle, "Prinzessin als Hirschkuh." ("The princess as doe.") in *Enzyklopädie des Märchens*, Berlin and New York: Walter de Gruyter, 2002.

Denis Sinor, "The legendary origin of the Türks." In *Folklorica: Festschrift for Felix J. Oinas*, edited by Egle Victoria Žygas and Peter Voorheis, Bloomington, Indiana: Research Institute for Inner Asian Studies, 1982.

Tadeusz Sulimirski, *The Sarmatians*, London: Thames and Hudson, 1970.

Piers Vitebsky, *Shamanism*, Norman: University of Oklahoma Press, 1995.

E. W. West, "Dâdistân-î dînîk," in *Pahlavi Texts* II, Oxford: Clarendon Press, 1882.

Heinrich Zimmer, "Four Romances from the Cycle of King Arthur." In *The King and the Corpse. Tales of the Soul's Conquest of Evil*, edited by Joseph

Campbell, Washington D. C. and New York: Pantheon Books, 1948.

Stefan Zimmer, *Die keltischen Wurzeln der Artussage. Mit einer vollständigen Übersetzung der ältesten Artuserzählung Culhwch und Olwen*, Heidelberg: Universitätsverlag Winter, 2006.

特雷斯及其他地区的萨尔马泰-凯尔特文化接触：欧亚中部的信仰、宗教概念及其他

Attila Mátéffy

摘　要

本文关注的问题是，凯尔特文化中的某些元素是否来自萨尔马泰文化，如亚瑟王传说中的“剑桥”传说（Sword Bridge）、高加索纳特史诗（Nart Epic）中的“如发窄桥”（bridge as narrow as a hair），以及琐罗亚斯德教神话中的钦瓦特桥（Chinvat Bridge）之间是否存在关联。这些故事的共同主题是，一座“危桥”连接起了我们的世界与彼岸世界。这一问题的解决有助于我们理解冈德斯特尔普大锅（Gundestrup cauldron，约公元前150年至公元前1年）上的一些图像的主题，这些主题最有可能是特雷斯地区的凯尔特人从萨尔马泰部落得来的。

关键词

萨尔马泰　钦瓦特桥　冈德斯特尔普大锅　种族-文化接触　凯尔特研究

东西语言接触史研究 >>>

明治初期汉语教科书中的句型教学

——以《官话指南》中的“把”字句为例

杨　昕*

摘　要

明治时期日本出版的大量的汉语教科书文献早已引起了国内外不少学者的关注，也取得了一定研究成果。由于这一领域的研究起步较晚，很多问题尚未解决，尤其是语言研究领域的价值并未受到重视。在近代汉语教学法这一领域，特别是句型教学法这一方面的研究，仅仅只有两三本教材的简单分析，还没有一个系统性的深入考察。本文试图从明治初期的汉语教科书《官话指南》入手，探讨这本书是如何处理汉语“把”字句句型，并通过分析这一句型勾勒出这一时期“把”字句的句型特点及其教学方法，为今后全面梳理明治时期汉语教科书中“把”字句的发展变化奠定基础。

关键字

句型教学　汉语教科书　“把”字句

众所周知，任何一种语言都存在大量的句子，而句型则是通过整理、归纳、演绎或抽象等方式总结出的常用的、典型的语言结构模式。在衡量学习外语成功与否时，我们往往通过是否熟练掌握和使用这一语言为衡量标准，而是否能够熟练使用对象国语言大多数情况下反映在能否掌握足够多的词汇和句型上。如今，学习外语的学生可以在掌握一些基本词汇的基础上，通过对句型的学习，达到可以进行简单对话的外语水平，由此可见，

* 杨昕，日本关西大学外国语教育学研究科在读博士生。

句型以及句型教学是一种可以提高语言运用能力的方法。

然而，在外语学习中，对于句型的学习并不是从一开始就有的，而是通过不断地实践与进步发展起来的。本文以明治初期的汉语教科书——《官话指南》中的“把”字句为例，考察这一时期的汉语教学中“把”字句都出现了什么种类的句型，它们是如何呈现在这一时期的教科书中的，教材的编写者和使用教材的教师和学生有没有意识到“把”字句句型。本文对这一时期的汉语句型教学进行了梳理。

一 “把”字句与汉语中的句型教学

关于汉语中“把”字句语法结构的讨论，开始于王力的《中國語法理論》一书，在书中他明确地给出了“把”字句的定义和构成。[①] 自此以后，关于“把”字句的研究和讨论取得了极大的进展和丰硕的研究成果。本文讨论的问题是“把”字句的句型，因此对于语法上的描述不做过多展开，仅做简单介绍。

自从王力将“把”字句命名为“处置式”以后，学界对“把”字句在语法层面的研究已经积累了大量的成果。例如，王力认为“处置式是汉语语法走向完善的标志之一。”[②] 关于“把”字句的来源，蒋绍愚等在整理前人的研究后认为，汉语中的“把”字句在唐代是以“将”和“以”作为标志的，随着“把”和“持”等动词的语法化，处置式的标记才渐渐转化为“把”。[③] 对于“把”字句中各个语法成分的讨论也是比较多的，尤其集中在“把”字句中的动词问题。例如，吕叔湘认为“把”字句中“把”之后的动词一般不可以使用一个字动词，特别是不能使用一个字的单音节动词，并且动词后必须跟着其他句子成分。[④] 刘月华则认为“把”字句中不能出现以下几类动词：（1）表示判断、存在、领有的动词，如“是”“像”“有”等；（2）能愿动词；（3）某些动作者不能控制的表示心理活动或感受的动词，如“赞成”“知道”“同意”等；（4）某些趋向动词（只能带处所宾

① 王力：《中國語法理論》，中华书局，1955，第 165 页。
② 王力：《汉语史稿》，中华书局，1980，第 405 页。
③ 蒋绍愚：《近代汉语研究概要（修订本）》，北京大学出版社，2017，第 244 - 286 页。
④ 吕叔湘：《现代汉语八百词 吕叔湘全集第五卷》，辽宁教育出版社，2002，第 9 页。

语），如“上”“下”“进”“出”等。①

综上所述，笔者认为对“把”字句的研究主要集中在历史语言学上的描写和单一的语法线性的论述这两个侧面。毫无疑问的是，现代汉语中“把”字句在句法层面的描写已经梳理得比较详细了，而关于为什么使用“把”字句，在句型教学上的讨论，特别是在明治时期汉语教科书中所记载的“把”字句的全貌尚未有系统的考察。

此外，关于汉语句型的讨论和汉语句型教学的讨论，在欧美行为主义语言学及结构主义语言学的影响下也发展了起来。例如，吕叔湘在借鉴欧美语法理论的基础上撰写了《中国文法要略》，这部书可以说是早期汉语句型研究的开山之作。② 书中将汉语句子分为 4 种（叙事句、表态句、判断句、有无句），而“把”字句被归入叙事句中进行讨论。自此之后对于汉语句型的研究也日渐多了起来。然而，对于现代汉语句型体系，目前学界还没有比较完整的方案，对汉语句型的分类也有较大的分歧。因此本文仅讨论“把”字句这一句型，对汉语句型体系的讨论不做过多的涉及。

我们在讨论汉语句型教学之前，可以简单地看一看其他语言中的句型教学是怎么处理的。有了对比和参照，可使我们对汉语的考察有更全面和深刻的认识，以便得出更符合汉语自身语言规律的研究结果。由于笔者能力所限，本文仅以英语句型和日语句型为例进行讨论。

翻开任意一本面向中高级外语学习者的英语词典，我们都可以看到这些词典在解释一个词的时候，不仅是单纯地告诉学习者词条本身的含义，除此之外还提供了大量的短语和例句，使学习者在掌握词义的同时，还可以通过例句的反复练习，掌握如何使用一个单词，进而在脑中留下一个固定的结构搭配，写出合乎语言规范的句子。毫无疑问，这里的固定搭配就相当于一个句型，学习者只有掌握了这个固定搭配，才能写出一个合乎语法规范的句子。

而在以日语为外语的学习中，句型更是无处不在。例如，《日本語文型辞典》③ 和《日本語基本動詞用法辞典》④ 就专门为日语学习者整理了日语

① 刘月华：《实用现代汉语语法》，商务印书馆，2001，第 745 页。

② 吕叔湘：《中国文法要略 吕叔湘全集第一卷》，辽宁教育出版社，2002，第 29 - 129 页

③ 〔日〕Group Jammassy 编《日本語文型辞典》，黑潮出版社，1998，第 1 - 851 页。

④ 〔日〕小泉保等：《日本語基本動詞用法辞典》，大修馆书店出版社，1989，第 1 - 565 页。

中常用的句型，以及日语中动词是如何造句的。这些成果在一定程度上帮助了外语学习者掌握目标语言。考虑到句型在英语和日语学习中发挥的重要作用，笔者认为在汉语学习中，特别是对外汉语教学中引入句型教学，是十分必要的。

总而言之，我们在讨论汉语句型的时候，可以参考其他语言中关于句型是如何讨论的，以便我们能以更科学的方法对汉语句型进行研究。此外，笔者认为，讨论汉语句型时，要避免模仿印欧语系语言的句型讨论方式，要从汉语自身出发，将汉语句型与句子的表达功能结合起来，才能全面认识汉语句型的特点。

二 《官话指南》中的“把”字句句型

在讨论《官话指南》中的“把”字句句型之前，笔者先对《官话指南》进行简单介绍。

（一）《官话指南》

《官话指南》（1882）由吴启太和郑永邦两个日本人共同编撰，经过中国人黄裕寿和金国璞的校订，于 1882 年在日本出版。这是一本面向日本汉语学习者的汉语会话教科书。这本书是明治初年日本汉语界第一本由日本人自己编写的教科书，被当时学习汉语的日本人和西方人作为入门教材而广泛使用。1882 年出版后，《官话指南》曾在 1886 年、1900 年、1903 年多次再版重刊，此外，以其为底本的各类改写本也不胜枚举，可以说《官话指南》在明治时期的汉语教育界具有重要的地位。笔者认为通过考察《官话指南》中的“把”字句句型，不仅可以看到当时“把”字句是如何被处理的，而且可以反映出这一时期“把”字句与现代汉语中“把”字句的差别。

《官话指南》全书由以下几个部分组成，分别是：序文两篇，凡例，目录，卷之一：應對須知，卷之二：官商吐屬，卷之三：使令通話，卷之四：官話問答。

关于《官话指南》的版本研究，可详参《官話指南の書誌的研究》一书，笔者在此不做过多展开。

(二)《官话指南》中的“把”字句句型

笔者以《官話指南の書誌的研究》(1882)[①] 中的词汇索引为基础，整理得出，第一版《官话指南》共出现259个“把”字句。笔者在分析《官话指南》中的“把”字句时，从语法结构层面展开讨论，也试图通过结合“把”字句的表达功能来讨论句型。

《官话指南》是一本初中级别的汉语教科书，在前人研究的基础上，笔者拟提出“把”字句的四个基本句型，以讨论《官话指南》中“把”字句是否使用科学合理。

第一是句型一。句型一形态构成比较简单：S+把+O+V。其中S代表主语，介词“把”是句型的标志，O代表宾语，V代表动词。

经过整理分析，我们发现在《官话指南》全书中只有14例由句型一所构成的“把”字句。

(1) 趕他把這銀子交還之後、上司自然派官来。[2-22-A45a-8][②]

(2) 今天天氣好、也沒風、把衣裳得曬曬。[3-10-Blla-9]

另外，值得我们注意的是，出现在这一句型中的动词几乎没有单音节动词。如果使用了单音节动词，至少都是采用了动词的重叠形式出现。

第二是句型二。句型二形态结构是：S+把+O+V+了/着/过。同样，S代表主语，介词“把”是句型的标志，O代表宾语，V代表动词，“了/着/过”是动态助词。

(3) 我求你千萬別把這個事給洩漏了。[1-16-A4b-3]

(4) 你這兩天、先把我的東西都歸着齊截了、好交代給新手兒、把外頭首尾的事、也都要算清了。[3-20-B25b-8]

经过整理分析，我们发现在《官话指南》中只有49例由句型二所构成的“把”字句。整理这一句型时，可以明显观察到句型二中的动态助词绝大多数是“了”；动态助词“着”仅出现了1例；动态助词“过”没有在“把”字句中出现。句型二中的动词绝大多数是单音节动词，双音节动词仅

---

① 〔日〕内田庆市：《官話指南の書誌研究》(文化交涉学与语言接触研究资料丛刊7)，好文出版社，2016，第105-299页。

② [2-22-A45a-8] 表示第2卷第22章(A为卷1-2，B为卷3-4)第45页a面第3行；下同。

出现几个。

此外，和 BCC 语料库[①]中的“把”字句比较来看，现代汉语中的“把”字句通常加动态助词“了、着、过”，“了、着、过”出现的频率相近，而《官话指南》中“把”字句加动态助词“了、着、过”这一句型中，使用最多的是“了”;“着”“过”几乎没有出现，这可看作这一时期“把”字句句型的一个特点。

第三是句型三。句型三形态结构相对于前两种句型较为复杂：S + 把 + O + V + OB。其中 S 代表主语，介词“把”是句型的标志，O 代表宾语，V 代表动词，动词后的 OB 代表谓语动词的另一个宾语。可以说对于汉语初学者来说句型三是不太容易掌握的。

(5) 你把這套書、給琉璃廠寶文堂書鋪裏送了去。[2 - 18 - A37a - 6]

(6) 你把這個十吊錢的票子、給破五個一吊一個五吊。[2 - 34 - A67b - 2]

《官话指南》全书中有 73 例由句型三构成的“把”字句。在句型三中谓语动词的宾语，既有表示宾语经过动作后所在的处所，也有表示“把”的宾语为整体和部分的关系等，可以说宾语的类型是比较丰富的。而句型三中出现的动词既有单音节动词，也有双音节动词，但占大多数的依然是单音节动词。

第四是句型四。句型四的形态结构类似于句型三，只是谓语动词后的成分变成了补语：S + 把 + O + V + B。其中 S 代表主语，介词“把”是句型的标志，O 代表宾语，V 代表动词，动词后的 B 代表谓语动词的补语。

(7) 這麼着他們就挑了三間屋子、把行李都搬進去了。[2 - 29 - A57b - 5]

(8) 你先把這零碎的東西、挪到院子裏去、把地毯那茶葉先掃一回捲起來。[3 - 9 - BlOb - 3]

(9) 他先到家去措辦水腳、晚上必回船上來、把欠下的銀兩、都要交清的。[4 - 7 - B38a - 2]

《官话指南》全书中有 121 例由句型四所构成的“把”字句，是全书中数量最多的一种句型。在句型四中谓语动词的补语，既有结果补语，也有趋向补语，有情态补语，也有数量补语，可以说出现的补语类型是比较齐

① 荀恩东、饶高琦、肖晓悦、臧娇娇：《大数据背景下 BCC 语料库的研制》，《语料库语言学》2016 年第 1 期，第 93 - 111 页。

全的。此外，句型四中出现的动词既有单音节动词，也有双音节动词，但占大多数的依然是单音节动词。在分析句型四时，还有一点值得注意的是，句型四的“把”字句不仅是一些单句，还出现了不少的复句。对于汉语初学者来说，恐怕是难以迅速掌握的。由此也可以推断出《官话指南》的编写者应该注意到了句型四这种“把”字句的难度，因而编写了较前三种句型还多一倍的例句放在教科书中，让学习者反复操练，直至掌握。

在全书259个“把”字句中有两个特殊的“把”字句，难以列入以上四种句型中，因此，将它们作为特例单独列出，作为参考。

（10）把批單一燒、就算沒這麼件事了。[2-19-A40a-10]

这个“把”字句不仅套用了句型一，而且还用了另外一个句型“一…就…”，在全书中仅有此一例。

（11）偺們把買賣一辭、一個人趕着一輛車就回家去了。[2-29-A58b-1]

这个“把”字句的句型为S+把+O+一+V。这种“一+V”的结构在现代汉语中不算少见，而在《官话指南》全书中也仅有此一例，因不具有代表性，在此就不展开讨论了。

由上所述的句型种类，如表1所示。

表1　《官话指南》中的句型种类分布

句型一	句型二	句型三	句型四	其他句型
S+把+O+V	S+把+O+V+了/着/过	S+把+O+V+OB	S+把+O+V+B	
14	49	73	121	2
5.4%	18.9%	28.2%	46.7%	0.7%以下

从表1中可以看出，明治初期《官话指南》中“把”字句的基本构成。首先句型四这种带有补语成分的“把”字句是最多的，可以看出句型四是明治初期汉语中较为常用的“把”字句句型；而句型三则是次常用的“把”字句句型，有73例。与之相反看似结构简单的句型二则很可能是当时汉语中不常用的“把”字句句型，仅出现49例，并且其中占绝大多数的是带动态助词“了”的“把”字句，带动态助词“着”的“把”字句仅有1例，而带动态助词“过”的动词则完全没有，与今天现代汉语中的“S+把+O+V+了/着/过”相比，有一定的差距，可以说是这一时期“把”字句的一个特征。看似结构最为简单的句型一，实则有可能是最难以掌握的“把”

字句句型，全文中有且仅有 14 例，这也正符合后来王力、吕叔湘等人对“把”字句的考察：“把”之后的动词一般不可以使用一个字的单音节动词，如果使用，则动词至少是以动词的重叠形式出现。

（三）《官话指南》中的“把”字句句型及其表达功能

我们在考察《官话指南》中的“把”字句句型时，不能单纯只考察其线性的语法结构，而要在考察其语法结构的同时，将句型的表达功能一并进行讨论，因为汉语的句型与西方语言的句型不完全相同，汉语的每一个句型都含有特定的表达功能，它是一种功能句型，而不单是语法结构句型。

汉语使用不同的句型来表达陈述、疑问、命令等功能。对于汉语中“把”字句的表达功能的讨论，从笔者所调查的资料来看，还不是很多。吕叔湘认为，从功能上来看“把”字句有五种表达功能，它们分别是（1）表示处置；（2）表示致使；（3）表示动作的处所或范围；（4）表示发生不如意的事情；（5）表示“拿”“对”等含义。[①] 而蒋绍愚认为，从“把”字句的历史发展来看，它的语义功能发生了重大的变化，也就是说，历史上的（特别是唐宋时期）“把”字句以表示处置为主，而现代汉语中的“把”字句主要以表示致使为主。[②] 结合前人的研究，笔者认为从“把”字句的原型语义——位移义出发，现代汉语中的“把”字句至少包含了以下四种表达功能，分别是：移动（位移）、状态变化、处置、失败。随着“把”字句的泛用，原来不需要用“把”字句的句子也开始使用“把”字句。为了考察这四种表达功能在现代汉语中的使用状况，笔者从 BCC 语料库[③]中抽取了 1000 个句子进行分析，除去语句不成立的“把”字句，结果如表 2 所示。

表 2　BCC 语料库中 1000 句“把”字句的表达功能分布

表达功能	句子数量
移动	236
状态变化	132

① 吕叔湘：《现代汉语八百词 吕叔湘全集第五卷》，辽宁教育出版社，2002，第 9 页。

② 蒋绍愚：《近代汉语研究概要（修订本）》，北京大学出版社，2017，第 244 - 286 页。

③ 荀恩东、饶高琦、肖晓悦、臧娇娇：《大数据背景下 BCC 语料库的研制》，《语料库语言学》，2016（1），第 93 - 111 页。

续表

表达功能	句子数量
处置	611
失败	16

从表 2 中可以看到，现代汉语中表示处置功能的“把”字句是最多的，超过了 50%；表移动功能的“把”字句句型排在第二，有 236 句；“把”字句中表示失败功能的句子是最少的，仅有 16 句。然而明治初期“把”字句的表达功能是怎样的也是值得讨论的，这有助于我们厘清汉语“把”字句的句型与表达功能的发展历程。

经过整理分析，《官话指南》中 259 个“把”字句的表达功能，可以得出以下数据（如表 3 所示）。

表 3　《官话指南》中“把”字句的表达功能分布

表达功能	句子数量
移动 、	108
状态变化	35
处置	106
失败	10

从表 3 的数据中不难看出，在以《官话指南》为代表的明治初期的教科书中出现的“把”字句里，最多的是表达移动的“把”字句，而表达处置的“把”字句居第二位，表达状态变化和失败的“把”字句则分列后两位。如果和表 2 对照来看，与现代汉语相比，明治初期汉语教科书中的“把”字句的表达功能的特点是表示移动功能的最多，而非现代汉语中表达处置功能的最多。由此可证明这一时期“把”字句的使用尚未泛化。其次，用“把”字句来表达失败这一功能，无论是在明治时期还是在现代汉语中均是最少见的，也就是说，“把”字句虽然可以用于表达失败，但是无论古今，它在“把”字句中都是一个不常用的表达功能。

从表达功能上我们可以粗略看出，明治初期的汉语“把”字句与现代汉语中的“把”字句的异同点，接下来笔者将“把”字句的表达功能依次带入前一节所述的四种句型中，探讨“把”字句的句型与表达功能的联系。

由于篇幅所限，笔者将分析过程从略，现仅将分析结果呈现如下（见表4），以便讨论。

表4 《官话指南》中“把”字句句型与其表达功能分布概况

数量

	句型一	句型二	句型三	句型四	其他句型
移动	3	16	30	58	—
状态变化	—	5	9	21	—
处置	11	22	31	40	2
失败	—	6	1	4	—

从表4中可以分析出明治初期《官话指南》中“把”字句的特征。首先是句型一，它是所有句型中结构最简单的，但从表达功能上来看，句型一最多用于表达的还是处置，其次才是表达移动功能，而完全不表达状态变化和失败功能这一特点是值得注意的。也就是说，句型一的表达功能集中在处置和移动上。从表4中的数据来看，句型二均具有表达“把”字句的四种表达功能，但是它主要的表达功能依旧是用于表达处置，其次才是表达移动，而仅有五六个例句表达状态变化和失败。由此可见，表达处置功能是句型二的主要表达功能。从句型三的统计结果来看，其表达功能集中在移动和处置；表达状态变化和失败的功能均是次要的，不显著的。但是，句型三与句型一和句型二不同的是，在表达移动和处置时，出现的例句数非常接近，也就是说，在这一时期汉语“把”字句第三类句型中，表达移动和处置是同等重要的功能，而表达状态变化和失败的这个功能几乎可以忽略。我们从句型四的数值可以看到，其主要用于表达移动功能，有58个例句，而在前三个句型中表达处置功能的例句最多，在句型四中仅处于第二的位置。表达状态变化和失败的功能，在句型四中也处于次要地位。最后由于仅有两句其他结构的“把”字句，在此仅标出其表达功能如何，而不做进一步讨论。

三 小结

通过对第一版《官话指南》（1882）中“把”字句句型的讨论，本文可以得出以下结论。

《官话指南》是明治初期第一部由日本人编撰的汉语教科书，并且由汉语为母语的校订者校订，保证了语言的准确性，而其中所出现的“把”字句较为丰富，既有单句，也有复句；既有陈述句，又有疑问句。可以看出“把”字句在这一时期已是必不可少的学习内容。

在考察《官话指南》中“把”字句句型及其表达功能的时候可以看到这一时期“把”字句句型的特点。从句型结构来看，句型结构看似简单，有可能是难以学习掌握的句型，而看似结构复杂的句型，实有可能是常用的，所以出现的例句较多，形式也有所变化。这样的特点也从侧面印证了当时编撰汉语教科书的著者仅是从实用的角度出发尽可能多地编入“把”字句，而没有考虑到学习者的学习层次，并未从难易性的角度排序，即从简单到复杂进行编撰，而仅是根据课文内容，杂乱地插入“把”字句，不利于学习者掌握这一句型。从表达功能上来看，《官话指南》中出现的“把”字句的表达功能是全面的，都具有移动、状态变化、处置、失败四个功能，在表达功能上已经高度接近现代汉语中的“把”字句了。然而，从数量上来看，明治初期汉语教科书所出现的“把”字句的表达功能最多的是表达移动，其次才是表达处置；这正好与现代汉语相反，现代汉语中“把”字句的处置功能是独占鳌头的。我们可以推论这一时期“把”字句的主要表达功能是处于移动向处置转移的一个时期，并且这个过程尚未结束。

The “把” in Sentence Strncture in Mandarin Chinese Textbooks in early Meiji Period of Japan：A Case Study on the *Kuan Hua Chin Nan*（官话指南）

Yang Xin

Abstract

The “把” in Sentence structure generally recognized as one of the most studied constructions in Mandarin Chinese. As we known, native speakers know how to use this pattern, but as a foreigner who wants to use disposal form well in Mandarin Chinese needs great efforts. Obviously, there is a huge gap between what a native speaker can do and what a foreigner can achieve. According to a huge quantity of publications for this construction, there is no doubt that the "把" Sentence Ba-Construction has been described and explained from every possible perspective. However, few of researches related to the sentence with "把" in Mandarin Chinese Textbooks, especially in the mid and late 19th century in Japan.

Kuan Hua Chin Nan, which was organized with conversations and some short articles, is an oral Chinese textbook used by Japanese in the early period of Meiji. As a preciously record of Mandarin Chinese in the mid and late 19th century, this textbook is highly valuable, and also gets a significant position in the research of both Mandarin Chinese and the history of Chinese Education in Japan.

With analyzing sentence structures with "把" which appears in *Kuan Hua Chin Nan*, we may be able to find the answers to these questions such as how does the concept of the sentence with "把" are accepted by Westerners, Japanese, Chinese, and how do they teach students to use it at that time and others. Furthermore, we attempt to distinguish the types of verbs, the sentences patterns which were used in these disposal form so that we can compare the results with Modern Chinese to clarify the differences. In conclusion, this research mainly discusses the changes of the sentence structures with "把" in *Kuan Hua Chin nan* to see its development in 19th century.

Keywords

Sentence Pattern　Chinese Textbook　Ba-construction

试析信原继雄著《清语文典》一书中对于日语语法概念的活用

卢　骁*

摘　要

明治维新后，近代西方语言学的传入促进了日本语言学的近代化。许多从事语言研究的学者将近代西方语言学的理论和方法引入日语研究，在参照了各种各样的洋文典的基础上，编撰了一系列带有西方语法学色彩的洋风日本文典。同时，在对近代西方语法学进行吸收和应用的过程中产生的近代日语语法学的研究成果给尚处于草创期的近代汉语语法研究带来了巨大影响，使得这个阶段的汉语语法研究无论是在理论框架上还是在研究方法上都呈现了与江户时代的汉文法研究截然不同的一面。从明治初期至昭和中期由日本学者所编撰的数十册汉语语法书中，受近代日语语法学影响最深的便是于1905年问世的《清语文典》。本文将以《清语文典》中的词论为研究对象，结合从江户末期到明治时期的日本文典，从术语的使用、下位分类的框架、词类范围的划定这三个方面对信原继雄将日本文典中的语法概念应用于汉语语法研究的情况进行具体分析。

关键词

《清语文典》　语法概念　术语　下位分类　词类范围

日本的汉语语法研究始于江户时代初期。元代卢以纬所著《助语辞》

---

* 卢骁，文化交涉学博士，云南大学外国语学院日语系讲师，日本关西大学东西学术研究所非常勤研究员。

一书的流入是日本开始汉语语法研究的重要契机。《助语辞》传入日本后，当时的汉学家们如获至宝，围绕《助语辞》进行了一系列的研究。此后，以荻生徂徕、太宰春台、皆川淇园、毛利贞斋等为代表的日本汉学家们陆续编写了许多研究汉语文语助词用法的著作，开创了具有日本特色的汉文法研究的新领域。但在日本，对于"文法"的理解还停留在对汉诗文中的修辞手法以及虚词的用法进行解释说明的近世时期。这一时期的汉文法著述，从严格意义上说并非基于近代"文法"概念撰写而成。

到了时势急剧变化的江户末期，以兰学、英学为中心的西学在日本逐渐盛行。特别是在明治维新以后，日本掀起了在政治、经济、文化等各个层面向西方学习的热潮。在语言学领域，近代西方语言学的传入促进了日本语言学的近代化，作为"文法是语言内部规则"的语法观也逐渐普及。许多从事语言学研究的学者将近代西方语言学的理论和方法导入日语研究，在参照了各种各样的洋文典的基础上，编撰了很多带有西方语法学色彩的洋风日本文典。同时，在对近代西方语法学进行吸收和应用的过程中产生的近代日语语法学的研究成果给尚处于草创期的近代汉语语法研究带来了巨大影响，使得这个阶段的汉语语法研究无论是在理论框架层面还是在研究方法上都呈现了与江户时代的汉文法研究截然不同的一面。

从明治初期至昭和中期由日本学者编撰的数十册汉语语法书中，受近代日语语法学影响最深的便是于 1905 年问世的《清语文典》。《清语文典》中有以下一段记述，明确指出，信原在编撰文典的过程中，对日本文典有所参照。

> 幸に日本文中には、漢字が用いられて居るために、日本文と比較して相発明することが出来ると云ふ非常なる便利がある。そこで、余は、毎に日本文典と対照しつつ、読者と共に研究しようと思ふ。①

《清语文典》由四个章节组成，包括介绍汉语性质、种类、历史发展的

① 信原继雄:《清语文典》，青木嵩山堂，1905，第 10 页。

"总论"，介绍汉语发音的"音韵论"，解释说明汉语词类的"单语论"，以及论述汉语句法的"谈话论"。其中，"单语论"所占篇幅最大，是全书的核心内容，也是著者试图重点说明的部分。因此，本文以《清语文典》中的词论为研究对象，结合从江户末期到明治时期的日本文典，从术语的使用、下位分类的框架、词类范围的划定这三个方面对信原继雄将日本文典中的语法概念应用于汉语语法研究的情况进行具体分析。

一　术语的使用

（一）助数词

信原继雄在对数词进行解释说明的过程中，同时提到了"助数词"。《清语文典》中关于"助数词"的定义以及词例如下所示。

> 助数詞は、数詞に附加して、形式を補助したり、内容を補助したりするもの
>
> 一個、一棵、一隻、一粒、一枝、一塊、一剤、一年、一天、一張、一雙、一桿[①]

信原认为，助数词附着于数词，在形式上以及内容上对其起到辅助作用，常用的助数词包括"粒""枝""塊""剤""年""天""張""雙""桿"等。由此可见，所谓"助数词"，即我们今天所说的量词。

"助数词"这一术语的产生和威廉·乔治·阿斯顿（William George Aston）所著 *Short Grammar of the Japanese Spoken Language*（1869）的问世具有十分密切的关系。在本书中，日语中的"匹""人""羽"等词被命名为"Auxiliary Numerals"。原文如下所示。

> Auxiliary Numerals — It is comparatively seldom that the numeral is joined immediately to the noun. What may be called Auxiliary Numerals are

① 信原继雄：《清语文典》，青木嵩山堂，1905，第81页。

much in use.

They correspond to the English phrases, six head of cattle, four brace of game, two pair of shoes. Ex. Kami ichi mai, one sheet of paper; hakimono issoku, one pair of shoes; Akindo ju ichi nin, eleven merchants.

Most of these Auxiliary Numerals are of Chinese origin, a few are Japanese words……①

著者举了“紙一枚”“履物一足”“商人十一人”的例子对“Auxiliary Numerals”的用法加以说明，并把“枚”“足”和英语中的“sheet”“pair”进行对照理解。同时，他还提到了，日语中大部分的“Auxiliary Numerals”源自汉语。具体用例如图1所示。

如图1所示，关于日语中来源于汉语的“Auxiliary Numerals”，威廉·乔治·阿斯顿列举了几个例子，如用于动物计数的“匹”，用于计算人数的“人”，用于鸟类计数的“羽”，通常和长而圆的物体搭配使用的“本”，和宽而平的物体搭配使用的“枚”，以及用于计算房子数量的“轩”，用于计数船只的“艘”，用于计量酒、茶等液体的“杯”，用于计算鞋子数量的“足”等。

首次将“Auxiliary Numerals”译为汉字词的“助数词”，并将其作为语法用语固定下来的是英语学家冈仓由三郎。他在1897年出版的著作《日本文典大纲》中正式提出了“助数词”的概念。

助数詞　これが後に付きて、もて其添ひて数を示さんとする事物の性質の一端を、知らしむるものなり。

シナ語にも、此助数詞一類のものあり。本数詞と共に、本邦に傳はり、本邦語中に多く用ゐらる。②

冈仓认为，“助数词”是用在数词之后表示数量单位的词。他还提到，汉语中也有“助数词”，这些词传入日本后在日语中也十分常用，并列举了

① William George Aston, *Short Grammar of the Japanese Spoken Language*, F. WALSH, 1869, p. 13.

② 冈仓由三郎：《日本文典大纲》，富山房，1897，p. 65.

The most common are:—

	FOR ANIMALS.	FOR MEN.	FOR BIRDS.
	Hiki.	*Nin.*	*Wa.*
1.	*Ip piki.*	*Ichi nin* or *hĭto ri.*	*Ichi wa.*
2.	*Ni hiki.*	*Ni nin* or *fŭtari.*	*Ni wa.*
3.	*Sam biki.*	*San nin.*	*Sam ba.*
4.	*Shi hiki.*	*Yottari* or *yo nin.*	*Shi wa.*
5.	*Go hiki.*	*Go nin.*	*Go wa.*
6.	*Rop piki.*	*Rokŭ nin.*	*Rokŭ wa.*
7.	*Shichi hiki.*	*Shichi nin.*	*Shichi wa.*
8.	*Hachi hiki.*	*Hachi nin.*	*Hachi wa.*
9.	*Ku hiki.*	*Ku nin.*	*Ku wa.*
10.	*Jip piki.*	*Ju nin.*	*Jip pa.*
	&c.	&c.	&c.

FOR LONG AND ROUND ARTICLES, SUCH AS PENCILS, TREES, ETC.

Hon.

1. *Ip pon.* 2. *Ni hon.* 3. *Sam bon.* 4. *Shi hon.*
5. *Go hon.* 6. *Rop pon.* 7. *Shichi hon.* 8. *Hachi hon.*
9. *Ku hon.* 10. *Jip pon*, &c.

FOR BROAD, FLAT OBJECTS, SUCH AS DOLLARS, SHEETS OF PAPER CLOTHING, ETC.

Mai.

1. *Ichi mai.* 2. *Ni mai.* 3. *Sam mai.* 4. *Yo mai.*
5. *Go mai.* 6. *Rokŭ mai.* 7. *Shichi mai.* 8. *Hachi mai.*
9. *Ku mai.* 10. *Ju mai*, &c.

	FOR HOUSES.	FOR SHIPS.	GLASSES OF WINE, CUPS OF TEA, ETC.	SHOES.
	Ken.	*Sō.*	*Hai.*	*Sokŭ.*
1.	*Ik ken.*	*Is sō.*	*Ip pai.*	*Is sokŭ.*
2.	*Ni ken.*	*Ni sō.*	*Ni hai.*	*Ni sokŭ.*
3.	*San gen.*	*San zō.*	*Sam bai.*	*San zokŭ.*
4.	*Shi ken.*	*Shi sō.*	*Shi hai.*	*Shi sokŭ.*
5.	*Go ken.*	*Go sō.*	*Go hai.*	*Go sokŭ.*
6.	*Rokŭ ken.*	*Rokŭ sō.*	*Rokŭ hai.*	*Rokŭ sokŭ.*
7.	*Shichi ken.*	*Shichi sō.*	*Shichi hai.*	*Shichi sokŭ.*
8.	*Hachi ken.*	*Hachi sō.*	*Hachi hai.*	*Hachi sokŭ.*
9.	*Ku ken.*	*Ku sō.*	*Ku hai.*	*Ku sokŭ.*
10.	*Jik ken.*	*Jis sō.*	*Jip pai.*	*Jis sokŭ.*
11.	*Ju ik ken.*	&c.	&c.	&c.

图 1　日语中源自汉语的“Auxiliary Numerals”

很多源自汉语的词例（见图 2）。

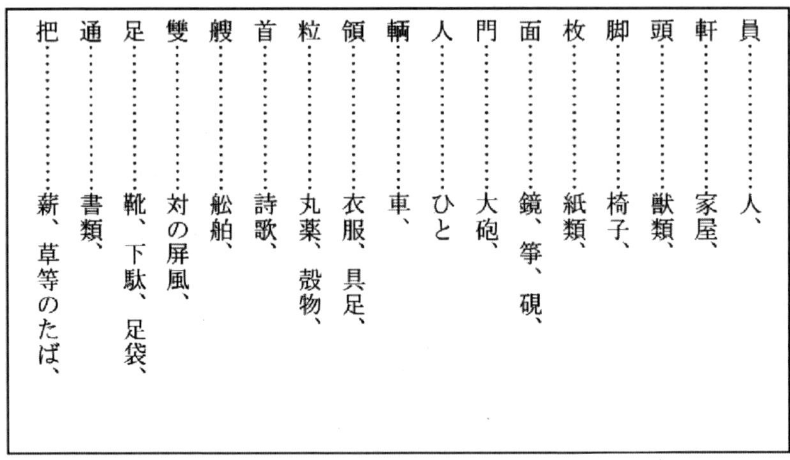
員……人、
軒……家屋、
頭……獣類、
脚……椅子、
枚……紙類、
面……鏡、箏、硯、
門……大砲、
人……ひと
輌……車、
領……衣服、具足、
粒……丸薬、穀物、
首……詩歌、
艘……舩舶、
雙……対の屏風、
足……靴、下駄、足袋、
通……書類、
把……薪、草等のたば、

图 2　日语中源自汉语的“助数词”

以上内容是用“助数词”对汉语量词进行描述的最早的记录。冈仓由三郎的《日本文典大纲》出版于 1897 年，信原继雄的《清语文典》刊于 1905 年，信原之所以将量词定名为助数词很可能是受到同时期日本文典的影响。

（二）后置词

信原还将“罷”“麽”“呢”“哪”“呀”“咧”等语气词命名为“后置词”，“后置词”则被认为是助词的下位分类之一。《清语文典》中关于常用语气词的解释如下。

> 罷　之れは、ヨに相當する。即ち命令の助詞である。去罷
> 麽　之れは、カヤ等に相當する、疑問の助詞である。不來麽
> 呢哪呀罷咧　之れ等は総べて、感歎の意を表するのであるが、感歎詞と違ふ所は、獨立して用ゐられないと雲ふ點である。上東京呢　好看哪[①]

① 信原继雄：《清语文典》，青木嵩山堂，1905，第 112－113 页。

可以看出，信原是通过套用日语语法中助词的概念来对汉语语气词进行理解和把握的。他把“罷”和日语中表示命令的终助词“よ”等同起来，把“麼”和日语中表示疑问的终助词“か”相对应。至于为何信原会将语气词称为“后置词”，其原因与“后置词”一词的由来有很大关系。

在明治时代初期的日本文典中，“后置词”是日语助词的称谓。而这一术语实际上是由“前置词”演化而来。“前置词”最早作为荷兰语“Voorzetsels”的日语译词被提出，而后频繁出现在江户时代的各类和兰文典以及和兰辞典中。《和兰文典前编》（嘉永 2 年）《和兰字汇》（安政 2 年）《和兰文典字类》（安政 3 年）《训点和兰文典》（安政 4 年）等都使用了“前置词”这一译词。其后，“前置词”作为“Preposition”的译词在英文典中也得到了广泛应用。《英和对译袖珍辞书》（文久 2 年）开成所版《英吉利文典》的译书《插译英吉利文典》等都沿用了这一称谓。

到了明治时期，随着在语法系统上全面模仿洋文典的洋风日本文典接连问世，“前置词”也作为语法术语被引入近代日语语法的研究，如在明治初期出版的太田随轩著《太田氏会话篇》等日本文典中，“前置词”被用来指称日语助词这一词类。但是，“前置词 = 助词”这一对应关系并没有持续太久，从《山田氏文法书》开始，助词称谓发生了从“前”到“后”的变化（见表 1）。

表 1　明治前期的日本文典中“助词”的名称

书名	品词名	著者	出版年份
《山田氏文法书》	后词	山田俊三	明治 6 年
《日本消息文典》	后词	藤沢亲之	明治 7 年
《日本文典》	后词	中根淑	明治 9 年
《小学科用日本文典》	后置词	春山弟彦	明治 10 年
《小学文法书》	后置词	中岛操	明治 12 年

至于为何会发生以上称谓上的变化，我们可以从江户末期到明治前期从事日语研究的西方人的记述中找到蛛丝马迹。

表 2　西方人所编写的日语语法书中“助词”的名称

书名	品词名	著者	出版年份
Arte de la Lengua Japona	preposiciones	Oyanguren，Fr. M	1738
Epitome linguae japonicae	praepositiones	Shiebold，Ph. Fr	1826
Introduction à l' étude de la langue japonaise	postposition	Rosny，L	1865
A Grammar of the Japanese Spoken Language	postposition	Aston，W. G	1888
Lehbücher Japanishen Umgangssprache	postposition	Lange，R	1890
Grammatica giapponese della lingua parlata	posposione	Gattinoni，G	1890

表 2 清晰地揭示了从幕末到明治时期，西方人所著日本文典中助词的名称从“前”到“后”的变化过程。阿斯顿指出，“The Preposition in Japanese should be called the Postposition，as it always follows the noun”。① 即，由于日语助词总是出现在名词之后，因此“前置词”在日语中应改称为“后置词”。此外，兰格（Lange. R，1890）也认为在日语中，与法语“前置词”相对应的词是“后置词”。

由此可以判断，西方学者出于对日语助词在句法位置上的考量，认为用“后置词”命名更合适。而深受西方语言学影响的日本学者可能也是出于同样的理由，将“前置词”改成了更加符合日语性质的“后置词”。

在梳理清楚“后置词”一词的由来之后，信原将其用来指称汉语语气词的理由也更加显而易见。“后置词”是基于日语助词在句中的位置，由“前置词”演化而来。而汉语的语气词常常用于句末，和日语助词在句法位置上存在一定程度的相似性。因此，信原才会将“后置词”选做汉语语气词的称谓。

二　下位分类的框架

（一）　代名词的下位分类

在《清语文典》中，信原将人称代词称为“人代名词”，并将其分为三类。详细解释如下文所示。

① William George Aston，*A Grammar of the Japanese Spoken Language*，Lane，1888，p. 159.

人代名詞は、自己の名の代りに用ゐる所の、私と云ふ意味の詞と、話相手の名の代りに用ゐる所のアナタと云ふ意味の詞と、自己や相手以外の人の名の代りに用ゐる所のアノヒトと云ふ意味の詞との三類に分たれる。①

第一类是代称自己的词，相当于日语中的“私”。第二类是代称听话方的词，相当于日语中的“あなた”。第三类是代称自己和对方以外的人的词，相当于日语中的“あのひと”。这三类词分别被命名为“自称”“对称”“他称”，各类中的人称代词词例分别对应“通称”“贱称”“尊称”三项（见表3）。

表3 《清语文典》中人称代词的下位分类

	自称	对称	他称
通称	我	你	他
賤称	我、小的	你	他
尊称	我	您老爺	他那位

以上分类方式在大槻文彦于1882年出版的《言海》卷头所附《语法指南》一文中已经出现。

人ニ就キテ用ヰル代名詞ヲ、人代名詞トイフ。而シテ、其称スル人ノ位置ニ因リテ、別ヲ起ス、コレヲ人称トイフ。其人称ノ第一ナルヲ自称トス。話スル人、自ラ、己ガ名ニ代ヘテ用ヰルモノナリ、即チ、「我、行カム」ノ我ノ如シ。第二ナルヲ対称トス、我ト相対シ我ガ話シ掛クル人ノ名ニ代ヘテイフモノナリ、即チ、「我、汝ト倶ニ行カム」ノ汝ノ如シ。第三ナルヲ他称トス、二人ノ間ニ話シ出ス他ノ人ノ名ニ代ヘテイフモノナリ、即チ、「我ガ汝ト倶ニ彼ヲ訪ハム」ノ彼ノ如シ。②

① 信原继雄：《清语文典》，青木嵩山堂，1905，第51页。

② 大槻文彦：《语法指南》，小林新兵卫，1882，第13页。

大槻将指称人的代名词称为“人代名词”。将因指称之人所处位置的不同而产生的区别叫作“人称”。“自称”指称代自己的词。“对称”是代称相对于我方而言的听我说话的对象。“他称”是代称双方对话中所提到的第三方对象（见表4）。

表4 《语法指南》中人称代词的下位分类

自称	吾、麿、朕、妾、僕、己、某、余、身
对称	汝、吾主、御身、御事、吾殿、吾邊、君、其許
他称	彼、そやつ、かやつ、あやつ
不定称	誰、某、何某

比较对照两种说法可以得出，首先，“人代名词”这一称谓本身就出自《语法指南》的可能性很大。其次，除了“不定称”之外，其他三项的用词完全一致，且给出的定义也极其相似。由此可见，信原很有可能照搬了大槻所提出的分类方式和分类项目。不仅如此，大槻提到，人称有古今、雅俗、尊卑之分。这也很有可能是信原将人称代词纵向分为“通称”“贱称”“尊称”的契机之一。

此外，信原在《清语文典》中对于指示代词的下位分类表述如下（见表5）。

> 指示代名詞も、亦三類に分たれる。手近な事物場所等を指し示す所の、近称代名詞と、中程のを指し示す所の、中称代名詞と、遠いのを指し示す遠称代名詞とである。①

表5 《清语文典》中指示代词的下位分类

指示代名詞			
	近称	中称	遠称
事物	這、這個（コノ）	那、那個（ソノ）	那、那個（アノ）
場所	這兒（ココ）	那兒（ソコ）	那兒（アソコ）
方向	這（コノ）	那（ソノ）	那（アノ）

信原将指示代词横向分为“近称”“中称”“远称”三类，并以日语

① 信原继雄：《清语文典》，青木嵩山堂，1905，第52页。

“こそあど”系列词中的“この”“その”“あの”与之一一对应。“近称”是指称近处的事物以及场所的词；“中称”用于指称距离适中的情况；“远称”指称远处的事物或者场所。同时，信原还将指示代词纵向分为表示“事物”“场所”“方向”这三种情况。

而以上分类方式同样也出自《语法指南》。在《语法指南》中，大槻对于指示代词的描述以及分类如下。

> 事物、地位、方向、等ニ就キテ用ヰル代名詞ニハ、近称、中称、遠称、不定称ノ別アリ。近称ハ、最モ近キニイフ、是、此處、此方、ノ如シ。中称ハ、稍、離レタルニイフ、其、其處、其方、ノ如シ。遠称ハ、遠キニイフ、彼、彼處、彼方、ノ如シ。①

表6　《语法指南》中指示代词的下位分类

	事物	地位	方向
近称	これ、こ	ここ	こなた、こち
中称	それ、そ	そこ	そなた、そち
遠称	あれ、あ、かれ、か	あしこ、あそこ、かしこ	あなた、かなた、あち
不定称	いづれ、なに、どれ	いづこ、いづく、どこ	いづかた、いづち、どち

大槻将表示事物、场所、方向的词分为“近称”“中称”“远称”“不定称”四种。“近称”用于近处的情况；“中称”用于稍远的情况；“远称”用于指代远处的事物。通过对比可知，《清语文典》中关于“近称”“中称”“远称”的划分和划分的依据，以及信原所提及的“事物”“场所”“方向”这三种情况，无一不出自《语法指南》中大槻文彦的论说。值得一提的是，信原不仅仅是照搬，还把这些分类项目和汉语中的指示代词巧妙地一一对应起来。

（二）动词的下位分类

1. 本来动词与转来动词

在《清语文典》中，关于动词的下位分类，信原提出了两种分类方法，

① 大槻文彦：《语法指南》，小林新兵卫，1882，第14页。

一种是按照形式来划分，另一种是按照内容来划分。首先，依据形式标准，动词可分为“本来动词”和“转来动词”。

> 本来動詞：走（歩ム）、去（行ク）、回（返ル）、聴々（聞ク）、瞧々（見ル）
>
> 転来動詞：花（費ス）、幹（為ス）、頑児（遊ブ）[①]

从信原给出的词例可以判断，所谓“本来动词”，即原本就是属于动词一类的词。“转来动词”则是由其他词类转用为动词的词。例如，“花”和“幹”由名词转化而来，“頑”由形容词转化而来。

根据福井（1907）的研究，日语语法史上首次将动词分为“本来”和“转来”的是冈仓由三郎。[②] 冈仓在《日本文典大纲》中，把动词分为“本来语”和“转来语”两种。

> 動作詞に書く、焼くの如き相傳の本来語とおぼしきもの、多き事、論を竢たざれども、これと同時に、相傳の転来語の尠からざるもの、亦事実なり。
>
> 一、名詞より来れるもの……やど（宿）-る、つな（綱）-ぐ、はら（腹）-む
>
> 二、形容詞より来れるもの……ひろ（廣）-む、たか（高）-まる
>
> 三、感詞より来れるもの……あはれ（嗚呼）-む
>
> 四、副詞より来れるもの……いな（否）-む[③]

如引文所示，冈仓不仅认为动词中存在“本来”和“转来”的区别，同时它还对转来动词按照其原本的性质进行了更为详细的分类，即以下四小类：由名词转化而来的词、由形容词转化而来的词、由感词转化而来的词、由副词转化而来的词。

① 信原継雄：《清语文典》，青木嵩山堂，1905，第 56 - 57 页。

② 福井久藏：《日本文法史》，大日本图书株式会社，1907，第 150 页。

③ 冈仓由三郎：《日本文典大纲》，富山房，1897，第 82 - 83 页。

前面已经提到，信原在对汉语量词进行论述的时候，很有可能参考了《日本文典大纲》中的相关内容。而在对动词的分类上，信原所提出的形式分类法与冈山所提出的分类方法也存在重合的部分，这也从另一个角度增大了信原参照过《日本文典大纲》的可能性。

2. 自动词与他动词

信原还依据“内容”，也就是动词所表示的意义，将其分为“自动词”和“他动词”。

> 自動詞とは、蝶が飛ぶ、花が散る、の飛ぶ、散る、の如く、動作が他物に、推及ぶ事の無い者を云ふので、他動詞とは、人が枝を折る、猫が鼠を捕る、の折る、捕る、の如く、動作が他の物に及ぶのである。
>
> 他動詞の付いて居る文章又は談話は必ず、其の動作を為す所の主人公を表はす名詞と其の主人公に処置せらるる所の或る物を云ひ表はす名詞との二の名詞が缺けてはならぬ。[①]

根据信原所给出的定义，“自动词”是动作不会波及其他事物的词。“他动词”是动作会给其他事物造成影响的词。他还补充到，在使用“他动词”的情况下，必须要有表示动作的施动者的名词，以及表示动作的承受者的名词，二者缺一不可。值得注意的是，信原在说明“自动词”和“他动词”的概念的时候，并没有列举汉语的例子，而是只给出了日语的词例。这也是他试图通过日语中相似的概念来对汉语语法进行解释的重要表现。根据引文中的日语词例，我们可以看出，“自动词”不带目的语[②]，而“他动词”是带有目的语的。因此，动作是否会影响其他事物，动词后是否跟有表示动作承受者的目的语，是信原所认为的区别“自动词”和“他动词”的重要依据。

通过对“自动词”“他动词”进行历时性研究发现，这种二分法起源于日本江户时代的洋学资料，而类似的说法最早见于《兰语九品集》。

① 信原继雄：《清语文典》，青木嵩山堂，1905，第 57－58 页。

② 日语中的语法概念，相当于汉语中的宾语，表示动作的承受方。

表7　江户时代的洋学资料中动词的下位分类

书名	动词的下位分类	著者名	出版年份
兰语九品集	动他词、自动词、被动词	中野柳圃	文化7年
谙厄利亚语林大成	动他词、自动词、被动词	木本正荣、楢林高美、吉雄永保	文化11年
英和对译袖珍辞书	他动词、自动词	堀达之助、西周、箕作贞一郎等	文久2年
洋学指针·英学部	他动词、自动词	柳河春三	庆应3年
英文典便览	他动词、自动词	青木辅清	明治4年

在《兰语九品集》中，动词被分为“动他词”“自动词”“被动词”三种。深受《兰语九品集》影响的《谙厄利亚语林大成》也采用了相同的三分法。其后，从《英和对译袖珍辞书》开始，三分法逐渐向二分法转变，包括《洋学指针》《英文典便览》等都采用了“自动词”“他动词”的二分法（见表7）。

明治前期以洋文典为范式的洋风日本文典也同样沿袭了把动词分为“自动词”和“他动词”的分类方式。

表8　明治前期的日本文典中动词的下位分类

书名	动词的下位分类	著者名	出版年份
日本小文典	自动词、他动词	黑川真赖	明治5年
小学日本文典	自动词、他动词	田中义廉	明治7年
日本消息文典	自动词、他动词	藤泽亲之	明治7年
日本文典	自动词、他动词、单用动词、重用动词、顺用动词、逆用动词、规则动词、不规则动词、助动词、分词	中根淑	明治9年
小学科用日本文典	自动词、他动词、受动词	春山弟彦	明治10年
小学文法书	自动词、他动词	中岛操	明治12年

从表8可以看出，将动词区别为“自动词”和“他动词”的二分法，在明治前期的洋式日本文典中已经基本固定下来，并具有一定的普遍性。

至于何谓“自动词”和“他动词”，大槻文彦在《语法指南》中给出了详细的定义。

自ラ動作シテ、他ノ事物ヲ処分スルコトナキ意ノモノヲ、「自動性」トス。例ヘバ、「花、飛ぶ」、「蝶、驚く」ノ「飛ぶ」、「驚く」ノ如シ、其動作、ソノママニテ通ズ。自動性ノ動詞ヲ略シテ、自動詞トモ言フ。

動作ノ、他ノ事物ヲ処分スル意アルモノヲ、他動性トス。例ヘバ、「蠶ハ、絲ヲ吐く」、「蜂ハ、蜜ヲ醸す」、ノ「吐く」、「醸す」ノ如シ。コレヲ、唯、「蠶ハ、吐く」、「蜂ハ、醸す」、トノミイヒテハ、其意、未ダ全ク通セズ、必ズ、「何を」ト問ハルベシ、然ルトキハ、其処分スベキモノヲ挙ゲテ、「絲を」、或ハ、「蜜を」ト答ヘズハアルベカラズ、而シテ後ニ、其意ヲ全ウス。他動性ノ動詞ヲ他動詞トモイフ。①

根据大槻的解说，“自动词”就是不具有处置其他事物意义的词。如，日语中的“飛ぶ”“驚く”。“他动词”就是含有处置其他事物意义的词。如，“吐く”“醸す”等。他强调，“他动词”若不带目的语，其意则不通，一定要带有由助词“を”提示的目的语，如用例中的“絲”“蜜”等，其意才得以完整。

将《清语文典》中对于自他动词的定义与上文比较可知，不论是从定义上来说还是从区分自他动词的标准上来说，两者的说法基本一致。由此可见，信原不仅借鉴了日本文典中“自动词”和“他动词”的概念，他将是否带有表示动作承受者的目的语作为区分自他动词的标准也是受到日本文典中相关记述影响的结果。

三　词类范围的划定

（一）将“的”“了”纳入助词一类的情况

“的”和“了”在现行的汉语语法体系中，分别被称作“结构助词”和“时态助词”。但它们并非从一开始就被归入助词一类。根据吕叔湘（1956）的研究，最早将“的”“了”等纳入助词的中国学者是赵元任。在

① 大槻文彦：《语法指南》，小林新兵卫，1893，第17－18页。

其著述《北京、常州、苏州语助词的研究》（1926）和《现代吴语的研究》（1928）中都可以看到相关的见解。而早在 1905 年出版的《清语文典》中，信原就已经将“的”“了”纳入助词一类，并做了如下解释：

> 的　これはノに相當する。例えば、「我の家」と云ふ事は、我的房子と書くが如きである。
>
> 了　これは、タに相當する、即ち過去を示す助詞である。去了、念了、完了。①

信原认为，“的”相当于日语中表示领属的格助词“の”。他举了“我の家”和“我的房子”的例子，以此表现“の”和“的”在语法功能上有着一定程度的相似性。因此，日本学者在考虑“的”应该被划归到哪一类词的时候，很有可能参考了“の”在日语语法中的性质与所属范畴。因此，日本学者把“的”纳入助词在很大程度上是受了日语语法的影响。

信原将“了”归为助词同样也是受到了日语语法的启发。他认为“了”和“た”相当，是一个表示过去的助词。“た”虽然在日语语法中是一个表示过去、完了的助动词，但日语助动词和助词在过去很长一段时间内被看作是同一类词，叫作“天爾遠波”。也就是说。信原将“了”划归助词，与“た”在日语语法中的所属范畴不无关系。

（二）将介词纳入助词的情况

信原还将“上”“打”“从”“由”“把”“给”等介词也纳入了助词的范围（见表 9）。

表 9　《清语文典》中被纳入助词的介词词例

例词	说明	例句
上	この字は日本語のへと云ふ助辞に相當して、「東京へ行く」、「西京へ行く」等の如く、東京、西京と云ふ名詞と、行くと云ふ動詞との関係を補助言明して居る	上東京去
打、従、由	之れ等は皆日本語のカラに相當する	打東京来

① 信原继雄：《清语文典》，青木嵩山堂，1905，第 110－111 页。

续表

例词	说明	例句
把	之れは、ヲ又はニテに相當する	把尺寸開出来
給	之れは、ニの字に相當する	給您請安来

信原认为，“上”相当于日语中表示方向或者目的的格助词“へ”。不仅如此，他把“打”“从”“由”等和日语中表示空间起点的格助词“から”等同起来。把“把”和日语中表示动作对象的格助词“を”相对应，把“给”和日语中表示动作目标的“に”相对应。他还强调，

> それから一言参考として云って置くが、予が兹に助詞と称へる者は、日本文典の助辞と、助語とのような性質の者が包含せられて居るのである。[①]

即，信原认为汉语“助词”中包含许多与日本文典中的“助词”性质相类似的词。而“へ”“から”“を”“に”在日语语法中都是格助词，因此信原将汉语中与之功能类似的“上”“打”“从”“由”“把”“给”等介词也归入助词一类。这是将日语语法中助词划分的概念直接套用到汉语研究中的结果。

四　结语

本文主要从术语的使用、下位分类的框架以及词类范围的界定这三个层面考察了在《清语文典》一书中，日语语法概念如何影响著者信原继雄对汉语的认识和理解。

首先，在术语的使用方面，信原在描述量词时所用到的“助数词”一词，出自冈仓由三郎的《日本文典大纲》（1897）。而汉字词“助数词”又源于威廉·乔治·阿斯顿在 *Short Grammar of the Japanese Spoken Language*（1869）中所提到的“Auxiliary Numerals”。冈仓由三郎在《日本文典大纲》

① 信原繼雄：《清语文典》，青木嵩山堂，1905，第 96 页。

中首次使用汉字词的“助数词”，并将其作为语法用语固定下来。而信原也借用了这一称谓，正式将汉语量词定名为助数词。

信原将语气词称为“后置词”，并且将汉语语气词与日语中与之具有同样功能的终助词相对应。在明治时代的日本文典中，“后置词”是日语助词的称谓。信原通过日语的终助词来理解汉语的语气词，是语气词被称作“后置词”的原因之一。此外，通过考察“后置词”的由来可以得知，这一术语实际上是基于日语终助词在句中的位置，由“前置词”演化而来的。而汉语的语气词在句法位置上和日语中的终助词一样，都用于句末。因此，信原才会将“后置词”选做汉语语气词的称谓。

其次，在下位分类的框架方面，在《清语文典》中，信原将人称代词称为“人代名词”，并将其横向分为“自称”“对称”“他称”三类。这是信原照搬了大槻文彦著《语法指南》（1882）中“人代名词”的下位分类模式的结果。大槻指出人称有古今、雅俗、尊卑之分，这也是信原将人称代词纵向分为“通称”“贱称”“尊称”的契机之一。此外，信原还将指示代词横向分为“近称”“中称”“远称”三类，并以日语“こそあど”系列词中的“この”“その”“あの”与之一一对应。而这种分类方式同样也出自《语法指南》。

关于动词的下位分类，信原首先依据形式标准，将动词分为“本来动词”和“转来动词”，而日语语法史上将动词分为“本来”和“转来”的最早记录出自冈仓由三郎的《日本文典大纲》。在本书中，冈仓首次将动词分为“本来语”和“转来语”两类。信原所提出的形式分类法与冈仓所提出的分类方法存在极高的相似性，这也从另一个角度增大了信原参照过《日本文典大纲》的可能性。此外，信原还依据动词所表示的意义，将其分为“自动词”和“他动词”。信原在对“自动词”和“他动词”进行说明时，并没有列举汉语的用例，而是给出了日语的词例。这也是他试图通过日语中相似的概念来对汉语语法进行解释的重要表现。通过对“自动词”和“他动词”进行历时性研究后发现，这种二分法最早起源于日本江户时代的兰文典，后被广泛用于各类洋文典中。明治前期以洋文典为范式的日本文典也同样沿袭了这一分类方式，并将这种分类方式固定下来。信原不仅借鉴了日本文典中“自动词”和“他动词”的概念，他将是否带有目的语作为区分自他动词的标准也是受到日本文典中相关记述影响的结果。

最后，在范围划定方面，信原早在1905年出版的《清语文典》中，便将“的”“了”纳入助词一类。信原认为，“的”等同于日语中的格助词“の”，而“了”和“た”相当。因此，信原在给“的”和“了”分类时参考了“の”与“た”在日语语法中的性质与所属范畴。

信原之所以将“上”“打”“从”“由”“把”“给”等介词也纳入助词的范围，是受到日语语法概念影响。信原认为汉语“介词”中包含许多和日本文典中的“助词”具有类似性质的词，于是他将这些介词与日语中与之功能类似的“へ”“から”“を”“に”等格助词一一对应起来进行理解。“へ”“から”“を”“に”等在日语中是助词的一种，因此这些与格助词性质类似的介词也被归入助词一类。

综上所述，在《清语文典》的词论中，频频出现将日语语法概念应用到汉语语法研究中的情况。信原继雄在对汉语的语法现象进行描述时，经常直接套用或者借鉴日本文典中与描述对象在某种程度上相对应或者相类似的语法概念。由此可见，在近代西方语言学的影响下，日语语言学在近代化的过程中所构建出的新的语法体系，对于尚处于草创期的日本近代汉语语法研究产生了巨大的影响。

参考文献

William George Aston, *Short Grammar of the Japanese Spoken Language*, F. WALSH, 1869.

William George Aston, *A Grammar of the Japanese Spoken Language*, Lane, 1888.

大槻文彦：《语法指南》，小林新兵卫，1882。

冈仓由三郎：《日本文典大纲》，富山房，1897。

信原继雄：《清语文典》，青木嵩山堂，1905。

福井久藏：《日本文法史》，大日本图书株式会社，1907。

An Analysis of the Use of Japanese Grammar Concepts in *Shingobunten* Authored by Nobuhara Tsuguo

Lu Xiao

Abstract

After the Meiji Restoration, the introduction of modern Western linguistics promoted the modernization of Japanese linguistics. The research results of modern Japanese grammar research produced in the process of absorbing and applying modern Western linguistics have also brought great influence to the study of modern Chinese grammar, which was still in the initial stage. This made the study of Chinese grammar in Japan advanced to a new stage in both the theoretical framework and the research methods.

Among the dozens of Chinese grammar books written by Japanese researchers from the early Meiji era to the middle of the Showa era, the most deeply influenced by modern Japanese grammar research was *Shingobunten*, which was published in 1905. There is also a description in *Shingobunten*, which clearly states that Nobuhara has indeed referenced many Japanese grammar books in the process of writing.

Therefore, this article focus on the description of parts of speech based on the Japanese grammar books from the end of the Edo era to the Meiji era. The paper analyzes how the grammatical concepts in Japanese grammar books are applied to the study of Chinese grammar from three aspects: the use of terms, the framework of the sub-category, and the delineation of the scope of the word class.

Keywords

Shingobunten　Grammatical Concepts　Terms　Sub-classification　Scope of the word class

历史比较语言学视野下的“把”字句和满语助词“be”的关系

崔香兰[*]　朴兴洙[**]

提　要

“把”字句作为处置式的一种，是汉语的一种重要的句法结构。因此一直以来都备受学界的重视。最早提出“处置式”这一概念的是王力先生，他讲道：“凡用助动词把目的位提到叙述词的前面以表示一种处置者，叫作处置式。”以往的研究表明，唐宋时期处置式的“将”字句的使用率明显多于“把”字句，而当金元明清时期北方方言逐渐奠定了作为标准语言的地位的时候，“把”字句的使用开始占据绝对优势，进而形成了北方方言只用“把”字句，南方方言只用“将”字句的格局。[①] 因此，我们提出疑问：汉语中“把”字句这种处置式句法跟北方的阿尔泰语言有什么关系？我们甚至可以大胆的假设，“把”这个词，其实就是来源于阿尔泰语言中的某个词语。本文的研究目的在于探讨“把”字句的起源及其与满语格助词“be”的关系。

关键词

“把”字句　满语　处置式　阿尔泰语言　格助词

* 崔香兰，韩国外国语大学讲师。

** 朴兴洙，韩国外国语大学中语中文系教授。

① 今天的北方方言处置式用“把”不用“将”，而粤、闽、客家等多数南方方言用“将”而不用“把”。参见蒋绍愚《近代汉语研究概况》，北京大学出版社，1994，第205页。

一　“把”字句的起源

部分学者提出，“把”字和“以”字的替换是在“以”字作为处置介词使用以后。单纯地把“把”替换成“以”，是处置介词替换的结果。对于上述意见蒋绍愚先生在《近代汉语研究概要》中指出，“词汇替换”只有在“被替换词”与“替换词”在词义或语法意义相同或相近的情况下才可能发生。因此，只有在“把”具备了与表示处置功能的“以”相近或相似的功能的时候，才会发生“词汇替换”。但是，蒋先生又进一步引用贝内特（P. A. Bennett）提出的观点，认为表处置的“把”是从连动式演变而来的。“作为动词的‘把’在连动式中处于次要动词的位置，因此有机会达到‘连动——处置’的重新分析，促使词义演变并发生语法化。”而对于上述“把”字的语法化过程，本文提出的看法如下。

首先，本文赞同“词汇替换”是需要词义及语法义的相似性作为前提。李宝嘉先生曾经说过“语言的演变从来没有无缘无故”的，特别是像处置式这种异于汉语正常语序的特殊的句法形式的演变更是如此。其次，本文认为贝内特提出的“连动式演变论”值得进一步探讨。我们都知道，在漫长的汉语发展史中，曾经历过多次大规模的变动，其中最具代表性的就是隋唐以后的近古汉语的南北差异。汉语在中塬士民迁徙与南北民族融合中“北杂夷虏，南浸吴越”，于是出现了北留中塬汉语的阿尔泰化或阿尔泰语的汉语化，出现了南迁中塬汉语的南方化或南方语言的汉语化。所谓汉语的“阿尔泰化”主要是指北方民族在换用北留中塬汉语的过程中，阿尔泰语的语音、语法特点改变了汉语，形成了阿尔泰语的表层；所谓汉语的“南方化”，主要是指南迁中塬汉语对南亚语言的不完全汉语化，残留了南方语。以上这些语言运动导致了近古南中北汉语的差异度。在这种多次移民和语言交融的文化历史背景中，东亚大陆形成了与欧洲语言演变模式不同的语言发展模式。换而言之，在过去的 2000 多年中，东亚大陆一直处于时起时伏、绵延不绝的汉语化运动中，华夏汉语在同化周边语言的过程中也异化着自己。在如此多元因素的影响下，表处置的“把”是否一定是从汉语固有的动词“把”演变而来的？如果不是，它又是从哪里来的呢？产生于唐宋时期的体助词“了”“着”，其语义和功能并不仅与完成或持续有关。“了”还具有表示开始、进行义的功能，“着”还兼有表示方位、目的、语气等多种功能。依据民族语言和汉语的参照研究，它们可能源于具有对应关系的阿尔泰语词缀。[①]“了”与阿尔泰语中表完成，将要、持续、开始进行、目的等词尾，特别是与蒙古语的未完成体具有惊人的相似之处。“了”的轻读［lə］/［la］等，和阿尔泰语词尾［rə］\［ra］等具有对应关系。表“完结”的“了”，在东汉仅有一例，且可以另解（宋金兰解作“明了”）。直到唐代，“了”才逐渐取代魏晋表完成义的动词“迄”“已”“竟”“毕”等而成为常用词。具有完结义的“了”和先秦的“已”“矣”之间没有语音演变关系，当另有来源。完结义的“了”大约是魏晋时期产生的一个口语词，它的出现或许和阿尔泰语的上述词尾有关。这个词尾可能最初变换成为一个汉语单音节词，其语法意义转为汉语词汇意义，并借用“了”的书写形式。随着阿尔泰语对汉语的日益渗透，又从词汇层进入语法层。作为汉语词尾的“了”，最早出现在唐代变文和诗词这类口语作品中。“宾+动+了”格式与阿尔泰的句法结构完全一致。

“着”与阿尔泰语的词尾-d、-dʒ具有一系列对应关系。从功能上看，“着”可以表示动作的持续、完成、处所、随同人物、目的、被动、工具和祈使语气等；从语音上看，“着”的中古音＊diak，与蒙古的持续体词缀和过去时词缀-dʒə：音近。作为方位介词的“着”相当于先秦汉语的“于”。二者的功能和分布的差异表明，“着”并非完全承袭了上古汉语的“于”，反而与阿尔泰语的位（与）格词缀存在许多共同点，而阿尔泰语的位格词缀，与时体词缀在语音上的相似性是显而易见的。王力等研究者认为“附着”的“着”是助词“着”外的间接来源，即“着”的演变轨迹是：附着的“着”—方位介词“着”—情貌助词“着”。表方位的虚词“着”的最早用法见于魏晋，当时的读音＊d-，与阿尔泰语的位格词尾音近。而后，方位介词“着”又逐渐具有了与位格词缀类似的一系列用法，并且演变为助词。在“着”的演变过程中，如果没有阿尔泰语对其的影响，单凭其内部潜在语义，未必能够发展成后来这样一个多语义、多功能的虚词。

如果仅就汉字内部的观察，时体助词“了”或“着”的出现确实像一

① 宋金兰：《汉语助词“了”、“着”与阿尔泰诸语言的关系》，《民族语文》1991年第6期第59页。

个实词逐步虚化的结果。但是，只要以语言接触和语主替换的观点进行考察，其实它们的产生和发展都与阿尔泰语的渗透密切相关。另外《元朝秘史》总译中的“了”“着”出现频率远远高于同时期的其他文献；今青海汉语中的“了”“着”使用频率，不仅高于其他北方话，而且与阿尔泰语词尾具有更加明显的趋同性。

这些都进一步阐明了时体助词“了”或“着”出现的汉语阿尔泰化背景。据研究，满语中的词语或短句加属格后缀-i＊能够独立形成很长的名词性结构，这种格式套到北方汉语上的结果就是“的”字结构的出现。《儿女英雄传》中的这类结构使用频率相当高，使用场合也比汉人用汉语更普遍，是满语结构对汉语结构影响的结果。以此类推，我们可以假设表处置的“把”字句可能同“了”“着”一样与汉语阿尔泰化有关。

二　满语助词“be”

“be”字在满语中除以实词表示“我们”及爵位中的“伯爵”等义外，其在句子中多以虚词的形式出现，在句子中起到连接宾语与谓词动词的作用。有“把”“将”等义。如，

(1) si ume niyalma be gidaxara
你 不要 人 把 欺负 （你不要欺负人。）

(2) muse urunakv gosihon mangga be eteme mutembi
我们 一定 困 难 把 胜 能
（我们一定能战胜困难。）

(3) bi manju hergen be taciha bihe
我 满洲 字 把 学了 曾 （我曾学过满文。）

(4) bi ubade sefu be aliyambi
我 在这里 师傅 把 等 （我在这里等师傅。）

(5) niyalma tome gemu siden jaka be hairambi
人 每 都 公 物 把 爱护
（每个人都要爱护公物。）

在《满语教程》中，“be”被称为宾格、对格、宾体格，表行为动作的直接受事者，有“把”“将”等意义。虽然，“be”在满语句法中非常重

要，但一些固定用法的宾格“be”可以省略。例如，

buda jembi 做饭　bithe hvlambi 读书　aniya arambi 过年

在上述固定用法中，“buda（饭）”“bithe（书）”和“aniya（年）”后面的宾格“be”可以省略不用。为了了解“把”字句和满语“be”的关系，我们首先需要厘清“be”在满语句法中的具体用法。

（一）引出宾语

“be”字在满语中以格助词的形式出现在句子中，其作用就是指代谓语动词所涉及的对象或事物，也就是为谓语动词引出宾语。宾语是受动词支配的成分，表示动作关涉的人或物，可以回答“把谁怎么”和“把什么怎么”的问题。满语属于拼音文字，直排竖写，其语言顺序与汉语不同，满语是主语在前，宾语在次，谓语在最后，即主宾谓之序也。例如：

(6) i　niyalma　be　tantaha.
他　人　把　打了　（他打人了。）

这句话中，“i”是主语，“tantaha”是动词谓语，“be”字前面的“niyalma”即为宾语。回答了动词谓语“tantaha”打了“谁”的问题。“be”字在满语句子中的一个作用，就是为及物动词的谓语指示宾语。在这种情况下，“be”字一般多按照汉语动宾之序的习惯直接翻译，“be”字不做显译。有时也可根据表达的需要将“be”字译成“把……，将……”。例如：

(7) ejenbe　be　belehe　eme　be　oktoloho
君主　把　弑杀了　母亲　把　毒死了

（《古文·讨武曌檄》）

可以译做“弑君鸩母”，也可以译成“把君主弑杀了，把母亲毒死了”。究竟如何翻译为好，要视具体情况而定，不能一概而论。

（二）引出致使义

动词为使动态时带有间接宾语，“be”字具有“使……如何……”之义。例如：

(8) bi　tere　be　gashūbumbi.
我　他　令/使　发誓

我令他发誓。（《满文讲义》）

该句中“gashūbumbi”的源形动词，在赋加了使动态的附加成分，变成“gashūbumbi”后，即具有了使令的对象，故而“be”字前面的“tere（他）”为宾语。后面的宾格助词“be”字，则起到了指示或引出宾语的作用。从例（8）中我们可以看出，当动词变成使动态时，由宾格助词“be”字引出。在以往清代讲析虚字的旧籍中，往往把引出宾语的“be”字译为“使、令”。其实，实译“使、令”的并非“be”字，而应当是动词的使动态、使令语气，而“be”字仅是起到了引出宾语，即使令对象的作用而已。

（三）引出受事宾语及受事宾语句

受事宾语，指承受动作的人或物。它与动词的关系是，强调承受动作的人或物受到怎样的动作行为的影响和作用，或者说某人、某物被什么动作怎么样了，是动宾关系的另一种表述。因而，受事宾语一般置于谓语部分的前面，给人一种宾语提前的感觉，其谓语动词往往带有补语、状语或更加复杂的短语和短句。也就是说，受事宾语的谓语部分不仅是一个简单的动词，往往还有其他句子成分。这是因为受事宾语是承受动作的人或物，因此，句子里不仅要有表示动作的动词，而且要有说明动作结果的成分，或是说明如何处置或影响动词的成分。但是，无论谓语部分如何复杂，受事宾语都与谓语动词存在着意念上的动宾关系，受事宾语仍然由宾格助词“be”字所引出。

受事宾语的谓语部分有以下几种情况。

1. 谓语动词带有补语

（9）dere be hūwa de guribufi teki. 将桌子挪到院子里坐着罢。（《清文启蒙》）

（10）uba be kemuni lioboju de jasifi. 将此仍寄信留保柱。（《乾隆四十八年寄信档》）

（11）uru be waka seci ojorakū 以是说非使不得。（《清文启蒙》）

（12）ai be temgetu obumbi ？以何为凭据？（《清文启蒙》）

（13）targiyan be ta an obuci ojorakūsere anggala ta an be yargiyan obuci inu ojorakū 别说以真作假使不得，以假作真也使不得。（《清文启蒙》）

以上句子中，“dere”“uba”“uru”“ai”“targiyan”“ta an”都是受事宾语，其动词“guribufi”“jasifi”“seci ojorakū”“obumbi”“obuci ojorakūsere”“obuci”都带有各自的补语“hūwa”“lioboju”“waka”“temgetu”“ta an”“yargiyan”。其中，“hūwa”是说明地点的，“lioboju”是说明人物的，“waka”是说明说话的内容的，“temgetu”和“ta an”“yargiyan”都是说明结果的。

2. 谓语动词前带有状语

（14）eiten baita be gūnin were eme icihiya. 看一切事务留心办理。（《乾隆四十七年寄信档》）

（15）suweni jurgan uthai garjaha efujehe babe gemu niyeceteme tasata. 尔部即将残破之处予以修补。（《顺治十六年上谕》）

（16）muse gūwa hacin i baita be yilgame faksalame karu ulhibuhebi.

我等已将其余事项分别回谕。（《乾隆朝满文月折档》）

以上各例中，“eiten baita”“garjaha efujehe”“gūwa hacin i baita ”都是受事宾语，而“gūnin were eme（动宾词组）”“gemu（副词）”“yilgame faksalame（并列词组）”皆为各自动词“icihiya”“niyeceteme tasata”“ulhibuhebi”的状语，分别修饰各自的动词，以说明是如何处置和影响动词的。

3. 谓语为短语

（17）age i ferguwecuke gūnin be bi wacihiyamesaha. 阿哥的盛情我尽都知道。（《清文启蒙》）

（18）ere baita be jiduji atanggi teni yargiyanmejige bahara ?

这个事情到底几时才能得实信？（《清文启蒙》）

以上例句中，“age i ferguwecuke gūnin”和“ere baita”均为受事宾语，而宾格助词“be”字后面的部分皆为短语，以说明受事宾语因动作、行为而受到的影响。从以上各例中，我们可以看到，受事宾语皆置于动词及其说明部分之前，而不仅在动词之前，这说明了受事宾语的被强调性，其作用类似于汉语的“把”字结构。故而，引出受事宾语的“be”字，一般多译成“把、将、以”等，与汉语的“把”字句颇为相似。

综上所述，笔者认为满语的宾格助词“be”字可以引出宾语，引出致使义，引出受事宾语及受事宾语句。“be”字在不同的宾语下面，起着连接谓语动词与宾语的作用，且有着不同的译法。厘清这些，可以帮助我们了解“把”字句可替代“以”字表处置及后来致使义处置式功能的演化缘由。

三　满语助词“be”到“把”字句的演化

上面我们简述了一下，满语助词“be”在句中的用法和功能。下面我们需要谈论一下，“把”字处置功能如何可以取代“以”字处置功能。

1. 语音特征

汉语中，表处置的“把”大约是魏晋时期产生的一个口语词，它的出现或许和北方阿尔泰语系中满语的格助词“be”有关。满语“be [pə]”和“把 [pa]”都属于“双唇音”；“be”的元音部分的/ə/发音位置在“中舌”而汉语的/a/也是“中舌”，两个元音的差异只在于，/a/舌位偏低，而/ə/的舌位比/a/高一些。这个词可能最初变换成一个汉语单音节词，其语法意义转为汉语词汇意义，并借用“把”的书写形式。进入明清时期后，以满语作为母语的满族在政治上的统治地位，致使这种“把”字处置式在汉语中的使用频度急剧上升，进而推动词汇层进入语法层，促成了现代汉语的“把”字句。此外，在满语中“i/i/”作为第三人称指示代词使用，意为“他（她、它）”，它跟汉语的“以”很容易在语音上形成撞车，导致语义表达上的歧义。为防止表达错误，采用“be [pə]”代为使用似乎更加适合。表处置功能的“以”字处置式的语音推演大概如下：“以 > be > 把”。

2. 结构特征

第一，在古代汉语“以 + O”结构可以放在动词前或动词后。满语的“O + be”结构一般放在谓语动词前面。例如：

（19）教人以善。

（20）尧以天下与舜。

（21）i　niyalma　be　tantaha.　（他打人了。）
　　　他　人　把　打了

在例（19）中，动词为“教”，“以 + O”位于谓语动词“教”后面。在例（20）中动词为“与”，“以”位于动词“与”前面。在例（21）中“niyalma（人）+ be”放在谓语动词“tantaha”的前面。在结构上，满语的“O + be”结构存在可代替“以 + O”结构的可能性。

第二，在古代汉语中“以”的宾语可以前置，满语的助词“be”通常放在后面。例如：

（22）君若以力，楚国方城以为城，汉水以为池，虽众，无所用之。（《左转·僖公四年》）

（23）si　ume　niyalma　be　gidaxara　　（你不要欺负人。）
　　　你　不要　人　把　欺负

在例（22）中“方城”在“楚国方城以为城”中置于“以”前面，而且“汉水”在“汉水以为池”一句中，也放在“以”前面。如例（23）中助词“be”放在宾语“niyalma”后。我们可以看出例（22）这种宾语前置型结构与满语非常相似。对古代北方汉语的处置式句型可做如下推测。首先，宾语前置“以”字处置式句型中的“以”在口语中用“be”代替，而书写方式上用与“be”在发音上相近的“把”字代替。其次，宾语后置“以”字处置式句型在口语上也用“be”代替，书写方式一样用“把”字。再次，因汉语中宾语后置，“以”字处置式在使用频度及范围上更占优势，进而促使“把”在汉语中的位置逐渐固定在宾语前的位置，最终形成了现代汉语中的“把”字句的处置式句型格式。

即，［O＋以］＞［O＋be（把）］

↓

［O＋以］＞［O＋be（把）］／［以＋O］＞［（把）be＋O］

↓

［以＋O］／［（把）be＋O］

↓

［（把）be＋O］

3. 用法特征

满语助词“be”在句中不仅可以引出宾语，还具备引出致使义及引出受事宾语及受事宾语句的功能。早期的“把”字句只是单纯的代替“以”字，发挥引出宾语的句法功能，形成“主＋（把）＋宾＋谓”的格式。但随着使用频度的增加，满语助词“be”所具备的引出致使义及引出受事宾语及受事宾语句的功能转移到汉语中，因此促成“把”字句增加了引出致使义及可引出受事宾语的功能。

综上所诉，本文通过语音、句中结构及用法三个方面的考察，认为满语助词“be”有充分的条件代替“以”字处置式，进一步演化为表处置的“把”字句。此外，满族具有悠久的历史，经历了漫长而复杂的变化历程。

在历史发展过程中，满族及其先人不断与其他民族接触，其中与汉族的接触更为频繁，因此语言相互之间的影响和借用便成为自然。在满汉人民的语言交流中，汉语的“主+谓+宾”句法结构和满语的“主+宾+谓”结构的相互冲突，促使满汉两族人民不得不为其寻找一个平衡点，以方便交流，因此，具有满语句法特色的“把”字句在北方被活跃使用。

据《竹书纪年·五帝纪》载：“帝舜二十五年，息慎氏来朝，贡弓矢”；“肃慎者，虞夏以来东北方大国也，一名息慎”。自古以来，东北是满族人民的故乡，是满语的发祥地。在北方，满族是处于统治地位的民族，而汉族是被统治的对象。正是这种统治的威望，不断影响着汉族人对居于统治地位者的语言的审美倾向，普遍对满语产生美感，这样的语言情感又化成强烈的语言动机，有力地促成了汉语向满语的借用，使东北地区产生了大量的满语特色的北方汉语。其中元代出现的“汉儿言语”[①] 一词就是指阿尔泰化的中塬汉语，即以宋元中塬汉人口语为目的语，用辽金人阿尔泰语言习惯大量换用后的北中国汉语。这也正是“把”字处置式开始活跃使用的时期。

唐宋时期用作处置式的“将”字句明显多于“把”字句，但随着满族的统治地位的巩固，明清以后，这种平衡被打破了，满族统治中国长达268年，汉语处置式中的“把”字句受其影响成了主流，“将”字句退位成为书面语。因此，“把”字句在汉语口语中的优势地位不是偶然形成的。

四 结论

关于“把”字句的起源问题，对汉语学界来说一直都是大难题。大部分学者在分析“把”字句时，都立足于把它看成一个汉语固有的语法形式，因受北方阿尔泰语影响发生了语法化或词汇替换等变异。本文综合各位学者的意见，试图证明表处置的“把”字句是由满语助词“be”演化而来的。虽然，列出的证据还有很多不足之处，但可以作为一个潜在研究方向。

① 元朝用“汉儿”指代契丹、高丽、竹因歹、浦姆等金朝治下的诸民。

参考文献

安双城，王庆丰，印丽雅：《满文讲义》，北京满文书院，1995。

胡增益主编《新满汉大词典》，新疆人民出版社，1994。

李葆嘉：《中国语言文化史》，江苏教育出版社，2001。

关嘉录：《简明满文文法》，辽宁民族出版社，2002。

蒋绍愚：《近代汉语研究概要》，北京大学出版社，2005。

蒋绍愚、曹广顺，《近代汉语语法史研究综述》，商务印书馆，2005。

赵杰：《满族话和北京话》，辽宁民族出版社，1996。

宋金兰：《汉语助词“了”、“着”与阿尔泰诸语言的关系》，《民族语文》1991 年第 6 期。

王小红：《浅析满语“be”字在句子中的作用及其汉译方法》，《满语研究》2002 年第 2 期。

The Relation Between the Sentence with Chinese Character of “把” and Manchu Auxiliary “Be”

Cui Xianglan, Piao xingzhu

Abstract

As a disposition, the Sentence with Chinese character of “把” is an important syntactic structure in Chinese. Therefore, it has always been recognized by academia. The earliest concept of “disposition” was put forward by Mr. Wang Li, that is, “Every person who uses auxiliary verbs to put the destination in front of the narrative to express a disposer is called disposition.” Previous studies have shown that in Tang and Song Dynasties, there were more sentence with the Character of “将” than the sentence with “把” used as disposal style. With the development of northern dialects in Jin, Yuan, Ming and Qing Dynasties, the use of "把" in sentences began to be frequent, and therefore forming a disposal style in which only sentences with "把" are used in northern dialects and only sentences with "将" are used in southern dialects. Then, A question is raised: what is the relationship between the disposal syntax with the Chinese character of "把" and the Altaic language in the north? We can list the hypothesis that the word "把" actually comes from a word in a northern Altaic language. The purpose of this paper is to study the origin of the sentence with "把" and its relationship with the Manchu auxiliary "be".

Keywords

Sentence with Character of "把" Manchu language disposition Altaic Language Case Auxiliary

以艾约瑟为例谈早期西方人眼中的汉语“大语法”*

魏兆惠** 魏兆玲***

摘　要

有人认为韵律、修辞均属语言之外，语法却属语言之内。早期许多西方传教士或学者研究汉语语法时，打破这个偏见，将韵律、修辞和语法都看作语言要素结合起来研究。19世纪英国传教士艾约瑟是其中的代表人物之一。他在多部著作中探讨了汉语语法，勾勒了汉语语法体系、字、词、字组、单句和复句系统，将汉语词分为八类，句型分为三大类，并发现了汉语“被”字句、非主谓句和双宾句等句式的特点，也论及修辞和韵律在构词和造句中的作用，他的汉语语法体系是一种“大语法”。黎锦熙、史有为、沈家煊等国人的语法思想与此有相合之处。

关键词

艾约瑟　汉语　“大语法”

一　早期西方人对汉语“大语法”的认识

我国第一部系统的语法学著作《马氏文通》对于汉语语法学的建立有

* 本文为北京社科基金项目“600年间北京官话副词研究”的阶段性成果，并受北京语言大学院级项目和国家社科基金重大项目“多卷本断代汉语语法研究”资助。

** 魏兆惠，北京语言大学人文社科学部/北京文献语言与文化传承研究基地教授。

*** 魏兆玲，江苏无锡江南影视艺术职业学院讲师。

着里程碑式的贡献，但是这个成就并不是突然出现的，是长期的积累、铺垫的结果。其影响来源主要有两方面，一是中国传统的语文学，二是 16 世纪以来的西方汉学家的不停研究和探索。“十六世纪中叶前，汉语研究只是国人自家的事，中叶以后则有所变，渐成世界的学问，其中海外研究的主体在西洋”（《海外汉语研究丛书》编委会序）。西洋自身的语法体系，以及西洋人对汉语语法体系的研究，对马建忠的学术思想有着或多或少，或直接或间接的影响。16 世纪至 20 世纪初的西方汉学家对于汉语语法的研究，可以说对汉语语法学这一学科的产生和建立有着不可磨灭的作用。但是“在一些中国语言学史家的笔下，西方人研究汉语的历史被大大缩短、简化了”（姚小平，1999）。早期西方传教士对于汉语语法的认识和描述固然受到了西方语法体系的影响，但是其中也不乏独到的见解。天主教传教士弗朗西斯科·瓦罗（Francisco Varo，1627 - 1686）的《华语官话语法》（1703）、基督新伦敦会罗伯特·马礼逊（Robert Morrison，1782 - 1834）的《通用汉言之法》（1811）等只关注汉语的词法，而基督教浸信会传教士约翰·马士曼（John Marshman，1768 - 1837）的《中国言法》（1814）不仅有词法，句法部分也占据了相当的分量。他在前言中强调了语序的重要性，他说“整个汉语语法就取决于位置”（On examining the various parts of speech，the reader will perceive，that the whole of Chinese Grammar turns on position）。深受马士曼影响的法国儒莲的《汉文指南》的法文标题就是“汉语新句法，立足于词的位置”。洪堡特（1826）甚至指出，印欧语言的语法由形态和句法两部分构成，而汉语的语法只有句法部分。

也有不少传教士在研究汉语语法时将词法、句法，甚至是韵律、修辞、语体结合起来进行研究，他们眼中的汉语语法是一个“大语法”。如美国南浸信传道会传教士高第丕（Tarlton Perry Crawford，1821 - 1902）和中国人张儒珍合作的《文学书官话》（1869），德国语言学家、汉学家乔治·德·甲柏连孜（Gabelentz，1840 - 1893）的《汉文经纬》（1881）等。还有一位重要的代表人物是英国传教士艾约瑟。

艾约瑟（Edkins Joseph，1823 - 1905），英国伦敦会传教士、汉学家。1848 年他来华协助麦都思（英国传教士）工作、传教。除 19 世纪 60 年代在天津、北京开辟教区，80 年代被北京总税务司赫德聘为翻译外，其他时间一直在上海活动。其间与中国人王韬合译了《光学图说》《中西通书》等多部著作，还撰写了大量哲学、历史、科学文章，由《万国公报》和广学会发表，其中《希腊罗马史》影响较大。他还精研中国文化，著有《中国的宗教》等英文著作。他对汉语语法的研究颇为翔实。19 世纪英国汉学家撰写的汉语语法书十余部，其中就包括艾约瑟的《上海方言口语语法》《汉语官话口语语法》《中国在语言学方面的成就》《汉语学习入门》及《上海方言词汇集》等至少五本。《上海方言口语语法》1853 年初版，1868 年再版，是第一部描写汉语方言白话的语法著作。该书对“19 世纪中叶开埠初 10 年时上海县城方言的语音、词语、语法做出了最早的忠实记录和全方位研究，有不少精辟的论述和独到领先的见解。尽管它是一本语法书，然其语音、语法并重，并提供了当时丰富的语言、社会和文化背景知识”（钱乃荣，2006)。《汉语官话口语语法》1857 年初版，1864 年再版。这本书不仅细致地介绍了汉语官话的历史起源、发音体系，还详细地介绍了官话和主要方言的联系及异同，直到今天，该书仍然可以作为我们研究汉语官话及方言历史的重要参考资料（董方峰、杨洋，2015)。

相比较而言，艾约瑟是早期西方对汉语语法理解最为深刻，研究领域最为宽泛的汉学家之一。艾约瑟的汉语语法既包括词法，也包括句法，既涉及单句，也涉及复句，既谈到修辞，又论及韵律，这些部分相对独立，又互相联系。他眼中的汉语语法可以说是一个“大语法”。

二　艾约瑟论汉语的词类和句法系统

（一）词类系统

艾约瑟建立了一个“字—词—字组—句子”的语法系统。字是汉语基本语法单位。词分为简单词和复合词，“天、夏、一、诗、我”等为简单词，“皇帝、衣裳、亮晃晃”这样由两个或两个以上的字构成的为复合词；汉语中字与字组合成的，在意义上又没有形成完整句子的结构称为“字组”，从字数上来看，“字组”由两个到多个不等的字组合而成，如“只得、仿佛、山羊、敬天地、游手好闲、不会跑路、打错了算盘等。

艾约瑟给汉语词分类时借鉴了中国人广泛使用的实字、虚字，死字、活字的概念，认为有实际意义的字是实字，辅助字或者没有实际意义的字是虚字，表达行为的是活字，表达事物的是死字。在此基础上，他将汉语的词类分为八类：名词、形容词、代词、数量词、小词、副词、连词、感叹词。有些词无法归入任何一类，称为小词，如“的、个、了、们、哩、呢、哪、啦、咯、阿（啊）、么（吗）”等。语序是重要的语法手段，词类因为位置的不同会发生转换，如“孝悌忠信、信实、相信”和“尽忠报国、忠臣、忠君报国”中的“信、忠”分别可以归入名词、动词和形容词三个类别。这种“词无定类”的思想后被证明是错误的。

艾约瑟的词类观受到两方面的影响。一方面，受中国传统语文思想的影响；另一方面，受西方语法体系的影响。他在《上海方言口语语法》提到了清代中国人毕华珍的《衍绪草堂笔记》。《衍绪草堂笔记》由“论文浅说”“论文续说”“余论四则”和“四言句格”四章组成。第一部分“论文浅说”中主要概述了“一实字四虚字”的词类观。

> 或问作文如何是法？余曰只一实字四虚字。如何是理？余曰只一实字四虚字。文不贵有意义乎？余曰无意义，只一实字四虚字。古今载籍极博，只虚实两字无已更益，宾主两字尽之矣。

艾约瑟在介绍当时中国人对汉语词类的划分时指出，一部分中国学者将动词和形容词归为实字，而另一些学者将它们视为虚字。雷慕沙认为动词是实字，而当地学者毕华珍认为除了名词以外的所有词都是虚字。

> Common teachers of the language in distinguishing words, only use two pairs of terms, viz. 实，虚，and 死，活. The former signifies words that have a meaning and such as have not. All substantives are 实字眼. Auxiliary words or particles receive the name of 虚字眼. Verbs and adjectives are placed by some writers in the first of these classes, and by others in the second. Remusat, says that verbs are 实字; a native author 毕华珍 treats, all words except substantives, as in the second class.
>
> The native writer just referred to, in a recent work, 衍绪草堂笔记, on the parts of speech and construction of sentences, has extended these divisions, by forming the 虚字, or words not substantives, into four classes:

adjectives 呆虚字，verbs 活虚字，口气语助虚字，空活虚字。

尽管一定程度上受到中国传统语文思想的影响，艾约瑟的语法术语系统和语法框架主要还是来源于西方。早在 17 世纪中叶，“Port-Royal 语法理论”由法国唯理语法学派提出，主张把拉丁语的九种同类分为两大类：表示“思想对象”（Objects of Thought）的是名词、代词、分词、介词、副词、冠词；表示“思想方法”（Manners of Thought）的是动词、连词、叹词。在这一思潮的影响下，英国传教士维尔金斯和库柏等学者开始从语义角度对词进行了二分，分为全义词（Intergrals）和小品词（Particles）两个主要类别，前者本身具有确定的意义，包括名词、动词和形容词；后者包括代词、冠词、介词、非派生词和连词。这和中国人的虚、实二分有异曲同工之处。以艾约瑟为代表的西方传教士基本都将这套语法体系套用在汉语上，对汉语的词类进行了八分，并将“格”“数”“性”等概念强加于汉语。

著名语言学家叶斯柏森清醒地认识到这种削足适履的做法的不适当性。他在《语法哲学》中说：“不幸的是，他们误以为拉丁语的语法是最完美的逻辑连贯性的典范，于是他们努力在每一种语言中寻找拉丁语语法所显示的特点。但庆幸地，通过推论和逻辑思维，他们无法在语言中找到上学时所学的拉丁语法找到的东西。”

西方语法思想影响深远，19 世纪末的中国人马建忠、20 世纪初的日本人广池千九郎、中国学者黎锦熙、杨树达等对汉语词类的划分都没有跳出这种西方词法系统的窠臼。无论是在对词法和句法的重视程度上，还是词的分类及标准上，无不如此。邢庆兰（1947）评价说：“它的成就，与其说在文法方面，不如说在训诂方面——一种受了西洋文法影响的新训诂学。”

（二）句法系统

艾约瑟对汉语的特殊句式有独到的认识。他指出汉语中“下雨”“下雪”“落潮”这些迥异于英语的句子是主谓倒置或者主语省略。省略主语的说法在国内语法学界被广泛接受，直到吕叔湘（1979）提出非主谓句的说法。吕叔湘认为“送他一本书”“拿一本书送他”“送一本书与他”这样的双宾句的出现是由于韵律的需要；他发现汉语有被动句，如“明被人欺”“我叫他闹乏了”“吃亏不小”“拨别人打（给别人打）”，表被动的句子中也有被动标记，同英语一样需要在谓语动词之前加助动词，被动标记有“被、叫、挨、受、吃、见、拨（上海方言词，同北京话‘给’）”。不过他将被动标记的词与英语中表被动态的“be”词性的作用视为相同，这又是套用西方语法的结果。他还发现被动标记在不同方言中使用不同，在中国北方的口语中，“被”不如“叫”普遍，上海方言中运用最多的为“给”字。这些发现都是难能可贵的。

艾约瑟将汉语的句子分为简单句、主从句和并列句三类，形成了如下句型系统。

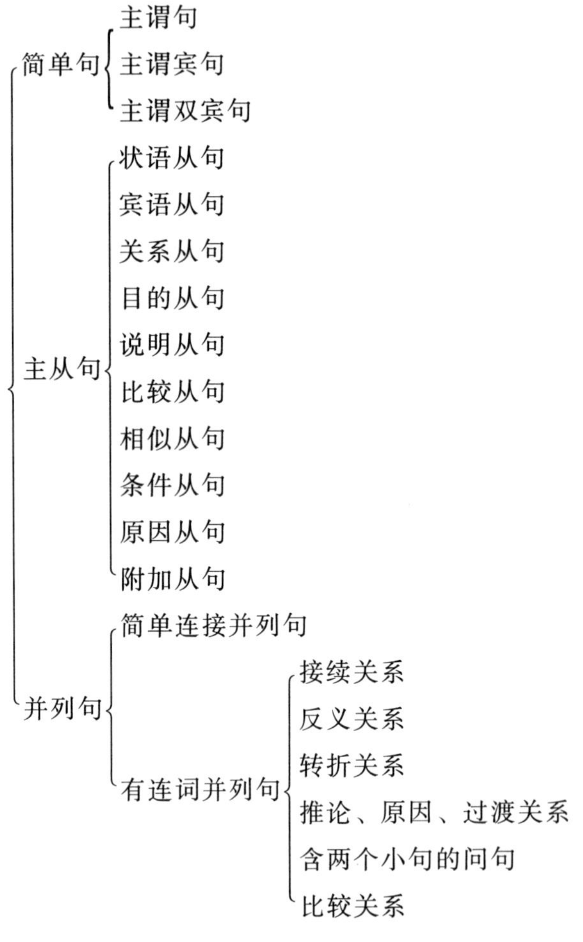

黎锦熙（1924）将复句分为三类——包孕复句、等立复句和主从复句，

后来在结合学界各种意见之后重新对汉语复句进行了划分。包孕复句被列入单句，对等立复句、主从复句中论述不当的地方做了适当的调整，单、复句系统如下：

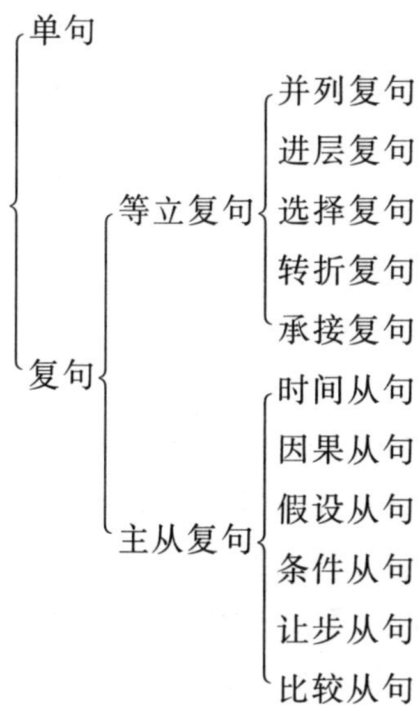

黎锦熙和艾约瑟一样，将句子分为单句和复句两大类，等立复句和主从复句与艾约瑟的并列句和主从句可分别相对应。当然调整之后他的单复句系统更为完善、准确，单复句划分比艾约瑟更为科学明晰。

三　艾约瑟论修辞与语法的关系

艾约瑟常将修辞手段的分析和句法分析融合在一起。《汉语官话口语语法》第九章指出“对话中常用的修辞手法里最值得关注的是省略、冗言（pleonasm）、重复和对偶（antithesis）”。

省略指的是略去根据语境可以理解的成分，以使句子更为简练。书中共列举了八种省略的情况，如表示敬称或者谦称的形容词用作所有格代词时，这些形容词前的代词通常省略。如恭维语，在不使用替代形容词时可省略，人称代词的省略也很常见，如“讨光”（南方表达）或“借光”（北方表达）、久仰、久慕、岂敢、谢谢等。

对偶的修辞手法在字组和句子的组合中均起作用。在字组中意义相对的两个词，在四字字组中出现在第一和第三，或者第二和第四的位置，例如“弃暗投明、左邻右舍”等。形容词和动词通过对偶构成名词，例如“万丈深浅地穴”，两组对偶的形容词可以构成一个四字字组，例如“长幼大小”。句子中的对偶，在汉语口语对话和书面语中都很常见，如“一个人唱百个人和。”很多成对的句子，以反义形容词或者其他词开头，如“上、下”等，例如“上有天堂下有苏杭”等。名词的重叠带来复数意义，如“父父子子、子子孙孙”；形容词和动词重叠的作用则在于韵律或者强调。

艾约瑟是当时将语法和修辞打通研究并处理得最好的汉学家之一。相比较而言，同时期的汉学家们常常将修辞独立于语法之外。如《文学书官话》修辞被称为“话色”,[①] 分为“婉转灵巧的说法，其中最要紧的，叫如生的（类似拟人）、借喻的（比喻中的借喻）、过实的（夸张）、讥诮的（反语）、比方的（寓言）”，仅仅列举了五个修辞格。《汉语札记》论及修辞的内容很多，既在语法第二章论述汉语语法特质时提到重叠、对偶和疑问三个修辞格，又在第四章下设七节，分述对偶、重叠、层进、反诘、素写、比喻等。这些汉学家主要涉及积极修辞，而没有讨论修辞在语法中的作用，没有涉及消极修辞。可与艾约瑟相提并论的是德国甲柏连孜的《汉文经纬》。在分析系统和综合系统的句子和句子成分的部分，都提到了修辞特征。在分析系统的词序规律部分，讨论了两种词的排列方式、叠音和反复。

艾约瑟将修辞和语法打通讨论的做法，无论在西方，还是中国古代，都有传统。戴维（2016）说：“早在公元4世纪，语法就已经侵入了修辞学的这个部分。多纳图斯《大技艺》的第三卷也是最后一卷讨论的是词形变异（metaplasms，即为了韵律修饰而对语词中的一个或多个字母进行添加、删除或互换位置）、修辞格和比喻，所有这些在散文中都是错误的，但在诗中却是允许的。”可见在西方早有学者不是将修辞看作语言之外的东西，而是看作语言的一部分，它和语法在语言的构成和表达中都起着作用。

中国古人虽然没有建立独立的语法学和修辞学，但是在讨论创作的时

① “话色”这个术语译自英语的“figure”，东京大学三学部公开发行的（井上哲次郎等编）1881年版《哲学字汇》，及黑岩大译述的《雄辩美辞法》都使用了这个术语来对译英语中的“figure”。

候常常谈及这两个方面的问题。比如古代汉语的活用现象，属于语法，也属于修辞。《文心雕龙》讨论章句时提到语法中的虚词现象：“至于‘夫’‘盖’‘故’者，发端之首唱；‘之’而‘于’‘以’者，乃札句之旧体；‘乎’‘哉’‘矣’‘也’者，亦送末之常科”。

马建忠的修辞研究也常和语法分析分不开，如分析“君子之交淡若水，小人之交甘若醴”（《庄子·山木》）时说：“‘淡’‘甘’两象静也，附诸名后，所以比也。其所比之两端，一则‘君子之交’与‘水’，一则‘小人之交’与‘醴’也。今以‘淡若’二字参诸‘君子之交’与‘水’之间，犹云‘君子相交之淡与水之淡无轩轾’也。”这既是修辞格的分析，也是论述由象静字（形容词）表示的比较对象的属性，是语法分析。

吕叔湘先生也认为，语法和修辞是邻近的学科。把语法和修辞分开，有利于科学的发展；把语法和修辞打通，有利于作文的教学。后者是中国的古老传统，也为许多学者所倡导。在这件事上，艾约瑟和《马氏文通》均可算是有承先启后之功。

四　艾约瑟论韵律与语法的关系

艾约瑟的《上海方言口语语法》认为汉语口语语法可以分为两部分讨论，语法的和韵律的，二者的关系是既互相独立又彼此联系。

魏兆惠（2016）论述了艾约瑟对韵律的认识。艾约瑟认为汉语和英语一样，也存在重音，不过英语的重音是在一个字内部，汉语的重音要在“字组”中体现。他对北京话、上海话的重音的认识和徐世荣（1980）、石汝杰（2006）有很多相似之处。

不仅如此，在认识到汉语轻重音的基础上，艾约瑟更是引进西方诗歌的音步理论分析上海话的韵律，认为在上海话中至少包括存抑扬格（轻重格）、抑抑扬格（轻轻重格）和扬抑抑格（重轻轻格）三种模式。

谈语法时论及韵律问题是英语语法的传统做法。郑梦娟认为“句法及韵律学”是英语语法其中的一部分，“包括做诗规则以及重音、停顿、音长、语调等韵律特征，是对韵律学内容的进一步探讨”。艾约瑟同时代传教士论及汉语语法时也将语法和韵律结合起来，《汉语札记》《通用汉言之法》和《语言自迩集》都是采取将韵律和语法结合的做法。

就中国而言，自诗歌产生以来，中国古人就有韵律感，如《诗经》鲜有不押韵的诗，对于诗歌中的韵律的研究由来已久。《马氏文通》谈到“之”字的作用时说：

> 偏正两次之间，“之”字参否否无常。惟语欲其偶，便于口诵，故偏正两奇，合之为偶者，则不参“之”字。凡正次欲求醒目者，概参“之”字。

马建忠也意识到句子中是否有“之”不仅是语法的问题，也有韵律作用。这种认识影响深远。关于韵律和汉语的句法关系，前有赵元任、吕叔湘、张斌等语法学界前辈的探索，后有端木三、冯胜利、王洪君等学者通过语音实验、理论阐释的进一步论述，证实了语法和韵律间密不可分的关系。如谈到现代汉语和“之”功能相似的虚词“的”，庄会彬、刘振前（2012）就指出“的”作为一个附着成分，本身在韵律上不能独立，而必须依附于毗邻的黏附组，“的”在构建汉语节律的过程中起到极其重要的作用。

五 现代中国人论汉语“大语法”

《马氏文通》“不愿意把自己局限在严格意义的语法范围内”（吕叔湘语，1980），已经在谈词法和句读的同时论及修辞和韵律的问题，虽然这些论述只是零星的。黎锦熙所著的《新著国语文法》内容繁复，包罗万象，不仅包括各种复句、段落篇章和修辞，还有连词、助词、叹词和标点符号等，还把修辞和段落篇章方面的内容囊入文法研究中。黄婉梅（2009）称其有“大语法”观。20 世纪 80 年代，人们开始重视口语研究，这使人们逐渐发现语音和语法之间的某种联系，不仅是语调，还有音节的协调。张斌、胡裕树提出语法“句法、语义、语用”三平面，张斌的研究进一步表明节律对句法的制约，节奏表现形式对句子的生成和理解的影响。陈昌来认为张斌对汉语语句节律的研究“从汉语语法学史来看具有开拓价值”。史有为（1991）指出人们甚至“开始认真考虑是否还有第四个平面：句法语音平面”。最为明确地阐述汉语大语法观念的是沈家煊（2005、2016、2017）。

他以唐诗的对偶为例，阐明印欧语的语法是狭窄的“小语法”，汉语的“语法”是个“大语法”，它同时是“语义语法”“语用语法”“声韵语法”，不是单纯的“语法”，印欧语观念的那种“语法”在汉语里实际是包含在“大语法”之中的，没有成为一个独立的领域，离开了语义语用声韵这个本源也就没有了那种狭窄的语法。大语法是语法、语义、语用甚至语音的综合，如果分开研究就破坏了它的完整性（沈家煊，2016）。他指出汉语的韵律语法是大语法的一个部分，而在西方，韵律和语法之间的关系是不互相包含的，只是有交集而已。韵律和语法的关系如图 1 所示。

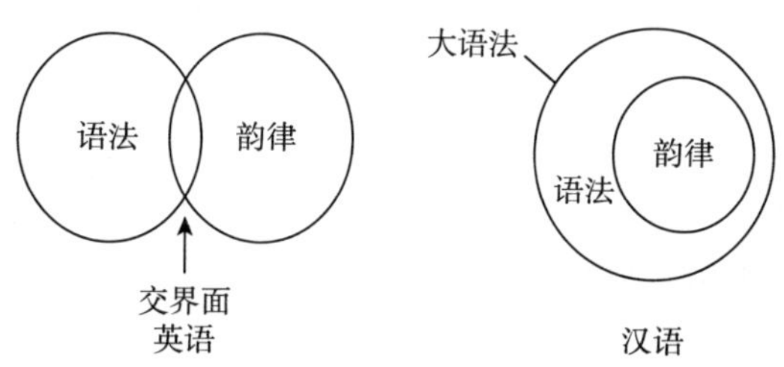

图 1　汉语和英语之间韵律和语法的关系

不过艾约瑟在 19 世纪中期所展现的汉语大语法内涵甚至比沈家煊的更宽广，可以用图 2 来表示。

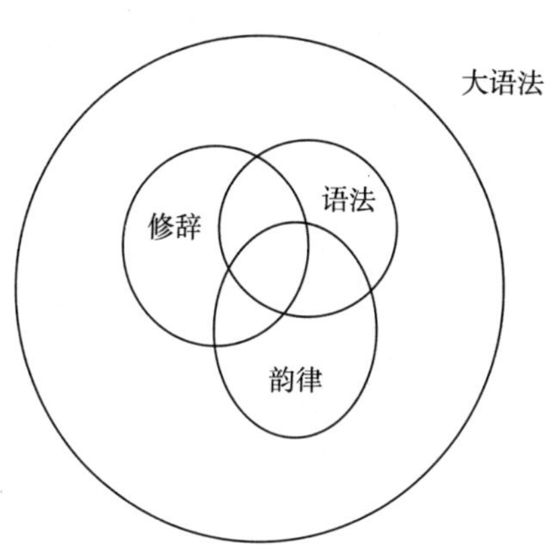

图 2　艾约瑟汉语大语法内涵

无论是黎锦熙，还是胡裕树、张斌、沈家煊，他们的“大语法”观都可谓 20 世纪以来对以艾约瑟为代表的早期西方人对于汉语研究的回应和发展。

参考文献

〔美〕戴维 L. 瓦格纳编《中世纪的自由七艺》，张卜天译，湖南科学技术出版社，2016。

〔英〕艾约瑟：《汉语官话口语语法》，董方峰、杨洋译，外语教学与研究出版社，2014。

〔英〕艾约瑟：《上海方言口语语法》，钱乃荣、田佳佳译，外语教学与研究出版社，2014。

〔英〕威妥玛：《语言自迩集——19世纪中期的北京话》，张卫东译，北京大学出版社，2002。

黄婉梅：《黎氏语法体系研究》，华中师范大学出版社，2009。

吕叔湘：《重印〈马氏文通〉序》，商务印书馆，1993。

马建忠：《马氏文通》，商务印书馆，1993。

沈家煊：《名词和动词》，商务印书馆，2016。

沈家煊主编《现代汉语语法的功能、语用、认知研究》，商务印书馆，2005。

石汝杰：《明清吴语和现代方言研究》，上海辞书出版社，2006。

徐世荣：《普通话语音知识》，文字改革出版社，1980。

姚小平：《海外汉语探索四百年管窥：西洋汉语研究国际研讨会暨第二届中国语言学史研讨会论文集》，外语教学与研究出版社，2008。

沈家煊：《从唐诗的对偶看汉语的词类和语法》，《当代修辞学》2016年第3期。

沈家煊：《汉语“大语法”包含韵律》，《世界汉语教学》2017年第1期。

魏兆惠：《英国传教士约瑟夫 艾约瑟论汉语的韵律》，《当代修辞学》2016年第3期

姚小平：《〈汉文经纬〉与〈马氏文通〉——〈马氏文通〉历史功绩重评》，《当代语言学》1999年第2期。

郑梦娟：《〈中国言法〉及其汉语韵律研究》，《修辞学习》2008年第6期。

庄会彬、刘振前：《“的”的韵律语法研究》，《汉语学习》2012年第3期。

史有为：《多元·柔性·主体——80～90年代语法研究大势之我见》，《世界汉语教学》1991年第4期。

邢庆兰：《中国文法研究之进展——〈马氏文通〉成书的五十年纪念》，《国学月刊》1947年第59期。

Chinese Grammar: From the View of Edkins Joseph

Wei Zhaohui, Wei zhaoling

Abstract

Some people thought that rhyme and rhetoric should be thought as language studies except for grammar. In 19th Century, Edkins, a British missionary and sinologist, studied grammar, rhetoric and rhyme in Chinese grammar. In a number of works, he gave an in-depth analysis of Chinese grammar, and outlined the system of Chinese grammar—word-word group, sentence and compound sentence system. He divided Chinese words into eight categories and while sentence patterns are divided into three categories. He put foward that the characteristics of Chinese "being", non-subject and predicate sentences and double object sentences and often discussed rhetoric and rhythm. The function of word formation and sentence construction reflected a kind of chinese grammar. Li Jinxi and Shen Jiaxuan agree with that.

Keywords

Edkins Joseph　Chinese　Grammar

《清文指要》时体助词“了”的相关句法格式及满汉对应[*]

李聪聪[**]　王继红

摘　要

本文以《清文指要》（百章）为考察对象，从“了”的句法格式入手，通过统计分析不同格式的句法位置和句法功能探讨清代旗人汉语中“了”的使用。经统计发现，在满汉合璧会话教材《清文指要》（百章）中“了”主要分为三大类，即动词性的“了”、“了”构成的复合词以及时体助词“了”。《清文指要》（百章）中时体助词“了”有九种主要的句法格式，其中“V+了”格式数量最多。《清文指要》（百章）有不同的修订与改编版本，通过版本对比可以看出这些句法格式中有些“了”被其他助词替换或整体格式发生变化，从满汉对应的角度来看，“了”相关格式的使用在一定程度上受到了满语的影响。

关键词

清文指要　满汉对勘　句法格式

所谓的满汉合璧，指满汉两种文字的并列。清朝建立之初，采用行政手段对其公文的书写形式进行规范，“所有的公文、奏章以及印鉴、城门等都要求满

---

* 本文得到中央高校基本科研业务费专项资金项目（*Supported by the Fundamental Research Funds for the Central Universities*）“基于满汉对勘的清代汉语句尾‘了’多功能性分析”（2017JX011）与北京市社会科学基金项目“基于满汉平行语料库的清中前期北京话时体标记研究”（14WYB018）的资助。通讯作者为王继红，北京外国语大学教授。

** 李聪聪，北京外国语大学中文学院在读博士生，研究方向为满汉合璧文献研究。

文和汉文并列书写。满文是竖写右行，汉文是竖写左行，两种文字并列书写，由此就形成了满汉合璧”。[①] 满汉合璧会话教材则是在满汉文化交融与冲突的背景下产生的一种语言教学材料。通过梳理和比较满汉合璧会话教材的语言现象，可以探求满语和汉语等不同语言相互接触和影响的过程。满汉合璧文献尤其是满汉合璧会话教材成为研究清代北京话和旗人汉语的宝贵材料。

本文选取清中前期具有代表性的满汉合璧文献《清文指要》（百章），将其中能够反映清中前期旗人北京话的会话部分作为主要的考察对象。除此之外，也将《清文指要》（百章）不同时期文本中时体助词“了”的句法格式变化作为研究的一个方面。《清文指要》（百章）是《清文指要》（上、下各25篇）和《续编兼汉清文指要》（上、下各25篇）的合称，常见的版本是嘉庆十四年（1809）三槐堂重刻本，也是本文主要使用的版本。此外，还有嘉庆二十三年（1818）西安将军署内存版校正重刻本、道光十年（1830）清人富俊撰《三合语录》收录《清文指要》（102章）五云堂刻本等，张美兰、刘曼（2013）对《清文指要》（百章）的七个不同汉译本进行了整理。本文采用《清文指要》的版本主要是嘉庆十四年（1809）的三槐堂刻本以及张美兰、刘曼（2013）的重订及改编文本。

《清文指要》（百章）中“了”的用法有三种。第一种是表示“完成、结束”的动词性用法，这些动词性的“了”在句子中并非单一动词的形式，而是与其他语素构成双音节词在句子中充当谓语；第二种“了”是与完成动词“完”等表示完成义的动词构成复合词，在整个篇章中充当话题标记；第三种是时体助词用法的“了”。本文从满汉对应的角度出发，对满汉合璧语料中的时体助词“了”的句法格式进行分析，动词及话题标记等用法另文讨论。

一　词尾“了”相关句法格式

（一）V+了+O

满汉合璧文献中词尾“了”句法格式“V+了+O”是其中数量较多的

① 包和平：《什么是满汉合璧》，《中国民族》1990年第3期。

一类，《清文指要》（百章）有 109 例。“V + 了 + O”格式所对应的满语语法形式主要以一般过去时和副动词为主，其中“了”的时体意义主要以完成体的结果性用法和先时性用法为主。这种格式在句法分布上主要有两种情况：一种是整个结构用于全句的结尾；另一种就是位于句中，且其后必须接有其他成分。

“V + 了 + O”格式在句子中可以单独充当谓语或者在复句中充当最后一分句，其内容是句子所要表达的主要信息。但是这类自由形式在满汉合璧文献中的实际用例较少。例如：

（1）后来说有阿哥的话，才急忙去。慌速去了，只拿了三套来，遗漏了一套。（《清文指要》，卷上，37）

amala age i gisun bi sere jakade teni ebuhu sabuhū genehebi，emu yohi duin dobton wakao，ekšeme saksime genefi，damu ilan dobton gajiha，tede emu（一）dobton（套）melebu-he（遗漏 - 一般过去时）

（2）阿哥，你别怪我嘴直，风闻说，你如今顽起钱来，作了好些账。（《清文指要》，卷下，52）

age si mimbe angga sijirhūn seme ume wakašara，urahilame donjici，si te jiha efire de dosifi，tutala（那样多）bekdun（债）ara-ha（作 - 过去时）se-mbi（表示强调）

以上例句中“V + 了 + O”均用于句子的末尾或者复句的后一分句，充当句子的谓语成分，表达句子的主要信息。但是从具体数量来看，这种类型的“V + 了 + O”在文献中的数量相对较少，这与词尾“了”的性质有一定关系。金立鑫（1998）指出，在中性语境也就是句子中没有任何时间成分的环境中，光杆形式的“V + 了 + O”格式作为句子的独立性很差，是因为词尾“了”具有延续性，总是表示所说的话未完。由此可以解释“V + 了 + O”这种独立型格式数量较少的现象。

“V + 了 + O”的另一种形式“V + 了 + O”后必须有其他成分承接其所负载的语义，否则从语感上来说一句话未说完或者句子的重点不突出。这种格式一般位于句中，整个结构可以充当修饰成分作定语，也可以在复句中的前一分句中单独充当谓语。例如：

（3）他那模样儿言语儿，与别的孩子们迥乎不同。穿上衣裳雄雄寔寔的，一见了人，端然正立，慢慢的进前问个好。（《续清文指要》，卷下，61）

tere baninwen, gisunhese, gūwa juse ci cingkai encu kurkar etufi, niyalma（人）be（宾格）sabu-mbihe-de（看见－进行时－时）, beyebe tobseme obufi, fišurseme elhei ibefi sain be fonjimbi

（4）我那个那里算得数？白是个褂子名儿罢咧，毛也磨了，火力完了，反穿不得了。关了俸银的时候，该买一件好的呀。（《续清文指要》，卷下，62）

mini tere ai, ton bai emu gebu dabala, funiyehe manaha, simen wajiha, tulesietuci ojorakū ohobi fulun（俸禄）ba-ha（得到－过去时形动词）manggi, giyani emu sain ningge udambi dere

有后续成分的“V+了+O”格式中的词尾“了”表示动作的完成并且已经结束，或者表示动作完成并且状态持续。例（3）中的“见了人”前有表示假设条件的“一”，表示后面句子实现或者完成的条件。句中动词“见”为非持续性动词，所以“了”表示的是动作完成并且结束，但是事件所形成的状态却在持续，非持续动词表示的是一种状态的形成并且延续；例（4）“关了俸银”充当整个句子时间状语的定语成分，句子的语义重心必然是后续句子的内容。动词“关”为弱持续性动词，“了”表示行为的完成，动词具有弱持续性，所以说“了”表示动作完成以及状态的持续。

（二）V（+O）+了+C

“V+了+C”格式在《清文指要》（百章）中有52例。这种格式中，“了”主要对应满语副动词和一般过去时，可以分两种情况进行讨论。

第一种，当“V+了+C”位于全句或者分句的末尾时，后面一般不需要其他成分，可以单独充当句子的谓语，在复句中一般处于最后一个分句的位置。例如：

（5）阿哥，你这个话不错了些儿吗？有“心专山可通”的话呀。（《清文指要》，卷上，2）

age sini ere gisun, majige（一点点）tašarabu-ha-kū（使出错－一般过去时－否定式）semeo（吗）hing sere oci, hada hafumbi sehebi

（6）相隔的很远，因为当日不能打来回，在那里歇了两夜。（《清文指要》，卷下，49）

sandalabuhangge umesi goro, ineku inenggi mudari amasi jici muterakū ofi tuba-de（那里－位置格）juwe（二）dobori（夜）inde-hebi（宿－肯定过去时）

（7）阿哥，你那盘朝珠，我说要拿了去，到底没拿了去。什么缘故呢？每逢来了，你全不在家，没见你的面，怎么说胡里胡涂的把你什么东西拿了去呢？所以我今日特来找见你，告诉了，好拿了去。（《续清文指要》，卷下，88）

age sini tere erihe be，bi gama-ki se-hei（拿去 - 情愿式 - 连续副动词）jiduji bahafi gamahakū turgun ai seci jihe dari si gemu boode akū simbe acahakū de ai hendume buksuri sini jaka be gamambi uttu ofi bi enenggi cohome sinde acafi alaha manggi gama-ki se-mbi（拿去 - 情愿式 - 现将时）

在以上三个例句中，“V + 了 + C”均处于整个复句的末尾，表示句子的核心内容，为整个句子提供了背景时间信息，“了”的语法意义是表示动作的完成或实现。例（5）中“了”是完成体的标记，属于典型的结果性用法，后面的补语是对谓词性成分程度的说明或补充；例（6）中“了”表示动作发生在过去并且已经完成，时量补语成分“两夜”是对动词持续时间的描述，“歇了两夜”的“了”表示的是“歇”状态的持续，“两夜”则是状态所持续的时间；例（7）“拿了去”与上述两例不同，补语为趋向补语，“了”同样表示动作完成。

第二种情况是有后续成分的“V + 了 + C”，该格式后面必须有一定的成分来承接语义，可以在句子中充当谓语，一般位于复句的前一分句中。例如：

（8）每日家念话就记得了，时刻的说，舌头就熟了。要这样学了去，至狠一二年间，自然任意顺口不打瞪儿的说上来了，又何愁不能呢？（《清文指要》，卷上，4）

inenggidari hūlaci gisun ejembi，erindari gisureci，ilenggū urembi uttu（如此）taci-me（学 - 并列副动词）ohode（如果…的话）manggai emu juwe aniya i sidende ini cisui gūnin i cihai anggai ici tang sembikai muterakū jalin geli aiseme jobombi ni.

（9）这些人都是作什麽的？僱了来的匠人们。（《续编清文指要》，卷下，64）

ese ainarangge turi-me（雇 - 并列副动词）gaji-ha（领来 - 过去时）faksisa

（10）就是铺里卖的没有好的，我也必定在各处转找了给你，你心里怎麽样？你还题什麽？不论怎麽拿了去也好来着，如何至于丢了呢？（《续编清文指要》，卷下，88）

uthai puseli de uncara sain ningge akū seme bi inu urunakū babade ulame baifi sinde bure sini gūnin de antaka si kemuni jondofi ainambi ine mene gama-ha（拿去－一般过去时）bici sain bihe ainahai waliyabumbini hairakan bodisu ningge ai yadara，damu tede isirengge umesi komso

以上的三个例句中，有后续成分的“V＋了＋C”一般位于单句的前半部分，一般是用来表示句子的背景信息，所以往往语义上不能自足，其后必须有其他成分来补足语义或者只能作为一个修饰成分出现。从格式的使用频率来看，满汉合璧文献中词尾“了”句法格式“V＋了＋O”的用例要高于“V＋了＋C”的格式，其中一部分原因是“V＋了＋C”格式与副动词对应的现象较多，满语副动词的使用数量较多，但是通过文本的对应来看，副动词的意义在汉语中主要是依靠句子成分的语义关系来体现，而非依靠某种格式。

二　句尾“了”相关句法格式

（一）V＋了

句尾“了”最常见的格式就是“V＋了”，在满汉合璧文献中数量较多，其中“了”对应过去时、现将时以及副动词等多种语法形式。

小句中的“V＋了”通常是位于分句或者全句的结尾，可以充当独立的谓语。如：

（11）再要是不念满洲书，不学繙译，两下里都至于耽搁了。（《清文指要》，卷上，1）

jai aikabade manju bithe hūla-rakū ubaliyambure be tacirakū oci juwe de gemusartabu-re（耽搁－现将时）de isina-mbi（到达－现将时）

（12）阿哥，你的清话什麼空儿学了？话音好又清楚。（《清文指要》，卷上，2）

manju gisun taci-re age sini manju gisun ai šolo de taci-ha（学习－一般过去时）mudan gai-rengge sain bime tomorhon

通过以上的例子我们可以看出，这种“V＋了”结构在句子中充当谓语，位于全句的结尾且后面没有接其他成分。“V＋了”所表示的事件信息是句子表达的主要信息，从全句来看是语篇的主要组成部分，主要用于提供新信息和确定语气。从统计来看，这种后续不加其他成分承接语义的“V + 了”形式表示的是句子提供的新信息，是句子所要表达的核心内容。

位于分句或者全句句尾的“了”表示动作的完成或者实现，是完成体标记。而完成体多与过去时和将来时标记共现。以上两个句子主要时态不同。例（11）的“耽搁了”表示假设条件中事件所造成的结果，其中的“了”表示动作发生在参照时间之前，根据句子中的“再要”等能愿动词来看，参照时间是将来的某个时间，所以在这个句子中“了”表示的是将来的完成。

“了”分别表示将来的完成和过去的完成，是强调一种结果性的状态，属于完成体结果性用法。根据胡亚、陈前瑞（2017）对于完成体结果性用法下位用法的细化，例（11）中的“了”属于将来完成的范畴，表示基于当前的事实和情况——“不念书，不学翻译”对未来情况的预测或者是主观假设——“耽搁”；例（12）中的“了”则是狭义的结果性用法，主要是指过去的动作行为——“学清话”造成的现在状态——“话音好又清楚”。

“V + 了”结构可以表达多种功能，并且几乎可以对应所有满语语法形式，所以在满汉合璧文献中词尾“了”句法格式“V + 了”的用例要高于其他几类格式的用例。

（二）V + O + 了

“V + O + 了”格式在满汉合璧文献中主要对应满语的一般过去时，并且数量相对不多。“V + O + 了”一般位于全句的句尾，可以独立成句，也可以在句中充当谓语。

（13）你们狠相好啊，如今怎麽了，总不登你的门槛子了？（《清文指要》，卷上，15）

suwe umesi banjire sain kai te ainaha fuhali sini duka（院门）i（属格格助词）bokson（门槛）de（方向格格助词）fehunji-r-akū（来往，踩 - 方向 - 现将时）o-ho-ni（可以 - 一般过去时 - 疑问式）

（14）直倾到晚，又彻夜至天明，总没有住。到今日饭时，才恍恍惚惚看见日光了。（《清文指要》，卷上，18）

yamjitala hungkerehe bime dobonio geretele umai nakahakū enenggibudai erin otolo teni buru bara šun（日）i（属格格助词）elden（光）be（宾格格助词）sabuha（看见-一般过去时）

位于全句句尾位置的“V+O+了”格式所表示的事件属于前景事件，是句子的主要部分。例句中“登你的门槛子了”和“看见日光了”所表达的事件内容是句子的主要信息，也是句子中所提示的新信息。这种自由形式的格式较少用于单一事件句中，通常用于复句的后一个分句中。

当“V+O+了”格式不用在全句末尾时，可以记为“V+O+了，……”，其中的“了”仍然属于句尾“了”。在这种格式中，“了”主要表示动作的实现或者完成，属于完成体的标记。例（13）中的“了”动作发生在过去的时间线索不明显，发生在过去的“怎么了”对现在所造成的影响是“总不登你的门槛子了”，这个“了”属于完成体中广义的结果性用法，具有现时相关性；例（14）“看见了日光”中的动词“看见”是典型的动结式复合词，本身就表示动作获得了结果。同时，从句子中“方才”“才”等表示过去的时间副词来看，“看见”的动作是发生在过去并且获得结果，所以例（18）中“了”的用法属于完成体典型的结果性用法。

通过统计发现，自由形式的“V+O+了”的句法位置相对来说比较一致，均处于全句句尾。处于分句句尾的“V+O+了”与全句句尾位置上的“V+O+了”有所不同，其后续部分必须有其他谓词成分来承接语义，使整个句子完整。

（15）你竟是一个说不尽的好人，心里沒有一点渣滓，但只嘴太直，知道人的是非了，一点分儿不留，就直言奉上。（《清文指要》，卷上，14）

si serengge emu wajirakū sain niyalma dolo majige hede da akū damu angga jaci sijirhūn niyalma（人）i（属格格助词）uru waka（是非）be（宾格助动词）sa-ha（知道-一般过去时）de（后置词，在……时候）majige ba burakū uthai kang seme gisure-mbi

（16）因为推脱不开，我所以应承了，明明白白的通告诉那个朋友了，不成望不是他一个人的事，说人多掣肘，沒肯应承。（《清文指要》，卷下，33）

anatame banjinarakū ofi tutu bi alime gaifi tere（那个）gucu（朋友）de（与格格助词）giyan giyan i（件件，详细）hafukiya-me（使通晓-并列副动词）ala-ha（告诉-一般过去时）gūnihakū ini emhun i baita waka niyalma geren mayan tatabumbi seme alime gaihakū

“V+O+了”结构处于分句的句尾时，后面有其他的谓词性的成分对前面表示的事件进行说明。这种格式的句法位置相对来说比较固定，通常处于句子的中间。“V+O”表达的是前一个事件，后面的成分紧接着表达后一个事件，组成一个连贯的复合事件。这种“V+O+了”则是句子中的背景事件，在句子中仅起到对主要信息进行补充说明的作用。例（15）句子中的主要信息或者所提示的新信息是“嘴太直”，后续的成分“知道人的是非，一点分儿不留”则是对于“嘴太直”具体表现的补充说明，属于背景信息；例（16）句子的主要信息是“不成望不是他一个人的事”，这个主要信息则是“告诉他那个朋友了”所“告诉”的主要内容，所以说这里的“V+O+了”格式是对主要内容的具体说明，同样属于背景信息。在这个格式中的“了”表示动作的完成或者状态的实现，均属于完成体的结果性用法。

（三）V/Adj（+O）+C+了

与之前几种格式不同，在统计的语料中，“V+C+了”后面不需要任何成分来承接语义，不存在“V+C+了……”的用例。“V+C+了”一般用于全句或者分句的末尾，后面不需要接其他成分，可以单独充当句子的谓语。例如：

（17）竟是把他的话截断来的，不然早来坐乏了。（《清文指要》，卷上，12）

inigisun be meitefi jihe secina akū-ci aifini ci jifi teme（坐下）šada-mbihe（疲乏来着－过去进行时）

（18）忽然一拿的时候，把窗户纸抓破了。拿住了看时，是一个家雀儿。（《续编清文指要》，卷下，75）

leb seme emgeri jafa-ra jakade fa i hoošan be fondo hūwaja-fi（破碎－顺序副动词）lakdari（正好）nambu-ha（拿获，被拿住－一般过去时）tuwaci emu fiyasha cecike

（19）喝了一碗凉茶的上，立刻的头就疼起来了，鼻子也囔了，嗓子也哑了，浑身发冷，狠觉得昏沉了。（《续清文指要》，卷上，56）

emu moro šahūrun muke omi-ha bi-ci ilihai-andande uthai uju nime-me（疼痛－并列副动词）deribu-he（开始－过去时）oforo inu wanggiyana-ha bilha inu sibu-ha beye tugi de te-he adali hūi-sembi

“V + C + 了”的补语成分通常为形容词，如例（17）（18），还有一部分就是趋向动词作补语。我们通过以上几个例子可以观察到，在“V + C + 了”中“了”的语义指向补语，表示补语的实现和完成。例（17）“了”的语义指向是补语成分“乏”，是指前面动作“坐”导致的结果，“乏”的状态已经实现；例（18）“了”指向补语“破”，指的是“抓”的结果——“破”状态的实现；与前两个例句不同，例（19）的补语是趋向补语“起来”，趋向补语表示动作的开始或者起点，“疼起来”也就是“开始疼”的意思。

“V + C + 了”格式表达的句子的主要信息是句子的语义重心。刘丹青（1996）指出，在汉语动结式的结构中，动词往往不是句子所提示的信息，而是做出预设，结果补语才是整个句子的信息焦点。所以，在以上两个例子中，“V + C + 了”表示的内容是整个句子的新信息。

“V + O + C + 了”与“V + C + 了”的形式类似，但是该格式中的宾语属于复杂宾语，或者并未与动词融合为复合结构，所以单独将其列为“V + O + C + 了”。这种有关“了”的句法形式与“V + C + 了”功能相似，值得注意的是，其中的“C”除例（20）为数量结构之外，其他例句中的补语全部为趋向补语“来”和“去”。例（20）“V + O + C + 了”结构表示的是背景时间信息，而其余例句相关结构表达的均是句子的主要信息。例如：

（20）我学汉书十多年了，至今并无头绪。（《清文指要》，卷上，1）

bi juwananiya funce-me nikan（汉人）bithe（书）taci-ha（学习——一般过去时）te-tele umai dube da tucirakū

（21）我初次打围去，骑的一匹马，颠的稳，跑的快，颉着撒袋，才放开围走着，从草里跑出一个黄羊来了。（《续清文指要》，卷上，51）

tuktan bi abalame genehede emu suru morin yalumbihebi katararangge necin feksirengge hūdun jebele ashahai teni aba sarafi genehede orhoi dorgici emu（一）jeren（黄羊）feksi-me（跑 - 并列副动词）tuci-ke（出来 - 一般过去时）

（四）Adj + 了

“Adj + 了”是句尾“了”句法格式中比较重要的一类，这类结构主要位于小句或者整句的末尾，表示状态的变化或者是现在状态。例（22）中的“熟了”表示状态的变化，属于完成体的结果性用法，而例（23）则表示目前呈现的状态。

(22) 每日家念话就记得了，时刻的说，舌头就熟了。(《清文指要》，卷上，4)

inenggidari hūlaci gisunejembi erindari gisureci ilenggū ure-mbi（熟 - 一般现在时）

(23) 每日拿着的上，汗全浸透的，狠光润了。(《续清文指要》，卷下，88)

inenggidari jafaša-hai gemu siberi daha umesi nilgiyan（光滑）o-hobi（及至 - 肯定过去时）

例（22）中，“每日家念”与“时刻的说”导致了“熟”的结果，是一种“不熟”到“熟”的变化。同样，例（23）中“汗全浸透”导致了“光润”的结果，也是现在所呈现的状态。

（五）N + 了

句尾“了”的另一种形式“N + 了”，这种格式的数量很少，在《清文指要》（百章）共有 6 例，主要表示结果性用法或现在状态。例如：

(24) 若大的年纪了，一点陰德儿不积，寡要行这样吃屎的事情，如今的天低啊，叫怎麼替你愁呀？(《续清文指要》，卷上，72)

utala（这么多）se（年纪）unu-fi majige butu-i erdemu-be isa-bu-ra-kū baibi ere gese hamu dunda-ra baita yabuci te-i forgon i abka fangkala kai absi sini funde jobošo-mbi kai

从例句中可以看出，这类格式在满语语法形式对应上表现为一种零形式对应。但是值得注意的是，在这一类的“名词 + 了”的结构中，名词之前均带有修饰成分，如例句中的“若大”，由此可以认为，这里“名词 + 了”并非现代汉语中具有描述性成分的名词与“了”共现的情况，而是带有修饰成分的名词结构与“了”共同表达现在状态。

三 双了句及其他

（一）V + 了 + O + 了

“V + 了 + O + 了”在现代汉语中是一类特征明显的句法形式，在满汉合璧文献中也是比较重要的一类。在现代汉语中，我们通常将这类格式称之为“双了句”。

第一种是处于全句或分句的末尾，后面一般不需要其他成分来承接语义，可以单独充当句子的谓语。现代汉语的“V＋了＋O＋了”句法格式表示完成体的结果性用法和持续性用法。持续性用法与时量宾语相关，《清文指要》中表持续性用法的典型“V＋了＋O＋了”格式仅有2例，其宾语为时量成分。例如：

（25）这一次考繙译，递了名字了没有？要考得自然好麽。但是文秀才未必使得。那格［个］的例呢？像你这样的八旗的都许考，有独不准你考的理吗？（清文指要，卷上，4）

eremudan ubaliyambure be simnere de gebu（名字）alibu-ha-o（呈送－一般过去时－疑问式附加成分）akūn（没有）

（26）阿哥，我不吃烟，长了口疮了。（《清文指要》，卷上，5）

age bi dambagu omirakū angga（口）furuna-habi（长口疮－肯定过去时）

从以上的例句可以看出，自由形式的“V＋了＋O＋了”是句子的主要内容，后续没有任何成分的是句子的语义重心。值得注意的是，例（25）中后续还有一个补语成分“没有”，但是我们依然将其列入自由形式。补语成分“没有”是对该格式所表达的内容的补充与确认，在删去“没有”时不影响其意义的表达。

另一种形式是有后续成分的“V＋了＋O＋了”，一般位于句子的中间位置或者复句的前一分句，后面必须有其他成分来承接使得语义完整。例如：

（27）汉子直过了五十岁了，并没有后，说要放妾使小，他就横躺着不依，要吊死，又是要自尽，各样的吓闹。（《续清文指要》，卷上，69）

eigen susai（五十）se（年纪）tuli-tele（超出－直至副动词）umai juse enen akū bime guweleku sindambi sulahehe takūrakiserede hetudedufi ojorakū fasime-buce-ki-se-re beye-be-beye-ara-ki-se-re acingga demun i gele-bu-me daiša-mbi.

（28）这里那里赶着拿的上，小人儿们听见说得了雀儿了，叫喊着磕磕绊绊的跑了来了。（《续清文指要》，卷上，75）

uba tuba jing amcame jafara sidende buya juse cecike（雀鸟）baha（得

到）sere be donjire jakade kaicaha gio i gese tuhere afarai sujume jifi.

以上的几个例句中的“V + 了 + O + 了”格式属于黏着形式，这种格式后面一定会有其他成分来承接使得语义完整。除此之外，根据《清文指要》（百章）不同时期的汉译本的文本内容对比发现，“V + 了 + O + 了”格式在不同的版本中有不同的形式变化。在《语言自迩集》中，“V + 了 + O + 了”格式中句尾“了”有一部分被语气词“咯”替换，郭锐、陈颖、刘云（2017）介绍了《语言自迩集》改“了”为“咯”的情况，并且指出《语言自迩集》将“了”改为“咯”，说明编写者明确意识到句末语气词的读音不是“liao”，句末“了”读为“lo/la”已经稳定，因此换用新字形来记录。

（二）V + 了 + C + 了

“V + 了 + C + 了”格式大多位于全句的末尾，表示句子中动作发生所造成的结果。其中的补语成分主要为趋向动词，如例（29）（30）；还有一部分补语为量化成分，如例（31）。

（29）——阿哥，你在这里住着麽？

——是，新近搬了来了。（《清文指要》，卷上，5）

——age si ubade tehebio

——inu jakan guri-nji-he（搬了来了 - 方向态附加成分 - 一般过去时）

（30）一定瓜搭着脸要，到底给了，才喜欢着跑了去了。（《续清文指要》，卷上，75）

lakdahūn i wasifi gaji sembi jiduji buhe manggi teni urgunje-fi（欣喜，高兴 - 顺序副动词）fekuce-hei（雀跃 - 连续副动词）gene-he（离去 - 一般过去时）

“V + 了 + C + 了”格式的补语一般是趋向动词“来”“等”，在这一类句法格式的满语对应中，有一类对应为满语的方向态，如例（29）中“-nji-”表示“来”，与趋向补语“来”意义相对应；有一类格式的补语如例（30），没有明显的满汉对应，整体结构的时态为一般过去时，其中没有表示趋向的词语以及相关语义蕴含其中，但是在汉语部分出现了表示趋向的补语“去”。以例（30）为例，这一类格式中出现趋向补语的情况，“跑了去了”中的“跑了”为状语，“去了”为句子的谓语。从满汉对应的角度看，“跑了”对应 fekuce-hei（雀跃——连续副动词），体现副动词的语法功能，而“去了”对应 gene-he（离去——一般过去时），是句子的主要动词、谓语。这一点，从后续的汉译本“V + 了 + C + 了”形式中的前部分被改写成“V 着”也能体现出来。例如：

a. 就死也不依，一定瓜搭着脸要，到底给了，喜欢着跑了去了。（《清文指要》）

a. 要放时，哭着喊着不依，尽命的拉着要，到底给了，才喜欢跳跃着去了。（《新刊清文指要》）

b. 抵死不依，打着坠儿要，到底给了的时候，才喜欢跳着去了。（《三合语录》）

c. 他一定不肯，打着坠毂辘儿的要，没法儿，给了他咯，他才跳跳钻钻的喜欢着去了。（《语言自迩集》）

d. 他一定不肯，打着坠轱辘儿的要，没法儿，给了他咯，他才跳跳钻钻的喜欢着去了。（《亚细亚言语集》）

与例（30）不同，例（29）中的“新近搬了来了”在后世具有互文关系的文本中被改写为如下形式：

a. 是，新近搬了来了。（《清文指要》）

b. 是，新近搬了来的。（《新刊清文指要》）

c. 是，才搬了来。（《三合语录》）

d. 是啊，新近才搬在这房子来的。（《语言自迩集》）

e. 是啊，新近搬了来的。（《亚细亚言语集》）

例（29）中“V + 了 + C + 了”的句尾“了”改写为“的”，在这里助词“的”表示肯定或判断语气，与表语气的助词“了”用法比较相近。除此之外，改写的原因除两者功能相近之外，还有就是“搬了来了”不符合汉语的表达。“V + 了 + C + 了”句尾“了”主要是表示事态出现变化，整个结构表示事态变化产生的结果，而从例（29）前半句中的“是”来看，句子突出的是肯定回答，所以换用表示肯定语气的助词“的”来表达，更符合汉语的习惯。

除此之外，在后续的几个版本中“V + 了 + C + 了”的改写形式也有很多种，例如省略句尾“了”，同时省略词尾和句尾“了”等变化。例如：

b. 这里那里正赶着拿的空儿，小孩子们听见说得了雀儿了，一齐都来到，大家赶的赶拿的拿，那一个拿一顶帽子一扣得了。（《三合语录》）

c. 满屋子里正赶着拏的时候儿，小孩子们听见说拏住雀儿了，一齐都来咯，赶的赶拏的拏，有一个小孩子使帽子扣住了。（《语言自迩集》）

d. 满屋子里我正赶着拿的时候儿，小孩子们听见说拿住雀儿了，一齐都来咯，赶的赶拿的拿，有一个小孩子使帽子扣住了。（《亚细亚言语集》）

e. 正在赶着拿的时候，那小孩子们听见说拿着雀儿，一齐的都推门进来，那雀儿满屋飞躲，赶的赶拿的拿，归根空空手都拿不着。后首有一个小孩子使帽子覆住，才又抓着拿去。（《参订汉语问答篇国字解》）

以上例句在不同版本中有不同的改写形式，从一定程度上也能体现出一部分的“V+了+C+了”是一种“非汉语表达”。也就是说，“V+了+C+了”形式中的一些表达被改写主要是因为不符合当时汉语的表达习惯。上文提到，副动词兼具有副词和动词的功能，而将格式中“V+了”部分与副动词相对应，很大程度上是一种汉语的“误用”或者受到满语的干扰。通过满汉合璧文献中满汉对应的整体结果来看，很大一部分副动词是以助词“了”的对应为主，出现在翻译时扩大了“了”的功能范围而误用的情况。

（31）我说这想必是存住食了罢，吃了一付打药的时候，把好歹的东西全打下来了，那个上才料料的松闲了些了。（《续清文指要》，卷下，87）

tede teni majige（稍微）sulakan（略松快）o-ho（可以，认为，到－一般过去时）

例（31）中的补语是量化成分“些”，用来补充说明“松闲”的程度。同样，在不同历史时期的版本中，“松闲了些了”也存在不同的改写形式，例如：

a. 我说这想必是存住食了罢，吃了一付打药的时候，把好歹的东西全打下来了，那个上才料料的松闲了些了。（《清文指要》）

a. 我说这必是存住食了罢，吃了一付打药，把肚子里所有的好歹东西都打下来了，那上头身子才畧松快了些儿。（《新刊清文指要》）

b. 我说这个想是停住食了，服了一剂打药的上头，好歹的东西都下来了，那上头才畧松快了些了。（《三合语录》）

c. 我想是停住食了，就服了一剂打药，把内里所有好啊歹的东西都打下来了，这心里才觉着松快些儿。（《语言自迩集》）

d. 因为那样儿，我说这想是停住食了，服了一剂打药，内里所有的好

啊歹的东西都打下来了，心里觉着才畧松快些儿。(《亚细亚言语集》)

e. 我想这是风火的病，吃一剂畧表散的药就是；若风能退散，那火自然的会平了。(《参订汉语问答篇国字解》)

g. 我想是停住食了，就腹［服］了一剂打药，把内里所有的好啊歹的东西都打下来了，这心里才觉着松快些儿。(《自习完璧支那语》)

四　结论

《清文指要》(百章）中“了”主要有九种句法格式，各自具有不同的句法分布和句法功能。从句法位置来看，“了”的相关句法格式一般是处于小句或者全句的末尾。一般来说，处于全句末尾的“了”格式是句子表达的主要内容。处于小句末尾的“了”格式属于黏着形式，语义上不自足，其后必须有其他成分来补足，一般是句子表达的背景时间信息，是句子发生的条件或者是背景。

《清文指要》(百章）中“了”句法格式的出现频率与其满汉对应的倾向性规律有关。“V + 了 + O”的使用次数要高于“V + 了 + C”的格式，重要原因之一是“V + 了 + O”大多对应顺序副动词，而“V + 了 + C”格式主要对应满语并列副动词形式，满语顺序副动词出现频率高于并列副动词。词尾“了”句法格式“V + 了”的用例要多于其他几类格式，原因不仅是在文本的统计中顺序副动词出现频率高于并列副动词，而更进一步的原因是副动词在汉语中的对应较少使用固定格式，而多用句子成分之间的关系，而“V + 了 + O”格式较“V + 了 + C”更普遍，使用频率会更高。词尾“了”句法格式“V + 了”的用例要多于其他几类格式，原因之一是“V + 了”格式在文本中对应时、态、副动词等多种语法形式，而某些格式在对应上存在明显的倾向性。

《清文指要》后来有多种修订或改写版本。“了”结构在《清文指要》改编文献中有各种变化。比方说，“V + 了 + C + 了”格式在《清文指要》三槐堂刻本中数量最多，后世改编本中数量减少，并且有相应的改写形式，改写的原因是，编者认为句子不符合当时北京话的表达习惯，而不符合汉语表达习惯出现的原因是满汉语言翻译导致的。

参考文献

刘丹青：《东南方言的体貌标记》，香港中文大学吴多泰中国语文研究中心，1996。

张美兰、刘曼：《〈清文指要〉汇校与语言研究》，上海教育出版社，2013。

包和平：《什么是满汉合璧》，《中国民族》1990 年第 3 期。

郭锐、陈颖、刘云：《从早期北京话材料看虚词“了”的读音变化》，《中国语文》2017 年第 6 期。

胡亚，陈前瑞：《“了”的完成体与完整体功能的量化分析及其理论意义》，《世界汉语教学》2017 年第 7 期。

金立鑫：《试论“了”的时体特征》，《语言教学与研究》1998 年第 2 期。

Syntactic Structures with the Aspect Auxiliary "*le*"（了）in *Qingwen Zhiyao* and their Expressions in Manchu and Chinese

Li Congcong, Wang Jihong

Abstract

This paper takes *Qingwen Zhiyao*（100 chapters）as case study. Starting from the syntactic structures of "*le*", it explores the use of "*le*" in Qing Mandarin through statistical analysis of the syntactic positions and functions of different structures. According to statistics, in the Manchu and Chinese bilingual conversation textbook *Qingwen Zhiyao*（100 chapters）, the "*le*" can be divided into three main categories, namely, the verb "*le*", the compound words composed of verbs "*le*" and the tense-aspect auxiliary word "*le*". In *Qingwen Zhiyao*, the aspect auxiliary "*le*" has a syntactic structures, of which "Verb + *le*" appears most frequently. There are different revisions and adaptation versions of *Qingwen Zhiyao*. Through the comparison of the versions, we can see that some of these syntactic structures have been replaced by other auxiliary words, or the whole structure has changed. From the perspective of Manchu-Chinese correspondence, to some extent, the use of the syntactic structures of "*le*" is influenced by Manchu.

Keywords

Qingwen Zhiyao　the proofread of Manchu and Chinese　Sentence Structures

“德国式拼音”考述

何玉洁*

摘　要

自西方人用罗马字拼读汉语利玛窦等耶稣会传教士名字始，晚清国门打开后，来华传教、经商、外交的西方人日益增多，拼写汉语的各语种罗马字方案因此盛行。本文研究对象是在华德国人中传播广泛的雷兴－欧特曼方案（Lessing-Othmer-System），又称“德国式拼音”。该方案自创制起便被广泛用于辞典和教材的拼读、名称和小说的译介以及汉学著作中，但目前鲜有此方案的系统研究。本文基于前人的研究，梳理该方案创制的背景及过程，通过考察该方案在各种著作中的使用情况，探究其在中德交流史上的价值与意义。“德国式拼音”虽然最终没有如威妥玛式拼音那样，被约定俗成为德语语种真正的统一方案，但是它的出现体现了德语使用者在汉语拼读上的努力尝试，它所促成的相关著作也丰富了德语区汉学及汉语的研究，极大促进了近代东西语言上的接触和交流。

关键词

德国式拼音　雷兴－欧特曼方案　汉语拼音方案　汉语拉丁化

用罗马字拼读汉语语音的历史可以追溯到16世纪，利玛窦、金尼阁等来华传教的耶稣会传教士将学习、翻译汉语的经验编撰成《西字奇迹》《西儒耳目资》等书，书中用各自的语言或者通用拉丁语拼读汉语。晚清国门打开后，中西交流活动日益增多，西方人在华经商、传教、处理外交事务

---

* 何玉洁，北京外国语大学历史学院在读博士生。

等过程中所从事的翻译、管理沟通、外语教学、汉学研究等活动催生了一批新的更适时的汉语拼音系统的出现。

随着19世纪各民族国家的形成，人们民族意识觉醒，语言作为民族身份认同的重要形式，影响了语种化的汉语拼音方案的创制。英、法、德相继开始了用本国语言拼读汉语的尝试，其中影响最大的是创制于1867年的威妥玛式拼音，该方案以英语的拼读习惯为基础拼读北京官话语音，1912年由翟理斯（H. A. Giles）稍做修订后以“威－翟式”（Wade-Giles System）拼音固定下来，流传最为广泛。在语种化汉语拼音方案实践的过程中，人们意识到地名人名不同的拼读方式，给处理外交信函、正式文件乃至杂志期刊等带来了极大的不便。汉语罗马化很难统一为一种形式，原因之一是作为描写对象的语音在变化，并且一些以传教为主要目的的拼音方案以汉语方言为对象，有很强的地域性，难以通用；其二在于方案本身的不足，即便是流通广泛的威式拼音也有自身的不一致性。

但他们并没有停止创制统一方案的尝试。为了方便各地的广大传教士学习汉语，内地会创始人戴德生（Taylor James Hudson）创建了内地会拼音系统，试图建立一种全国标准音。[①] 但该方案以南方官话为对象，主要用于中国的中部和西部。法国驻华外交官、汉学家的微席叶（Arnold Jacques Antoine Vissière，1858－1930）认为法语字母能够标出大多数的汉语官话的发音，也认为重新创立或统一汉语法式标音系统是非常有必要的。他于1902年创制的拼音方案参考了儒莲（Stanislas Julien，1797－1873）、于雅乐（C. Imbault-Huart，1857－1897）和威妥玛（T. F. Wade，1818－1895）等人的方案，实施中因受到了法国外交部的大力支持，因而得到颇具效力的推广。[②] 这套法式拼音方案也几乎全部被法国远东学院（l'ecole française d'Extrême-Orient）采用，因此该方案也被称为法国远东学院拼音，在法国汉学界流传较广，并一直沿用到二十世纪中期。

以德语拼读为基础的汉语拼音方案也同样经历了这一过程。德国的硕特（Wilhelm Schott，1794－1865）、甲柏连孜（H. G. v. c. Gabelentz，1840－

① 岳岚：《晚清时期汉语注音罗马化系统的演进——从“北京大学”的英译谈起》，《贵州社会科学》2017年第4期，第52页。

② 温利燕：《微席叶〈北京官话：汉语初阶〉研究》，上海师范大学硕士学位论文，2010，第6页。

1893）和穆麟德（P. G. von Möllendorff，1847 - 1901）等汉学家曾创建出一套拼音方案，但均未得到广泛使用。统一德语拼音方案的尝试中最为成功的是雷兴 - 欧特曼方案（Lessing-Othmer-System），该方案源自雷兴和欧特曼于 1912 年合著的教科书《汉语通释》（*Lehrgang der Nordchinesischen Umgangssprache*）。该书出版后在德语世界广为流传，该拼音方案也因此作为德语式拼音方案的代表被广泛使用。在随后中国的汉语拉丁化和拼音运动中，该方案也提供了重要参考。至今，一些地名人名的德译仍采用这一方案。在目前各类文献资料中的“德国式拼音”均指该方案。

被称作“德国式拼音”的雷兴 - 欧特曼方案在各种著作中被零星提及，关于该方案的研究目前仅有德国学者孙敏学（Michael Schön）的《19 至 20 世纪的中德拼写系统》（*Chinesich-deutsche Transkriptionssysteme im 19. und 20. Jahrhundert*，2013）一书，书中介绍了该方案的创制过程。本文从雷兴 - 欧特曼方案的创制理念出发，通过对其使用情况的考察，探究其在中德语言文化交流史上的价值与意义。

一 “德国式拼音”的创制

雷兴 - 欧特曼方案的创制背景及过程与青岛德占区的德语教育发展息息相关。雷兴 - 欧特曼方案的前身是卫礼贤 - 雷兴方案（Wilhelm-Lessingsche Vorschlag），该方案于 1911 年在青岛德语教师大会（Zusammenschulss deutscherLehrkräfte）[①] 上经由投票，选为德语区教师使用的“统一方案”。19 世纪 60 年代，教会开始在华创办德语教会学校，既传授基督教义，又开展语言教学。[②] 1897 年德国强占胶州湾后，殖民统治当局致力于将其建立成一个模范殖民地，开始重视文化输出。德督府成立了学务委员会，负责改造原有的私塾和创办蒙养学堂；胶州湾总督府无偿将土地赠送给教会组织，

① 青岛市档案馆编《青岛开埠十七年——〈胶澳发展备忘录〉全译》，中国档案出版社，2007，第 714 页。该档案关于这一集会的记录：在青岛特别高等专门学堂的召集下，1911 年 7 月德国在华教师在青岛集会。会议就德国在华教育活动的目的和目标以及有效的教育和教学手段问题进行了座谈。集会结束时决定 1912 年于青岛再次举行集会，这表明青岛也开始成为德国在华文化活动的中心。

② 毛小红：《中国德语文教育历史研究（1861 - 1976）》，上海外国语大学博士学位论文，2014，第 9 页。

鼓励教会办学。反过来，教会也游说政府外交及军事部门重视对华语言文化政略，努力使德语成为中国学校课程里的一门主要外语。[①] 在此背景下，著名传教士卫礼贤（Richard Wilhelm，1873 - 1930）与其妻子卫美懿（Salome Wilhelm）出于为中国孩子办学的目的，由瑞士同善会资助，于1901年6月在青岛创办礼贤书院；1905年，卫礼贤以妻子的中文名字创设女校“美懿书院”，又于1911年开辟新校舍“淑范女子学堂”。卫礼贤创立的三所学校课程均实行中西合璧的教学方式，开设德语课程和教授中国经典文化的课程。

殖民地内一所大学的建立也与卫礼贤息息相关。随着租借地中小学教育体系的建立，在租借地内建立一所高等学堂的呼声越来越高。1904年，卫礼贤出于对学院毕业生升学考虑，向中德政府申清合办青岛高等学校。[②] 1909年，青岛的特别高等专门学堂（Deutsch-Chinesische Hochschule）（又称为德华大学）在这一背景下得以创办。该校教学模式基本上以德国现代大学制度和教学内容为主，结合中式教学形式，形成中西合璧的教学体系。除了必修的中文课程（经学、文学、人伦道德等）外，其他各科均以德文授课。1913年上半学期，学堂共有26位德籍教师，其中正式教员15名，兼职教员11名。[③] 而雷兴[④]和欧特曼[⑤]正是正式教员中的两名，分别担任讲师和预科教务长。

德占区学校的创办促进了德语教育的发展，德语师资因此形成一定规模。更为规范、统一的汉语拼音方案，逐渐成为中德语言教学和交流中追求的目标。因此，1911年在青岛举办的德语教师大会上，与会者商讨了统

① 毛小红：《中国德语文教育历史研究（1861 - 1976）》，上海外国语大学博士学位论文，2014，第38页。

② 转引自翟广顺《半个世纪风雨——1891 - 1949青岛教育大事记述》，青岛出版社，2009，第33页。

③ 刘金玲：《特别高等专门学堂研究》，山东经济学院硕士学位论文，2010，第24页。

④ 雷兴（Ferd Lessing，1882 - 1961），德国汉学家（后去往美国），时任青岛特别高等专门学堂讲师。1907年来华学习，在北京翻译学校担任讲师，1909年之前转到青岛德华大学任教。1925年成为柏林东方语言研究所汉学教授，主要从事汉语语言和佛教研究。

⑤ 欧特曼（Wilhelm Othmer，1882 - 1934），1904年获得博士学位，1907年成为外交部候选人前往北京，负责管理德国学校里的中国人。通过一系列的教学和管理活动，欧特曼学会汉语。因为名望，他于1909年转到青岛特别高等专门学堂任职，直至1914年，其间，他和雷兴创制新的以德语拼读习惯为基础的汉语拼音方案，并合著汉语教材《汉语通释》。

一汉语拼音方案制订一事。这一过程载于刊物《德文学报》（*Ostasiatische Lehrerzeitung*）[①]。

（一）卫礼贤-雷兴方案

1911年7月，时任《德文新报》（*Ostasiatischen Lloyd*）[②] 的编辑卡尔·费希（Karl Fischer，1881－1941）在《德文新报》上发表了一篇题为《官话汉字统一拼写方案——卫礼贤-雷兴方案》[③] 的文章。该文论述了当前所遭遇的拼写问题以及统一拼音方案亟待出现的必要性，并展示由时任德汉研讨会主持者卫礼贤和特别高等专门学堂的讲师雷兴共同创制的拼音提议草案（见图1）。作者卡尔·费希为了鼓励大会成员提出其他更为科学、完整的提案，在其中附上了新系统所含的各种基本元素及其相关说明。[④]这篇文章对新的统一的对德拼音方案的出现起到较强的推动作用。图1草案为一套以德语发音为基础的汉语音节表。其中个别音节尚未确定，以问号标出。

在1911年7月26日至29日于青岛举办的在华德语教师大会上，卫礼贤和雷兴的草案经过修订后被票选为"统一方案"（Einigungsumschrift），又称卫礼贤-雷兴方案（*Wilhelm-Lessingsche Vorschlag*）（见图2）。根据议程报告，经过与会人员一系列讨论和投票后，该方案被一致通过，附于28日会议记录中。[⑤]"统一方案"确定了此前草案中一些不确定的音节，改进了个别音节的拼写，添加上遗漏掉的汉语音节，调整了音节表顺序，相比之下更为完善。

卫礼贤-雷兴方案（*Wilhelm-Lessingsche Vorschlag*）最突出的特点之一

① 编辑部在上海，创办于1910年，1913年停办。

② 《德文新报》是近代中国第一份德文报刊。1886年创刊于上海，每周发行一次，主要读者对象为远东地区德国侨民。第一次世界大战期间，中国加入协约国阵营，对德宣战，由此缘故，《德文新报》于1917年8月被迫停刊。该周刊连续出版近31年，是近代中国出版时间最长的德文报刊。

③ *Einheitliche Umschreibung der chinesischen Zeichen der Mandarinsprache. Zum Wilhelm-Lessingschen Vorschlag*, Ostasiatischen Lehrerzeitung, 1911.

④ Ibid.

⑤ 报告刊载于《德文学报》Anlage 1 zum Protokoll: *Verzeichnis der von der Versammlung deutscher Lehrer an chinesischen Schulen zu Tsingtau am 28. Juli 1911 angenommenen Umschrift* in: Ostasiatische Lehrerzeitung 2/3 (Oktober 1911), pp. 3－17. 转引自 Michael Schön, *Chinesich-deutsche Transkriptionssysteme im 19. und 20. Jahrhundert. Abriss der Enwicklung einschliesslich wichtiger Transkriptionstabellen*, Berlin, 2013, pp. 49－55.

In Folgendern ist das von den beiden Herren vorgeschlagene System wiedergegeben:

A	阿	Ding	定	Dsï	子	Fĕng	風
Ai	愛	Diu	丟	Dsi	祭	Fou	否
An	安	Do	朶	Dsiä	姐	Fu	夫
Ang	昂	Dou	豆	Dsiän	賤		
Au	傲	Dsa	雜	Dsiang	將	Ga	蛤
		Dsai	在	Dsiau	焦	Gai	改
Ba	巴	Dsan	贊	Dsin	進	Gan	甘
Bai	拜	Dsang	葬	Dsing	井	Gang	剛
Ban	板	Dsau	早	Dsiu	酒	Gau	告
Bang	邦	Dscha	乍	Dso	坐	Ge?	格
Bau	包	Dschä?	這	Dsö?	責	Gĕn	根
Be	倍	Dschö?	這	Dsou	走	Gĕng	更
Bĕn	本	Dschai	齋	Dsu	祖	Gi	記
Bĕng	崩	Dschan	占	Dsuan	鑽	Gia	家
Bi	比	Dschang	章	Dsü	聚	Giä	揭
Biä	別	Dschau	兆	Dsün	俊	Giän	見
Biän	扁	Dsche?	責	Dsüö	爵	Giang	江
Biau	表	Dschĕn	真	Dsui	嘴	Giau	交
Bin	賓	Dschĕng	正	Dsun	尊	Gin	金
Bing	兵	Dschï	知	Dsung	宗	Ging	經
Bo	波	Dscho	著	Du	妒	Giu	救
Bu	布	Dschou	晝	Duan	短	Giung	窘
		Dschu	主	Dui	對	Go	哥
Da	大	Dschua	抓	Dun	敦	Gou	狗
Dai	歹	Dschuai	拽	Dung	冬	Gu	古
Dan	單	Dschuan	專	E? Ŏ?	額	Gua	爪
Dang	當	Dschuang	壯	En	恩	Guai	怪
Dau	道	Dschui	追	Eng	哼	Guan	官
De? Dö?	德	Dschun	準	Fa	法	Guang	光
Dĕng	等	Dschung	中	Fan	反	Gü	居
Di	地	Dse	賊	Fang	方	Güan	捐
Diä	爹	Dsĕn	怎	Fe	非	Gün	君
Diän	店	Dsĕng	增	Fĕn	分	Güö	腳
Diau	吊						

图 1　提议草案

是它基于业内实践经验和广泛的交流设置而成。该大会不是官方政府部门，方案属于共同约定而不具有强制性。随后，该方案很快便运用在卫礼贤自己的译著《庄子：南华真经》① 中；此外，德国汉学家许勒（Wilhelm Schüler）于 1912 年出版的《中国近代史概论——以山东省为例》② 一书中，

① Richard Wilhelm, *Dschuang Dsi: das wahre Buch vom südlichen Blütenland*, Jena, 1912.

② Wilhelm Schüler, *Abriss der neueren Geschichte Chinas unter besonderer Berücksichtigung der Provinz Schantung*, Berlin, 1912.

Anlage 1 zum Protokoll.

Verzeichnis der von der Versammlung deutscher Lehrer an chinesischen Schulen am 28sten Juli 1911 zu Tsingtau angenommenen Umschrift.

A	阿	Diau	吊	Dsï	子	Fang	方
Ai	愛	Ding	定	Dsi	祭	Fe	非
An	安	Diu	丟	Dsiä	姐	Fen	分
Ang	昂	Do	多	Dsiän	賤	Föng	風
Au	傲	Döng	等	Dsiang	將	Fou	否
		Dou	豆	Dsiau	焦	Fu	夫
Ba	巴	Dsa	雜	Dsin	進		
Bai	拜	Dsai	在	Dsing	井	Ga	蛤
Ban	板	Dsan	贊	Dsiu	酒	Gai	改
Bang	邦	Dsang	髒	Dso	坐	Gan	甘
Bau	包	Dsau	早	Dsöng	增	Gang	剛
Be	倍	Dscha	乍	Dsou	走	Gau	告
Ben	本	Dschä	這	Dsu	祖	Ge	格
Bi	比	Dschai	齋	Dsuan	纘	Gen	根
Biä	別	Dschan	占	Dsü	聚	Gi	記
Biän	扁	Dschang	章	Dsün	俊	Gia	家
Biau	表	Dschau	兆	Dsüo	爵	Giä	揭
Bin	賓	Dschen	真	Dsui	嘴	Giän	見
Bing	兵	Dschï	知	Dsun	尊	Giang	江
Bo	波	Dscho	著	Dsung	宗	Giau	交
Böng	崩	Dschöng	正	Du	妒	Gin	金
Bu	布	Dschou	周	Duan	短	Ging	經
		Dschu	主	Dui	對	Giu	救
Da	大	Dschua	抓	Dun	敦	Giung	窘
Dai	歹	Dschuai	拽	Dung	冬	Go	哥
Dan	單	Dschuan	專			Göng	更
Dang	當	Dschuang	壯	E	額	Gou	狗
Dau	道	Dschui	追	En	恩	Gu	古
De	德	Dschun	準	Eng	哼	Gua	爪
Di	地	Dschung	中			Guai	怪
Diä	爹	Dse	賊	Fa	法	Guan	官
Diän	店	Dsen	怎	Fan	反	Guang	光

图 2 “统一方案”——卫礼贤 - 雷兴方案

考虑到拼音方案研究的新发展及其书的通用性，除了采用穆麟德拼音方案[①]外，还另外附上卫礼贤 - 雷兴方案以供读者选择，并肯定了后者对于个别拼写形式的改进。例如，当时大部分地区将“胶州”拼写为 Kiau tschou；汉语中的送气音和不送气音沿袭了威妥玛式拼音的方法，即用送气符号

① P. G. *Möllendorff*, *Praktische Anleitung zur Erlernung der hochchinesischen Sprache*, Kelly& Walsh, 1906.

‘表示送气音。德语中有类似发音的字母组合可以用于区分两者，如 tsch 和 dsch，该设置也为卫礼贤－雷兴方案所参考（卫礼贤－雷兴方案中“胶州”为 Giau-dschou）。这种拼写表达以及中间用于分隔汉字的横线均在《中国近代史概论——以山东省为例》一书的“拼写方案”部分中得到著作者的认可。[①]

（二）雷兴－欧特曼方案

同在青岛德华大学任教的雷兴和欧特曼，于 1912 年合著出版了两卷本汉语教科书《汉语通释》。该教材出版后满足了当时人们对一本系统、实用的汉语教材的需要。该书在德语区通行多年，受到德语学习者的广泛欢迎，1933 年于上海再版。该教材中使用的汉语拼音系统是对卫礼贤－雷兴方案的继承与发展，被后来的使用者称为雷兴－欧特曼方案，即广为流传的“德国式拼音”。

《汉语通释》引论中的“拼写方案”称，“我们以卫礼贤和雷兴的‘统一方案’为基础，希望创制出一种拼音方案，使学习者能够在语言学习时产生尽可能少的困扰。相对于‘统一方案’，该方案产生的偏差并不明显”。[②] 因此该教材将两种拼音方案同时展示出来，以音节表的形式标识出其与“统一方案”的不同之处。如图 3 所示，图中为《汉语通释》中“统一方案”与威妥玛式方案的对比。

图 3 的对比中，汉字后面的第一列为“统一方案”，其中几个用逗号隔开并以斜体表示的音节为该教材修改了的形式，即雷兴－欧特曼式方案（书中被雷兴等称为“不规则形式”）。第二列为英式拼音方案——威－翟式拼音，这种方案以及与其相似的方案大多使用于英语类书籍和报刊。[③] 为了精确起见，作者还在此表上括号里添加了汉字的其他不常用发音。

雷兴和欧特曼在其著作《汉语通释》中没有直接沿用卫礼贤和雷兴的“统一方案”，而是以其为基础进行了修改和添加，原因之一是由于“统一

---

① Michael Schön, *Chinesich-deutsche Transkriptionssysteme im 19. und 20. Jahrhundert. Abriss der Enwicklung einschliesslich wichtiger Transkriptionstabellen*, Berlin, 2013.

② Ferd. Lessing, Dr. Wilh. Othmer, 漢語通釋 *Lehrgang der nordchinesischen Umgangssprache*, Deutsch-Chiesische Druckerei und Verlagsanstalt (Walther Schmidt), Tsingtau, 1912.

③ Ibid.

II. Vergleichende Umschrifttabelle.

In der ersten Spalte hinter dem Z. steht die Einigungsumschrift (vgl. I, 1, Einl. S. V—VI, bes. V, Anm. 2), jede abweichende Schreibung dieses Buches ist in schrägen Lettern beigegeben. In der zweiten Spalte steht die englische Umschrift von Wade, wie sie sich, in Kleinigkeiten verändert, in dem grössten chin.-engl. Lexikon, dem von H. A. Giles, a Chinese-English Dictionary, Schanghai, 2. Aufl., 1909—1912, findet; dieselbe oder eine ganz ähnliche Umschrift benutzen die meisten englischen Bücher und Zeitungen. — Zu der Einigungsumschrift mussten einige wenige unberücksichtigt gebliebene Z. hinzugefügt werden; sie sind der Genauigkeit halber in eckige Klammern gesetzt worden.

阿	a	a	爹	diä	tieh
爱	ai	ai	店	diän	tien
安	an	an	掉	diau	tiao
昂	ang	ang	定	ding	ting
傲	au	ao	丢	diu	tiu
			多	do	to
巴	ba	pa	等	dŏng, *dĕng*	têng
拜	bai	pai	豆	dou	tou
板	ban	pan	雜	dsa	tsa
邦	bang	pang	在	dsai	tsai
包	bau	pao	贊	dsan	tsan
貝	be	pei	葬	dsang	tsang
本	ben, *bĕn*	pên	早	dsau	tsao
比	bi	pi	乍	dscha	cha
别	biä	pieh	這	dschä, *dschö*	chê
扁	biän	pien	窄	dschai	chai
表	biau	piao	占	dschan	chan
賓	bin	pin	張	dschang	chang
坡	bŏ	po	眞	dschen, *dschĕn*	chên
崩	bŏng, *bĕng*	pêng	知	dschĭ	chih
布	bu	pu	著	dscho	cho
			正	dschŏng, *dschĕng*	chêng
大	da	ta	箒	dschou	chou
帶	dai	tai	主	dschu	chu
單	dan	tan	爪	dschua	chua
當	dang	tang	拽	dschuai	chuai
道	dau	tao	專	dschuan	chuan
德	de, *dö (de)*	tê (tei)	壯	dschuang	chuang
地	di	ti	追	dschui	chui

图 3 《汉语通释》中“统一方案”与威妥玛式方案对比（部分）

方案”中大部分音节拼读的是山东地区方言的发音。例如声母组 gi-dsi，ki-tsi，hi-si 等，在《汉语通释》中均被以北京官话为基础的声母替换。如 dji 对应 gi 和 dsi，tji 对应 ki 和 tsi，hsi 对应 hi 和 si。此外，还有一些微小的变化，例如 jën、mën、wën 替换了 jen、men、wen 等。编排上，作者在每篇课文生词表部分，仍旧在改动过的音节下面附上“统一方案”原来的形式，以供读者对照参考。将两种拼音方案对比来看，“统一方案”设定更多是因为受到青岛地区德语教师大会需求的影响，侧重于当时的时效性和实用性；而《汉语通释》作为一本教授北京官话的教材，使用的拼音方案以北京官话为对象，面向德语世界所有汉语学习者，其影响远远超出了德占青岛地区。高本汉（K. B. I. Karlgren，1889－1978）1917年出版的《官话注音读本》（*A Mandarin Phonetic Keader in the Pekinese Dialect*）一书中便列举了《汉语通释》的雷兴－欧特曼方案作为英、法、德、俄四种拼音方案中德语语种的代表。[①] 该书客观上为德国式统一拼音方案这一目标的实现提供了可能性，随之流传的汉语拼音方案也为德语世界的汉语研究及教学提供了重要工具。

二 “德国式拼音”的使用情况

雷兴－欧特曼方案的前身卫礼贤－雷兴方案的设定旨在统一山东地区混乱的汉语拼读情况，因此最初的名称也为“统一方案”。该方案虽经过集体商讨投票的形式制定而成，但其在实际使用中并没有以固定不变的形式沿袭下去。雷兴－欧特曼方案自创制以来，便广泛运用于各种汉语教材和双语词典中，其中就有谋乐的《德汉教程》（1914）、利定白的《华德辞典》（1924）和石密德、陆懿的《标准国语教本》（1939）这三本著作。这三本书分别是初级口语汉语教材、双语词典和综合性汉语教材，出版时间跨越25年，作者和面向的读者对象呈现多样性的特点，但都选择雷兴－欧特曼方案拼读汉语。本文以这三本书为例，分析雷兴－欧特曼方案在使用中所呈现的变化及其原因。

（一）谋乐的《德汉教程》

谋乐（F. W. Mohr，1881－1936），德国法学博士，德占胶澳总督，盐务协理官。1907年他由德国科隆步兵团派往青岛，1907年至1913年任胶澳总督翻译官，期间也曾在特别高等专门学堂任兼职德语教师。谋乐于1913年春天担任过德侨家庭妇女们和女传教士们的汉语老师，他于1914年出版的汉语教科书《德汉教程》（*Deutsch-Chinesische Unterrichtsstunden*）的初稿就

① 倪海曙：《中国拼音文字运动史简编》，时代出版社，1950，第29页。

曾作为教学讲义。谋乐在此基础上进行整理，在其担任山东盐务稽核分所协理期间，在济南完成终稿并出版。[①]《德汉教程》全称《德汉教程，初级汉语学习简要指南》，结合实践中的教学对象，可将该教程看作一本偏重初级口语的实用性汉语教材。在序言里，作者推荐了两本适合高级汉语学习的用书，即卫礼贤的《德汉语言课程》以及雷兴和欧特曼合著的《汉语通释》。[②]

《德汉教程》中教学对象是北京官话，基本沿用雷兴－欧特曼方案，只稍做改动。两者声母系统完全一致，韵母系统区别如下：（1）因教程选材的原因，文本中缺少［uəŋ］韵的汉字；（2）用“ˆ”“ˊ”表示元音的长短及诵读时的停顿；（3）将雷兴－欧特曼方案中用“ä”表示的韵母全部改成“ë”表示。从改动来看，谋乐基本认可雷兴－欧特曼方案的设定，细节改动是因为教学对象不同：《德汉教程》面向初级汉语口语学习者，以编排常用词语和句子为主，并增添了帮助理解的辅助符号。雷兴与欧特曼在《汉语通释》中对“ë”有这样的描述：“‘ë’是介于‘e’和‘ö’之间的模糊的音，它在‘ng’之前读出的音是类似‘ong’的音。”[③] 据高兰（2017）推测，“ë”是为了准确描写出介于“e”“ö”之间的音而大胆创制的元音，以更准确地标注北京官话音。谋乐的《德汉教程》在雷兴－欧特曼方案创制不久后立即投入使用，该书充分结合了教学实践，可见雷兴－欧特曼方案在实际教学中也经受住了考验，能满足德国人在日常生活中准确拼读汉语的需求。

（二）利定白的《华德辞典》

利定白（Werner Rüdenberg），德籍犹太人，1881 年 11 月出生于德国下萨克森州的州府汉诺威，后成为著名的商人和辞典编撰者。他在上海住过 16 年，前后时间跨度长达 30 年，这为他编写《华德辞典》（*Chinesischen-Deutsches Wörterbuch*, 6400 *Schriftzeichen mit ihren Einzelbedeutungen und den gebräuchlichsten Zusammensetzungen*）奠定了基础。除了官话之外，他对上海

① 高兰：《谋乐〈德汉教程〉研究》，上海师范大学硕士学位论文，2017，第 11 页。

② Friedrich Wilhelm Mohr，德漢教程 *Deutsch-Chinesische Unterrichtsstunden*，Druck und Verlag von Adolf Haupt，Tsingtau，1914.

③ 参见高兰《谋乐〈德汉教程〉研究》，上海师范大学硕士学位论文，2017，第 17－22 页。

话也颇有研究。1938 年他在伦敦大学亚非学院教过几个月的汉语，并编纂了《英汉词典》（英语 - 上海方言词典）。1940 年他曾被拘禁在马恩岛的俘虏营中，后来他在德国的西菲尔德学院任教，并且继续与中国人做生意。[①] 利定白的《华德辞典》序言中提及，这本辞典广泛参考与借鉴了此前出版的各种优秀辞典，并大量搜罗了当时多种类型报纸及刊物上的语料。[②] 结合作者自身丰富严谨的汉语教学及研究经验，该辞典成为德语区汉语学习者最为全面且便捷的学习工具书之一，并于 1936 年简单修订后推出第二版，1963 年汉学家施翰基（Hans O. Stange，1903 - 1978）在该辞典基础上主持修订后出版第三版《华德辞典》。

《华德辞典》也采用了雷兴 - 欧特曼方案。利定白同时考虑到威妥玛拼音的广泛性以及使用者对其的熟悉程度，在"德国式拼音"的每个音节下以括号形式另附上威妥玛式拼音，以供对照参考。利定白没有原封不动沿用雷兴 - 欧特曼方案，而是在它的基础上作了一些改动：（1）声母系统中，《华德辞典》里用 sh 替代雷兴 - 欧特曼方案中的声母 sch；（2）韵母系统中的［uei］韵，雷兴 - 欧特曼方案并没有给出一个统一的形式，ue、ui 和 oe 是通用的（多用 ue）；而《华德辞典》里除了声母 g、k 后为 ue 外，其他声母后为 ui，如 gue（贵）、kue（揆）；（3）《汉语通释》里 iu、iou、eo 三种形式等同，其中除了 djiou（就、九、酒）外，多用 iu，音节 yo 和 yu 相同；而《华德辞典》里取 iu 和 yu 为固定拼写形式，yo 另表示"岳"这个音。

《华德辞典》1924 年出版时距《汉语通释》出版已经有 12 年。利定白在《华德辞典》中改动了雷兴 - 欧特曼方案的个别音节形式，主要固定了一些灵活性较大的韵母拼写形式，更利于读者查阅辞典。相比《德汉教程》，《华德辞典》对雷兴 - 欧特曼方案的改动更多。

（三）石密德、陆懿的《标准国语教本》

《标准国语教本》（*Einführung in das moderne Hochchinesisch. Ein Lehrbuch*

---

① 李雪涛：《利定白〈华德辞典〉识小》，《世界汉学（第 15 卷）》，中国人民大学出版社，2015，第 112 页。

② Werner Rüdenberg, *Chinesischen-Deutsches Wörterbuch*, 6400 *Schriftzeichen mit ihren Einzelbedeutungen und den gebräuchlichsten Zusammensetzungen*, Zweite verbesserte Auflage, 1936.

für den Unterrichtsgebrauch und das Selbststudium nebst chinesischem Zeichenheft）是一本教授标准国语（新国音）的汉语教科书，由波恩大学汉学家石密德（Erich Schmitt，1893－1955）博士和中国留德博士陆懿于 1939 年合著出版。石密德为陆懿的博士导师，两人均有研究和教授汉语及中国文化的经历。石密德一直在为编写一本《汉德词典》而准备，他在 1930－1931 年第一次来华时，便收集整理了 1200 多条歇后语，但在 1955 年去世时也未完成《汉德词典》的编写工作。有这一经历，《标准国语教本》因此参考了利定白的《华德辞典》。正如其序言里写到的那样，该书参考了《汉语通释》中的语法和《华德辞典》中的汉语拼音方案。通过考察发现，《标准国语教本》一书实则沿用了雷兴－欧特曼方案，并且在前人的基础上也做了修订。

在华所有标注北京官话音的拼音方案中，威妥玛式拼音一直因其审音准确、简便通用等特点而流传甚广，在 1939 年《标准国语教本》出版时，已经被国内外广泛地运用于邮政电信、海外图书馆中文藏书编目、外交护照之中文人名及地名的译音等。同时，自 1912 年雷兴－欧特曼方案产生起，中国通用语经历了老国音到新国音这一变化，《标准国语教本》教授的是新国音。在这一背景下，本文认为《标准国语教本》对雷兴－欧特曼方案的改动，在以新国音为对象的基础上充分参考了威妥玛式拼音的设计，具体改动如下：

声母系统：（1）《标准国语教本》沿袭了利定白的《华德辞典》，改 sch 为 sh，和威妥玛的音节一致；（2）［i］音位的变体舌尖前元音－i［ɿ］，在威妥玛拼音方案中由 ǔ 表示，威妥玛为了吸引大家对这个特殊元音的关注，单独为变体元音 ǔ［ɿ］设立了声母 tz、tz'、ss（即汉语拼音方案里的 z、c、s），这三个声母在和其他韵母相拼时，为 ts、ts'、s，只有在和 ǔ 相拼时，才改为 tz、tz'、ss，例如 tzǔ^1（字）。① 而在雷兴－欧特曼方案中，表示 z、c、s 三个声母的始终为 ds、ts、s，韵母［ɿ］由 ï 表示，两者相拼声母不变。《标准国语教本》将雷兴－欧特曼方案和威妥玛式拼音结合，用 ds、ts、s 表示 z、c、s 三个声母，和变体元音［ɿ］相拼时，变体元音［ɿ］由 e 表示，ts 和 s 变为 tz 和 ss，例如磁 tze^2、四 sse^4。而声母 ds 不变，以示和 tz 区分。

---

① 黄畅：《威妥玛〈寻津录〉研究》，上海师范大学硕士学位论文，2015，第 61 页。

韵母系统：(1) 汉语拼音方案中的韵母 i ［i］ 和声母 z、c、c 相拼时会变为舌尖前元音 -i ［ɿ］，和声母 zh、ch、sh、r 相拼时为舌尖后元音 -i ［ʅ］。对此雷兴－欧特曼方案将两者统一用韵母 ï 表示，例如 schï（事）、sï（四）、jï（日）等。而《标准国语教本》对此在拼写上使用了不同的字母以示区分，［ɿ］为韵母 e，［ʅ］为韵母 ih，如 sse（四、死）、dse（子、字）、shih（十）等。而［ʅ］韵采用 ih 这点与威妥玛式拼音相同；(2) 改韵母 e 为 ei。石密德在《标准国语教本》引论中说道：“需要注意的是，每个汉字的拼写方式都有其德语音值，每个汉字都是单音节的；ai 发音如德语词 Kaiser 里的音，对此韵母 ei 中的 e 音长而 i 的余音短，所以利定白选择的方案中的 e 并不完全正确。”因此将此前雷兴－欧特曼方案里的韵母 e 改为 ei。雷兴欧特曼选择 e 表示韵母 ei ［ei］ 音，是因为北德方言中 e 带 i 的尾音，但用一个字母表示复合元音的发音的方式并不十分科学；(3) 改韵母 au 为 ao，iau 为 iao。雷兴－欧特曼方案使用 au 是因为德语里 au 有其固定发音，类似 ao 音；(4) 改韵母 üa 为 üan。雷兴－欧特曼方案用 üa 表示汉语中韵母 üan ［yɛn］，但 üa 没有表现出前鼻音韵母 üan 的鼻音，这是个误差比较大的拼写方式。石密德针对这点选择 üan 来表示，显得更为清楚标准，也和现代的汉语拼音方案相同；(5) 改韵母 ëng 为 êng。石密德认为利定白的辞典中的音节 mën 和 mëng 中的 ë 代表两种不同的发音，第一个发音像 mönn，而后者像 mong。所以用不同的字母代表 ën 和 êng 两个音。但其实现代汉语拼音方案中同为鼻音韵母的 en ［ən］ 和 eng ［əŋ］ 中的音素 e 一致，都是央、中、不圆唇元音 ［ə］，无差别。ën 和 êng 仅有前后鼻音的差别；(6) 同样对于 ［uei］ 韵，《标准国语教本》既不同于雷兴－欧特曼方案，也没有采用利定白的改动，而是与威式拼音相同。威妥玛对汉语审音相当仔细，为了向初学者展示发音的细微差别，设定 uei 只能和声母 k、k‘相拼，其他情况用 ui。① 《标准国语教本》中声母 g、k 后用 uei，其他声母后为 ui，如 shui（水、睡）、tui（腿）、dui（对）、hui（会、回）、sui（随），kuei（愧）、guei（贵）等。该韵母自成音节时为 wei（位、畏）。

可以发现，《标准国语教本》一书吸纳了威妥玛式拼音里一些审音更为细致准确的拼写形式。跟谋乐的《德汉教程》和利定白的《华德辞典》相

① 黄畅：《威妥玛〈寻津录〉研究》，上海师范大学硕士学位论文，2015，第 69 页。

比，它对雷兴－欧特曼方案的改动是最大的。但需要指出的是，《标准国语教本》所用的拼写方案仍旧基本沿袭了后者的设定。雷兴－欧特曼方案最初的设定是以北京官话音为对象，以德语发音习惯为基础而创制的规范、统一的拼音方案。一方面，谋乐、利定白、石密德和陆懿的三本著作对该方案的沿用证实了雷兴－欧特曼方案的实用性，并且认为雷兴－欧特曼方案在一定程度上达到了德语世界汉语拼音方案的规范统一。这个过程也推广了雷兴－欧特曼方案，使其影响更为深远。另一方面，三者都对该方案做了或多或少的修改，随着时间的推移，变动越多。因此雷兴－欧特曼方案并没有实现德语世界里汉语拼音方案的完全统一和规范。

三　重新审视"德国式拼音"

雷兴－欧特曼方案及时满足了在华德国人对汉语拼读、翻译、写作、研究的需要，也被一些著作所使用，影响广泛，因此之后被称为"德国式拼音"。雷兴－欧特曼方案并不是最早用德语字母去拼写汉语的方案，肖特（Wilhelm Schott，1794－1865）、甲柏连孜、阿恩特（Carl Arendt，1838－1902）和穆麟德都在自己的著作中进行了这一尝试，但没有哪个方案达到雷兴－欧特曼方案的传播程度。本节重新审视"德国式拼音"，认为相对其他拼音方案，"德国式拼音"具有以下特点。

1. 更准确地标注官话发音，拼写形式更符合德语使用者习惯

"德国式拼音"汲取了前人的经验和成果，并在它们基础上做出改进。例如，相较于穆麟德方案，它改进了送气音和非送气音的区别方式。穆麟德方案和威妥玛式拼音方案一样，使用送气符号"ʻ"来区别，而"德国式拼音"用德语中已有的类似发音的字母来表示，因为以往总表示浊音的拉丁字母 b、d、g 等在德语里就可以读成清音［p］、［t］、［k］。这种方法在国际间不是孤立的，因其简单、便利，国人自己拟定的拼音方案也有长达半世纪的使用时间，汉语拼音方案也采纳了这三个字母。[①] 而其他组别的送气音和不送气音，也相应使用了德语里的字母组合标注，例如 dj［tɕ］和 tj［tɕʻ］、ds［ts］和 ts［tsʻ］。又如，相较于其前身卫礼贤－雷兴方案，前者

① 周有光：《汉语拼音文化津梁》，三联书店，2007，第 119 页。

主要是满足德占胶澳区的需要，受到青岛方言发音的影响，而“德国式拼音”以官话为发音标准，扩大了德语拼音方案的使用范围，更易于德语世界学习者对官话的阅读和学习。

2. 是德语使用者拼读汉语的一次较为成功的尝试

威妥玛式拼音具有审音准确、简洁实用等特点，广受欢迎，在经过翟理斯在其《英华词典》（*Chinese English Dictionary*，1912）中的修订后，在国内外流传更为广泛。但对于在华的西方人中的其他非英语使用者来说，威妥玛式拼音并不是最为理想的汉语拼读工具。“德国式拼音”的前身卫礼贤－雷兴方案，源于德占区人们的需求而产生，经过了讨论和投票，得到了德语教师们的认可，而“德国式拼音”的创制更多归功于雷兴和欧特曼两位作者的深入研究和普遍修订。“德国式拼音”以德语发音习惯为基础，力图舍弃对威妥玛式拼音等英式拼音方案的依赖，基本做到了德语拼读习惯的自洽和完善。“德国式拼音”基本做到了统一纷繁混乱的德语世界内部各种拼音方案分江而治的情况。随着各种书籍和报刊的应用和推广，该方案受到一定认可和使用。学习者可以不用再为了阅读一本书籍去习惯一种新的拼写方式，著作者也不用像许勒一样在自己的著作里放入两种拼写方案以供参考。

3. 为中国汉字拉丁化运动和《汉语拼音方案》提供重要参考

西方人拼读汉语是从明末利玛窦、金尼阁为代表的来华传教士开始，中国人自清末时期开始汉语拉丁化运动。自 19 世纪末以来，许多爱国人士认为国势孱弱，教育不普及；教育不普及，又是因为汉字繁难。于是提倡汉字改革。[①] 因考虑到国际通用性，许多先进人士开始了用拉丁字母拼读汉语的尝试，是为中国汉字拉丁化运动。其中影响最大的是 1928 年由中华民国政府组织制订的国语罗马字和 1931 年由瞿秋白等人在苏联制订的拉丁化新文字。新中国成立后继续展开文字改革运动，简化汉字的同时拟订拉丁字母式的汉语拼音方案。汉语拼音方案的制订与此前汉语拉丁化运动的一系列成果一脉相承，都充分参考了英法德等字母的读音习惯。正如罗常培（1957）所述，国语罗马字、拉丁化新文字和汉语拼音草案三者都用 b、d、g 和 p、t、k 两组声母，这与雷兴所作的拼音方案一致，因为南德方言对于

① 罗常培：《汉语拼音方案的历史渊源》，《罗常培语言学论文集》，2004，第 405 页。

b、d、g 的读音，本来是介乎清浊之间的半浊音，和北方话的方音相近。①

威妥玛式、邮政式等重要的西方人拼音方案为该运动提供了重要参考。1955 年 2 月中国文字改革委员会设立拼音方案委员会，着手拟定拉丁字母式拼音方案草稿。汉语拼音方案主要制定者之一周有光，在其《中国拼音文字研究》（1952）的“北方话方案的比较研究”章节中，罗列了“从利玛窦到拉丁化二十四种重要方案的比较表”，其中便有雷兴 - 欧特曼方案。同样，在其《汉字改革概论》（1961）“汉语改革运动的历史发展”章节后也附上了“汉语拼音方案拉丁字母式演进比较表”，该表中 17 种外国人拟定的拼音方案有 3 种德国式拼音，分别是甲柏连孜、阿伦特和雷兴 - 欧特曼式。正如罗常培（1957）所言：“现在公布的‘汉语拼音方案草案’，正是近 300 多年来拉丁字母拼音运动的结晶。”

重新审视“德国式拼音”——雷兴 - 欧特曼方案的创制缘起和其后的使用情况，该方案创制后没有“一劳永逸”，而是被使用者根据准确性和通用语音的变化不断进行修订，而方案的不足之处也随着改动而不断显现。“德国式拼音”虽然使用广泛，但没有如威翟式拼音那样，被约定俗成为德语语种真正的“统一”方案。但以该方案为基础出版的汉语教材、辞典、汉学研究著作、译著等却丰富了德语世界的汉学研究，促进了对德汉语教学的发展。此外，作为德语语种化汉语拼音方案的代表，“德国式拼音”也为其后的汉语拉丁化运动以及《汉语拼音方案》的制订提供了有效参考。“德国式拼音”及其促成的相关著作不仅促进了近代东西语言上的接触和交流，也是近代中德交流史的重要组成部分。

参考文献

Michael Schön, *Chinesich-deutsche Transkriptionssysteme im 19. und 20. Jahrhundert. Abriss der Enwicklung einschliesslich wichtiger Transkriptionstabellen*, Berlin, 2013.

倪海曙：《中国拼音文字运动史简编》，时代出版社，1950。

周有光：《汉语拼音文化津梁》，三联书店，2007。

① 参见罗常培《汉语拼音方案的历史渊源》，原载于 1957 年 12 月 18 日《人民日报》，《罗常培语言学论文集》，2004，第 410 页。

周有光：《汉字改革概论（修订本）》，文字改革出版社，1961。

周有光：《中国拼音文字研究》，上海东方书店，1952。

罗常培：《罗常培语言学论文集》，商务印书馆，2004。

高兰：《谋乐〈德汉教程〉研究》，上海师范大学硕士学位论文，2017。

黄畅：《威妥玛〈寻津录〉研究》，上海师范大学硕士学位论文，2015。

刘金玲：《特别高等专门学堂研究》，山东经济学院硕士学位论文，2010。

罗颖男：《论福兰阁对德华青岛特别高等专门学堂的贡献》，北京外国语大学硕士学位论文，2013。

毛小红：《中国德语文教育历史研究（1861－1976）》，上海外国语大学博士学位论文，2014。

温利燕：《微席叶〈北京官话：汉语初阶〉研究》，上海师范大学硕士学位论文，2010。

李雪涛：《利定白〈华德辞典〉识小》，《世界汉学（第15卷）》，中国人民大学出版社，2015。

岳岚：《晚清时期汉语注音罗马化系统的演进——从"北京大学"的英译谈起》，《贵州社会科学》2017年第4期。

周兆利：《德华大学：中德政府合办的第一所大学》，《山东档案》2012年第6期。

青岛市档案馆编，《青岛开埠十七年——〈胶澳发展备忘录〉全译》，中国档案出版社，2007。

Study on "Lessing-Othmer-System"

He Yujie

Abstract

Since Matteo Ricci and other Jesuit missionaries began to spell Chinese with Roman characters, and after the door of China was opened in the late Qing dynasty, more and more westerners came to China to preach and do business, thus the Chinese Romanization for all languages became popular. Lessing-Othmer-system, also known as "German-style Pinyin", which was widely spread among

Germans in China, is discussed in the paper. Since its creation, the system has been widely used in dictionaries and textbooks, translation of titles and novels, as well as sinological works. Based on previous studies, this paper reviews the background and the emergence of this program, and explores its value and significance in the history of Sino-German communication by investigating the application of this program in various works. Although "German-style Pinyin" was not finally established as a true unified system for German languages as Wade-Giles, its appearance reflected the efforts of German speakers in Chinese spelling. The related works it contributed to also enriched the sinology and Chinese language studies in German areas, strengthening the communication between eastern and western languages in modern times.

Keywords

German-style Pinyin　Lessing-Othmer-System　Scheme for the Chinese Phonetic Alphabet　Chinese Romanization

波列地《华英字录》及其价值

潘瑞芳[*]

摘　要

外国人来到中国后，掌握汉语是必须的交际工具。1881 年出版的《华英字录》是专为外国人汉字速成而编纂的袖珍字典。其作者是意大利人波列地（P. Poletti）。这是一本尝试对汉字进行科学编码的创新之作。首创的“双部首法”对汉字进行重新归类排序，便于检索；其将数字应用于汉字的编排中，具有独创性的意义，提升了汉字检索和编码的科学性。《华英字录》的编纂出版，是近代“汉语热”以及字典、教材编纂热潮的产物，对于外国人的汉语学习和应用具有重要的参考价值，在东西语言接触史上具有重要意义。直至现代，采用其方法编纂的系列词典还在被不断翻印出版。

关键词

波列地　《华英字录》　双部首法　双语词典编纂

1866 年，晚清派往欧洲的首个游历使团——斌椿使团在英国伦敦参观了英国皇家邮政公司（Royal Mail）（斌椿，1985）。1878 年 3 月 9 日，清政府决定在北京、天津等五地首批设立送信官局，也称为“海关书信馆”，并于同年开展书信邮寄业务。此后，中外之间的交流日盛。

与此同时，来华的西方人为了提高汉语学习的效率，进行了各种各样

* 潘瑞芳，北京外国语大学历史学院在读博士生，外语教学与研究出版社有限责任公司副编审。研究方向为全球史与中国、近代中国与世界。

的探索。尤其是中西文字的差异日益显现，汉字识字难、查字难的矛盾更直接阻碍了彼此的沟通与了解。于是，在汉语的学习与使用中，一些有经验的汉语学习者尝试用西方通行的字典编纂法给汉字编次序。其中，有代表性的是意大利人波列地（P. Poletti）。1876 年，他到中国海关工作。1881 年，天津新海关书信馆出版了他采用“双部首法”（Bi-Radical System）编写的汉英对照速查字典——《华英字录》，便于海关工作的外国人快速查找并理解汉字对应的英语意义，从而快速提高汉语水平。

可惜的是，目前学界对其研究寥寥无几。刘正（2005）在《图说汉学史》提到了这本字典，但是将原书的《华英字录》（*An Analytical Index of Chinese Characters*）书名错误地翻译成了《汉字分析索引》。谢康（2015）在其硕士论文中提到了《华英字录》的出版社“社标”，并没有涉及《华英字录》的内文。傅永莹（2016）研究了波列地《华英字录》的后续新版本《华英万字典》，并对其体例、编写特点等进行了详细描述，但未涉及《华英字录》。除此之外，鲜有对《华英字录》深入研究的，对其“双部首检字法”的开创性价值也没有足够的挖掘。因此，本文通过对《华英字录》的作者、文本本身的考察，指出其独创的“双部首法”“数字编码法”在汉字检字法上的重要价值，以及《华英字录》对汉字的科学分析和认识方面的价值。

一　波列地及其代表作品

波列地（P. Poletti，1846 - 1915），晚清海关意大利籍洋员，曾在天津、上海等地担任海关下级职员。1846 年出生在意大利科莫省，1876 年进入中国海关工作，1915 年在上海逝世。其名字被翻译成“普勒特”“布列地”“保列第”“珀勒第”“巴立地”等（王澧华，2015），这些不同的译法应该都是来自二手材料，因为在《华英字录》里清清楚楚地写着作者波列地。

波列地曾是位科学家，精通意大利语、英语、沃拉普克语、世界语等多种语言，也是一位中国语言学者和汉学家。19 世纪 80 年代作为一位著名的沃拉普克语专家，他热衷于支持这种语言的传播和推广，先后在厦门和上海授过课，出版了一些沃拉普克语（Volapuk，即世界语）的课本教材，正是他从中国厦门寄出了第一张世界语的明信片。[①]

他的主要作品包括《华英字录》《华英万字录》《华英万字典》《邮用语句辑要》《无师一目了然英文》等。

二 《华英字录》的构成

在互联网上检索时，在日本早稻田大学图书馆古典籍“洋学文库”查到了目前仅可见到的《华英字录》，是日本近现代词典学者勝俣銓吉郎收藏一册刻本，高 27 厘米。出版时间是光绪 6 年，也就是 1881 年。出版地为天津。图书的发兑公司是高林洋行（天津）[②] 和香港上海别发公司。

《华英字录》的整体构成包括封面/封二 1 页、扉页 1 页、部首表 1－2 页、正文 53 页、附录和封三/封四等几个部分。具体情况如表 1 所示。

表 1 《华英字录》的内部构成

封面/封二	扉页	部首表	正文	附录	封三/封四
1	1	1	1－53（上）	53（下）	1

在日本早稻田大学图书馆藏的这本《华英字录》的扉页上，署名作者为 P. Poletti。目录上有明确的“天津新海关书信馆波列地藏版”，这是作者自己所使用的中文名字，也证明了这本字典的版权归属。

关于页码的说明是，由于该字典是线装本，因此，页码标记在折页中间，所有一个跨页为一个页码，可以分为上和下两页。

（一）封面/封二、封三

在《华英字录》的封面上，印有这样一句富有挑战性的广告语：“如有比此书查字再快者作者送银一百两”。可见，作者对其检字法相当自信。至

① 郑俊明，新浪博客《一百多年前厦门人学习的外语——讲述世界最早的人造语在厦门的那些事儿》。链接地址：http://blog.sina.com.cn/s/blog_5fb272c80100yv6z.html，2019 年 10 月 2 日。

② 高林洋行，即 Collins & Co.，由英国商人高林于 19 世纪 70 年代末在天津创办，经营羊毛、皮革制品海外销售。

于有没有人去应征验证，有待新史料的发现以进一步挖掘分析。

字典的封二上印有书名的英中对照，即 *Analytic Index of Chinese Characters: List of Chinese Words with the concise meaning in English*《华英字录》。主书名和副书名一起也表明了本书汉英对照的特点。这种编排方法也是近代以来双语词典化的一种表现。

封二上还有字典的出版信息：上海别发公司（Shanghai: Messes, Kelly and Walsh）。也称"别发印书馆"，俗称别发洋行。别发印书馆是近代西人在上海开设的一个重要印刷出版机构，出版的书刊大多与中国有关，通过汉学研究领域的专家和长期侨居在中国从事传教、外交、贸易、教学活动的作者直接向西方读者介绍中国的各个方面，在西方世界引起了较大反响，涌动起一股"东学西渐"的潮流，推动晚清欧洲和西方对中国更为全面、客观的认识（孙轶旻，2008）。

字典的购买渠道也在封二上有了交代：天津紫竹林新园南式盆塘掌柜孙宝善发兑（发行）。

作为一本字典，波列地在封二上用简单的一句话说明了查找汉字的方法："为了找到一个汉字，首先需要找到并确认其部首，然后再确认剩余部分的'次部首'"（In order to find a Character, it is necessary first to ascertain its radical, and then to ascertain the radical of the rest of it）。这也就是波列地创造的"双部首检字法"。不过，这样的说明简单明了，不经过详细的说明，使用者也许会需要一定的学习时间。

（二）扉页

扉页上是中文书名和英文书名（*Analytic Index of Chinese Characters: List of Chinese Words with the concise meaning in English*）。同时，注明了《华英字录》的出版时间为光绪六年，即1881年，出版地为天津。

值得注意的是，封二和扉页上还钤有一枚徽章——一个早期自行车的标志（见图1）。这可能是中国境内较早使用徽章的出版机构（谢康，2015）。

（三）总目（部首表）

总目，也就是本字典的目录。总目之前，写有字典的版权所有者："天

图 1　波列地《华英字录》封二和扉页

津新海关书信馆波列地藏版”。

而“天津新海关书信馆”，成立于 1878 年初，就是波列地办公的地方。现在位于营口道 2 号（何玉新，2015）。

波列地对 214 个部首按照从 1 到 214 的顺序进行固定编码。例如（见表 2）：

表 2　《华英字录》的部首编号举例

部首	一	丨	丶	丿	乙	亅	二	亠	人	儿
编号	1	2	3	4	5	6	7	8	9	10

这样，每个部首就有了独立且唯一的固定编码，在检索汉字时，就可以使用固定的编码进行检索了。在检索时，每个汉字都要首先确认其主部首，剩下的主要部分作为次部首进行组合。两相结合就可以形成一个编码，就能够确定该汉字的位置。

（四）正文

正文包括 53 个页码，每个页码分为上和下。其中 53 下为字典的附录部分。

常用字就是经常使用的汉字，如阅读一般报刊书籍所必须掌握的汉字。其数量通常有数千字。根据《现代汉语常用字表》现代汉语的常用字和次常用字共 3500 字。《华英字录》每页收录 40 个汉字，共收录 4200 字左右，比较接近汉语的常用字数量。收字量超过了夏德

（Friedrich Hirth，1845 – 1927）的《文件小字典》（*A Vocabulary of the Textbook of Documentary Chinese*）的 2000 多个汉字，也多于 1874 年司登得（Stent，1833 – 1884）的《司登得中英袖珍字典》（*A Chinese and English Pocket Dictionary*）。

在正文的最后，波列地用拉丁文写了一句“Deo gratias.”，意思是说“托天之福，一切顺利”。可以想见，作者在写完最后这一部分的时候，也是长出了一口气。如此创新地对汉字进行科学的研究与分类，对于汉字的科学化具有重要的价值。

（五）附录部分

附录包括两个部分，第一部分是通过汉字举例，展示了检索汉字的方法。比如“丟（1，28）”“以（9，3）”“寅（40，12）”“官（40，49）”等。

第二部分是形近字辨别，共列举了 98 组字形相似的汉字。比如“旦—且”“王—玉”“亻—人”“氵—水”“扌—手”等。这些字有些是异体字，有些是字形相近的汉字，对使用者来说容易认错，给理解和检索带来困难。因此，这 98 组形似字的辨别，对汉字的检索和速查大有裨益。

（六）收藏钤章

在《华英字录》的目录钤有“勝俣氏旧蔵書”收藏印章。研究发现，这枚收藏章的持有者是日本著名词典学家胜俣铨吉郎（Senkichiro Katsumata）先生。他的词典代表作是由他主编的《研究社新英和活用大辞典》（*Kenkyusha's New Dictionary of English Collocations*），由日本东京株式会社研究社（Kenkyusha）于 1958 年出版。

这本书也是胜俣铨吉郎（Senkichiro Katsumata）先生的私人善本藏书，也是其大辞典编纂的知识来源之一。

三 《华英字录》的编写特点

（一）独创的“双部首法”与数字编码方法

《华英字录》创新了汉字的检索方法，采用主部首和次部首相结合的

"双部首法"，并将数字检字法应用于汉字检索中。这是对汉字检索方式的重大创新。每个汉字都有一个主部首，按照《康熙字典》的 214 部排列，每个部首有一个编号，按照部首的笔画数进行分类，从 1 划到 17 划，共 17 类。汉字主部首之外的其他部分也按照康熙字典的部首分类作为次部首。波列地认为，只要识别一个汉字的主要部首，就能很快地结合次部首进行组合，两者结合起来，一个汉字就有了一个数字编码，使用者按照编码就能快速而精准得查找到该汉字并确认其英文的对应意义。

比如，"十"的前面有一个数字"〢〤（24）"就是这个部首的编号，这个部首之下收录了所有"十"部首的汉字，包括"十""千""午""升""卒""半""南""协""博""卑""卉"，共 11 个汉字。其中，"千""午""升"三个字，是主部首"十"和次部首编号为"〤（4）"的"丿"组合。通过主部首编号"〢〤（24）"和次部首编号"〤（4）"，马上就可以定位这三个汉字。其他汉字的定位方法，同理可推。

和中国传统字典的检字方法相比，波列地的双部首检字法省去了计算整个字笔画数的麻烦，检字者只要找到对应的部首就能够很容易地检字识字。简单地汉字和部首，可以比较容易地记住编号。而较为复杂的部首，也只需要将主部首、次部首结合起来就能快速而精确地定位了（傅永莹，2016）。另外，在《华英字录》的附录部分所列举的难字检索和形近字检索，也便于检字者解决疑难问题，快速解决汉字学习和应用中的问题。

这种采用数字编码的方式，是对汉字整体笔画数检索的革命和升级，也是近代欧洲科学精神指引下的产物。波列地采用了更为科学的分类方法和计数方法，对汉字的部首和构成进行拆解，这是对汉字科学化认识的一大进步。

另外，这种"数字编码法"的数字序号采用的不是阿拉伯数字，而是来自中国民间的数字——"苏州码子"（见图 2）。这是一种传统在中国民间流行的数字，产生于中国苏州，起源自算筹。因为苏州码子容易学习，书写便捷，一串数字能连笔写出（阿拉伯数字就不能），而且写法如同算珠，可以配合算盘使用，所以曾经广泛使用于商业中，因此在账簿和发票等商业场合中均有使用。和马礼逊（Robert Morrison，1782 - 1834）在《通用汉言之法》（*A Grammar of the Chinese Language*）中的用法一样，波列地也采用了这种记数方法。从现在来看，也体现了晚清时期中国知识界和民间所使用的计数方法。

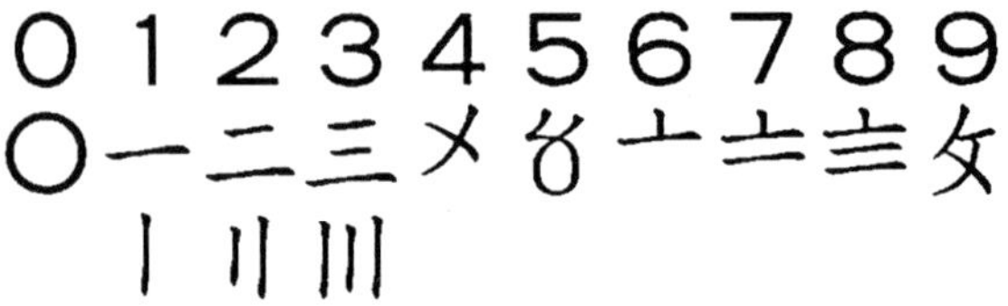

0 1 2 3 4 5 6 7 8 9
〇 一 二 三 〤 〥 〦 〧 〨 〩
〡 〢 〣

图 2 苏州码子和阿拉伯数字的对应关系

之后，波列地又于 1896 年、1907 年在上海美华书馆出版《华英万字典》（*A Chinese and English Dictionary*）时，都延续了其独创的检字方法，但是部首的数字编码已经采用了阿拉伯数字进行编排。

1925 年，商务印书馆的王云五在充分调查和研究了中外检字法的历史与现状的基础上，客观分析它们编排的优点与不足。其中，专门提到了普勒特（即波列地）的“按旧法检到部首之后，将剩余的部分再按部首或小部首顺序检查”法（王云五，1925）。这种对汉字进行拆分以及使用数字的方法，使王云五得到了一定程度的启发。在综合各种汉字检索法的基础上，博采众长，发明了“四角号码检字法”，为中国现代索引的发展做出了巨大的贡献。平保兴（2010）认为，波列地采用数字编码的“双部首法”也启发了现代出版家、商务印书馆总经理王云五“四角号码检字法”的发明，推动了近代汉外字典编纂的科学化进程。

（二）汉字的多种处理方式

《华英字录》共收录 4200 多个汉字。波列地在字典的编排过程中，对汉字采用了多种不同的处理方式。

（1）形近字、形似字和异体字等的处理

形近字、形似字和异体字，在字典的正文中，标记为“同”。例如：

傲 9，66 同敖（3 上）；

備 9，102 同備（3 上）。

（2）多音字的处理。对于当时北方官话的多音字，波列地对多个读音进行分别注音和翻译。

乾 5，4 ch’ien^{2} heaven kan^{1} dry（1 上）；

剥 18，48 pao[1]，bo[1] flay，peel（4 下）；

喉 30，9 hou[2]，ou[4] throat（6 下）。

（3）某些部首下只有一个字。

在 214 个部首里，有多个部首下面只收录了一个汉字。比如部首“夂”下只收录了“夏 39 hsia[4] summer（9 下）”；“屮”下只收录了“屯 45 t’un[3] village（12 下）”等。

（三）汉字注音方式

为方便来自欧洲的外国人学习汉语在晚清帝国海关任职的英国人威妥玛（Thomas Francis Wade，1818－1895）为方便来自欧洲的外国人学习和掌握汉语，将北京官话的读音用拉丁字母制定了拼音方案给汉字注音，并对汉字的读者进行标准化标记。在《语言自迩集》，威妥玛中明确指出，他所教授的汉语是“通行于中国首都及各大都会官场上的汉语口语，是当时的北京音”。

同在海关工作的洋员波列地完全采用了威妥玛的注音方法。在《华英字录》里，可以完整地看到威妥玛的注音系统，包括按照威妥玛注音方法给每个汉字用阿拉伯数字标记了 1、2、3、4 共四个声调。有多个发音的，还注释了多种发音，如“剥 pao[1]，bo[1]”。

采用的北京官话的发音，因此可以看到近代北京词汇的发音方法（张卫东，1998）。比如“谁”字的发音，现在存在着争议。在《华英字录》里，注音标记如下：

谁 149，172shui[2] who？ what？（43 下）

在最近出版的《现代汉语规范词典》收录了“谁 shei[2]”和“谁 shui[2] 的发音（李行健，2016）。但是，在汉字的解释上，以“谁 shei[2]”为主。因此，我们也可以看到随着时代的变化，汉语字词的发音也在跟随着发生变化。

（四）英语翻译问题

《华英字录》收录的每个汉字都有对应的简明的英文翻译，总结起来包括以下几种情况：

（1）明确为动词的，带有动词标记“to”。例如：

抽 64，102 chou[1] to pull out（19 上）；

押 64，102 ya^1 to guard（19 上）；

拨 64，105 bo^1 to transfer（19 上）；

咽 30，31 yen^4 to swallow（19 上）。

其他汉字，很少带有较为明显的词类标记。只有叹词的翻译为“interjection”。如“哟 30，122 interjection（8 上）”等。

（2）有多个意义的，列出 2－3 个翻译，用“，”隔开。例如：

乞 5，4 ch'i^3 beg，give（1 上）；

也 5，2 yeh^3 and，even（1 上）；

于 7，6 yu^2 in，to，as（1 下）；

伺 9，30 tz'i^4 wait，spy（2 上）。

（3）多个字有同样的含义的，使用同样的英语进行注释。在波列地后来出版的字典中，也延续了这一做法。

乞 5，4 ch'i^3 beg，give（1 上）；

丐 1，20 kai^4 beg（1 上）；

父 88 fu^4 father（28 上）；

爹 88，35 tieh^1 father（28 上）；

爸 88，49 pa^4 father（28 上）；

爷 88，128 yeh^2 father（28 上）。

不过，这样的对应翻译注释对使用者来说还好，但对于学习者来说，可能就会产生很大的问题了。

有部分英语的翻译具有浓厚的文化内涵。比如：

英 140，37 ying^1 brave，England（39 上）

对“英”这个汉字的英语对译中，将 England 作为注释英文，也反映了当时中英交往的情况，更说明了波列地所在天津书信馆中，中英之间交往的丰富性。至于其他国家的名字，如法国、德国、葡萄牙、荷兰等国家的名字的注释，则没有这种注释方式。然而，这一注释方式在 1896 年和 1907 年出版的《华英万字典》中已经见不到了。

（五）出版与传播特色

晚清时期，来华的外国人增多，因此出现了汉语学习和汉语词典、教材编写的"汉语热"。《华英字录》是这个大潮中的一朵浪花。但是，该字典在近代的汉外出版史也很有特色，前文已有论及，在图书的封二和扉页上，钤有出版机构的标志——一辆自行车。

另外，《华英字录》也较早地使用了欧式标点符号，主要在疑问词和感叹词的翻译中。例如：

谁 149，172 shui² who？ what？（43 下）；

岂 151，46ch'i³how？（43 下）；

何 9，30he²who？ why？（2 上）；

呸 30，1 p'ei¹ pish！ pooh！（6 上）。

另外，鉴于海关总税务司赫德对海关洋员汉语学习的要求，汉语学习材料的简洁实用、可操作性强就是当时的一个重要需求。如何短时间内通过集中训练提高汉语水平，并能够适应在中国的工作，就是海关洋员们首要解决的问题。因此，波列地这本简单、明了、速成、实用的汉英小字典在当时的汉语学习领域，可以说是备受欢迎的。也正是满足了洋员们的实际需求，波列地才将这本小册子进行了不断修正、升级，并很快在赫德的支持下于 1896 年、1907 年出版了《华英万字典》《华英万字录》，将 12650 个汉字进行了重新编排，方便海关洋员们使用。

四 《华英字录》在中西语言接触中的价值

首先，《华英字录》是来华洋员的重要汉字学习作品，更是 19 世纪汉语学习探索"高峰期"的一个作品，方便了海关洋员的汉语学习，也便于海关洋员的工作开展。尤其是，波列地之后系列字典的延续出版使海关洋员的汉语学习突飞猛进。

其次，波列地创造的"双部首法"和"数字编码法"采用近代的科学分析方法，对汉字进行拆分，推动了汉字的科学认知，是汉字科学化的一种探索，也使外国人的汉字学习更为科学。同时，《华英字录》也是汉英简易检索字典的重要代表，在汉外字典编纂史上具有重要理论和实践价值。

第三，《华英字录》不仅留存了中华文化里的"数字"应用，也记录并反映了中西文化交流的一些情况。"苏州码子"的应用，让我们今天还可以系统地观察到其记数的方法和科学性。关于“英”字采用“England（英国）”的翻译，也展示了当时中国和英国广泛而深入的交流与互动情形，对中西语言接触研究具有重要的参考价值。

最后，《华英字录》采用威妥玛拼音的注音方法对每一个汉字进行注音，保留了当时北京官话的汉字发音情况，对北京方言语音历时研究极具史料价值（张卫东，1998）。

五 结论

语言是交流的工具。近代以来，随着国门的打开，中外交流日益丰富。外国人来到中国，不管从事外交、贸易，还是科学考察，了解并掌握汉语都有助于其生活和工作的顺利开展。而汉字是最大的难点。面对来华外国人的这一强烈需求，编写双语词典、语言教材、汉字教材等是当时知识界的重要责任和当务之急。

《华英字录》正是晚清这一“汉语热”和工具书、教材编纂高峰期的代表性作品之一。对于今天我们了解晚清时期的中外文化交流、语言交涉、海关洋员的汉语学习、方言语音研究、近代词汇变迁等领域的研究都具有重要的史料价值，有待于进一步的深入、比较研究。

参考文献

Heming Yong, Jing Peng, *Chinese Lexicography*: *A History from* 1046 *BC to AD* 1911, Oxford University Press, 2008.

斌椿：《乘槎笔记》（外一种），长沙：湖南人民出版社，1985。

傅永莹：《布列地〈华英万字典〉研究》，见王澧华、吴颖主编《近代海关洋员汉语教材研究》，广西师范大学出版社，2016。

何玉新：《天津往事：藏在旧时光里的秘密地图》，北方文艺出版社，2015。

李行健主编《现代汉语规范词典（第三版）》，外语教学与研究出版社，2016。

李兆麟：《谈常用字词的选取及其等级划分》，《辞书研究》2014 年第 2 期。

刘正：《图说汉学史》，广西师范大学出版社，2005。

平保兴：《王云五索引成就及其学术思想探究》，来源：http://www.cnindex. fu-dan. edu. cn/zgsy/2010n2/pingbaoxing. htm

孙伟杰：《“威妥玛式”拼音研究》，吉林大学硕士学位论文，2009。

孙轶旻：《别发印书馆与近代中西文化交流》，《学术月刊》2008 年第 7 期。

王澧华、吴颖主编《近代海关洋员汉语教材研究》，广西师范大学出版社，2016。

王澧华：《赫德的汉语推广与晚清洋员的汉语培训》，《上海师范大学学报（哲学社会科学版）》2015 年第 6 期。

王云五：《号码检字法》，《东方杂志》1925 年第 12 期。

谢康：《中国大陆出版社社标研究》，河北大学硕士学位论文，2015。

张卫东：《威妥玛氏〈语言自迩集〉所记的北京音系》，《北京大学学报（哲学社会科学版）》1998 年第 4 期，第 135 - 143 期。

朱洪：《晚清海关洋员汉语学习初步研究》，南京大学 硕士学位论文，2013。

邹振环：《近代西学翻译由南而北的地域扩散——以澳门华英校书房、宁波华花圣经书房和上海美华书馆为例》，《东方翻译》2010 年第 1 期。

P. Poletti's *Hua Ying Zilu* and Its Value

Pan Ruifang

Abstract

When foreigners come to China, they get to know that Chinese is necessary for communication. *Huaying Zilu* published in 1881, which is a pocket dictionary that helps people quickly learn Chinese characters. The dictionary is authored by a Italian, called P. Poletti. It is an innovative work that attempted to encode Chinese characters. The dictionary uses an original Bi-Radical Method, which reclassifies and sorts Chinese characters for easier retrieval. It applies the numbers to the arrangement of Chinese characters for the first time, which makes the retrieval and coding more user - friendly. *Huaying Zilu* is a product of the "fever" in Chinese study and in the compilation of dictionaries and textbooks in modern times. It has important value for studying Chinese, and is of great significance in the history of language contact between the East and the West. Until modern times, dictionaries using its original method are still being reprinted.

Keywords

P. Poletti *Huaying Zilu* BiRadical Method Bilingual Dictionary Compilation

开启俄国汉语教学现代之窗的教科书

——彼得·施密特《汉语官话语法试编》（1902）

罗　薇*

摘　要

19世纪末至20世纪初，随着俄国在远东势力的增强和符拉迪沃斯托克东方学院的建立，俄国需要大批的东方语言实用人才。包括施密特在内的一批汉学家对俄国的汉语人才培养做出了重大贡献。除上述历史原因外，该时期语言学本身由历史比较语言学、普通语言学向现代语言学过渡的导向也为此时汉语学家和教授们提供了必要的学术土壤。施密特的汉语研究成果《汉语官话语法试编》（Опыт мандаринской грамматики с текстами для упражнений）正是在这样的历史背景下应运而生。《汉语官话语法试编》作为该时期东方学院初级汉语学者的教科书，在俄国汉语教学和研究历史上产生了划时代的影响，该书不仅是俄国汉学家对普通语言学的首次尝试，而且还结束了近百年来俄国汉学和汉语学习界由比丘林的《汉文启蒙》主导的俄国汉语教学的历史，从而开启了俄国汉语教学的现代阶段。

关键词

俄国汉学　官话语法　东方学院　语言学　汉语口语

一　施密特生平及汉语研究概况

俄国汉学家施密特及其汉语研究成果《汉语官话语法试编》在俄国汉

* 罗薇，北京外国语大学历史学院博士生。

语教学和研究历史上产生了重要影响。在这部著作中，施密特从语言学的角度研究汉语，比较汉语同其他语言的异同，对俄国学者的汉语研究具有重要的启发意义，并且使俄国汉语教学进入现代阶段。

（一）施密特生平

彼得·彼得洛维奇·施密特（Пётр Петро́вич Шмидт，1869 – 1938），著名东方学家（尤其擅长满汉学研究），民族志学家，民俗学家，著有多项关于学术理论与方法论的著述。俄罗斯现代著名民族学家和历史学家列舍托夫[①]（А. М. Решетов）对施密特的评价如下："施密特教授——杰出的俄罗斯及拉脱维亚学者——其学术遗产数量巨大、内容多样。他是汉学家、满学家、编年史学家、语言学家、民族学家、民俗学家、宗教学家、教育家、宣传家和科普家，并且在其从事的每一个具体领域都获得了深湛的成果。"[②]

1869 年 12 月 25 日，施密特出生于当时俄罗斯帝国（现位于拉脱维亚境内）里夫梁茨省（Лифляндская губерния）文津县（Венденский уезд）拉乌尹斯卡乡（Раунская волость）的一个农民家庭。1891 年，时年 22 岁的施密特毕业于里加省城中学（Рижская губернская гимназия）后赴莫斯科继续深造。

在莫斯科大学（Императорский Московский университет）学习一年之后，于 1892 年转入圣彼得堡大学（Императорский Санкт-Петербургский университет）东方语言系学习。1896 年 4 月，大学毕业，并于同年十二月被派往中国见习，时年 27 岁。

年轻的施密特曾被列为第一批北京大学俄文教师成员。在北京实习三年后，施密特顺利获得俄国境内大学教师的从业资格。1899 年至 1920 年，施密特长期在俄从事东方学及民族学的研究工作，这段时期可以看作其学术生涯的辉煌时期，许多代表著述均在此期间完成。

1920 年春，施密特移居拉脱维亚首都里加，并于 1923 年至 1925 年先后担任里加国立大学（创立于 1919 年）哲学与语文系的教授及系主任，并

---

① 亚历山大·米哈伊洛维奇·列舍托夫（Александр Михайлович Решетов）（1932 – 2009），著有《20 世纪俄国民族学家及人类学家目录汇编》（Материалы к биобиблиографическому словарю российских этнографов и антропологов. XX век）。

② А. М. Решетов，"Петр Петрович Шмидт（1869 – 1938）"，*Восток*（*Oriens*），2009，p. 103.

尝试在此开设东方学课程。在里加，施密特常年致力于年代学领域的研究，尤其在研究拉脱维亚民间信仰与民间文学方面颇有建树。

1938 年 6 月 5 日，病逝于里加，葬于森林墓地（Лесное кладбище），享年 69 岁。

（二）施密特的汉语研究

从 1899 年起，施密特开始担任符拉迪沃斯托克（海参崴）东方学院教师，并在此开设汉语课程。1901 年，成为阿穆尔地区研究会（Общество изучения Амурского края）成员之一；1902 年，时年 33 岁的施密特因编写《汉语官话语法试编》这一教材而获得满汉语文学硕士学位（Магистр китайской и маньчжурской словесности），进而获得教授席位；1909 年，入选哈尔滨俄国东方学会（Общество русских ориенталистов в Харбине）成员；1919 年至 1920 年，担任远东国立大学历史语言系（Историко-филологический факультет Дальневосточного государственного университета）系主任。

在俄任教期间，除了使之声名鹊起的《汉语官话语法试编》外，他还撰写了一系列有关通古斯满语的论文。1908 年，他开始着手研究俄罗斯远东地区的通古斯—满族，与之相关的材料在俄罗斯未能发表，直至 1920 年到任拉脱维亚大学，才陆续发表了此前在远东从事研究工作时有关通古斯—满族语的著作。与此同时，还曾参加国际东方学大会，并在当地期刊上发表了若干有关东方学研究的文章。

总之，施密特对于汉语和满语的研究在俄国汉语界占有重要位置，为后人留下了近 20 部著作，其作品被视为开创俄国汉学“新学术实践派”（Новая научно-практическая школа российского китаеведения）的奠基之作。

施密特一生著作颇丰，其中与汉语教学研究相关的作品主要有：

（1）《中国经典读本》（Китайские классические книги. -Известия Восточного института. Т. II. Вып. III. -Владивосток，1901.）；

（2）《汉语学习之语言学导论》（Лингвистическое введение в изучение китайского языка -Известия Восточного института. Т. II. Вып. IV. -Владивосток，1901.）；

（3）《初级汉语阅读》（Начальные чтения по китайскому языку. С приложениями китайских текстов для упражнения. -Известия Восточного института Т. III. Вып. Ⅰ，Ⅱ，III. 1902.）；

（4）《初级汉语教学文选》（Китайская хрестоматия для первоначального преподавания. Вып. 1. -Владивосток，1902.）；

（5）《官话语法试编》（Опыт мандаринской грамматики с текстом для упражнений. Пособие к изучению разговорного китайского языка Пекинского наречия. Владивосток，1902. Изд. 2 – е. -Владивосток，1915.）；

（6）《汉语官话课本》（Тексты к Мандаринской грамматике. -Владивосток，1903.）。

二 《汉语官话语法试编》的成书背景

在《19－20 世纪中国的史学思想》① （Историческая мысль в Китае в XI—XX вв.）一文中，作者指出，引起远东地区新局势的重大事件之一便是于 1899 年在符拉迪沃斯托克成立东方学院。② 学院致力于培养掌握汉语、

① В. И. Кузищин，“Историография истории Древнего Востока：Иран，Средняя Азия，Индия，Китай”，Историческая мысль в Китае в XI—XX вв.，СПб.：*Алетейя*，2002，p. 148.

② 本文根据需求对其进行了删减，原文如下：Одним из мероприятий，призванных ответить на вызов новой ситуации на Дальнем Востоке，явилось открытие в 1899 г. Восточного института（ВИ）во Владивостоке，нацеленного на подготовку практических работников со знанием китайского，японского или другого дальневосточного языка. Его первым директором（1899 – 1903）стал А. М. Позднеев，переведенный туда из ПУ，а преподавателями — ученики Васильева，выпускники того же университета：П. П. Шмидт，А. В. Рудаков，возглавлявший институт в 1907 – 1917 гг.，Н. В. Кюнери др. ВИс самого начала своего существования обладал единственной в России типографией с восточными шрифтами：монгольским，маньчжурским，затем китайским，японским и пр.，а начиная с 1907 г. печатавшей книги и на русском языке. Им же издавались《Известия Восточного института》. Все это способствовало научному творчеству его сотрудников и студентов. Из более значимых работ можно назвать：Шмидт П. П.《Опыт Мандаринской грамматики...》（1902，II издание — 1915）；Рудаков А. В.《Материалы по истории китайской культуры вГиринской провинции》（1903）；《Образцы маньчжурского официального языка》（1908）；Позднеев А. М.《Опыт собрания образцов маньчжурской литературы》（1904）；Кюнер Н. В.《Коммерческая география Китая》（1903，（转下页注）

日语及其他远东国家或民族语言的实践人才。首任院长（1899－1903）是波兹涅耶夫（А. М. Позднеев），在此期间，来自圣彼得堡大学的毕业生和进修生中有两位成为刚成立的东方学院的教授，他们是鲁达科夫（А. В. Рудаков）和施密特（П. П. Шмидт）。值得一提的是，东方学院定期出版《东方学院院报》并刊登学校师生的学术成果。其中最著名的有：施密特的《汉语官话语法试编》（1902 年成书，1915 年第二版），鲁达科夫的《吉林中国文化史料》（1903）等。

由此我们可以看出，施密特的汉语教学研究经历及其著作《汉语官话语法试编》均与当时的历史背景相关。笔者认为其中与之有直接关联的便是符拉迪沃斯托克的地理要义以及东方学院的成立背景。此外，从语言本身来讲，该书的撰写还受到了世界语言学发展的进程以及中西方汉语研究已有成果等方面的影响。

（一）海参崴与西伯利亚大铁路

历史上的海参崴曾自唐、辽、金起，这里已渐见人畜活动。17 世纪中期，沙俄东侵，在远东地区寻找不冻港口，与清朝曾有多次领土纠纷。虽然在清康熙年间清朝和沙俄签订的《尼布楚条约》指明海参崴属清朝，但随着清朝国势日衰，在两次鸦片战争后，清政府先后与沙俄签订《瑷珲条约》和《中俄北京条约》，割让乌苏里江以东包括库页岛在内的 40 万平方千米的领土给俄国，其中包括海参崴。随后其成为沙俄在远东地区的一个重要军事基地。

1891 年，西伯利亚大铁路① 开通至此，开始有海运路线自此往返日本神户、长崎及中国上海等地。西伯利亚大铁路竣工后，给俄国带来了政治、

（接上页注②）1907，1908－1909），《Лекции по истории Китая》（1903，1919），《Исторический очерк развития основ китайской культуры...》（1909），《Описание Тибета》（ч. 1－2，1907－1908）. Часть этих трудов и в первую очередь《Описание Тибета》— энциклопедия знаний об этой стране — не утратили значения и поныне. Кроме того，ВИ издал большое количество разного рода учебных пособий. Его деятельность оставила заметный след в истории российского китаеведения.

① 西伯利亚大铁路是世界上最长的铁路，已运行超过 100 年，全长 9288 公里。它被称为俄罗斯的“脊柱”，对俄罗斯乃至欧亚的经济、安全有举足轻重的影响。西伯利亚大铁路的修建对当时的远东国际局势和当时的中国产生了重大影响。开工后不久，俄国财政大臣维特就主张大铁路干线应通过中国东北直达海参崴，这样就可拉近中国东北与俄国之间的距离。

经济、军事、人口、文化等各个领域的重大效益。在远东大开发的势头下，急需东方语言人才，于是东方学院应运而生。

（二）东方学院的成立

1899 年，海参崴成立了东方学院，并迅速发展成俄国在远东的第一个中国学研究中心。它充分利用海参崴远东门户的地理优势，发挥与俄国在远东的政策和活动相辅相成的社会功能。其汉语教学以实用为目的。学院章程第一条规定，东方学院是为俄国东亚地区及其相邻地区的工商行政机构培养人才的高等学校，主要任务是根据现实的需要培养汉语、日语、朝鲜语、蒙古语和满语人才。学制为 4 年，第一年为汉语学习，第二年学生按四个不同的专业方向进行学习：汉日方向、汉朝方向、汉蒙方向和汉满方向，同时学习第二种东方语言。此外还有一些必修课，如英语、中日朝历史、地理、人类学、经济地理、政治经济、法学、商品学、会计学等课程。

东方学院在为沙俄培养远东实用人才的同时，对于汉语和中国文化在远东的传播也发挥了极其重要的作用。

（三）施密特自身的学术背景

在较为开放的学术氛围之下，施密特勤于钻研、严谨治学，终于在到任后三年内完成了《汉语官话语法试编》的撰写工作并将其运用到教学当中，取得了巨大的成果。而本书的撰写离不开作者在此前受到的专业学术训练，以及其自身优秀卓越的治学精神。

据圣彼得堡中心历史档案馆（Центральный государственный Исторический Архив Санкт-Петербурга）记载，1896 年 4 月，施密特大学毕业并获得圣彼得堡大学的学位证书，他于 1892 年被东方语言系满汉蒙语班录取之后研修了中国文学、中国历史、满语、满族文学史、蒙古语、蒙古文学史、卡尔梅克土语、东方历史通论、中亚东部地区史、印欧语语言学、立陶宛语、罗马法律史、法律学导论、国家法、国际法、政治经济学以及英语等课程，还曾参加过德语考试。

在中国，施密特系统学习了满语，并对汉语的方言有所研究。他还在 1898 年 5 月成立的北京大学教授过俄语。在北京，施密特出版了自己的第一部学术著作，这部著作显示出他对语音问题的强烈兴趣（Schmidt,

1898）。

（四）语言学的发展及中西方汉语研究的基础

这部著作当中很多章节的论述和思路都是基于语言学的相关理论，可见语言学对施密特的写作产生了巨大影响。在19世纪末20世纪初，语言学应当是这样一个时期：历史比较语言学趋于成熟，普通语言学形成体系，现代语言学正在萌芽。因此，19世纪和20世纪之交的语言学应当是受到上述三者共同影响下的语言学。作者的汉语研究也受到了青年语法学派、俄国喀山学派、莫斯科语言学派等派别的语言学思潮的影响。

从已有的汉语教学与研究的角度来看，施密特在《汉语官话语法试编》的撰写中引用了相当丰富的例句，从前人已有的经验中总结归纳、去粗存精、推陈出新。书中引用的汉语课本有：《语言自迩集》（*Progressive Course of Colloquial Chinese*，T. F. Wade，1886）；《官话手册》（*Einführung in die Nordchinesische Ümgangssprache*，C. Arendt，1894）；《铅椠汇存》（*Manuel de langue mandarine*，A. Théophile Piry，1895）；《官话萃珍》（*A Character Study in Mandarin Colloquial*，C. Goodrich，1898）；《汉语入门》（*Rudiments de Parleret de Style Chinois*，Léon Wieger，1899）；《官话类编》（*A Course of Mandarin Lessons Based on Idiom*，C. W. Mateer，1900）；《西蜀方言》（*Western Mandarin*，A. Grainger，1900）等，以及当时供中国人学习的《官话指南》《正音撮要》《北京风土编》《清文启蒙》等。同时还引用了相当多的汉语字典如《华英字典》（*A Dictionary of Chinese Language*，R. Morrison，1815），以及中国古代著名的字典：《尔雅》《说文》《类篇》《五音类聚》《字汇》《五音集韵》《佩文韵府》《经籍纂诂》《清汉文海》《五元方音》《李氏音鉴》《经韵集字谱》《康熙字典》。

三 《汉语官话语法试编》的内容概要

《汉语官话语法试编》全书共330页，成书于1902年，其主体内容分别登载于《东方学院院报》（Известия Восточного института）第二、三卷。该书的封面上明确指出：本书作为教材适用于北京方言（即当时的“北京官话”）的口语学习（Пособие к изучению разговорного китайского языка

Пекинского наречия）。此外，该书还可作为汉语研究领域的语言学导论和初级汉语阅读教材。

全书拟分为三部分。第一部分包括序言、目录、附录及书末修订；第二部分为汉语学习的语言学导论（Лингвистическое введение в изучение китайского языка）；第三部分为初级汉语阅读讲义（начальные чтения по китайскому языку）。其中，二、三部分为本书的核心内容。

在序言中，施密特主要陈述了两方面的内容。第一，编写这部教材的原因；第二，本教材的板块设置意图。通过两方面的逐层递进，施密特为读者和学习者打开了一扇重新认识和学习汉语语法的窗口。

第一，编写这部教材的原因。简单来说可以用“推陈出新”一词来概括。开篇作者便指出：“近来，用欧洲语言所著的汉语语法书和教科书相当之多，以至于出版新的这类教材可以认为是不大必要的。进一步了解这些书籍之后，我确信它们并非全都符合我们的需求……鉴于上述所有的问题，相比于仅从外语教材那里翻译一些东西，我认为编写一部全新的语法书更为必要。我从其他人那里借鉴的东西，将会在适当的地方标出，此外我自己不但要补充一些旧规则，还得再设立一些新的。”① 随后，作者又一次强调语法在汉语研究学习中的特殊地位。

第二，本教材的板块设置有两大部分。其中作者特别强调了第一部分“导论”的重要性：“也许有人会责问我，与篇幅不大的实践语法相比，我却首先写了相当详尽的学术概论。这部教材是针对东方学院学生的学习需求而设定的，而在高等院校中，将学术和实践进行严格的划分未必合理。”②

另外，作者还指出导论部分的两个重要作用：“要着手学习一门新的语言可以不需要任何学术引论，这是因为对于所有印欧语系的语言来说，语法体

① П. П. Шмидт, *Опыт Мандаринской грамматики. Пособие к изучению разговорного китайского языка Пекинского наречия*, Известия Восточного института. Томы LI-LII, p. 1. (Владивосток Издание и печать Восточного института 1915г. 482 с. Картонный твердый переплет, Увеличенный формат.)

② П. П. Шмидт, *Опыт Мандаринской грамматики. Пособие к изучению разговорного китайского языка Пекинского наречия*, Известия Восточного института. Томы LI-LII, p. 1. (Владивосток Издание и печать Восточного института 1915г. 482 с. Картонный твердый переплет, Увеличенный формат.)

系的一般特征是一致的，而想要更具体地了解语言史，也可以在我们的语言学文献中找到解释。但是，汉语相当独特的语法、语音、声调及文字却无疑要求我们在开始语言的实践学习之前，对其进行更加详细的初步阐释。”[①]

四 《汉语官话语法试编》的开创性初探

为什么说这是一部“开启俄国汉语教学现代之窗的教科书”？在它之前的俄国汉语教学是什么样？它又在哪些方面开启了新的时代？这是一个需要深入思考的问题。

19 世纪的俄国汉学中心是圣彼得堡大学，在汉语学习者中广泛使用的著作有：В. П. 瓦西里耶夫的《汉字分析》《汉字笔画系统——俄汉词典试编》，Д. А. 佩休罗夫的《华俄词典》和巴拉第、П. С. 波波夫的《汉俄大辞典》，而称得上第一部真正系统的汉语语法教科书是比丘林为其主持的恰克图汉语学校所编写的教科书《汉文启蒙》。其中，作者从“汉语和汉字的基本概念”和“汉语的语法规则”两部分出发，分别从语音和语法的角度描写汉语，问世之后在半个多世纪里一直沿用，其中的语法部分主要是从西方语法学的角度对汉语进行词类划分并逐类描述，并从训诂学实字和虚字呈现汉语的语法意义，[②] 但缺乏从现代语言学角度深层剖析重要的词法和句法，因此逐渐无法适应新的学习和研究要求。

我们先从体例和内容上考察施密特的这部语法著作有什么特点。序言中已经提到，“供研习使用的只是语言讲义部分，而语言学导论部分应当主要用于阅读和查询”。导论和讲义的作用相辅相成，互为补充。

（一）导论——汉语学习的语言学导论

该部分共 105 页，总标题为“汉语学习之语言学导论”。在本卷中，施密特用长达十三章的篇幅为汉语学习者详细介绍了汉语在世界语言中的地

① П. П. Шмидт, *Опыт Мандаринской грамматики. Пособие к изучению разговорного китайского языка Пекинского наречия*, Известия Восточного института. Томы LI-LII, p. 1. (Владивосток Издание и печать Восточного института 1915г. 482 с. Картонный твердый переплет, Увеличенный формат.)

② 柳若梅：《俄国汉学史上第一部汉语语法书——〈汉文启蒙〉》，福建师范大学学报（哲学社会科学版）2010 年第 2 期，第 138－147 页。

位、方言、前辅音与后辅音、元音及其音变、汉语各方言区的形成、词根、音调（元音音高差）、重音、汉字、部首、词典体例以及汉语的拼音、音标和注音等内容。值得一提的是，在最后一章的附录部分，施密特还运用表格的形式将此前通用的八种汉语官话拼音方案做出了较为全面的总结，使学习者能在一张表格中清晰地辨明各拼音方案的异同。这八种汉语官话拼音方案包括现代俄语拼音方案；比丘林《汉文启蒙》拼音方案；弗莱斯（S. Ritter von Fries）和穆麟德（Paul Georg von Möllendorff）拼音方案；威妥玛（Thomas Francis Wade）拼音方案；卫三畏（Samuel Wells Williams）拼音方案；顾赛芬（Seraphin Couvreur）拼音方案；晁德莅（Angelo Zottoli）拼音方案；旧式葡萄牙语拼音方案。

（二）讲义——初级汉语阅读

该部分共 205 页，总标题为“初级汉语阅读”。这一部分是全书的核心内容，囊括了初级汉语学习者所能遇见的大部分语法问题。该部分也可看作是施密特的汉语课程讲义汇编。总体来看，每课设有语法点讲解、字词讲解、句子拼读、俄译汉练习、注释五个板块。

全卷共六十四课，每一课都有一个鲜明的语法主题，内容几乎已经涵盖了北京官话口语中的所有词类和句法成分，其中涉及的词类归纳如下。

（1）名词（第十课 名词概述；第十三课 名词的格；第二十三课 部分名词的理解与运用；第三十二课 名词复数）；

（2）动词（第十一课 动词概述；第二十四课 自然界的现象和动词“下”“打”“刮”的运用；第二十八课 动词的时态；第四十课“有”和“是”；第四十五课至第五十六课 对口语常用动词如当、打、发、放、弄、出、可、住、开、起、到、动、倒、来、去等十余个动词及词组的详细解说；第六十二课 完成动作的可能性表述方法）；

（3）形容词（第十二课 形容词概述）；

（4）代词（第二课 人称代词；第三课 指示代词；第五课 代词“这”/“那”；第六课 常用人称代词）；

（5）数词（第一课 数词和量词；第四课 基数词和序数词；第七课 约数和分数；第九课 不带量词的数词）；

（6）量词（第一课 数词和量词；第十四课 金钱 尺度 重量；第三十四

课 量词）；

（7）副词（第三十六课 副词概述；第六十课“刚”和“才”）；

（8）介词（第三十八课 介词概述）；

（9）连词（第五十七课 和）；

（10）助词（第二十九课“了”的用法；第三十课 过、来、着的用法；第四十一课“的”的用法；第四十四课“得”的用法）；

（11）语气词（第三十九课 句末语气词）

此外，在句法成分方面，《汉语官话语法试编》中涉及了如疑问句（第二十六课）、祈使句与命令式（第二十七课）、被动句与被动式（第三十七课）、否定句与否定式（第五十九课）、词序问题（第六十四课）等主题。

最后还要特别指出的一点是，在讲义中还出现了第二语言学习中的功能与话题导向，如第十六课至第十九课就分别列举了服装、家具、食物和知识学问相关话题的语言材料。

（三）编写理念的开创性例析

上文已经就本书的编写体例和内容架构的创新之处做出了说明，本节着重从编写理念探讨本教材的开创性。同样地，也是从语法理论和实践语法两个角度分析施密特在汉语语法研究中的创新之处。

1. 在语法理论方面，运用历史比较语言学和普通语言学方法对汉语重新定位

在这里有必要将20世纪之前的西方语言学史进行一个简单梳理。在世界语言学史的进程中，19世纪和20世纪之交的时期是一个相对复杂的阶段，经历了19世纪初的历史比较语言学时期，人们重视各种语言的外部比较研究，在各种语言的历史比较研究基础上产生了普通语言学，即从理论概括的角度出发研究和比较各种语言。19世纪跨入20世纪时，从语言内部的结构主义观点出发研究语言的观念迅速席卷各界，从而使语言研究进入现代语言学时期。施密特的书成书于20世纪初叶，其中处处渗透着普通语言学和历史比较语言学的理念，不乏大师和各主要门派的主要观点：洪堡特的汉语观——“既没有形态也没有词类”“标记词的联系的手段是虚词和词序”等；19世纪后期出现的青年语法学派语言观——“研究活的现代语言及方言”“语言规律的对比和类推”等；19世纪末俄国喀山学派语言观提出的观点包括："音位和词素是基本的语言原子""语言是社会心理现象"；19 世纪末俄国莫斯科语言学派认为"语言学的研究对象是现代的语言及其他的历史""词的形式（词干和词尾）""词组学说和句子学说"等。①

我们以青年语法学派有关"研究活的现代语言及方言"和"语言规律的对比和类推"的理念为例，考察施密特是如何在自己的教材中应用并丰富这一学派的思想。举一个简单的例子。在序言中作者就特别强调了研究"活"的语言的重要性："最近一段时间，就连语文学家也认为更重要的是鲜活的语言，而不是一味地依照词典对比已经僵化的词。"在"导论·第5章 元音及其音变"中，作者立足历史比较语言学思维，对比当下的官话、周边方言及印度支那语系部分语言的发音，对元音的音变现象做了梳理，尽管其中有不少对各方言及周边语言的认知错误，但不能否认的是，他的确在教材语言观的层面上践行了青年语法学派"研究活的现代语言及方言"的理念。现将引用的例文翻译如下。

在《康熙字典》的《字母切韵要法》中，官话里的开头辅音［*ž*］（*ж*）、［*š*］（ш）、［*tš'*］（*ч*）和［*tʂ*］（*ч ж*）没有丢失其后的元音［*i*］（*u*），在单音节中，［*i*］（*u*）的发音实际为前述的［ɨ］（*ы*）。现在的官话中，接在上述唏辅音之后的原始词尾［*in'*］（*инь*）和［*in*］（*инъ*）分别音变为［*εn'*］（*энь*）和［*εn*］（*энъ*）。具体参见表 1。

表 1　汉字及其发音

汉字及其意义	根据《字母切韵要法》的字音	客家话发音	朝鲜语发音	日本语发音
人［žεn'2］（жэнь2）человѣкъ	［＊r'in'］（＊ринь）	nyin	［in'］（инь）	［p'in］（пин）
眞［tʂen'1］（чжэнь1）настоящій	［tš''in'］（чинь）	chin	［tš''in'］（чинь）	［s'in］（син）
瞋［tš'εn'1］（чэнь1）сердиться	［tš''　'in'］（ч'инь）	chin	［tš''in'］（чинь）	［s'in］（син）
葚［šεn'2］（шэнь2），［žεn'4］（жэнь4）ягода тутового дерева	［dž'im］（джим）	shim	［s'im］（сим）	［s'in］（син）
身［šεn'1］（шэнь1）тело	［š'in'］（шинь）	shin	［s'in'］（синь）	［s'in］（син）

① 林玉山：《世界语言学史》，湖南人民出版社，2009。

续表

汉字及其意义	根据《字母切韵要法》的字音	客家话发音	朝鲜语发音	日本语发音
甚［šɛn'²］（шэнь²）весьма	［ž'im］（жим）	shim	［s'im］（сим）	［s'in］（син）

对于语言规律的对比和类推，我们可以用“导论·第7章 词根”一节来举例。从下面的举例可以看到，每一组词和“词根”的发音及意义有相关性，作者把“词的派生法”的相似性规律在汉语中类推，得出了相似的结论。相关译文如下。

诸如此类的例子在汉语中非常多，我们现在几乎完全没有遵循词的派生规则，因此连词语的比较目前也只能是基于推论，尽管某些词的相似性的确一目了然，而且现在不少词的来源也已经可以确定。例如：

词根＊［tš'a］（ча）——раздѣляться，развѣтвленіе（分成、分岔）。

叉［tš'a⁴］（ча⁴）——развилина（椏杈）；鍤［tš'a²］（ча²）——вилка（金属叉子）；扠［tš'a³］（ча³）——взять вилками（用叉子）；杈［tš'a⁴］（ча⁴）——развилина дерева（树杈）；岔［tš'a⁴］（ча⁴）——развѣтвленіе дороги（路的分支）；汊［tš'a⁴］（ча⁴）——раздѣленіе рѣки（河的分流）；差［tš'a¹］（ча¹）——разниться，ошибаться（有差异、犯错误）；拆［tš'aj¹］（чай¹）——разломать（拆毁）；奓［tşa¹］（чжа¹）——раскрыть，разсширать（打开、扩张），摘［tşaj¹］（чжай¹）——рвать，срывать（采摘、撕扯）。

词根＊［da］（да）——большой，увеличиваться（大、增大）。

大［da⁴］（да⁴）——большой（大的），也读作：［daj⁴］（дай⁴）——великій（伟大的），［dɔ⁴］（до⁴）——большой，огромный（大、庞大）；泰［taj⁴］（тай⁴）——великій，весьма（伟大的、极其）；多［dɔ¹］（до¹）——много（很多）；台［taj²］（тай²）——высокій，почтенный（高大的、可敬的）；太［taj⁴］（тай⁴）——весьма，слишкомъ（极其、非常）；臺［taj²］（тай²）——терраса（露台）。

词根＊［s'aɔ］（сяо）——маленькій，уменьшиваться（小、减少）。

小［s'aɔ³］（сяо³）——маленькій（小的）；銷［s'aɔ¹］（сяо¹）——расплавить，покончить（熔化、消灭）；消［s'aɔ¹］（сяо¹）——растаять， истощаться（融化、耗尽）；少［šaɔ^{3}］（шао^{3}）——мало（数量少），也作［šaɔ^{4}］（шао^{4}）——молодой（年幼的）；稍［šaɔ^{3}］（шао^{3}）——уменьшать，ничтожный，малый（减少、微小的、小的）；捎［šaɔ^{1}］（шао^{1}）——искоренить，отряхать（根除、抖掉）。

2. 在语法实践方面，积极总结归纳前人的研究成果，去粗存精，推陈出新

在第二部分的语法讲义中，每一个语法点的讲解都达到了较高的清晰度和准确度，很多观点在汉语研究日趋成熟的今天看来也丝毫不过时，甚至比今天还要超前。在这里我们选取第四十九课——“弄”的基本用法，说明施密特对语法现象的敏感和归纳。译文如下：

“弄”［nun^{4}］（нунъ^{4}）一词的原始义是：玩耍、用以消遣，其字形也是描绘一双拿着玉的手。但在当代口语中，“弄”通常表达人的一般动作，尤其是手部的动作。这个词在官话中的意思可以分为四类。

（1）与名词连用时，“弄”［nun^{4}］（нунъ^{4}）表示：приготовлять，производить，собирать（准备好、制作、收集）。例如：

弄菜［nun^{4} – tsàj^{4}］（нунъ^{4} – цàй^{4}）—— стряпать，готовить（做饭、做菜）；

弄飯［nun^{4} – fàn'^{4}］（нунъ^{4} – фàнь^{4}）—— id.（同上）；

弄花兒［nun^{4} – xuà（– ε）r］［нунъ^{4} – хуà（– э）ръ］—— рвать，собирать цвѣты（采摘、收集花）；

弄錢［nun^{4} – ts'an'^{2}］（нунъ^{4} – цянь^{2}）—— нажить деньги（нечестно）（赚钱，一般指不正当的）。

（2）“弄”［nun^{4}］（нунъ^{4}）与形容词连用表示：дѣлать такимъ – то（做的结果怎样）。如：

弄臟［nun^{4} – tçàn^{1}］（нунъ^{4} – цзàнъ^{1}）—— запачкать（弄污）；

弄好［nun^{4} – xa ɔ̀^{3}］（нунъ^{4} – хаɔ̀^{3}）—— поправить（纠正、改正）。

（3）作中间动词时，“弄”［nun^{4}］（нунъ^{4}）使行为具有实际意义，并位于其前。例如：

弄來［nùn^{4} – łaj^{2}］（н ỳнъ^{4} – лай^{2}）—— принести（拿来）（如下所见，该类的俄语动词释义均为完成体动词，强调行为的结果意义。——译注）；

弄去［nùn^{4} – ts'uj^{4}］（н ỳнъ^{4} – цюй^{4}）—— унести（拿去）；

弄沒了［nun^{4} – m ὲj^{2} – ła^{1}］（нунъ^{4} – м э̀й^{2} – ла^{1}）—— потерять

（丢失）；

弄滅［nun^{4} – m' ɛ̀^{4}］（нунъ^{4} – мѐ^{4}）—— потушить，погасить（扑灭、熄灭）；

弄壞［nun^{4} – xuàj^{4}］（нунъ^{4} – хуàй^{4}）—— портить（毁掉）；

弄翻［nun^{4} – fàn'^{1}］（нунъ^{4} – фàнь^{1}）—— опрокинуть（使倾倒）；

弄死［nun^{4} – s ɨ̂^{3}］（нунъ^{4} – с ы̀^{3}）—— убить，заиучить（杀死、虐死）。

（4）如果“弄”［nun^{4}］（нунъ^{4}）位于动词之后，则不含一般意义。例如：

戲弄［s'ì^{4} – nun^{4}］（с ѝ^{4} – нунъ^{4}）—— играть，забавляться（游戏、娱乐）；

哄弄［xù^{4} – nun^{4}］（ху ? ^{4} – нунъ^{4}）—— обманывать（欺骗）；

擺弄［bàj^{3} – nun^{4}］（бàй^{3} – нунъ^{4}）—— играть，заигрывать，вертѣть（玩耍、挑逗、转动）；

掇弄［d ɔ̀^{2} – nun^{4}］（дò^{2} – нунъ^{4}）—— обращаться，держать въ порядкѣ（使用、整理）。

属于以上第一类的还有“弄火”［lun^{2} – x ɔ̀^{3}］（лунъ^{2} – хò^{3}）—— зажечь，затопить（点火，生火），这种情况下“弄”一直读作［lun^{2}］（лунъ^{2}），并且还能用另一个字——“籠”［lun^{2}］（лунъ^{2}）替换。

可以看出，作者对词类搭配具有很强的意识，对“弄”与名词、形容词、行为动词的搭配做了严格的区分，总结出一套较为完整的“弄”的使用方法。课后翻译中选用了部分来自富善、阿恩德、戴遂良、狄考文以及威妥玛等人的教科书中的例句。我们并没有在他们的书中找到像施密特这样完整清晰的语法说明，他们的教科书还停留在将句子和课文铺陈在读者面前的阶段，几乎没有有关语法规律的专门说明。由此我们可以看出，施密特的语法书真正实现了运用已有的语言学观念解析语法、研究语法并表述语法现象的目的。

五　《汉语官话语法试编》的影响及评价

（一）前人的积极评价

《语言百科辞典》（Лингвистический Энциклопедический Словарь）的

“苏俄汉学（Китаистика в России и СССР）”词条写道：“俄苏汉学拥有久远的历史传统。有关汉语的专门学术研究从十九世纪上半叶比丘林（Н. Я. Бичурин）的《汉文启蒙》（Китайская грамматика，1837）开始便已初具规模。到十九世纪，瓦西里耶夫（В. П. Васильев）等汉学家先后研究了汉字书写系统。二十世纪伊始，阿列克谢耶夫（В. М. Алексеев）尝试对汉语语音进行系统研究。在卫国战争前的一段时期内，俄罗斯已经出现相当规模的汉语词典。20 世纪初期，俄国开始出现有关汉语语法的著作，例如波波夫（П. С. Попов）和施密特（П. П. Шмидт）的汉语语法著作。在施密特的《汉语官话语法试编》一书中，首次提出汉语中存在词类（части речи）的观点”。①

从本书中句法成分和词类划分来看，有学者从微观研究的角度对此做出了注脚，其中有代表性的包括如莎特拉夫卡（А. В. Шатравка ）在《现代汉语语法中方位词的学习方法》②（Грамматические способы выражения места в современном китайском языке）所做的注脚。他指出：“现代汉语语法方位词和空间关系表述的特点问题在各个时代诸多语言学家和语法学家的著作中均有提及。”俄罗斯汉学界的许多著名学者都对这一问题给予了特别关注，如施密特（П. П. Шмидт）、龙果夫（А. А. Драгунов）、吉普金娜（Н. И. Тяпкина）、卡列洛夫（В. И. Горелов）等。从中看出，作者对施密特在现代汉语语法方位词的提出和界定成就方面持有积极肯定的态度。

---

① В. Н. Ярцева. , ed. , *Лингвистический энциклопедический словарь*, Москва, Советская энциклопедия, 1990. 原文如下：Русская и советская китаистика имеет давние традиции. Научное изучение китайского языка восходит к работе Н. Я. Бичурина《Китайская грамматика》(1837) . В 19 в. русские китаисты В. П. Васильев, С. М. Георгиевский и другие изучали иероглифическую письменность, В. М. Алексеев (1910) — фонетику китайского языка. В начале 20 в. появились работы по грамматике (П. С. Попов, П. П. Шмидт) . В《Опыте мандаринской грамматики》Шмидта (1915) проводилась идея о наличии в китайском языке частей речи. В предреволюционный период в России были созданы крупные словари китайского языка.

② А. В. Шатравка, http://www. synologia. ru/, 2018 - 10 - 28. 原文如下：Описание особенностей выражения пространственных отношений и указания местоположения в современном китайском языке можно найти в работах многих филологов-грамматистов, которые рассматривали данный вопрос в различные периоды времени. Так, в отечественном китаеведении этой проблеме уделяли внимание такие известные учёные, как П. П. Шмидт [5], А. А. Драгунов [3], Н. И. Тяпкина [4], В. И. Горелов [2] и др. ; в китайском языкознании это Ли Цзиньси [8], Ван Ли [7], Чжао Юаньжэнь [10], Люй Шусян [9], Чжу Дэси [11], Ван Сяоцинь [1] и др.

在《汉语学习的现代语言学方法》[①]（Методы современной лингвистики для изучения китайского языка）一文中，作者指出，19 世纪的俄罗斯汉学受到历史比较语言学的影响，采用语言外部结构的比较方法进行研究。与此相关的包括施密特在内的多位汉学家均在此列。临近 20 世纪的俄罗斯汉学因受到历史比较语言学的影响而在汉语研究方面有了长足进步。当时的汉学研究已经引进了语言材料的系统知识（语音、词汇、语法等），并且对现代语言学中的结构划分概念有了初步的认识，有关这一方面的例证在包括施密特的《汉语官话语法试编》在内的诸多汉学家、语言学家的著述中有所体现。正是在这一时期，俄国的专业汉学研究产生，为随后按照学科进一步分化的汉学研究提供了基础。

---

① 该文章来源于网络，作者不详。https://habr.com/post/135074/，2018－10－28. 原文如下：Российская китаистика в 19 веке（в рамках сравнительно-исторического языкознания，с применением метода внешней реконструкции）тесно связана с именами таких ученых как Петр Иванович Кафаров（Палладий）（《Китайско-русский словарь》，1888），Василий Павлович Васильев（《Графическая система китайских иероглифов》，1867，《Анализ китайских иероглифов》1866，1884），Сергей Михайлович Георгиевский（《Анализ иероглифической письменности как отражающей в себе историю жизни древнего китайского народа》，1888；《О корневом составе китайского языка в связи с вопросом о происхождении китайцев》，1888），Алексей Осипович（Иосифович）Ивановский（《Материалы для истории инородцев Юго-Западного Китая》，1888，《Юньнаньские инородцы в период династий Юань，Мин и Дайцин》，1886），Дмитрий Алексеевич Пещуров（《Китайско-Русский словарь по ключевой системе》，1897，《Китайско-Русский словарь по графической системе》，1891），Павел Степанович Попов（《Китайско-русский словарь》，1879，《Краткое введение к изучению китайского языка》，1908），Дмитрий Матвеевич Позднеев（《Новый иероглифический японо-корейско-китайский словарь как попытка определения минимального числа иероглифов，общих для трех языков》，1910），Апполинарий Васильевич Рудаков（《Практический словарь служебных слов литературного китайского языка》，1927），Петр Петрович Шмидт（Петерис Шмитс）（《Опыт мандаринской грамматики》，1915，《Лингвистическое введение в изучение китайского языка》，1900/1901）. Представляется возможным утверждать，что к началу 20 века китаистика в России была развитой отраслью знаний о языке，в которой применялся метод сравнительно-исторического языкознания. Китаистика того времени обладала системными знаниями о языковом материале（фонетике，лексике и грамматике китайского языка）и была готова к восприятию идей структурной лингвистики（в подтверждение данного утверждения смотри работы — Алексея Ивановича Иванова，Василия Михайловича Алексеева，Александра Евграфовича Любимова，Георгия Феофановича Смыкалова）. Именно в тот момент зарождается национальная структурная школа китаистики，продолжается дальнейшая специализация китаистов，занимающихся различными проблемами китайского языка.

在列舍托夫（А. М. Решетов）所写的施密特小传《彼得·彼得罗维奇·施密特（1869 - 1938）》中，作者引述了汉学家斯卡奇科夫对其的评价："我觉得，用不着笃信对这位受人敬重的汉学家的某些热评，而是应当听取一些其他观点。汉学史领域的杰出专家——斯卡奇科夫（П. Е. Скачков）高度评价了施密特出版的汉语教程、文选读本和满语教科书，尤其是在俄罗斯汉学史上构成了一个时代的《汉语官话语法试编——汉语学习的语言学导论》（Скачков，1975，с. 182）。他认为，"对施密特这部分学术遗产有这样的看法是准确且公正的……他的每一部著作都有新的观点，对于当代研究者来说都不失自身价值。而且我今天要强调的是，他在《汉语官话语法试编》当中叙述和总结的关于汉语口语多样性的观点在学术角度上具有一定程度上的重要性和现实性……施密特提出的有关汉语在词法学及谱系学分类上之地位的观点具有历史性意义，而且他还使印度支那语系的概念得到了发展，据他所言，该语族包括汉语在内的一系列语言——藏语、缅甸语、暹罗语（泰语）和其他语言"。①

（二）研究不足

《不同语言系统中的生物学术语构词法——基于现代汉语及塔吉克语语料的研究》②（Словообразование терминов（биологических）в разносистемных языках：на материале современных китайского и таджикского языков）一文指出，施密特在《汉语官话语法试编》一书的开篇就从汉语发展的根源上描述了汉语在世界其他语言谱系中的地位，但是有关汉语语法体系的问题，施密特仅用略少的篇幅进行了粗略的解释，并没有形成系统、完备的论述。

另据列舍托夫考证，1902年10月，施密特就这部著作进行硕士论文答辩时，主要受到了佩休罗夫教授（Д. А. Пещуров）和波波夫教授（П. С. Попов）的批评。前者不赞成学位论文答辩人（这里指施密特）对汉语中

---

① А. М. Решетов，"Петр Петрович Шмидт（1869—1938）" *Восток*（*Oriens*），2009，pp. 97 - 98.

② Аслитдинова Раксана Насритдиновна，*Словообразование терминов*（*биологических*）*в разносистемных языках*：*на материале современных китайского и таджикского языков*：диссертация кандидата филологических наук：10. 02. 20，Душанбе，2007，p. 169.

存在语法的有关论证，后者认为他过分夸大了汉语和世界其他民族语言的亲缘关系（Новое время，1902）。[1]

（三）结论

19 世纪末至 20 世纪初，随着俄国在远东势力的增强和符拉迪沃斯托克东方学院的建立，俄国需要大批的东方语言实用人才。包括施密特在内的一批汉学家对俄国的汉语人才培养做出了重大贡献。除了历史原因之外，语言学本身由历史比较语言学、普通语言学向现代语言学过渡的导向也为当时的汉学家和教授们提供了必要的理论支撑。施密特的汉语研究成果《汉语官话语法试编》正是在这样的历史背景之下应运而生。

通过文本分析，我们得出：《汉语官话语法试编》作为该时期东方学院初级汉语学习者的教科书，对俄国汉语教学和研究历史产生了划时代的影响。该书的主体部分分为“汉语学习的语言学导论”和“初级汉语阅读”两部分，分别从理论和实践两个角度对汉语语法做出了独到的分析。其中，施密特尝试从语言学的角度研究汉语，不仅运用历史比较语言学方法，在语音、语法、词汇等方面比较汉语同其他语言、汉语内部方言的联系与区别，在世界语言中重新定位了汉语的坐标，而且还较为成功地运用了普通语言学的理念和方法，分析、归纳、讲解官话口语的各种语法现象。同时，作者还善于在中外学者对汉语语法研究的基础上推陈出新，在纷繁的课文和句子中提炼语法精要，并配以适度的练习。

总之，无论是从教材的体例、内容，还是理念上来看，《汉语官话语法试编》都不失为一部实用性与理论性兼具的高校汉语初级教科书范本。它结束了近百年来俄国汉学由比丘林的《汉文启蒙》主导的俄国汉语教学的历史，开启了俄国汉语教学的现代阶段。在俄国汉学，乃至世界汉语教学的历史上，施密特都代表了一个新的时代。

参考文献

Гридина Н. П.，Первый вуз на Дальнем Востоке России. Становление и развитие

---

① А. М. Решетов，“Петр Петрович Шмидт（1869—1938）”，*Восток*（*Oriens*），2009 p. 94.

центра востоковедения // Россия и АТР, 1996.

Известия Восточного Института. Владивосток, Т. I, вып. 1, 1900.

Кочешков Н. В. Они были первыми. Профессор Петр Петрович Шмидт // Россия и Азиатско-Тихоокеанский Регион, N 2. Владивосток, 1999.

Решетов А. М. Петр Петрович Шмидт (1869—1938) . // Восток (Oriens), 2009.

Шмидт П. Опыт Мандаринской грамматики. Пособие к изучению разговорного китайского языка Пекинского наречия. Известия Восточного института. Томы LI - LII. Владивосток Издание и печать Восточного института 1915г. 482 с. Картонный твердый переплет, Увеличенный формат.

〔俄〕П. Е. 斯卡奇科夫,〔俄〕В. С. 米亚斯尼科夫,《俄罗斯汉学史》,柳若梅译,社会科学文献出版社,2011。

贝罗贝:《二十世纪以前欧洲汉语语法学研究状况》,《中国语文》1998 年第 5 期。

董海樱:《西人汉语研究述论——16 - 19 世纪初期》,浙江大学出版社,2005。

林玉山:《世界语言学史》,湖南人民出版社,2009。

柳若梅:《俄国汉学史上第一部汉语语法书——〈汉文启蒙〉》,《福建师范大学学报(哲学社会科学版)》2010 年第 161 卷第 2 期。

张西平:《世界汉语教育史》,商务印书馆,2009。

A Textbook that Opens a Window of Chinese Teaching in Russia

Attempt of Mandarin Grammer with Texts for Exercises by P. P. Schmidt

Luo Wei

Abstract

In the late 19th and early 20th centuries, with the increasing power of Russia in the Far East and the establishment of the Oriental Institute in Vladivostok,

Russia needs a large number of practical oriental language experts. In addition to the aboved historical reasons, the orientation of linguistics from comparative and general linguistics to modern linguistics in this period also provided necessary academic soil for the development of Chinese teaching and research in Russia . In this historical background, Schmidt's Chinese research achievements—*Attempt of Mandarin Grammer with Texts for Exercises* came into being. As a textbook for junior Chinese scholars in the Oriental Institute during this period, it had an epoch-making influence in the history of Russian Chinese teaching and research. This book is not only the first successful attempt to general linguistics in Russian sinology, but also regarded as the end of the nearly one hundred years of Russian Chinese learning circles dominated by *Chinese Grammer* (Я. Бичурин, 1835) . Since then, Chinese teaching in Russia stepped into a new and modern stage.

Keywords

Russian Sinology Mandarin Grammar Oriental Institute Linguistics Spoken Chinese

浅谈司登得的《汉英合璧相连字彙》

李晶鑫*

摘　要

司登得（George Carter Stent，1833 - 1884）是 19 世纪末杰出的在华外国学者之一。他所编纂的《汉英合璧相连字彙》（*A Chinese and English Vocabulary in the Pekinese Dialect*）既借鉴了前人的诸多成果，又与当时其他传教士们所编纂的汉英、英汉辞典截然不同，辞典内几乎没有收录任何专业术语，所收词条绝大多数为日常生活中的高频词汇，涉及生活中的方方面面。从当时来看，这样的辞典无疑是非常新颖的。此外，该辞典特殊的编排方式以及所收录词汇特性影响了其后出版的汉外口语辞典。本稿以初版《汉英合璧相连字彙》为基础，对该辞典的结构及其特征逐一描述，在此基础上简单梳理该辞典的底本与其后续版本，并探讨辞典对日本的影响。

关键字

司登得　汉英合璧相连字彙　结构特征　石山福治

司登得（George Carter Stent，1833 - 1884）是 19 世纪末杰出的在华外国学者之一。他所编纂的《汉英合璧相连字彙》（简称《字彙》）与当时其他传教士们所编纂的汉英、英汉辞典截然不同，它几乎没有收录任何专业术语，所收录的词条绝大多数都是日常生活中的高频词汇，涉及生活中的

* 李晶鑫，关西大学东亚文化交涉学研究科博士在读生。

方方面面。但是目前为止，关于司登得其人以及《字彙》的研究并不多见。[①] 本稿以初版《字彙》为基础，对该辞典的结构与其特征逐一描述，并且对该辞典的底本与其后续版本做简单梳理。

一 司登得其人[②]

1833年6月15日，司登得在英国的坎特伯雷出生。他有两个哥哥：詹姆斯·威廉（James William）、查尔斯·弗雷德里克（Chailes Frederic）与一个姐姐朱丽叶·艾伦（Julia Ellen）。[③] 其父亲经营了一个水果市场与一个蔬菜农场，但他的家庭状况似乎并不是很好，而且也没有资料可以证明他曾接受过高等教育。1855年，司登得离开家乡，参加了英国第14国王轻骑兵团，并随军来到印度。关于司登得的兵旅生活，在他的回忆录中有详细的记述，但是归国时间不详。[④] 1860年，司登得与她的妻子结婚，但是由于长期的两地分居（司登得婚后不久便来到中国），二人于1878年离婚。1879年，司登得与萨拉（Sarah Ann Page）同居。次年，萨拉诞下一名男婴，孩子取名为佩奇（George Carter Albert Page）。

1860年中期，司登得以英国大使馆警卫的身份来到中国。[⑤] 来华后，司登得开始学习汉语。当时的英国大使馆首席书记官威妥玛（Thomas Francis Wade，1818－1895）对司登得的语言学习能力，特别是口语方面的才能非

---

① 相关研究包括：那须雅之：《G. C. Stent，とその著书について—— *A Chinese and English Vocabulary in the Pekinese Dialect*（《汉英合壁相连字彙》）を中心として》，《中国语学》，1993年第240期，第122－131页；宫田和子：《英华辞典の総合的研究——19世纪を中心として》，白帝社，2010，第254－257、307－308页；沈国威：《近代英华华英辞典解题》，关西大学出版部，2011，第153－162页；高永伟《辞海茫茫——英语新词和词典之研究》，复旦大学出版社，2012，第274－284页；韩一瑾：《司登得〈汉英合璧相连字彙〉谱系考》，《国际汉语》2017年第4号，第115－120页。

② 关于司登得生平与著作的具体内容，参见李晶鑫《ステント（George Carter Stent）の生涯と著作》，《文化交涉东アジア文化研究科院生论集》，2017年第7号，第79－96页。

③ 司登得的遗嘱记录了其兄弟姐妹3人与同居女友的姓名，但是对司登得的学习工作等信息并未提及。遗嘱中除了司登得本人的签名外，还有两位证明人的签名，分别为：马士（Hosea Ballou Morse）与泰勒（F. E. Taylor）。

④ G. C. Stent，*Scraps From My Sabretasche*，W. H. Allen & CO，1882.

⑤ 我们对司登得的现有材料做了整理和分析后认为，司登得的来华时间应在1860年中期（1865年前后）的可能性极高；参见李晶鑫《ステント（George Carter Stent）の生涯と著作》，《文化交涉东アジア文化研究科院生论集》2017年第7号，第81－86页。

常欣赏，开始帮助他学习汉语。随着学习的逐步深入，司登得对中国的小说、诗歌和戏曲产生了浓厚兴趣。1869年，司登得进入清政府海关工作，并在赫德（Robert Hart，1835－1911）的资助下继续学习汉语。自1869年起，他辗转于上海、烟台、温州、汕头等地从事海关工作。1881年，司登得来到台湾高雄打狗关，第二年任代理税务司长。1884年9月1日司登得在高雄病逝。

1871年6月9日，司登得在《皇家亚洲文会北中国支会会刊》（*Journal of the China Branch of the Royal Asiatic Society*）发表了他的第一篇文章："《中文诗歌》（*Chinese Lyrics*）"。[①] 从那时起，司登得发表了45篇文章，其中绝大多数为中国诗歌、歌谣、戏曲以及小说的英文译本。除此之外，司登得还出版了11本著作（包含死后他人所著的增订版及改订版），其中最著名的就是1871年11月于上海出版的《汉英合壁相连字彙》（简称《字彙》）。

二 初版《汉英合壁相连字彙》

（一）图书馆馆藏情况

1871年的初版《字彙》是司登得的第一本著作。我们以宫田和子（2010）[②] 所描述的馆藏情况为基础，在日本图书馆寻找到三本该辞典，另外通过调查，在欧美的两所图书馆也各寻找到一本。具体馆藏情况如表1所示。

表1 初版《字彙》馆藏情况

《汉英合壁相连字彙》（*A Chinese and English Vocabulary in the Pekinese Dialect*）				
图书馆	册数	尺寸	记号	说明
东洋文库	1	22＊14	贵III－12－D－a－21	情况良好

① G. C. Stent, "Chinese Lyrics", *Journal of the China Branch of the Royal Asiatic Society*, No. VII Art. IV, 1873, pp. 93－135. 此文章虽发表于1871年，但是在1873年才被刊载。

② 宫田和子：《英华辞典の総合的研究——19世纪を中心として》，白帝社，2010，第254－255页。

续表

图书馆	册数	尺寸	记号	说明
天理大学图书馆	1	20.5 * 14.8	823//2 (3)	扉页欠缺
东京大学综合图书馆	1	21 * 14	D100: 450	情况良好
那不勒斯国家图书馆	1	22 * 15.7	BIB. PROV. 20. 192	情况良好
加利福尼亚大学图书馆	1	不明	712b. S826 c. 2	PDF 版

日本方面，东洋文库藏本与东京大学综合图书馆藏本的保存情况良好，天理大学图书馆藏本扉页欠缺，其他部分相对完好。欧美方面，意大利那不勒斯国家图书馆藏有一本初版《字彙》。此书保存十分完好，图书馆也已将其制作成 PDF 版并上传至互联网档案馆①（初版《字彙》书影见图 1）。

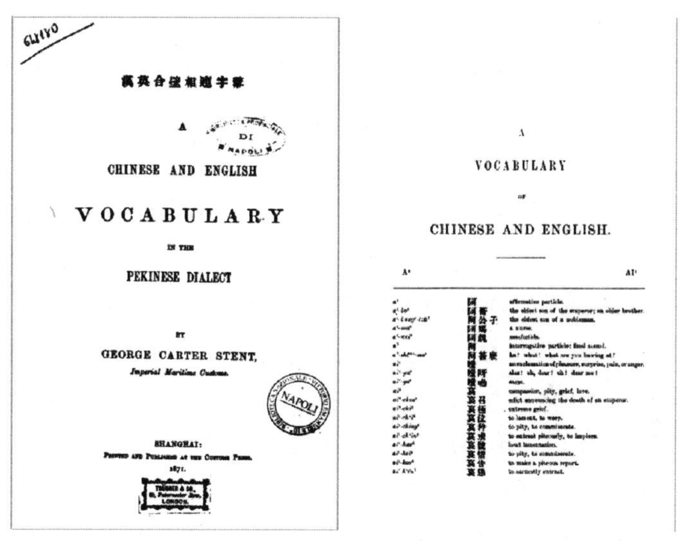
漢英合璧相連字彙

A

CHINESE AND ENGLISH

VOCABULARY

IN THE

PEKINESE DIALECT

BY

GEORGE CARTER STENT,

Imperial Maritime Customs.

SHANGHAI:

PRINTED AND PUBLISHED AT THE CUSTOMS PRESS.

1871.

A

VOCABULARY

OF

CHINESE AND ENGLISH.

初版《字彙》扉页书影　　初版《字彙》第一页书影

图 1　初版《字彙》扉页（左）与正文第一页（右）书影

（二）辞典结构及特征

初版《字彙》分为八个部分：扉页、献词、序言、正文、索引、部首

① 互联网档案馆（Internet Archive）中另藏有一本加利福尼亚大学图书馆藏本的 PDF 版。Internet Archive 中加利福尼亚大学藏本的网址为：https://archive.org/details/achineseandengl01stengoog；那不勒斯国家图书馆藏本的网址为：https://archive.org/details/bub_gb_ib9hORjFeUcC。

表、笔记以及正误表。具体信息如表 2 所示。

表 2 辞典结构

扉页	献词	序言	正文	索引	部首表	笔记	正误表
1（1）①	1（1）	5	1 - 572	发音排列索引 575 - 624 部首 - 发音排列索引 627 - 650	651 - 658	659 - 673	674 - 677

1. 扉页

本书的扉页内容如下：

漢英合壁相連字彙 / A / CHINESE AND ENGLISH / VOCABULARY / IN THE /PEKINESE DIALECT / = = = = = / BY / GEORGE CARTER STENT, / Imperial maritime Customs / = = = = = / SHANGHAI: / PRINTRD AND PUBLISHED AT THE CUSTOMS PRESS / 1871. ②

从扉页中我们可以看出，该辞典的中文名为《汉英合壁相连字彙》，司登得在编纂该书时并未将此书定义为“辞典”，而是一本“词汇集”。关于“合壁”③ 与“相连”二词，我们认为“合壁”即是“汉”与“英”之合璧，而“相连”有“头字”与“词汇”相连之意。本书的英文名为 *A Chinese and English Vocabulary in the Pekinese Dialect*，明确指出该辞典选词基准为北京官话。因此可以确切地说，本书是一本以北京官话为基础的汉英对照词汇集。这也是自马礼逊（Robert Morison 1782 - 1834）的《字典》④ 以来在中国本土出现的第一本明确表明以北京官话为主体的汉英辞典。另外，在扉页最后写明该书出版于上海，时间为 1871 年。

2. 献词

司登得 1869 年来到清朝海关，自此开始了长达 14 年的海关生涯。在这段时

① “（1）”表示该页的背面为一页空白页。

② “/”表示改行。

③ 基本古籍库中“合壁”一词共计 299 条，其中大多数词条都有“合璧”之意。如《官场现形记》中第 55 卷中即有：“……掏了半天，摸出一个东西来，翻译在旁边，看得明白，原来是一套华洋合壁的履历，倒很拜服他想到周到……”因此我们断定此处应不是错写，而是司登得有意为之。

④ Robert Morison，《字典》，The Honorable East India Company's Press，1815.

期内，特别是辞典的编纂过程中司登得受到了赫德的全力援助，才使《字彙》最终得以出版。因此在该辞典的序言前他将最诚挚的感谢与敬意献给了赫德。

3. 序言

序言共包含六点信息：编纂的缘由及方法、辞典的结构、采用威妥玛拼音编纂、如何排列量词、采集词汇的标准以及为何使用两个索引。[①]

4. 正文

辞典整体采用了“注音—词汇—译文”的结构进行编纂。注音系统采用了威妥玛拼音，所有词条按字母顺序进行排列。正文中司登得首先列出一个单字，之后引出以该单字为头字的词汇与短语。这样的排版方式在现代汉外辞典中已经成为主流，但是首先提出这种排版方式的是司登得。[②] 在序言中司登得是如此描述这种新式排版法的：

> “The book, as the reader will perceive, is on an entirely new principle, and in a different style from any hitherto published, being an attempt to bring Chinese characters into words and syllables, or words of syllables, assimilating it as near as possible to an English dictionary; so simplifying it that characters, and any combinations of characters it may contain, can, by this plan, be as readily found as words in an English dictionary…”

如序言所述，这种全新的排版方法使人们更易于在《字彙》中找出他们所需的单词，极大地提高了效率，并且对汉语初学者也非常友好，更易于上手。

全文一共收录单字 4222 个（包含多音字）[③]，并且收录了与其相关的词

---

① 本稿将在下文中结合具体信息对此六点做逐一解释说明。另外，沈国威（2011）将初版《字彙》的序言译成中文，并对初版《字彙》做了解题与短评。沈国威：《近代英华华英辞典解题》，关西大学出版部，2011，第 153 - 162 页。

② 在初版《字彙》之前，所有的汉外辞典在排版时虽然也会首先列出一个单字，但在随后引出的词条中该单字不仅会出现在词头，也有可能出现在词尾或短句中间，甚至会出现与该单字本体完全无关但意思相近的词汇（类似于类语辞典或近义词辞典）。这种排版方式更适合有一定汉语基础的人使用，但是对初学者来说并不一定友好，查找效率也较低。

③ 该辞典的索引部分共记录单字 4222 个，但是有 3 个单字并未在正文中出现，分别是“惆”“湘”和“坷”。这三个单字及其关联词汇随后在第二版《字彙》正文部分的第 103 页、203 页、271 页中出现。

汇与短语约20000条。全文包含单音节（单字）、双音节词汇与短语、三音节词汇与短语以及四音节词汇、短语及成语俗语。通篇未收录五个音节以上的长句。举例如表3所示。

表3　辞典中所收录的词汇举例①

双音节		
词汇	家庭	爱人，侧室，丈人，丈母，长弟，长子，季父，继嗣，契父，家人……
	行为	张伞，撑船，乘凉，骑马，寄信，砌墙，加衣，浇花，剪发，捡柴……
	用品	袄儿，钗钏，常服，罩子，潮脑，车轿，鍼線，几案，角梳，铅笔……
	饮食	熬酒，茶酒，常饭，炒肉，蒸肉，酱菜，饺子，煎饼，饯菓，忌口……
	法律	案件，案情，章程，章法，掌囚，招罪，证见，呈词，缉捕，监禁……
	自然	潮水，潮泾，七星，畦田，气候，江河，降水，节气，涧沟，金星……
	生物	阿魏，蚱蜢，沉香，陈皮，鸡子，寄生，漆树，家雀，结菓，蛟属……
	经济	债累，产业，帐目，帐单，招租，折兑，寄贮，交易，借贷，钱局……
	军事	安营，战场，将令，起兵，枪药，交战，剿灭，校尉，捷报，建功……
	教育	启蒙，及第，讲书，教学，教官，教授，教书，解元，借喻，切韻……
	民俗	招魂，超度，乩卜，吉星，祭祀，祈赐，叫魂，解梦，签语，请仙……
短语	挨著，爱病，按著，差著，这个，几回，几岁，起来，弃了，假的，交给，瞧瞧……	
三音节		
词汇	安息日，安南国，茶壶嘴，搀抢星，帐目单，丈母娘，照日葵，千里镜，千字文……	
短语	挨了打，闸上水，宅天命，差来了，差了来，气高帽，价钱贵，胶粘得，叫什麼……	
四音节		
词汇	按察使司，掌院学士，牵头老婆，谏议大夫……	
成语	爱民如子，安居乐业，暗箭伤人，侧耳旁听，撤水拏鱼，珍馐美味，借刀杀人……	
短语	唉的一声，碍你何干，张罗张罗，著儿不错，将才去了，悄悄儿的，值得多少……	

《字彙》与当时其他汉英-英汉辞典不同，所收词条几乎没有专业词汇或术语，绝大多数为日常生活中的高频词（常用语），其内容涉及生活中的

① 我们以沈国威（1994）的分类方法为基础（政、经、人、自、教、工、军、宗、他，共计九种），将类别扩展为21种，对初版《字彙》中的词汇进行分类。由于篇幅原因，本表仅展示了其中11个分类，其余10个分类分别为：政治、哲学、地理、宗教、艺术、建筑、工农业、医学、缩略语、科学。另外，单音节单字在本表中也并未展示。沈国威：《近代日中语彙交流史》，笠间书院，1994。

方方面面，对初到中国生活的外国人来说实用性极强。至于该辞典为何会表现出如此特点，我们认为这与司登得的学习动机与学习方法以及对常用词的特殊理解不无关系。首先，司登得并不是传教士，[①] 他没有传播教义、理念或者西洋科学知识的义务，也就是说，司登得是为了兴趣、交流或者仅为了生存而学习中文。那么，他所关心的一定是具有实用性并且会被经常使用的词汇。其次，司登得是通过阅读大量汉语小说来学习中文的，并且曾经一度想尝试将这些小说翻译成英语。[②] 然而，司登得在翻译的过程中发现很多词汇非但不能直接用英语来解读，而且这些词汇自身也携带着大量的信息，如许多奇怪的习俗，生活场景，亦或外国人并不了解但在中国民间却是每天都会发生的事情等。除此之外，他还发现许多仅在小说中出现的词汇与短语。司登得在阅读小说的同时将这些词汇逐一做了英语解释。《字彙》就是通过这样的日积月累，再经整理和编纂后才得以出版。因此，以这种方式编纂出的辞典，所收录的词汇必然是极具生活气息，非常贴近大众生活的。最后，司登得对“什么是常用词”这一问题有自己特殊的理解。在《字彙》的序言部分，司登得对辞典的选词原则有如下描述：“这本词汇集中收录有许多辞典里找不到的常用汉字。我采用它们，是因为我认为它们是必不可少的……本书的另一个原则，就是只收录我的老师无需查阅参考书籍就认识的那些汉字。该原则是基于这样的考虑，如果一个见识多广的中国人不借助参考书都无法知道某个字或者词的意思，那么他一定不可能是常用字词。”[③] 从序言中我们不难看出，司登得对常用词的理解非常独到，而且准确，同时也可以看出，司登得在学习

① 司登得是共济会成员，职位为“Craft（职人）”，加入时间不详。

② 司登得的遗物明细中共有汉语小说、诗歌与杂文 314 本，但是并未给出明确的书目。我们虽然无法证明他确实使用这些书籍，并将其用于编纂辞典，但是我们可以确定他当年确实阅读过大量的汉语读物。

③ 原文为：“Many characters in common use will be found in this book that are not recognised by dictionaries. I have used them, however, as I consider them indispensable, and placed them under the radicals they naturally belong to. It has also been a principle with me not to admit any characters but those actually known is my teacher without reference to books—a principle adopted on the ground that if a well informed Chinese did not know a character or word and its meaning without such reference, it could not possibly be in common use, and was therefore superfluous to my present purpose and not necessary for a foreign beginner to learn. . . ” G. C. Stent, *A Chinese and English Vocabulary in the Pekinese Dialect*, Shanghai, 1871. 沈国威：《近代英华华英辞典解题》，关西大学出版部，2011，第 153 – 162 页。

汉语时，对实用性是非常看重的，这一点也完全体现在了他的《字彙》中。

除实用性之外，收录的词汇还具有北京官话特征。我们以太田辰夫（1950）所描述的12个北京官话特征为基础，[①] 将之与《字彙》做简单对比，其结果如表4所示。

表4　辞典中表现出的北京官话特征

特征	出现情况	特征	出现情况	特征	出现情况
儿（←见，里）	O	别（禁止，推量）	O	[ ] 得慌	O
喒（咱）们	O	得（需要）	O	[ ] 是，似的	O
您	O	多喒	O	来著	X
俩（仨②）	O	给（介词）	O	罢咱	X

另外，与太田辰夫（1995）[③] 所描述的北京官话语法特征相符合的词汇举例如下：

"儿"：

"袄儿""渣儿""罩儿""辙眼儿""记号儿""起头儿""气味儿"；

"您"：

"您""您纳""你纳"；

"得"：

"必得""得有"；

"爱"：

"爱争论的""爱抬槓""爱媚""爱病"；

"给"：

"给我写""给我买""给我做"；

"让"：

"让他进来""让我过去"；

---

① 太田辰夫：《清代の北京语について》，《中国语学》1955年第34期，第1－5页。

② 《字彙》中并没有收录"仨"这一单字，而是收录了"三"，注音为"sa1"和"san1"。

③ 太田辰夫：《北京语の文法特点》，太田辰夫编《中国语文论集语学编》，汲古书院，1995，第243－265页。

“别”：

“别管我”“别生气”“别做”；

副词：

“乍来”“冷不防”“冷乎丁的”“抽冷子”“底根儿”

其他：

“多咱”、“罢了”、“程子”、“吃不了”、“老没看见”、“挤得慌”

因此我们基本可以判定《字彙》是具备北京官话特征的。但是是否所有词汇都属于北京官话，目前为止还无法确认。另外，由于该辞典是一本词汇集，通篇没有超过五个音节以上的长句出现，因此如“来著”“咖”“得了”等具有北京官话特征的助词在该辞典中并未收录。①

对于词汇的解释部分，司登得基本摒弃了那些原先就有的，但是现在已经不使用的释义，而给出了它们目前实际正在使用的定义。这样一来，《字彙》的词汇解释部分更加精练，汉语初学者在汉语学习过程中能够更加精准地把握每一个字词最常用的意思，不会因为过多的废弃词义而产生迷茫。但是，由于当时司登得学习汉语的时间并不很长，因此直译和误译相对较多。具体举例如表 5 所示。

表 5　直译与误译现象

词条	译文
展诵	to open and read
企望	to stand on tiptoe; looking with expectation
宅兆	to divine respecting a grave and the day of burial
期服	one year's mourning (for uncles or elder brothers.)

5. 索引

本书包含两个索引，分别是发音排列索引及以部首顺序为基础的发音排列索引。司登得认为这样做的优点在于，使用者只要掌握关于汉语的发音或者部首相关知识中的任何一种，就能在该辞典中找到他所需要的内容。值得注意的是，该辞典的发音排列索引中一共包含了 4222 个单字以及 404 个音节。由于司登得在序言中指出自己使用的是威妥玛拼音，而威妥玛拼

① 太田辰夫：《清代の北京语について》，《中国语学》1955 年第 34 期，第 264 页。

音在当时实际并存着两个版本，我们遂将两版威妥玛拼音同初版《字彙》内所含音节做对比，其结果如表 6 所示。

表 6 《字彙》与《寻津录》《语言自迩集》的音节收录情况

书名	《寻津录》（1859）①	《语言自迩集》（1867）②	初版《字彙》（1871）
所收音节数	397	420	404

从表中我们可以看出，虽然司登得表示自己完全采用威妥玛拼音，但实际上并非如此。初版《字彙》所收录的音节数要略高于《寻津录》，而又少于初版《语言自迩集》。③ 那么此处我们需要明确司登得在编纂辞典的过程中具体参考的是哪些书。

1859 年，威妥玛出版了《寻津录》。书中共收录了 397 个使用威妥玛拼音标识的音节。威妥玛不仅花费了很大的篇幅对所有音节做了逐一分析，而且还附加了音节表、多音字发音表、声韵母拼写表，所用例字也相当丰富，甚至该书中所有汉语部分也全部标注了拼音，④ 足见威妥玛对该发音系统的重视。1867 年，《语言自迩集》出版。在该书中威妥玛在原有的 397 个音节的基础上增加了 23 个音节，使威妥玛拼音达到 420 个音节。相对于《寻津录》，《语言自迩集》对音节部分的说明要简单一些，并且每个音节也只附加一个例字。除了增加音节数外，书中还增加了《练习燕山平仄篇》。

司登得在《字彙》中并没有直接说明自己是以哪本书作为参考对象的。为了解决这一问题，我们将三套发音系统做了详细的比对。⑤ 首先是《字彙》中并未收录而其他两本书均有的音节，共计 5 个（如表 7 所示）。

① Thomas Francis Wade, *Hsin Ching Lu*: *Book of Experiments Being the First of A Series of Contributions to The Study of Chinese*, Hong Kong, 1859, pp. 63 – 86.

② Thomas Francis Wade, *A Progressive Course*, *Designed to Assist the Student of Colloquial Chinese*, *Part* 1 *Sound Table or List of Syllables*, London, 1867, pp. 8 – 11。

③ 其未被收录的 16 个音节分别为：ch ‘iai、chüo、ch ‘üo、ê、êng、hsio、hsüo、k ‘uo、k ‘a、lio、lüeh、nüeh、nüo、nun、pou、ya。

④ 《寻津录》中有两个部分内容使用了汉语，分别为《天类篇》与《圣喻广训》。

⑤ 由于《寻津录》与《语言自迩集》的共有部分并不能看出司登得是如何参考这两本书的。所以我们在对比过程中主要针对三本书的区别部分，即初版《字彙》未收录的 16 个音节，以及《语言自迩集》中增加的 23 个音节为着手点进行对比。

表 7 《字彙》中未收录而《寻津录》《语言自迩集》收录的音节

	音节	例字	《字彙》	《寻津录》(《语言自迩集》)①
1	ê	额	o	ê、o
2	hsio	学	hsiao、hsüeh	hsio、hsiao、hsüeh、(hsüo)
3	lio	略	liao、lüo	lio、lüeh、liao、(lüo)
4	lüeh	略	liao	lio、lüeh、liao
5	yai	涯	ya	yai、ya

这五个音节所对应的汉字，均为多音字。在《寻津录》中这五个音节全部用"*"做了标记，并且在多音字字表"Appendix I. to the Peking Syllabary"中全部列举了出来。从上表中我们可以看出，司登得并不是完全按照《寻津录》或《语言自迩集》所记录的音节进行标音，而是选择最常用的发音进行标注。

另外，对于《语言自迩集》中增加的 23 个音节，司登得只收录了其中的 12 个，另外 11 个并未被收录。具体信息如表 8 所示。

表 8 《语言自迩集》中增加的 23 个音节

	音节	收录	例字	《字彙》	《寻津录》	《语言自迩集》
1	ch ‘iai	X	楷	k ‘ai	k ‘ai	k ‘ai、ch ‘iai
2	chüo	X	君	chün	chün	chün、chüo
3	ch ‘üo	X	羣	ch ‘ün	ch ‘ün	ch ‘ün、ch ‘üo
4	êng	X	哼	‘hêng	‘hêng	‘hêng、êng
5	hsüo	X	学	hsiao、hsüeh	hsio、hsiao、hsüeh	hsio、hsiao、hsüeh、hsüo
6	nun	X	嫩	nên	nên	nên、nun
7	pou	X	不	pu	pu	pu、pou
8	nüeh	X	虐	nio	—	nio、nüeh、nüo
9	nüo	X	虐	nio	—	nio、nüeh、nüo
10	chiung	O	壮	chiung	—	chiung
11	ch ‘ua	O	欻	ch ‘ua	—	ch ‘ua

① 括号内为《语言自迩集》中增加的音节。

续表

	音节	收录	例字	《字彙》	《寻津录》	《语言自迩集》
12	ch ‘uo	O	擉	ch ‘uo	—	ch ‘uo
13	Jê	O	热	Jê	—	Jê
14	lüan	O	恋	lüan	—	lüan
15	lüo	O	略	liao、lüo	—	lüo、lio、lüeh、liao
16	nin	O	您	nin	—	nin
17	nio	O	虐	nio	—	nio、nüeh、nüo
18	nou	O	耨	nou	—	nou、
19	p ‘ou	O	不	p ‘ou	—	p ‘ou
20	sên	O	森	sên	—	sên
21	tsên	O	怎	tsên	—	tsên
22	k ‘a	X	卡	ka、ch ‘ia	ch ‘ia	k ‘a、ch ‘ia
23	k ‘uo	X	阔	kuo	—	k ‘uo

从表 8 中我们可以看出，在一个字有多个发音并存的情况下，司登得往往更倾向于从《寻津录》中寻找合适的音节（表中 1－7 号）；另外，遇到《寻津录》没有收录该单字的音节的情况出现时，司登得会直接从《语言自迩集》中选取合适的音节进行补充。司登得在选取的过程中并不是机械式地照搬《语言自迩集》，而是有自己的考量。比如“虐”字在《寻津录》中没有给出合适的音，在《语言自迩集》中则给出了“nio”“nüeh”“nüo”三个音。司登得并没有全部采用，而是在多个发音中最终选择了“nio”。值得注意的是“nio”一音并没有收录在现代汉语词典中，这应该是 19 世纪末北京话特有并且很常见的一个发音。

综合上述两个表格，我们认为司登得在编纂辞典的注音部分时，有极大可能是先以《寻津录》为基础进行编写。只有在《寻津录》无法解决注音问题时，才会在《语言自迩集》中寻找合适的音节。理由有二：其一，《寻津录》中对于威妥玛拼音的解释与分析最为详细，例字例句也最为丰富，这种特性更方便司登得进行辞书的编纂；其二，如前文所述，司登得应是 1860 年中期来到中国的，那时市场上只有《寻津录》，而《语言自迩集》要在几年后才会出版。换句话说，司登得来华后接触到的第一本汉语教科书很有可能就是《寻津录》。司登得对此书的理解要比后面的其他教科书更加深刻，反之该书对司登得对汉语的理解等方面的影响也应是相当巨大的。因此在多个选项并存时，司登得自然会更倾向从《寻津录》中寻求答案。

另外，在表 8 中还有两个特殊例子。“卡”和“阔”二字在《语言自迩集》中的标音都是正确的，而在《字彙》中却标为“ka”和“kuo”。这应是司登得对汉语发音方法的认识不足造成的。这一错误在其他的擦音与塞擦音之中也会出现，尤其是在多音字的情况下更加明显。

以初版《字彙》中的“重”词条为例。在汉语中“重”字有“chung4”与“ch‘ung2”两种发音，但是司登得并没有明确地将两者分开(见图 2)。而实际上，在《寻津录》的多音字列表中已经将“重”字的两个发音明确地区分开了（见图 3)。这种错误在其他以送气音与不送气音为区分的多音字中多次出现，如“长”“传”等。但并不是所有的此类多音字都不能很好地区分开，比如“朝”字就被很好地分为“ch‘ao2”和“chao1”。另外，有明显发音区别的多音字在《字彙》中也很好地被区分开来，如“差”被标注为“cha1”和“chai1”，“行”被标注为“‘hang2”和“hsing2”等。从中我们可以看出，虽说司登得对汉语的造诣非常高，然而对汉语发音方法的认识还是有所欠缺的。

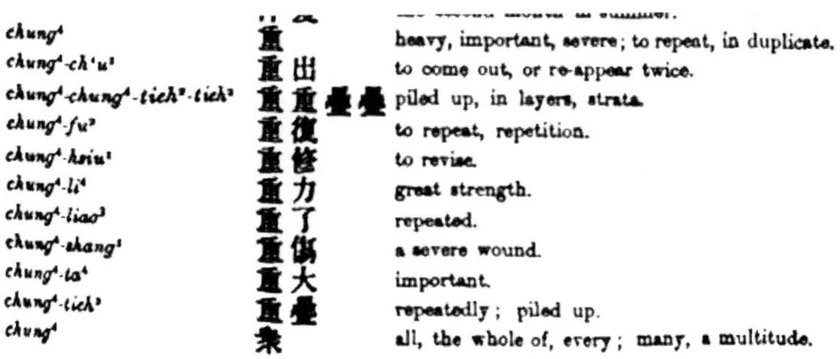

chung^{4} 重 heavy, important, severe; to repeat, in duplicate.
chung^{4}-ch'u^{1} 重出 to come out, or re-appear twice.
chung^{4}-chung^{4}-tieh^{2}-tieh^{2} 重重疊疊 piled up, in layers, strata.
chung^{4}-fu^{3} 重復 to repeat, repetition.
chung^{4}-hsiu^{1} 重修 to revise.
chung^{4}-li^{4} 重力 great strength.
chung^{4}-liao^{3} 重了 repeated.
chung^{4}-shang^{1} 重傷 a severe wound.
chung^{4}-ta^{4} 重大 important.
chung^{4}-tieh^{2} 重疊 repeatedly; piled up.
chung^{4} 衆 all, the whole of, every; many, a multitude.

图 2　《字彙》中“重”词条的记录情况①

① George Carter Stent, *A Chinese and English Vocabulary in the Pekinese Dialect*, Shanghai, 1871, p. 117。

CHUNG. 71.				CH'UNG. 72.			
中	○	…	中	中	虫	寵	…
忠	…	…	仲	沖	蟲	…	…
…	…	…	…	翀	…	…	…
鍾	…	腫	重	…	重	…	…
…	…	種	種	衝	崇	…	…
鐘	…	踵	…	充	…	…	銃
終	…	…	衆	沖	…	…	…

* Characters so marked will also be found under other syllables.

图 3 《寻津录》中“重”词条的记录情况①

6. 部首表

初版《字彙》共收录 214 个部首及其英文解释。内容与初版《语言自迩集》(1867)② 完全一致。

7. 笔记

笔记部分一共有 104 个记述项，涉及 417 个词汇的解释，其内容绝大多数为关于中国民俗的解释文。在这一部分中，司登得明确记述了引用其他书籍的信息。

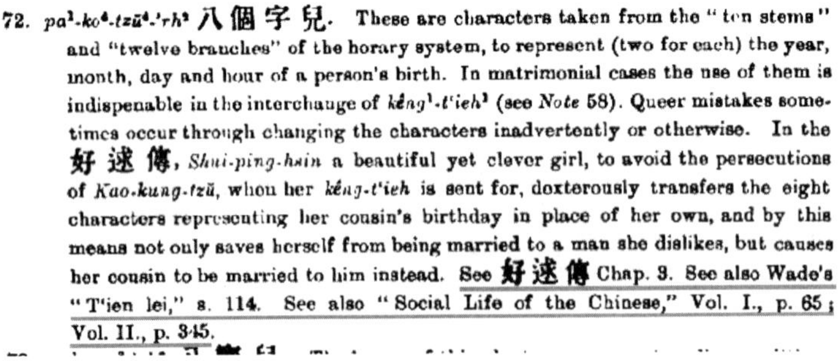

72. *pa¹-ko⁴-tzŭ⁴-'rh²* 八個字兒. These are characters taken from the "ten stems" and "twelve branches" of the horary system, to represent (two for each) the year, month, day and hour of a person's birth. In matrimonial cases the use of them is indispensable in the interchange of *kêng¹-t'ieh³* (see *Note* 58). Queer mistakes sometimes occur through changing the characters inadvertently or otherwise. In the 好逑傳, *Shui-ping-hsin* a beautiful yet clever girl, to avoid the persecutions of *Kao-kung-tzŭ*, when her *kêng-t'ieh* is sent for, dexterously transfers the eight characters representing her cousin's birthday in place of her own, and by this means not only saves herself from being married to a man she dislikes, but causes her cousin to be married to him instead. See 好逑傳 Chap. 3. See also Wade's "T'ien lei," s. 114. See also "Social Life of the Chinese," Vol. I., p. 65; Vol. II., p. 345.

图 4 《字彙》笔记部分中“八个字儿”词条的记录情况③

图 4 是笔记部分的第 72 个记述项“八个字儿”。在该项中，司登得对

① Thomas Francis Wade, *Hsin Ching Lu*: *Book of Experiments Being the First of a Series of Contributions to the Study of Chinese*, Hong Kong, 1859.

② Thomas Francis Wade, *A Progressive Course*, *Designed to Assist the Student of Colloquial Chinese*, London, 1867, pp. 15－22.

③ George Carter Stent, *A Chinese and English Vocabulary in the Pekinese Dialect*, Shanghai, 1871, p. 668.

彙》，但并未说明参考的是哪个版本。我们通过三个版本的《字彙》与之相比较，认为石山福治参考了 1898 年第三版《字彙》的可能性最大，而且《辞彙》是直接从第三版《字彙》改编而来的可能性也是存在的。[①]

关于为什么石山福治会在众多汉英辞典中选择司登得的辞典作为编纂辞典时的参考依据，我们认为主要有以下两个原因。

第一，《辞彙》的编纂受到当时日本汉语教育大环境的影响。在日本，汉语教育最初是指南京官话教育。1873 年，日本政府寻找北京官话翻译人员时发现，大学中根本没有设立北京官话学科，驻华使馆也没有正规的北京官话学习制度，导致整个日本国内很难寻找到一位精通北京官话的学者。为改变这一现状，1876 年，第一批专门学习北京官话的留学生被派往北京，同年九月，东京外国语学校汉语科正式将北京官话作为教学对象，并且引入威妥玛的《语言自迩集》作为教学课本。自此，在日本汉语教育体系正式从南京官话教育转型为北京官话教育。[②] 但是自 1876 年教育体系转型至 1904 年《辞彙》出版，这 28 年日本国内竟无一本以北京官话为基础的辞典出现。反观教科书领域，这段时期内，如《亜细亜言语集支那官话部》《総訳亜细亜言语集》等以《语言自迩集》为基础的教科书层出不穷，因此导致日本的教育界以及市场上极其迫切地需要一本与《语言自迩集》极为贴切的并以北京官话为基础的汉日辞典，用以满足汉语学习者们的需求。石山福治亲自来到中国收集词汇的初衷极有可能就是希望能够填补这段空白。在中国，石山福治发现了司登得的《字彙》，而《字彙》又正好满足了所有要求：（1）北京官话为基础；（2）与《语言自迩集》极为贴近。因而石山福治引入《字彙》也就成为一件水到渠成的事情。

第二，石山福治在他的第一本语法书《支那语独案内》（1905）中除提出了北京官话的重要性外，还指出日本人在学习汉语过程中的最大优势在于在记忆词汇方面相较西洋人来说更得法，并且认为如将同一类词汇聚集在一起，采取类推的方式进行记忆的话效果更好。[③] 而司登得的辞典正是以

---

① 我们选择第三版《字彙》作为参考对象的理由有以下两点：（1）韩一瑾（2017）中记述了石山福治很有可能在编纂辞典时参考了第三版《字彙》；（2）第三版《字彙》与初版《支那语辞彙》的编纂时间最为接近（分别为 1898 年和 1904 年）。韩一瑾：《司登得〈汉英合璧相连字彙〉谱系考》，《国际汉语》2017 年第 4 号，第 115 – 120 页。

② 六角恒广：《中国语教育史の研究》，东方书店，1988，第 119 – 134 页。

③ 石山福治：《支那语独案内》，文求堂，1905，第 1 – 6 页。

此理念进行编纂的。这样使得石山福治在挑选众多汉外辞典时，更加容易接受《字彙》。

事实证明，石山福治选用《字彙》为参考底本是极其正确的，自《辞彙》出版后便极受日本各界人士的欢迎。1906 年，石山福治便出版了第二版《辞彙》,① 与初版相比第二版增加了笔画顺序索引，其余部分内容一致。至 1917 年第七版《辞彙》② 出版发行，该版辞典一共出版了 6 次。随后，石山福治对《辞彙》做进一步修订，更名为《增订改版支那语辞彙》③ 并于 1921 年在东京出版。自该版起，序言部分中正式删除了所有关于司登得以及《字彙》的信息。通过粗略比对，我们发现此次修订与《字彙》也有所关联。

除《辞彙》外，1914 年石山福治还编纂出版了《支那语大辞彙》④，该版辞典的结构与《字彙》完全相同。桥本洋行（2018）经过比对，发现该版辞典所收词条与 1907 年版《字集》的关联最为紧密。不仅如此，《辞彙》所收《字集》之词汇及其释文绝大多数被再次收录到石山福治后期著作《最新支那语大辞典》⑤ 中，并最终延续至《大汉和辞典》⑥。上述几个版本辞典的具体信息见表 13。

表 13　《字彙》《字集》与石山福治所著辞书的结构对比

	1898 年版《字彙》	1907 年版《字集》	《辞彙》	《大辞彙》	《增补大辞彙》
扉页	1 页	1 页	1 页	2 页	2 页
序言	5 页	8 页	5 页	3 页	3 页
正文	740 页	924 页	496 页	924 页	924 页

① 此版为六角恒广（2003）所收录的影印版。六角恒广：《中国语辞典集成》（第一册），不二出版，2003。

② 石山福治：《支那语辞彙》（第七版），文求堂，1917。

③ 石山福治：《增订改版支那语辞彙》，文求堂，1921。

④ 1916 年，石山福治增订并出版《增补支那语大辞彙》，增添了 32 页内容（第 925 – 956 页），但其具体增补情况不详。为行文方便，后文均简略为《大辞彙》。石山福治：《支那语大辞彙》，文求堂，1914；石山福治：《增补支那语大辞彙》，文求堂，1916。

⑤ 《最新支那语大辞典》为石山福治前期作品《新支那大辞典》的缩印版。

⑥ 桥本洋行：《〈大汉和辞典〉所収现代中国语の依拠资料——石山福治の中日辞典とその典拠となった华英辞典—》，《近代语研究》2018 年第 20 期，第 179 – 203 页。

续表

	1898 年版《字彙》	1907 年版《字集》	《辞彙》	《大辞彙》	《增补大辞彙》
补遗	—	—	—	—	32 页
索引	部首 - 笔画	部首 - 笔画	1. 五十音 2. 部首 - 笔画	部首 - 笔画	部首 - 笔画
部首表	8 页	8 页	—	2 页	2 页
笔记	15 页	14 页	—	63 页	63 页
表	—	4 页	—	—	—
正误表	4 页	—	—	—	—
书目	—	2 页	—	—	—

四　结论

《汉英合璧相连字彙》凭借独特的编排方式以及极强的实用性，从当时众多的汉外辞典中脱颖而出，成为一个独立谱系的源头，并深深影响了其后众多的汉外辞典。但是反观现在对于司登得及其《字彙》的研究现状发现，研究明显不够。除了《字彙》本身对周围辞典的影响外，受到其影响的辞典对其他辞典的二次影响依然十分重要。其中比较典型的例子是佐藤留雄所著《支那时文大字彙》（1920）[①]。佐藤留雄与石山福治同为正则支那语学会的成员，他编纂的辞典从内容上看与石山福治所编的《辞彙》不尽相同，辞典结构与编纂理念受石山福治影响的可能性极大。除此之外，《支那语辞彙》与《日华语学辞林》[②]，《支那语大辞彙》与《井上支那语辞典》[③] 以及《支那时文大字彙》均受到较大影响（见图 6）。虽然新的辞典层出不穷，所收词汇也不尽相同，但是从中我们依然能够看到《字彙》的影子。这一现象也间接证明了司登得的辞典，尤其是辞典结构与编纂理念，在当时得到了汉语学习者的广泛认可。接下来我们将继续关注司登得系列辞典，对辞典对东亚的影响进行更深入研究。不仅如此，石山福治所编日

① 佐藤留雄：《支那时文大字彙》，同文社，1920。

② 井上翠：《日华语学辞林》，东亚公司，1906。

③ 井上翠：《井上支那语辞典》，文求堂，1928。

汉辞典与《字彙》的关系，以及该辞典对其他日汉辞典之间联系的探讨也是很有必要的。

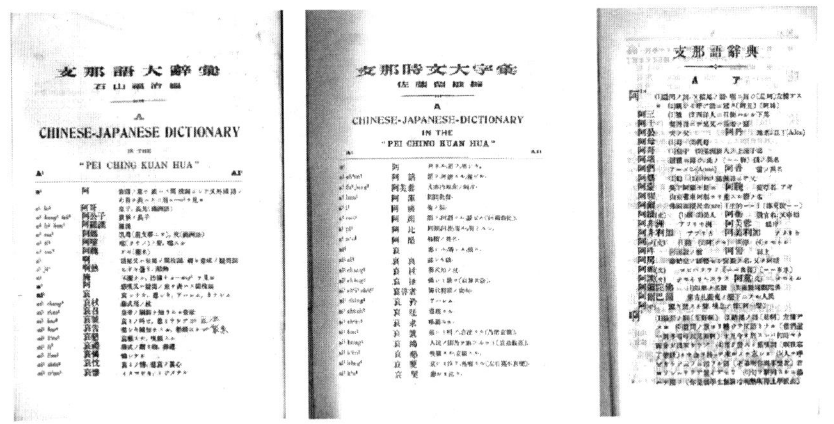
支那語大辭彙
石山福治編
A
CHINESE-JAPANESE DICTIONARY
IN THE
"PEI CHING KUAN HUA"

支那時文大字彙
A
CHINESE-JAPANESE-DICTIONARY
IN THE
"PEI CHING KUAN HUA"

支那語辭典

《支那语大辞彙》，第 1 页　《支那时文大字彙》，第 1 页　《井上支那语辞典》，第 1 页

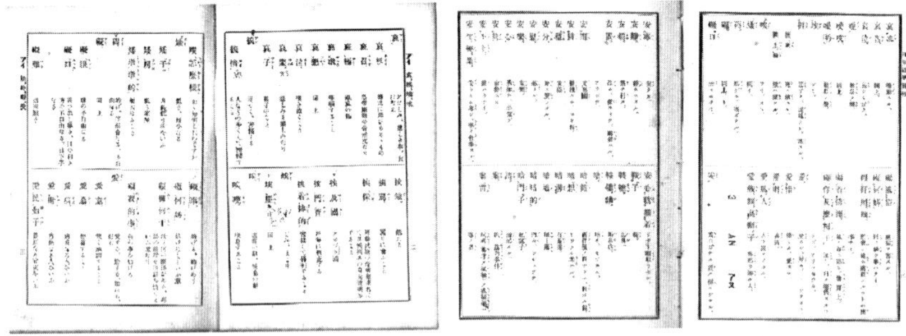

《支那语辞彙》，第 2 页　《日华语学辞林》，第 2 页

图 6　日本近代主要汉日辞书书影

参考文献

井上翠：《井上支那语辞典》，文求堂，1928。

井上翠：《日华语学辞林》，东亚公司，1906。

六角恒广：《中国语辞典集成》（第一册），不二出版，2003。

六角恒广：《中国语教育史の研究》，东方书店，1988。

石山福治：《增补支那语大辞彙》，文求堂，1916。

石山福治：《增订改版支那语辞彙》，文求堂，1921。

石山福治:《支那语辞彙》, 文求堂, 1904。

石山福治:《支那语辞彙》(第七版), 文求堂, 1917 年。

石山福治:《支那语大辞彙》, 文求堂, 1914。

石山福治:《支那语独案内》, 文求堂, 1905。

石山福治:《攷定中原音韻》, 东洋文库, 1925。

佐藤留雄:《支那时文大字彙》, 同文社, 1920。

宫田和子:《英华辞典の総合的研究——19 世纪を中心として》, 白帝社, 2010。

桥本洋行:《〈大汉和辞典〉所収现代中国语の依拠资料—石山福治の中日辞典とその典拠となった华英辞典—》,《近代语研究》2018 年第 20 期。

太田辰夫:《清代の北京语について》,《中国语学》1955 年第 34 期。

太田辰夫:《北京语の文法特点》, 太田辰夫编《中国语文论集语学编》, 汲古书院, 1995。

那须雅之:《G. C. Stentとその著书について——*A Chinese and English Vocabulary in the Pekinese Dialect* を中心として》,《中国语学》1993 年第 240 期。

G. C. Stent, "Chinese Lyrics", *Journal of the China Branch of the Royal Asiatic Society*, No. VII Art. IV, 1873.

G. C. Stent, D. MacGillivray, *Chinese and English Vocabulary in the Pekinese Dialect* 3rd, Shanghai, 1898.

G. C. Stent, K. E. G. Hemeling, *A Dictionary from English to Colloquial Mandarin Chinese*, Shanghai, 1905.

G. C. Stent, *Scraps From My Sabretasche*, W. H. Allen & CO, 1882.

Herbert A. Giles, *A Chinese-English Dictionary*, London, 1892.

Justus Doolittle, *A Vocabulary and Hand-book Chinese Language*, London, 1872.

Robert Morison,《字典》, The Honorable East India Company's Press; Walter Henry Medhurst, *English and Chinese Dictionary*, Shanghai, 1847 - 1848.

S. Wells Williams,《汉英韻府》, Shanghai, 1874, 1896, 1906.

Thomas Francis Wade, *A Progressive Course, Designed to Assist the Student of Colloquial Chinese*, London, 1867.

Thomas Francis Wade, *Hsin Ching Lu: Book of Experiments Being the First of A Series of Contributions to The Study of Chinese*, Hong Kong, 1859.

Journal of the China Branch of the Royal Asiatic Society, Vol. XX, Shanghai, 1885.

韩一瑾:《司登得〈汉英合璧相连字彙〉谱系考》,《国际汉语》2017 年第 4 号。

李晶鑫:《ステント(George Carter Stent)の生涯と著作》,《文化交涉东アジア文化研究科院生论集》2017 年第 7 号。

沈国威：《近代日中语彙交流史》，笠间书院，1994。
沈国威：《近代英华华英辞典解題》，关西大学出版部，2011。

Research on *A Chinese and English Vocabulary in the Pekinese Dialect*

Li Jingxin

Abstract

G. C. Stent, as a guard of the new British Legation, came to China in 1860s and translated many Chinese literature works to English, published three dictionaries. Among these dictionaries, *A Chinese and English Vocabulary in the Pekinese Dialect* of George Carter Stent has its own distinguish feature.

In the first edition of *A Chinese and English Vocabulary in the Pekinese Dialect*, Stent recorded his experience of studying Chinese language by reading Chinese novel and his wishes of translating those novels into English. Finally, he found the difficulties in translating and summarizing his own theory of translation.

However, it had very little research on Stent's dictionaries, and there are still many research left to be solved, for example, the characteristics of the dictionary's structure, the vocabulary of the recording condition, the features of vocabulary and others.

This paper gives an in-depth analysis of characteristics of *A Chinese and English Vocabulary in the Pekinese Dialect.* Based on this, the paper explores the impact of the dictionary on the other dictionaries of Chinese.

Keyword

G. C. Stent *A Chinese and English vocabulary in the pekinese Dialect* Characteristics of Structure Ishiyama Fukuji

日本明治早期汉语教科书《亚细亚言语集》语言意识初探

——与《问答篇》《语言自迩集》比较为基础

大槻美幸[*]

摘　要

《亚细亚言语集》是日本明治时代早期的汉语教科书，日本汉语教育者广部精以英国外交官威妥玛编《语言自迩集》为底本编译。为满足从初级到高级不同学习阶段的日本学习者的需求，《亚细亚言语集》还加入了《六字话》《常言》《欧洲奇话》等作者认为对日本学习者有益的内容。

《亚细亚言语集》在当时的日本很受欢迎，被视为名著，相当长的一段时间内被认为是上乘的北京话教科书之一，有着相当大的影响力。它为什么能够成为日本学习者学习汉语的名著呢？本文推测有两个主要原因：(1) 威妥玛编的《语言自迩集》确定了《亚细亚言语集》的框架；(2)《亚细亚言语集》充分体现了作者广部精为日本学习者着想，编写得适合初级学习者。

本文在此对《亚细亚言语集》与《语言自迩集》以及其原本之一的《问答篇》进行对勘，初步探讨了受到威妥玛语言意识影响的广部精对北京话的语言意识，探讨了日本人眼里的当时北京话的形态。

关键词

亚细亚言语集　日本明治时代　语言自迩集　汉语教科书

* 大槻美幸，北京外国语大学中国语言文学学院博士生。

一 广部精与《亚细亚言语集》的产生

（一）概述

《亚细亚言语集》是日本明治时代早期的汉语口语教科书，日本汉语教育者广部精以英国外交官威妥玛编的《语言自迩集》为底本编译，再加上为满足从初级到高级不同学习阶段的日本学习者的需求，还加入了《六字话》《常言》《欧洲奇话》等广部精认为对日本学习者有益的内容。广部精编写汉语教科书的目的是让日本学习者更好地掌握汉语（北京话），本书序言中提道："此本书多参考英国威妥玛公使编写的《语言自迩集》以及德国翻译官阿氏所著《通俗欧洲述古新篇》等书籍内容而成，为了适合日本人的阅读习惯改变了顺序，在此基础上还添加了《语言自迩集》中没有的内容。"

《亚细亚言语集》在当时的日本很受欢迎，相当长的一段时间内被认为是上乘的汉语教科书之一，有着相当大的影响力。它为什么能够成为对日本学习者具有影响力的汉语教科书呢？本人推测有两个主要原因：（1）威妥玛编的《语言自迩集》确定了《亚细亚言语集》的框架；(2)《亚细亚言语集》充分体现了作者广部精为日本学习者着想，编写得适合初级学习者。

本节阐述了广部精编写《亚细亚言语集》的时代背景以及广部精的生平，浏览明治早期学习汉语的情况，从而分析明治时期日本学习者对汉语的需求。明治初期的日本还沿袭江户时代长崎唐通事学习唐话（南京话）的传统，而在明治 4 年 1871 年明治新政府与清朝政府签订《日清修好条约》，在北京开设驻华公使馆之后发现，在北京的中方官员说的不是南京话，而是北京话，日本意识到当前通用的汉语是北京话，以及学习北京话的重要性。此后，日本陆续开办新的汉语学校，编写新的汉语教科书，编写《亚细亚言语集》的广部精也参与开办汉语学校、编写教科书等活动。本文阐述了时代的变化对日本汉语界带来的影响及广部精的生平。

此外，本文研究了《亚细亚言语集》的结构。作者认为《亚细亚言语集》是按照《语言自迩集》编译改编的，而其结构、内容等并不完全相同，在此研究《亚细亚言语集》的编写目的、内容编排结构以及收录《语言自迩集》内容之外的内容，从而分析广部精编写课本的思想以及对汉语的认识。广部精在《亚细亚言语集》序言中说道："该教科书是为日本人学习汉语更加便利而编写的"。他的思想体现在《亚细亚言语集》中。

此外，本文通过《亚细亚言语集》与《问答篇》《语言自迩集》进行对勘，研究三个课本的儿化词、称谓词的使用。本文列举具体例句分析广部精对课本选择采纳的语言，从而初步探讨广部精对汉语的语言意识。

（二）《亚细亚言语集》编写的时代背景

当时的日本，经过封建政权江户幕府末期的动荡和明治维新（1868）后，新政府急需推进改革，通过引入欧美各种制度推行日本国内的体制改革，谋求将国家带入近代化阶段。1871 年（明治 4 年），日本与清政府缔结《日清修好条约》，两国正式建外，考虑到以后与中国之间的往来增多，外务省以培养翻译为目的开设汉语学校"汉语学所"。东京外国语学校在 1873 年成立，开始讲授汉语，但这一时期教授的汉语都是南京官话。1874 年日本派遣首任驻华公使到北京，发现北京的中国官员说的都是北京官话，于是日本公使要求外务省派遣会北京官话的翻译，但当时日本学习的都是南京官话，只好从中挑选几个年轻的日本人派到北京学习，其中有后来任外务大臣秘书官的中田敬义（なかた たかのり）。1876 年（明治 9 年）来到北京的中田敬义等人发现中国官员确实是说北京官话，但几乎没有可以学习的教材，仅有英国公使威妥玛编写的昂贵的《语言自迩集》，于是他们抄写《语言自迩集》，把此手抄本作为课本使用，同时雇用中国老师，跟着中国老师学习北京话。中田敬义跟着满洲旗人英绍古学习北京话。

在日本国内，官方开设的东京外国语学校开始教授北京话，还从北京请来中国教师专门教授。民间组织的汉语教育机构也陆续诞生。其中开办"日清社"的广部精得到开设私塾"同人社"的中村正直赠送的威妥玛的《语言自迩集》，当时在没有其他适合日本人学习汉语的教材的情况下，广部精决定编写以《语言自迩集》为基础的北京官话教材。

（三）广部精本人

日本明治时期汉语教育家、《亚细亚言语集》编译者广部精（廣部 精/ひろべ くわし，1854－1909）出生于日本上总国（かずさのくに：现千叶县)，他父亲是上总国请西藩（じょうざいはん）的藩士，广部精从小在私塾学习汉学，受到良好的教育。

广部精出生的那年，在美国政府强迫下，日本江户幕府不得不放弃闭关锁国方针，与美国签订了开放港口的条约，从此开始江户幕府末期的动乱，为明治这一新时代打开门窗。广部精身在这样巨变的社会中，逐渐认识到国家需要开放，日本应与清朝等亚洲国家、地区携手起来反抗英美的压迫，挽回衰运，共同对付强国，他决心学习清朝的语言，将来开办汉语学校，培养致力于中日友好发展的人才。

他首先学习的汉语是南京官话，他的第一任汉语老师是周幼梅（苏州人)。之后，他知道当前的汉语是北京官话，于是跟着在东京外国语学校教北京话的薛乃良学习北京话，同时编写北京话教材。

1876 年，广部精在日本东京开办汉语学校“日清社”教授汉语，1877 年日本国内发生内乱（西南事变)，日清社无法维持，广部精只好将日清社并入中村正直开办的私塾“同人社”，之后广部精在同人社或汉语会等组织继续从事教学工作，同时着手编译中村正直赠送的以威妥玛《语言自迩集》为基础的北京话教材。

广部精编写《亚细亚言语集》《总译亚细亚言语集》等后，在日本陆军省会计局开始教授汉语，随后在会计局从事财务工作，不再教汉语。

(四)《亚细亚言语集》编写目的

六角恒广在其著作《日本近代汉语名师传》[①] 中提到广部精，广部精当初学习汉语以及教汉语的目标是期望挽回整个亚洲陷入的衰运，期望亚洲人互相增进理解，想要编辑一套涵盖亚洲所有语言的系列教材，所以起了《亚细亚言语集支那语官话部》这一书名，但这个愿望没能实现。尽管如此，《亚细亚言语集》作为一本从初级到高级不同阶段的学习者都可以使用的教科书，在明治时期被广泛使用。

广部精编写汉语教科书的目的是让日本学习者更好地掌握汉语（北京话)，他在其序言中提道：“此本书在英国威妥玛公使编写的《语言自迩集》以及德国翻译官阿氏所著《通俗欧洲述古新篇》等书籍的基础上而著，为

① 六角恒广：《日本近代汉语名师传》，王顺洪编译，北京大学出版社，2002。

了适合日本人的阅读习惯改变了顺序，在此基础上还添加了《语言自迩集》中没有的内容。”可见，他保留了《语言自迩集》的精华之处，还对其进行了适当修改，再添加他自创的内容，以便日本学习者学习。

广部精出版《亚细亚言语集》后，接下来就出版了《总译亚细亚言语集》。《总译亚细亚言语集》是将《亚细亚言语集》中的散语、常言、问答等汉语课文翻译成日语而成书，其体例先是汉语课文，后是日语翻译文本，就其日语翻译文本，广部精力求“尽可能通俗一点”。《总译亚细亚言语集》中没有收录《六字话》《欧洲奇话》的内容。日语翻译版《总译亚细亚言语集》在当时没有足够的汉语教科书的情况下，很受初学者的欢迎。

二　《亚细亚言语集》区别于《语言自迩集》《问答篇》的特点

（一）从体例结构看《亚细亚言语集》与《语言自迩集》的不同

《亚细亚言语集》是广部精以英国外交官威妥玛编《语言自迩集》为底本编写的，《亚细亚言语集》的框架以及课文内容基本遵循《语言自迩集》和广部精认为对日本学习者有益的内容，如《六字话》《常言》《欧洲奇话》等也加入《亚细亚言语集》中。（《亚细亚言语集》的成书体例和出版年份可参见表 1。）

表 1　《亚细亚言语集》的成书体例和出版年份

	出版年份	课本内容
第一卷	1879 年 （明治 12 年 6 月）	卷头有副岛种臣题“善邻”二字，王治本的序和广部精的自序；凡例和五音图 正文为散语 40 章； 上栏有六字话 118 句、欧洲奇话 13 条
第二卷	1880 年 （明治 13 年 2 月）	卷头有龚恩禄的序；续散语 18 章；常言 7 条； 上栏收录欧洲奇话 6 条
第三卷	1880 年 （明治 13 年 3 月）	卷头有中村正直的序；问答 10 章； 上栏收欧洲奇话 4 条

续表

	出版年份	课本内容
第四卷	1880 年 （明治 13 年 5 月）	卷头有刘世安的序；谈论 50 章； 上栏有欧洲奇话 3 条；续常言 1 条
第五卷	1880 年 （明治 13 年 5 月）	续谈论 52 章； 上栏有续常言 9 条
第六卷	1880 年 （明治 13 年 5 月）	例言（由广部精讲解的发音注释）； 平仄篇：总共收录了 420 个音节的相应汉字
第七卷	1880 年 （明治 13 年 8 月）	言语例略 15 段； 上栏有续常言 11 条

《亚细亚言语集》参考的《语言自迩集》是英国外交官威妥玛经过几十年完成的汉语课本的集大成，威妥玛编写《语言自迩集》前，先编写成为其雏形的《问答篇》《登瀛篇》，而后细心斟酌修改后才出版《语言自迩集》。本文围绕《亚细亚言语集》语言意识开展研究，它的底本《语言自迩集》以及《语言自迩集》的雏形《问答篇》是《亚细亚言语集》写成的基础。因此，本书梳理了《问答篇》《语言自迩集》《亚细亚言语集》的编排章节结构（见表 2）。

表 2　《问答篇》《语言自迩集》《亚细亚言语集》的编排章节结构

《问答篇》	《语言自迩集》	《亚细亚言语集》		
		照搬《语言自迩集》部分		广部精自创添加部分
×	第一章 发音	×	没收录	
×	第二章 部首	×	没收录	
×	第三章 散语 40 章	○	第一卷 散语 40 章	凡例和五音图； 上栏收录六字话 118 句、欧洲奇话 13 条
×	第五章 续散语 18 章	○	第二卷 续散语 18 章	（续散语后有）常言 7 条； 上栏收录欧洲奇话 6 条
×	第四章 问答 10 章	○	第三卷 问答 10 章	上栏收录欧洲奇话 4 条
问答篇 103 章	第六章 谈论篇 100 章	○	第四卷 谈论 50 章 第五卷 续谈论 52 章	上栏收录欧洲奇话 3 条；续常言 1 条； 续常言 9 条

续表

<table>
<tr><th rowspan="2">《问答篇》</th><th rowspan="2">《语言自迩集》</th><th colspan="3">《亚细亚言语集》</th></tr>
<tr><th colspan="2">照搬《语言自迩集》部分</th><th>广部精自创添加部分</th></tr>
<tr><td>×</td><td>第七章 练习燕山
平仄篇（声调练习）</td><td>○</td><td>第六卷 平仄篇</td><td>例言（广部精用日语解释汉语发音）</td></tr>
<tr><td>×</td><td>第八章 言语例略</td><td>○</td><td>第七卷 言语例略</td><td>上栏收录续常言 11 条</td></tr>
</table>

注：“×”表示没有收录；“○”表示被收录

由此可见，《亚细亚言语集》基本遵循《语言自迩集》的结构，即《语言自迩集》第三章散语 40 章与《亚细亚言语集》第一卷的散语 40 章一致；《语言自迩集》第五章续散语 18 章与《亚细亚言语集》第二卷的续散语 18 章一致；《语言自迩集》第四章问答 10 章与《亚细亚言语集》第三卷的问答 40 章一致；《语言自迩集》第六章谈论篇 100 章与《亚细亚言语集》第四卷的谈论 50 章以及第五卷续谈论 52 章一致；《语言自迩集》第七章平仄篇与《亚细亚言语集》第六卷的平仄篇相同；《语言自迩集》第八章言语例略与《亚细亚言语集》第七卷的言语例略相同。

但其中，为了使日本学习者更加易于理解，广部精调整了顺序，如《语言自迩集》是以“散语→问答篇→续散语”的顺序开展课文，而《亚细亚言语集》是以“散语→续散语→问答篇”的顺序开展课文。因为这样更适合日本学习者的思维方式，“续”的内容就不需要隔开，直接接着展开“续”的内容，这样更容易理解。

从上述表格可见，广部精为日本学习者添加很多内容，这些都是他认为对日本学习者有益的，如《六字话》《常言》《欧洲奇话》等，但广部精又因考虑增加的内容会影响整体课文的节奏，遂将这些添加的内容在正文的上栏中收录。

日本人同样使用汉字，所以广部精认为对日本学习者不需要的一些内容都删除了，如《语言自迩集》“部首”部分。而对日本学习者很难掌握的就是“语音”，所以广部精在《亚细亚言语集》第六卷中特意设置“例言”环节，用日语解释汉语发音时的一些注意事项。

本文研究的《问答篇》《语言自迩集》《亚细亚言语集》以日本关西大学内田庆市教授所提供的版本为准，《语言自迩集》《亚细亚言语集》的封面见图 1 及图 2。

語言自邇集

YÜ-YEN TZŬ-ERH CHI,

A PROGRESSIVE COURSE

DESIGNED TO ASSIST THE STUDENT OF

COLLOQUIAL CHINESE,

AS SPOKEN IN THE CAPITAL AND THE METROPOLITAN DEPARTMENT;

In Eight Parts;

WITH KEY, SYLLABARY, AND WRITING EXERCISES;

BY

THOMAS FRANCIS WADE, C.B.

SECRETARY TO H.B.M. LEGATION AT PEKING.

LONDON:

TRÜBNER & CO., 60, PATERNOSTER ROW.

MDCCCLXVII.

图1 《语言自迩集》第一版封面①

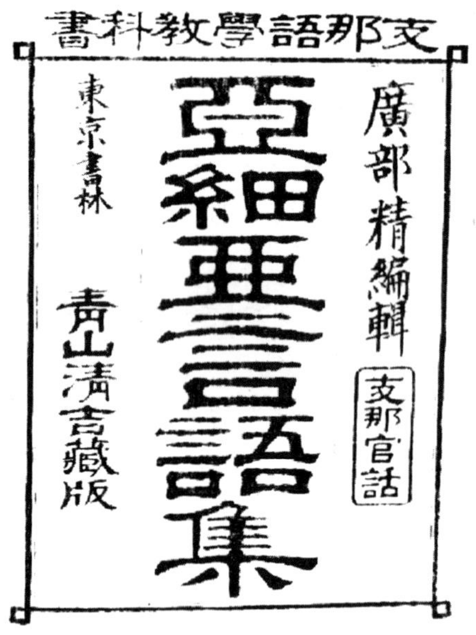

图2 《亚细亚言语集》封面

① 内田庆市、冰野步、宋桔，《語言自邇集の研究（文化交渉と言語接触研究・資料叢刊4)》，関西大学アジア文化センター，好文出版，2015。

（二）《亚细亚言语集》对日本传统教科书的传承与改变

广部精在《亚细亚言语集》中采用了对日本学习者有益的内容，如《六字话》《常言》《欧洲奇话》等。

早在日本江户时代，为应对以日本长崎为中心开展的中日贸易培养了汉语翻译人才，江户时代中期汉学家、汉语教育家冈岛冠山编写的《唐话纂要》① 等汉语教本中已使用日语片假名标注汉语读音这一方式来教授汉语。之所以广部精在《亚细亚言语集》中沿用这些日本传统学习方式是为了使日本学习者更加容易适应汉语学习环境。

但广部精采用的不是简单的传承，而是适当加以改变，试图使《亚细亚言语集》更加完善。广部精采取的对日本传统教科书的传承和改变可分为以下几个方面。

1. 注音方式

《亚细亚言语集》是汉语课本，全篇用汉语写成，只有第一、二、三卷，即《散语 40 章》《续散语 18 章》《问答 10 章》的开头有注音解释，是用日本片假名标注汉语读音。用日语片假名标注汉语读音这一方法是沿用日本人学习语言的传统学习方法之一，冈岛冠山编写的《唐话纂要》等汉语教材中已采用日语片假名来标注汉语读音这一方式。

广部精不仅用日语片假名标注汉语读音，还在汉语声调的标注方面下一番功夫，用圆点“。”来标注声调。具体来说，左下角的圆点表示阴平——第一声；左上角的圆点表示阳平——第二声；右上角的圆点表示上声——第三声；右下角的圆点表示去声——第四声。

以《散语 第一章》为例看一下具体的表示方式：

两°ﾘﾔﾝ；。三ｻﾝ；第。ﾃｨ；四。ｽｳ；五°ｳｰ；六。ﾘｳ；。七 ﾁｰ；九ﾁｭｰ；
几°ﾁｰ；。千ﾁｪﾝ；数。ｽｳ；百°ﾊﾟｰｲ；万。ｳｱﾝ；°零ﾘﾝ；°来ﾗｲ；
。多ﾄﾞｦ；少°ｼｬｦ；有°ﾕｰ；好ﾊｰｦ；。些 ｼｪｰ；个。ｺｦ

---

① 冈岛冠山（おかじま かんざん：1674－1728），日本江户时代（1603－1868）中期的汉学家，出生于长崎，精通唐话（汉语），当任唐通事，为推广唐话编写《唐话纂要》《唐译便览》《唐话便用》《唐音雅俗语类》等汉语教科书，同时研究《水浒传》等中国白话文学，翻译成日语推出《通俗忠义水浒传》等。

2.《六字话》+日语翻译

广部精以英国外交官威妥玛所编《语言自迩集》为底本编写《亚细亚言语集》，其结构、课文内容基本沿用《语言自迩集》的内容，但广部精为不同学习阶段的日本学习者着想，添加了《语言自迩集》中没有的《六字话》等广部精自创的课文。《六字话》的形式是以六个字构成的短句表达出简单的平时可以经常使用的会话内容，再配上日语翻译，为初学者的日常交际提供便利。

表 3 为《散语 第一章》上栏中收录的《六字话》具体表示方式。

表 3 《六字话》具体表示方式

	《六字话》	广部精的日语翻译
1	那书铺篠山来	アノホンヤノ、シノヤマガ、マイリマシタ
2	他说要见大人	カレノイフニハ、ダンナニ、ヲメニカカリタイ
3	你让他进来吧	ナンヂハカレヲコチラエ、トーセロ
4	老爷让你进来	ダンナガ、ヲマエヲ、トヲセロー、モーシマス
5	今儿天气不好	コンニチハ、ワルイヲテンキデ、ゴザヒマス
6	是，下得雪不少	サヨー、ユキガ、ダイブ、フリマシタ
7	你有洋书没有	ヲマエハ、ヤウシヨガ、アリマスカ、アリマセンカ
8	要什么洋书呢	ナンオヤウシヨガ、ゴヨウデ、ゴザヒマスカ
9	我是要英国书	ワタクシハ、インギリスノシヨガ、イリヨウデゴザル
10	英国书都没有	インクリスノシヨハ、イツコーゴザヒマセヌ
11	这个书好不好	コノホンハ、イカガデ、ゴザヒマス

对于《六字话》的日语翻译文本，广部精在其序言中提道："以日语的俗语翻译其意。"《六字话》中表达的日语翻译反映当时（明治时期）男性说话的语气，广部精意识到《六字话》是对话，所以翻译文本也采用口语的通俗语气。

《六字话》这种以六个字构成的短句来学习语言是日本传统的学习方法之一，冈岛冠山《唐话纂要》等汉语教本中已有《二字话》《三字话》《四字话》《五字话》《六字话》等从词汇、短语到短句的分段递进学习方法，由此可见，《六字话》等形式的学习方法是日本在学习语言时普遍被采纳的方法之一。但《唐话纂要》和《亚细亚言语集》《六字话》的内容不同，广部精采用的是其形式。

3.《常言》

《常言》也是广部精自创的《亚细亚言语集》独有的课文。《常言》收录在第二卷《续散语 18 章》之后的正文栏目中，《续常言》收录在正文课文的上栏。为什么特意收录《常言》，广部精在《常言第七》结束后，也就是在《亚细亚言语录》第二卷的最后提道：“常言七条，皆系将余所记俗谚信笔书之，自知杂乱无章，不免贻笑博雅，故不敢记初见字，以加四声圈点与出气点与汉音也。蓋使读者自取其可取，而非欲使人尽学习之也。或曰：‘然则何刻出世?’余曰：‘饥者不择食，寒者不择衣。’余之欲广汉话于世，殆如饥寒之于衣食，亦不暇论其糟糠与襤褸也，切望博雅君子订误正谬，以为锦绣，以为膏粱，则幸甚矣。”

在此以《常言第一》为例看一下具体的课文内容。

無風三尺土，下雨一街坭。東怕餓，西怕丟，鄉下怕累著。人要實，火要虛。天上下雨，地下滑。三人抬不過理字去。三人出外小的兒苦。水中撈月。

比上不足，比下有餘。行路防跌，喫飯防噎。大攔指小攔。狼叼餧狗。狗拿耗子，銕打房樑磨綉針。蔴稭棍兒打狼。不怕慢，只怕站。欲要生富貴，須下死工夫。千日蔓來，一日賣。貪多嚼不爛。把官路當人情。耳傍風。借花供佛。慢工出巧。多一智多一憂，多一物多一愁。家醜不可外揚。小題大作。圖錢買老牛。不経一事，不長一智。無窮歲月增中減，有益詩書苦後甜。蝦蟆在天井裡，想天鵝肉喫。文不成，武不就。窮文富武。酸文加醋。武不善坐兒的。文文縐縐的。文武一齊來。寧可以信其有，不可以信其無。中看不中喫。太平之年文官好，離亂時節武將高。好事不如無。羊群丟了羊群。羊毛出在羊身上。

羊群裡跑出了駱駝來。不信羊上樹。好事不出門，惡事傳千里。鼠肚雞腸。狐朋狗友。走三家不如坐一家。狼心狗肺。猫咬尿泡。惡醉強酒。人心總在人心上。惡死亡樂不仁。賣蓆睡土炕，賣扇兒手搧凉。指桑說槐。

4.《欧洲奇话》

广部精在《亚细亚言语集》序言中提道："此本书多采用英国威妥玛公使编写的《语言自迩集》以及德国翻译官阿氏所著《通俗欧洲述古新篇》等书籍内容而成书，为了考虑适合日本人的阅读习惯而改变了顺序，在此基础上还添加了《语言自迩集》中没有的内容。"可见，《亚细亚言语集》收录《欧洲奇话》的构思来自《通俗欧洲述古新篇》。与生活有关的读物收录为教材内容这一方式是日本江户时代的唐通事教材。

《亚细亚言语集》收录的《欧洲奇话》共有 24 条，内容是寓言故事，用比喻性、讽刺性强的故事来描述意味深长的道理。题材是狗、鸟、羊、狮子等动物，或父亲和儿子，或波斯、小亚细亚等古中东国家的国王和王子等，收录的内容从篇幅很短的故事开始，后面收录了篇幅较长的故事，可以满足不同阶段的学习者的阅读需求。在此以《欧洲奇话》第一条、第十六条为例，看一下其故事。

第一条：动物（狗）的故事

我有个笑话，说给你听，当日有一条狗，叼着一块肉过河瞧见河里的影儿，它想错了当是真的去抢那块肉，就把嘴里的肉松了，可见不但没得着那个，倒先把这个丢了，这是劝人不要贪心的意思。

第十六条：罗马国的故事

罗马国有位将军和士子相好，常常来往。这天，士子到将军的家里找他去，进门儿就问他的丫头："你主人在家没有？"那丫头进去一会儿，又出来告诉说："没在家。"那士子明知他在家，故意不见，也就回去了。有天那将军又去找士子，到了门口，就拍着门儿问："老爷在家没有？"那士子在里头答应说："老爷没在家。"那将军是听惯他的语声儿的，就说："明明是你说话的声儿，怎么说没在家？"那士子说："上回我上你家去，我还信你家的丫头的话，怎么今儿你就不信我的话呢？"

三 《亚细亚言语集》的语言意识

（一）广部精对北京官话的选择

广部精编写《亚细亚言语集》时，他对"汉语""北京官话"是如何认识的？广部精首先学习的是南京官话（江淮官话），后来跟着从北京来的薛乃良学习北京话。由此猜测，广部精在编写《亚细亚言语集》时，应该意识到其底本威妥玛《语言自迩集》的北京官话和他之前学过的南京官话的差异。

广部精在其"凡例"中，这么介绍《亚细亚言语集》的课文内容："一、支那言语分为四部，第一官话，第二南边话，第三满洲话，第四岭南话。一、官话部分十类：曰六字话；曰散语；曰欧洲奇话；曰续散语；曰常言；曰问答；曰谈论篇；曰平仄编；曰言语例略；曰东西事情。"他还在《亚细亚言语集》第六卷《例言》解释汉语语音时说："京话的四声虽然和寻常的四声有所不同，但是其发声的技巧都是大同小异……"可见，广部精认识到北京官话和南京官话的差异，有意编写《亚细亚言语集》，使其成为北京官话的教科书。

六角恒广在其著作《中国语学习余闻》提到，在当时的日本被认为官话的是北京官话。六角还引用当时在日本文部省从事编辑词典工作的大槻文彦所著的《支那文典 例言》解释说："官话是支那官府使用的通用语言，是其国当前的普通话，以其语音为正音，除了浙江、福建、广东、广西、云南等省之外，支那北部被广泛使用……我国人应该学习此语言。"①

广部精第一次看到《语言自迩集》时，注意到课本是从容易到难的层层递进的结构和学习方式，以及北京话特点"儿化"词及在说话开头经常使用的称谓词。因此本文将对儿化词、称谓词等方面进行对比研究。对比的版本是广部精编写《亚细亚言语集》时作为底本参考的《语言自迩集》和《语言自迩集 谈论篇》的底本《问答篇》。有关威妥玛编写的汉语课本《问答篇》《语言自迩集 谈论篇》的成书过程，内田庆市（2015）在其论文中详细地提到②，在此不多提及。

（二）从儿化词看三个课本

1.《问答篇》《语言自迩集》《亚细亚言语集》都相同的儿化词

有很多儿化词，尤其是名词在《问答篇》《语言自迩集》《亚细亚言

① 六角恒广：《中国语学习余闻》，同学社，1998，第215页。

② 内田庆市，『語言自邇集』の成立と伝播一解題に代えて一，《語言自邇集の研究》（文化交渉と言語接触研究・資料叢刊4）（内田庆市、冰野步、宋桔），関西大学アジア文化センター、好文出版，2015，第9－11页。

语集》都相同的（见表4）。

表4 《问答篇》《语言自迩集》《亚细亚言语集》中相同的儿化词

	问答篇	语言自迩集	亚细亚言语集
表时间	明儿	明儿	明儿
	前儿	前儿	前儿
	一会儿	一会儿	一会儿
表量	一点儿	一点儿	一点儿
指示代词	这儿	这儿	这儿
表场所	地方儿	地方儿	地方儿
名词 + 儿	花儿	花儿	花儿
	作伴儿	作伴儿	作伴儿
	媳妇儿	媳妇儿	媳妇儿
动词 + 儿	坐坐儿罢/坐了一坐儿	坐坐儿罢/坐了一坐儿	坐坐儿罢/坐了一坐儿
副词 + 儿	顺便儿	顺便儿	顺便儿
	明明儿	明明儿	明明儿

2.《问答篇》《语言自迩集》《亚细亚言语集》都不一样的儿化词

三个课本都采取不一样的儿化词的情况也存在，但并不多，而且不仅是单纯的词汇取舍的问题，整句结构都不一样（见表5）。

表5 《问答篇》《语言自迩集》《亚细亚言语集》儿化词区别（一）

章节	问答篇	语言自迩集	亚细亚言语集
62；61；62	忽然因为一半句话上，记了过去，	就是因为一半句话上，也不犯记在心里，	抽冷儿的，因为一半句话上记住了，
74；73；74	大哥，你纳在这儿住着么？	兄台，你纳在这左近住么？	大哥，你纳在这住着么？

3.《问答篇》和《亚细亚言语集》相同，而《语言自迩集》不同的儿化词

广部精在《亚细亚言语集》序言中提到，《亚细亚言语集》是参照《语言自迩集》编写的，但对上述三个课本进行仔细对比就会发现，《亚细亚言语集》的课文内容很多地方与《语言自迩集》不同，更接近于《问答篇》。

这一点，内田（2015）也指出过。[①]

在此提出的儿化词是《问答篇》和《亚细亚言语集》相同，而《语言自迩集》不同，而且不是选择不同的儿化词，而是整个句子被修改，甚至不采用儿化词（见表6）。

表6　《问答篇》《语言自迩集》《亚细亚言语集》儿化词区别（二）

章节	问答篇	语言自迩集	亚细亚言语集
1；1；1	至今还摸不着一点儿头绪儿呢	至今还摸不着一点儿头绪呢	至今还摸不着一点儿头绪儿呢
	二则我还有求哥哥的去处儿呢	二则还有奉求的事情呢	二则我还有求哥哥的去处儿呢
3；3；3	料想也就差不远儿咯	料想也就差不多儿咯	料想也就差不远儿咯
20；20；20	除了学马步箭的空儿	除了学马步箭的工夫	除了学马步箭的空儿
62；61；62	我所遇见的都是这个样儿的朋友，	我所遇见的朋友都是这个薄情的，	我所遇见的都是这个样儿的朋友

4.《问答篇》和《语言自迩集》相同，而《亚细亚言语集》不同的儿化词

有的儿化词，在《问答篇》《语言自迩集》都使用，而在《亚细亚言语集》中不使用（见表7）。

表7　《问答篇》《语言自迩集》《亚细亚言语集》儿化词区别（三）

章节	问答篇	语言自迩集	亚细亚自语集
62；61；62	预备点东西儿	预备点东西儿	预备东西呢

5.《语言自迩集》和《亚细亚言语集》相同，而《问答篇》不同的儿化词

有的儿化词，在《语言自迩集》《亚细亚言语集》使用的是一样的词汇，而在《问答篇》使用的不一样（见表8）。

表8　《问答篇》《语言自迩集》《亚细亚言语集》儿化词区别（四）

章节	问答篇	语言自迩集	亚细亚言语集
1；1；1	满州话是咱们头等头儿的要紧的事情，	满州话是咱们头一宗儿要紧的事情，	满洲话是咱们头一宗儿最要紧的事情，

① 内田庆市，『語言自邇集』の成立と伝播—解題に代えて—，《語言自邇集の研究》（文化交渉と言語接触研究・資料叢刊4）（内田庆市、冰野步、宋桔），関西大学アジア文化センター、好文出版，2015，pp. 16－20。

（3）从称谓词看三个课本

作为称谓词，广部精大部分采用《问答篇》的“哥哥”“大哥”，而《语言自迩集》采用的“兄台”“老兄”“弟台”“老弟”几乎不采纳。内田（2015）指出，“阿哥”“大哥”“哥哥”等具有满语特征的称谓词，《语言自迩集》基本不使用（见表 9）。①

表 9 《问答篇》《语言自迩集》《亚细亚言语集》称谓词

章节	问答篇	语言自迩集	亚细亚言语集
5、10、23、33、37、38、39、42、45、46	大哥	兄台	大哥
9、12、20、31、50、51	哥哥	兄台	哥哥
36	哥哥们	兄台们	哥哥们
27、37	哥哥	家兄	哥哥
3、4、5、19	阿哥	老弟	阿哥
3	阿哥	弟台	阿哥
20	那个阿哥	那个人	那个阿哥
32	阿哥	老弟	您纳

（四）“哪”和“那”

在《问答篇》《语言自迩集》《亚细亚言语集》中都使用“那”表达指示代词和疑问代词的语义。“哪”作为语气词使用（见表 10）。

表 10 《问答篇》《语言自迩集》《亚细亚言语集》指示代词

章节	问答篇	语言自迩集	亚细亚言语集
1；1；1	永远不敢忘了恩哪	我再不敢忘了恩哪	永远不敢忘了恩哪
7；7；7	你是懂得汉书的人哪	你是明白汉字的人哪	你是懂得汉书的人哪

《问答篇》《语言自迩集》《亚细亚言语集》都用“那”表示指示代词疑问代词，但广部精已认识到表示“那”有两种不同的用法，因此他用圆

① 内田庆市，『語言自邇集』の成立と伝播—解題に代えて—，《語言自邇集の研究》（文化交渉と言語接触研究・資料叢刊 4）（内田庆市、冰野步、宋桔），関西大学アジア文化センター、好文出版，2015，p. 18。

点标注声调，区分指示代词或疑问代词的语义，即如表示指示代词语义时，采用圆点“那。”来标注，表示疑问代词时，用“那°”来标注其声调。如《亚细亚言语集》的《续谈论二十四章》中有：“你纳往那°儿去来着，我往那边儿”这一对话，第一个“那”表示“哪儿”语义，所以用“°”标注，提醒念三声；第二个“那”是指示代词，通常念四声，所以没有特别标注。

（五）“是”与“最”

《问答篇》《语言自迩集 谈论篇》《亚细亚言语集 谈论》第一章中有如下例句。

问答篇：满州话是咱们头等头儿的要紧的事情，就像汉人们各处儿各处儿的乡谈是一个样儿。

语言自迩集：满州话是咱们头一宗儿要紧的事情，就像汉人们各处儿各处儿的乡谈一个样儿。

亚细亚言语集：满洲话是咱们头一宗儿最要紧的事情，就像汉人们各处儿各处儿的乡谈是一个样儿。

“是”是日本人学习汉语的难点之一，日语中有主格标记的“は（wa）”，日本人容易认为“是”等于“は（wa）”。《亚细亚言语集》在此使用“是”和“最”，是因为这样容易被日本学习者理解。

四　结论

本文总结了广部精编写《亚细亚言语集》的时代背景以及广部精的生平，介绍了明治早期学习汉语的情况，阐述了广部精编写《亚细亚言语集》的目的，《亚细亚言语集》的成书结构，分析了《亚细亚言语集》对日本传统教科书的传承和改变。《亚细亚言语集》在采用英国人编写的《语言自迩集》的先进语言体系的同时，还传承了日本传统教科书中适合日本学习者学习习惯的方式，即注音方式，此外还收录了《六字话》《欧洲奇话》等《语言自迩集》中没有的作者广部精自创的内容。从此可以看到，广部精为日本学习者着想考虑编排课文内容，从初级到高级不同阶段的学习者都可以使用《亚细亚言语集》来学习。广部精的编写宗旨是使日本学习者更好地掌握汉语（北京话），本着此原则他基本保留了《语言自迩集》的优秀之处，即从易到难层层递进的学习方式，还增加了他认为需要的内容，从而试图满足从初级到高级不同学习阶段学习者的需求。

广部精参考了这种教科书的编排方式、教学理念，更注重的是语言本身。通过《亚细亚言语集》与《问答篇》《语言自迩集》的对勘发现，广部精在编写《亚细亚言语集》过程中为了使日本学习者更加容易理解，采取了在语言方面有所取舍的方式，如“是”“最”等的添加。《亚细亚言语集 谈论篇》中有句对话：“满洲话是咱们头一宗儿最要紧的事情，就像汉人们各处儿各处儿的乡谈是一个样儿，不会使得么?”，而在《问答篇》《语言自迩集》相同章节的对话中没有看到“最”“是”的使用，由此可猜测是否为广部精为日本人学习者考虑添加的受母语迁移的语言成分。本文只看儿化词“哪”和“那”、“是”等，但这些选择的根据是什么？广部精是在日本学习北京话的，虽然他背后有从北京来的旗人老师，但他“在日本学习的汉语”这一因素是否对《亚细亚言语集》的编写有影响？对于这些问题，今后还需要进一步的研究。

参考文献

六角恒广：《中国语学习余闻》，同学社，1998。

六角恒广：《日本中国语教学书志》，王顺洪译，北京语言文化大学出版社，2000。

六角恒广：《日本近代汉语名师传》，王顺洪编译，北京大学出版社，2002。

鲁宝元、吴丽君编《日本汉语教育史研究——江户时代唐话五种》，外语教学与研究出版社，2009。

内田庆市、冰野步、宋桔：《語言自邇集の研究（文化交渉と言語接触研究・資料叢刊4)》，関西大学アジア文化センター、好文出版，2015。

奥村佳代子：《唐話の伝播と変化：岡島冠山の果たした役割》，《東アジア文化交渉研究》*Journal of East Asian cul tural interaction studies*，2008。

冰野善宽：《19~20世紀の中国語教育史を研究するための資料—鱒澤彰夫氏寄贈図書の目録編纂作業とその特徴，《関西大学東西学術研究書紀要》，2016。

内田庆市：《『語言自邇集』の成立と伝播—解題に代えて—》，《語言自邇集の研究》(文化交渉と言語接触研究・資料叢刊4)（内田庆市、冰野步、宋桔），関西大学アジア文化センター、好文出版，2015。

藤田益子，《トーマス・ウエードと漢語会話テキスト—『語言自邇集』の言語観一（二）》，《新潟大学国際センター紀要》，2008。

《亚细亚言语集》：明治13年（1880）8月出版，明治25年5月再刻出版。

《语言自迩集》（第一版），1867。

《问答篇》，哈佛大学燕京图书馆藏，1860。

A Preliminary Study on the Language Consciousness of the Early Meiji Chinese Textbook *Asia Gengo-shu*

Based on Comparing with *Wenda Pian* and *Yü-yen Tzŭ-erh Chi*

Miyuki Otsuki

Asia Gengo-shu is a Chinese textbook in the early Meiji Age in Japan, Japanese Chinese educator Kuwashi Hirobe compiled from *Yü-yen Tzŭ-erh Chi* by British diplomat Thomas Francis Wade, in order to meet the needs of Japanese learners at different stages of learning from primary to advanced level, and also added contents such as *Six-character Talks*, *Common Sayings* and *European Tales*, which he thought were beneficial to Japanese learners.

Asia Gengo-shu was very popular in Japan at that time and was regarded as a masterpiece. It was identified as one of the excellent textbooks of Beijing dialect for quite a long time and it has maintained a considerable influence. Why can it become a masterpiece for Japanese learners to learn Chinese? I speculated that there are two main reasons: first, the excellence of *Yü-yen Tzŭ-erh Chi* compiled by Wade determines the framework of *Asia Gengo-shu*; second, the carefulness of the author's attention to Japanese learners is fully reflected in *Asia Gengo-shu*.

This papler is based on a preliminary study of the language awareness of Beijing dialect in *Asia Gengo-shu*, *Yü-yen Tzŭ-erh Chi* and one of its original works *Wenda pian*, and also focuses on exploring the language awareness of Beijing dialect in the perspective of Japanese people at that time.

Keywords

Asia Gengo-shu Meiji Age in Japan *Yü-yen Tzŭ-erh Chi* Chinese Textbook

赛兆祥《官话口语》的价值和局限

——兼论19世纪西人汉语语法书的互文性*

郭利霞**

摘　要

《官话口语》是19世纪末一部英文写成的汉语语法书，通过与同期其他语法著作进行比较，可以清楚地看出此书跟之前几部西人语法书有明显的互文性，同时也有赛兆祥对汉语语法的独立思考和认识。《官话口语》虽以北方官话为基础，但也记录了不少南方官话的现象。19世纪还有大量跟《官话口语》一样尚未进入学界视野的语法著作，挖掘、整理和研究仍有很大空间。

关键词

赛兆祥　《官话口语》　互文性

一　赛兆祥本人

赛兆祥（Absalom Sydenstricker，1852－1931）生于美国弗吉尼亚州，是美南长老会〔American Presbyterians（South）〕江北教区（North Kiangsu Mission）的开创性人物，1880年偕妻子到杭州布道兴学，1883年奉派至江苏镇

* 本研究受2016年度国家社科基金重点项目“十九世纪来华传教士记录的官话方言及其历时演变研究”（16AYY002）暨南开大学2019年度科学学位精品课程建设项目（91922176）资助。曾在“语言互动史研究——近代东西语言接触研究学术会议2018”（北京外国语大学，2018年12月22日）上宣读，有幸得到内田庆市、李无未等先生的指点，谨致谢忱。

** 郭利霞，南开大学汉语言文化学院副教授。

江立会设堂，1887 年抵达江苏清江浦（今淮阴），1891 年回美度假，1892 年赛兆祥夫妇与初生女儿赛珍珠（后成为美国第一位获得诺贝尔文学家的女性作家）返华布道，驻清江浦。此后又陆续开辟了宿迁（1893）、徐州（1895）、淮安（今淮安市楚州区，1904）等传教站，还曾到江苏泰州布道（1902）。

赛兆祥在华传教五十载，撰述主要集中在汉语方言及传教士汉语学习等方面，1887 年至 1888 年有多篇关于汉语方言、区域语言等文章在《教务杂志》（*The Chinese Recorder and Missionary Journal*）上刊出，如《扬子江与大运河地区方言》（“The Dialect of The River and Grand Canal”，1887）《中国北方与中部口语的区别》（“Variations in the Spoken Language of Northern and Central China”，1887）《官话的罗马字化》（“Romanizing the Official Dialect”，1888）《官话》（“The Official Dialect”，1888）《南方官话》（“Southern Mandarin”，1887）等。赛兆祥提倡传教士学习和掌握复杂的汉语时，以小说等文学文本作为学习材料。1908 年，他在《传教士汉语学习中的几个原则》（“Some principles which should guide the missionary in his study of the Chinese language”，*The Chinese Recorder and Missionary Journal*，1908）中提出，传教士在能阅读普通圣经书籍的同时，应该还要能阅读由中国人写的本土官话和白话书籍（colloquial books），而汉语白话大多数都是小说（沈梅丽，2017）。

17 世纪至 19 世纪欧美汉语语法专著经历了两个阶段。17、18 世纪缓慢前行，19 世纪快速发展，特别是鸦片战争后 60 年，欧美汉语语法专著呈现“井喷”式发展，三分之二的专著都出现在这个时期（叶锋，2014）。赛兆祥的《官话口语句子结构和习语》（*An Exposition Of The Construction And Idioms Of Chinese Sentences: As Found In Colloquial Mandarin. For The Use Of Learners Of The Language*）（简称《官话口语》）出版于 1889 年，正处于叶锋所说的“井喷”期。目前尚未见到对此书的系统研究，只有岳岚（2015）提到了赛兆祥对量词的三分法。笔者手头的版本是斯坦福大学图书馆的影印本，缺失第 15 章，即第 62、63 页。

二 《官话口语》的内容

《官话口语》分前言、正文和附录三部分，后两部分共 88 页，正文共

19 章，第一章讲的是构词法，第二章是词语的分类，把词分成死字、活字、虚字，第三章到第十九章分成死字、活字、虚字三部分。两个附录分别是量词表和汉语音节表。各章内容如表 1 所示。

表 1 《官话口语》的内容

	章节	内容
	第一章 词语分析及构造	讨论了单纯词（单音节、多音节词，如“咳嗽、阿嚏、哈哈、嘭嘭”）；合成词以及构词法，包括派生法（“子”尾、“儿”尾、“头、处、家”尾）；重叠法（哥哥、妹妹）；复合法（并列式：朋友、埋葬、轻重；偏正式：草料）。
	第二章 词类	“死字”在句中用法和位置均固定，如体词、名词和代词等；“活字”即谓语，位置和用法均不固定；“虚字”本身无实义，包括连词、感叹词、句尾助词等。
第一部分 带修饰语的『死字』或『体词』	第三章 体词	包括名词和代词，名词除加“们”外另有四种复数表达法。 代词分人称代词、反身代词、疑问代词、关系代词，疑问代词五种不定用法。
	第四章 同位语	描写性的同位语（Descriptive Apposition），如：中国皇帝光绪； 代词性同位语（Pronominal Apposition），如：我们两个； 数量同位语（Quantitative Apposition），如：他们众人都来了。
	第五章 名词的定语	定语有五种：数词（numerals）、量词（classifiers）、所有格（possessives）、指示词（demonstratives）、形容词（adjectives）； 数词分为基数词（cardinal numbers）、序数词（ordinals）、分数（fractionals）、约数（approximate numbers）； 量词（classifiers）分为描写性量词（descriptive classifiers），如用于长而柔软的事物的“条”；集合量词（collective classifiers），如“群、班”；量度量词（quantitative classifiers），如“斤、两、斗”； 形容词分为数量短语（quantitative terms）、性质形容词、动词性形容词（verbal adjective）。
第二部分 活词：带有修饰词的谓词	第六章 谓语概说	谓词可分为未完成式（incomplete form）和完成式（complete form），前者如：这个东西好。我们做买卖。后者如：我们明日去了。他再不来了。 时态和语气：时态分现在时、过去时、完成时、将来时。每种均分肯定、否定、特指三式，特指式即谓语前有时间副词，如现在时中的“现在、如今、现今、现时、这会儿、今天、此刻、正”；过去时中的“从前、以先、以前、头前、先前、早日、头里、曾、前天、去年、前几天、昨日”；完成时中的“已经、曾经”等，将来时中的“将来、往下，此后；过晌、明天、四年后”等。

续表

	章节	内容
第二部分　活词：带有修饰词的谓词	第六章 谓语概说	语气分为陈述（indicative）、可能（potential）、祈使（imperative）、不定式（infinitive）四种。
	第七章 谓词的分类	谓语有三类：形容词谓语，动词谓语，名词谓语。本章主要描写形容词谓语句。 形容词表比较，比较对象不出现的情况，如：这个大。那三个人呢那一个年岁大。可加“再、又、更、顶、最、及、至”加强比较，如：这件衣裳更贵。比较项间的区别量通过在谓语后加结果表示，如：这张椅子轻些。我的病好一点。短三尺。 比较对象出现用“似乎、仿佛、（好）像、好比、如（同）”等，如：那个人如同牲口。差比的方式一是用“似、如、（过）于、胜过/似、起”等，如：他强似我。这本大起那本。一是“比、有、较比”置于比较项间，如：这个法子比那个好。这本书有那本书好。
	第八章 动词性谓语	讨论的问题有： 1. 补语（Completive）：用于动词后表行为完成（complete the action）。“上”用在动词后可表提高、添加、增长，如：抬/按/添/题上。“住”表固定，如：站/立/钉/抓/钉/捆/锁/捉住。 动词后可跟不同补语，如：走来/了/过/上/下/进/出/通/到/开；看见/透/出/进/上/下/通。 2. “来”是朝说话人移动，“去”是离开说话人的移动。找出来，看出来，拿出来，抬过去，拿过椅子来，赶出那条狗去，领他去，你送过信去了吗？ 3. 时态和语气 语气：动补结构间加“得”的可能式表有能力完成，如：看得见，听得出来，找得着，听得懂他的话来，他戒得掉鸦片。 否定式表没有能力完成，动补间加“不”，如：看不懂，拿不过去，抬不动，街上热闹挤不动。 时态： （1）过去时（Aorist）：“过”表示行为完结，如：我见过他。他前年去过。我昨天买过一本。到明年他必死过了。 否定式：没到过。到明日晚上他必不到过。 （2）进行体（Continued action）：“着”在动词后表示动作正在发生。有时相当于英语的现在分词：站着，坐着。在书房里念着书。进行体多用于从句，表主句谓语发生时这个动作正在进行，如：他骑着马来了。用床抬着送他来。 （3）终止体（cessative），通常由“不 + V + 了”构成，如：不念书了。不见了，他们不听讲了。
	第九章 名词谓语	名词谓语需要用系词“是，做、作、当、为”连接主语和谓语。

续表

	章节	内容
第二部分 活词：带有修饰词的谓词	第十章 谓语的修饰语副词	副词的分类： 1. 单音节副词：包括典型副词“再、狠、甚、太、最、才、不”等和来自其他词类的副词，如“先、后，上，至”。 2. 双音节副词，包括： (1) 单音节副词重叠或跟其他词语结合，如：刚刚、刚才、然后、后来、本来等。 (2)“然”结尾的副词，如：徒然、枉然、偶然、忽然、自然、显然等。 (3) 名词、数词跟其他词组合成的副词，或形名组合及类似组合，如：竭力、加倍、同心、一直、笔直、一块儿、一路等。他枉然做工。要一直往前走。我们一同走。 (4) 形容性的副词：修饰名词时是形容词，修饰动词时是副词，如“快刀”的“快”是形容词，“快走”的“快”是副词。 (5) 指称副词：“这、那”加上“么、样”就构成了指称性副词，么着，么样，这样，这么着，这么样，这样，那么，那么着，那么样办事不行，这么看起来。 (6) 疑问副词：“怎、多”加上“么、样”，怎么样说呢？昨天怎么没来过？多么大？ (7) 处所副词：“这、那”加上处所短语“里、边、面、头”，如：这里，那边/面，这头等。在“边、面、头”前加“前、后”也可有类似组合，前边、前面、后面、后头。
	第十一章 状语从句	介词从句 1. 处所介词（locative preposition），书面语色彩的“于、乎”，指时间的“在、当”，还有“自、从、自从、打、等，到，等到，至，临，向、望，往，上，下，对”，书面语色彩的“与”，同，和，在天上，从关东来了，自古至今，这个和那个比量，同他说话，对他说话，向他说话，望我讨钱。 2. 受益介词（preposition of advantage）“给、把（南方）、与、因、为、因为、因着、为/的/着；替、代、替代”。如，给我做工，与你无益，为他做的。替你做工。 3. 方式介词“按、按着、照、照着、凭、据、依、在”，按着规矩办事，照着律法，凭他说，依你的话，在我看来。 4. 手段、施事前的介词“使、永、被、拿”：用力杀他，拿钱买东西，被他杀掉，使枪被他打杀，被强盗抢夺。 5. 方位从句： (1) 空间方位从句：结构是“介词 + 体词 + 处所词”。 (2) 时间方位从句：方位词，如“里、间、先、后、以上、往下”。“时（候）；先，后”通常跟前面的名词用“之、以”连接起来。“时候”则用“的”连接，他来的时候，创造天地以后，他来之后，康熙年间，六月里。 6. 普通引导从句（General introduction clause）： (1) 双音节或多音节副词，如原来、本来、究竟、到底、如此、这么着”。原来不是这么样，到底你有什么意思？

续表

	章节	内容
第二部分　活词：带有修饰词的谓词	第十一章 状语从句	（2）时间方位从句，康熙年间天下大兴旺了。当他来的时候我有病。 （3）普通主语（general subject）：由“论到、讲到”等引介。
	第十二章 谓语的不同形式	汉语动词没有及物和不及物之分。及物不及物取决于是否带宾语。 1. 总的原则是官话口语中的动词后从来不带介宾结构，如：走路，坐轿子，上京，走外江，走中间；地点除外，如：煤盛袋子里了。 2. 宾语及其修饰语位于动词后，如：他盖着一处好看的房子。时态标记“了、过、着”被当作动词的一部分，位于宾语前。我见过他。他到了家。他赶着车子。 间接宾语（secondary object）位于直接宾语前，如：送他一管笔。间接宾语带动词时，均位于直接宾语后，如：送我上船。赶狗子到门外。直接宾语不出现时，两个动词均位于间接宾语前，如：分给他们。把银子送给难民。 第二个宾语在第一个直接宾语后说明动作行为的范围（extent），如：罚他十块洋钱。
	十三章 主动和被动结构	动作行为由以下成分补足时，动词带宾语是主动态，不带宾语是被动态。（1）了；（2）完成式（completive）；（3）动果式（a sequent）或（4）表终结的间接宾语。如“他搁了书在桌子上”是主动态，“书搁在桌子上”是被动态。 1. “是”可引介施事者，如：这话是你说的吗？是他说的。 2. “被”做被动标记，主语出现与否均可：被他杀了。被你所爱。他们都被兵丁杀尽了。被贼掠了。被害。受害。 3. 有些主动结构具有被动意义。如：受，蒙，挨，见，奉，他挨了打。受苦。蒙恩典。奉命令。他见好。
	十四章　疑问结构	非极性问句，参见疑问代词和疑问副词。 极性问句主要有两种结构： 1. 重复谓语，并加否定词。现在时和将来时用“不”，过去时用“没，没有”。如：他来了没有？没来。你去不去？不去。他今天念书不念？念书。 问句中至少要重复否定副词和谓语（形容词、动词或名词）。否定回答只需要否定副词，不过也可重复整句。那个人是不是他？不。他今天来了没有？ 2. 动词带宾语时重复谓语，如：你信不信他？也可重复宾语：你信他不信他？ 问题长且复杂时，通常期待肯定回答，否定部分只用“不是”，你今天要去明天回来不是？他要买不是？回答是“是，不是”或重复谓语。
	十五章	缺失

续表

	章节	内容
第二部分 活词：带有修饰词的谓词	十六章 动结式	补语是词，短语或从句，指谓语的趋势、程度或结果。他们和副词的区别在于他们表明（indicate）结果等，而副词指谓语动词的方式，如“他明说”指说的方式，“他说明”指说的特点。 分类如下： 1. 趋势补语（sequents of tendency）：指谓语行为的趋向，不暗示（intimate）结果真的达到。用于现在或过去时所有语气，尤其多用于祈使语气，说明，好极，罚他很重，写字清楚等。 2. 结果补语（sequents of result）：结构为“句子 + 得/的 + 结果补语”或“句子 + 结果补语 + 了”，用于过去时间，如：写得清楚。重的叫人抬不起来。压硬了。穿破了。打伤了。 3. 程度补语（sequents of extent），这本书好得多。那张桌子高些。那座墙壁高一丈。 4. 数量补语（sequents of number）：指动词行为发生的次数。趟、次、顿、回等，可以翻译成“次”等，去过一趟。来了三次。来过几回。要去屡次。
	第十七章　强调的位置	描写了五种强调的方式，下文单独讨论。
第三部分　虚词	第十八章 连词	连词可连接及词、短语、句子： 1. 连接体词（名词和代词） 连接谓语和修饰语（形容词和副词） 选择连词（disjunctive connection）：包括“或，或是，或者”“不是……就是……”“无论，不论”。 对立的分离连词（antithtical disjunction）：“不但，非但，惟独……就是，并且……” 2. 连接从句 连词分为表推进的“就、便（书面）、于是、才、方才、刚才”以及“此后、以后、然后”等；表补充的“还、又、再、也、且”；表转折的“却、乃、仍然、无奈、反、倒、反倒”；引出结果的“到了儿、末了、末末了儿、到底、究竟”。 3. 连接主句和从句 1）从句在主句前 条件句（protasis）和结论句（apodosis）同时发生时，任何副词或连词都不用。时间有先后时，结论句用“就、才、必”等，你要去我送你。有病才好吃药。 条件句可分成不同种类： （1）时间条件句（temporal protasis）： a. 用“了”的，如：到了城里才好。到了天亮就去了。 b. 时间方位（locative）：我来的时候他已经去了。三年之后他才回家去了。 c. “几时……就/才/几时”：我们几时再来就要告诉你。几时能几时去。

续表

	章节	内容
第三部分 虚词	第十八章 连词	(2) 假设条件句 (conditional protasis)：用"若是、倘若、倘或、如若"等，如：若是他不来我不去。倘若你不信我可以问旁人。若见他就罢了。 (3) 转折条件句 (concessive protasis)："虽，虽然，既、既然……却，然而，到底……"：这个法子虽然拉到了还有个法子。他既然死了你不用去。 (4) 选择条件句："宁、宁可……" 或 "与其……不如"：宁肯多用几两银子买好的。不如去告诉他才好。 2) 从句在主句后 可分为目的从句和结果从句。 让步句 (Fartori)：用"尚且，何况，怎么，那里"：尚且不可杀别人何况倒可杀自己呢？我的话尚且当不起何况神的咒诅呢？ 因果句："因、为……所以、因此、故此……"：因为有许多的事所以我不能去。为的人多所以挤不动。
	第十九章 叹词和语气词	列举了常用叹词"哎呀、哎哟、咳、噫、啊"和语气词"吗、了、罢；啊、呢"。

赛兆祥对语法观察细致，如定语、状语、宾语及连词的分类和用法。语法描写多从表达着眼，如如何比较，如何表被动，如何表强调等。下文将分析其创见及局限。

三 《官话口语》的贡献和局限

赛兆祥认为掌握汉语有三点是至关重要的：一是正确的发音，二是正确使用词语，三是正确认识和使用句子的习语和结构。

《官话口语》中的前言提到，在掌握了词语和它们的用法之后，一定会有连词成句的普遍规则。可见，赛兆祥词法和句法兼顾。

(一)《官话口语》的特点和地位

《官话口语》既有词法描写，也有句法范畴的分析；词类包括名词、动词、形容词、代词、数词、量词、副词、介词、助词、感叹词、连词、语气词等；构词法有附加式和复合式；语法范畴如比较、疑问、可能、主动、被动、时态、语气等；句子成分有主语、谓语、宾语、同位语、定语、状语、补语等；句式有"连"字句、"把"字句、"被"字句、双宾语句等；补语涉及结果补语、可能补语、趋向补语、动量补语、程度补语。《官话口语》的特点包括：

1. 比较的视角

跟其他西方人一样，赛兆祥也天然具有比较的视角，包括英汉比较、方言比较等，表 2 中的比较均有助于了解汉语，有的是比附英语，如：不定式用于形容词或动词后，如好看、难看、容易明白、来看、去喊他（见表 2）。

表 2　《官话口语》中的比较

比较对象	比较内容
英汉比较	疑问词在句中的位置不变，跟英语的疑问词不同。 “要”指愿意，“必”指义务和必要，像英语的 will 和 shall “一”相当于英语的不定冠词。 “这、那”涵盖了英语定冠词的用法。 跟英语 in、un 等类似，形容词否定式在前面加“不”，不义、不信的、不会、不能等。 动补结构跟英语的“动词 + 方位副词”类似，如 come up，throw out，cast down 等。
方言比较	北方说“咱”，复数形式是“咱们”（缩写成“偺”），“俺”多用于第一人称。 “谁”（北方官话）、“那个”（南方官话）。 北方“不要”常常合音为“别、败”，南方官话的“莫”指“不、不要”。 和（在北方官话普遍）、同（南方官话普遍）
语体比较	书面形式“彼、此”。书面语词“如此”常常用于口语，如此看来，也是如此。书面疑问词还有“如何、何以”，口语化一些的有“岂、难道、难说”；“把”用得最多，“将”用于书面。
词语辨析	“两”和“二”、“呢”跟“啊”、“能”和“会”

2. 对语序的描写和论述

表 3　对语序的描写

	说明及用例
语序影响词性	一个词的词性取决于在句中的位置，而非形式。
语序影响语义	处于修饰位置和谓语位置的处所从句的区别是前者描述动作的范围（sphere），后者指动作的倾向或结果。如，在桌子上摆书，摆书在桌子上。在屋里走，走在屋里。

续表

	说明及用例
修饰语的语序	修饰语必须在修饰的体词前。
	副词位于所修饰的动词前。
	“将、要、就、必、将要、必要”位于副词前，除非副词修饰它们。
	多重定语的顺序：领属定语 + 指示定语 + 数量定语 + 量词 + 形容词，如：你这三本大书，他们的那些四个小学生，你的三处大房子。例外有二：（1）指示词提前，如：那块白的石头；（2）动词性形容词或介词短语位于代词后，如：你昨日来的朋友，你所买的那所顶高房子。
	一般来说，长的或重要的副词位于句首，后来他说。这么着我不去。（第 49 页）
连词在句中的语序	“就、便（书面）、于是、才、方才、刚才”以及“此后、以后、然后”中，只有“于是”和处所“以后”用于主语前，其他词都在主语后。如：他就说。读书上进便可以做官。次日才去了。这个法子方才好。我们到了城门他刚才出来了。
	“还、又、再、也、且”用于主语后，“再者、此外、还有、而且、况且”用于主语前，如：还有一样。又有一个人。我也有一句话。此外他也不肯来。况且他说有病。
	表转折的“却、乃、仍然、无奈、反、倒、反倒”，除了“无奈”均用于句中主语后。“但、但是、只、只是、不过、然而、其实”都用于主语前，如：他说要来却没有来。医生能救别人倒未必能救自己。我们来传道无奈你们不听道。我固然错了但责备的话太厉害。
	“所”在分句中的位置如下：分句主语 +（时间副词）+ 介词短语 + 所 + 其他词语。
词序	有些词语序两可，如：葬埋、埋葬，查考、考查等。
	反身代词位于人称代词后，如：我自己、他自己。

重视语序也是西人共性，这一点应该是受到了中国学者的影响，赛兆祥对语序的描写和论述又弥补了前人研究的不足。

3. 学术史中的《官话口语》

（1）《官话口语》跟其他语法著作的互文性

正如李葆嘉（2008）所言，西洋学者的汉语语法论著内容上具有互文性，如上文所述比较的视角，又如语法描写主要基于词类划分及其形态和范畴。普遍区分实词、虚词，活字、死字是吸收了中国学者的研究成果，这些在赛兆祥的《官话口语》中均有体现（内田庆市先生指出，当时用“活字、死字”分法的并不常见，李无未先生也提醒笔者注意查阅相关文献。细阅文本，“死字”是指位置和用法固定的体词性词语，包括名词和代词，事物及行为的名称；“活字”指位置及用法均不固定的词语，“虚词”则指本身无实义，意义依赖于语境的词语，包括连词、叹词、语气词等）。换言之，赛兆祥虽然用了中国传统的概念，但其核心还是以词类为纲。

《官话口语》前言提到，此书参考了所有能找到的用英语写成的短语书和语法书。赛兆祥之前英语写成的汉语语法书主要包括：

马礼逊《通用汉言之法》（*A Grammar of the Chinese Language*，1815），这是第一部用英语写成的汉语语法著作；艾约瑟《官话口语语法》（*A Grammar of the Chinese Colloquial Language*，*Commonly Called the Mandarin Dialect*，1857）；萨默斯《汉语手册》（*A Handbook of the Chinese Language*，1863）；罗存德《汉语语法》（*Grammar of the Chinese Language*，1864）；文璧《北方口语语法》（*Grammatical Studies in the Colloquial Language of Northern China*，1880）

董方峰（2011）认为《通用汉言之法》立足于英语语法，像是一部英语语法的汉译本。《汉语语法》是罗存德为中国南部地区尤其是粤语区来华传教士学习汉语而编的语法书。艾约瑟《汉语官话口语语法》是影响最大的一部，也是研究内容最多的，其中语音占三分之一多的篇幅。《通用汉言之法》《汉语手册》《汉语语法》也均有独立的语音部分，《北方口语语法》和《官话口语》均无单独的语音部分，不过后者例句中的词语有注音。

就词类而言，从《通用汉言之法》到《官话口语》六本书均包括名词、形容词、代词、数词、量词、动词、介词、副词、连词、感叹词十类词。艾约瑟、文璧、赛兆祥均把语气词称作 terminal，文璧和赛兆祥描写了拟声词。虽然均未单独分出助词，但在动词时态部分均有对“着、了、过”的描写，“的”通常被描写为属格的标记。

赛兆祥深受文璧的影响，文璧区分了体词、谓词、小词三大类，并据此构架全书，《官话口语》步其后尘，且大量例句重合，不少描写照搬《北方口语语法》，如“在”的用法（第 51 页），区别仅在于赛兆祥给词语注了音。《官话口语》附录 1 的 47 个量词包括了文璧书中（第 9 页）列出来的 45 个量词，后者主要引自艾约瑟《官话口语语法》，《官话口语》中的量词除了“辆”，均出现在《官话口语语法》中，萨默斯《汉语手册》中的量词也跟《官话口语语法》大同小异。文璧把“这、那 + 里/面/边”归为处所名词，赛兆祥则归为处所副词。显然不如前者合理。

文璧完全按照英语语法的框架以“拴”为例给出了动词的各种形态及其不同语气。赛兆祥对时态的处理大大简化，区分了肯定式、否定式，肯定式又有一般时态和特指时态之分。文璧文白兼顾，不仅多处提及文理的说法，如文理“而”连接形容词（第 93 页），文理感叹词用“哉”（第 99 页），句末虚词“乎、欤”表疑问，另外“也、矣、已、耳”各有不同用法（第 100 页），而且最后一章专门说明文理的特点。赛兆祥则完全着眼于口语，只有少量书面语的描写。

《官话口语》受文璧的影响最大，同时也受到了艾约瑟的影响，文璧说自己受到马若瑟、马士曼、马礼逊、艾约瑟、儒莲、威妥玛的影响，艾约瑟也在前言里提及了马若瑟、雷慕莎、马礼逊、马斯曼。可以说，赛兆祥也直接或间接受到了这些语法著作的影响。

孟柱亿（2004）认为文璧的《中国北方口语语法》反映了 19 世纪中叶外国人汉语研究水平，董方峰（2015）认为这个评价言过其实。类似现象并非孤例。原因之一在于学界对 19 世纪西方人编写的官话论著的挖掘仅是冰山一角，很多资料尚未面世；同时也跟学者的学术视野和旨趣不无关系。因此，进行单部论著的梳理和研究时，必须把它放入语法史、学术史的框架之中，否则只见树木，不见森林，很难客观评判其功过得失。

（2）《官话口语》的独创性

既然《官话口语》跟其他语法著作有互文性，能否说它模仿甚至抄袭了前人的著作，尤其是《北方口语语法》？答案是否定的。

跟《北方口语语法》相比，《官话口语》例句丰富得多，而且更加彻底地贯彻了“口语语法”的原则；《官话口语》的描写也更细致，每种格式均给出肯定式、否定式，时态的描写上也略胜一筹，具有独创性。

《官话口语》的独创性首先表现在立足于汉语的描写，如对平比和差比的描写；如“的”的隐现，总的原则是，“的”只在名词前出现一次。关于“的”的使用，作者总结了四点：

1）两个或多个形容词在名词前修饰，后一个形容词加“的”。如：年老学问大的那位先生，他灵巧聪明的小儿子；

2）一个领属词和一个形容词修饰名词时，领属词加“的”。如：学生的高桌子。但是如果指示词在代词后，或者形容词是动词性的，那么“的”放在形容词后。如：他那条顶厉害的狗、我这个不好的学生。

3）动词性修饰语（verbal adjective）优先带“的”。如：你所买的那本大书、所来的那些年老人。

4）如果短语很长，每个修饰语后都可以带“的”。如：昨天所来的那位年轻体面的先生。

对三种可能表达式的描写如下：

1）最常见的是“来”。如：做不来、买不来。这件事情做得来。

2）其次是“了”。如：多不了、五点钟晚不了。假不了。这处房子你们两家住不了。这口袋子盛得了吗？注意“了”读 liao 不读 la。

3）第三种“得”比前两种用得都少，说明谓语行为可不可以做。如：这本书是少不得的。这个饭吃不得。他那样光景实在看不得。这个了不得。

有些涉及语用，指人所在地而非人时需要用方位副词“这里、那里”。如：在你那里，在我这里。

上文提到，语序很重要，但强调式可改变语序，强调成分置于句首（见表4）。

表4　强调式

语序改变	用例
定名结构定语（从句）提前	洋布红的黄的蓝的都有；教友男女都来了；本地先生那用功的可以能进达
主语位于句首	李大哥他已经五十岁了；那个人我认识他的父亲；山东人大概是大个子的
谓语置于句首	好是好的；病必病死你了；走是走得马上快
动词有宾语时，宾语也可提前	打扫地板要打扫干净；做工要出力
宾语置于句首	那个灯笼你得找出来；世上的人他都能爱
补语提前	快走很快；结实他绑得不大结实
不定式提前	锄地呢无力；讨饭呢怕耻

赛兆祥区分了逻辑主语和语法主语。从句通常在句首，处于最强调的位置，形成句子的逻辑主语；语法主语可能在它们后面插入适当的位置。

两次提到普通主语（general subject），如：普通主语可由“论到、讲到”等介引。如：论外国人他们大概有些学问。普通主语一般由“论到、讲到、至于”介绍，如：论到这件事。以上均可看作话题句。赛兆祥说的强调正是话题化的方式，《大辞海（语言学卷）》对话题化的定义是：语义表达转换为句法表达时，将重要信息和强调部分置于适当位置（一般是句首）以提高其已知程度和受注意程度的过程。如：“雷锋的名字传遍神州大地”可以话题化为“雷锋，他的名字传遍神州大地”。甲伯连孜的《汉文经纬》（1881）比《官话口语》略早，则称此为“心理主语”。

在讲到句尾虚词“呢”时，赛兆祥认为，“呢”不是疑问词，但是可用于任何需要强调的词语或句子后。显然就是话题标记。

4.《官话口语》的语言性质

19 世纪的语法著作普遍重视方言差异，《通用汉言之法》《汉语语法》中均有大量对粤语的描写，《官话口语语法》中也有不少区域或地点方言的描写，如山东、直隶、徽州、福建“我”的说法或读音；《北方口语语法》也有对直隶、山东、河南，多处有登州、北京话的记录。相比而言，《官话口语》涉及方言的篇幅很小，而且只提到南北差异。目前学界通行的看法是，19 世纪中叶，西方人学习的对象从南京官话转变为北京官话，那么《官话口语》是否是纯粹的北京官话呢？答案是否定的。书中有不少南方官话特点，具体如下。

（1）附录二的音节表记录了入声字，表现的是南方官话的特点。

（2）全文无一处对北京话的记录，但有大量反映南方官话特点的记录，表示比较的方式，如：他强似我；这本大起那本；爱父母过于爱兄弟；一层高一层；一天好一天。

反复问句格式有 v-neg-vo、vo-neg-vo、vo-neg-v、vp-neg（neg 包括“不、没（有）、不是”）。同时期北方官话反复问句主要有三种格式：vp-NEG-vp、vp-NEG-v、vp-NEG，19 世纪后期以 vp-neg-v 为主，赛兆祥记录的 v-neg-vo 反映的是南方官话的特点。

（3）话题优先，特别是谓语和补语提前做话题反映，这是南方官话的特点。

（4）再次，赛兆祥主要在江苏地区传教，虽然当时主流是学习北京官话，但是赛兆祥由于工作和生活原因，很自然地有更多南方官话的记录。

（二）《官话口语》的局限

混淆语法单位和范畴，既包括词类的混淆，也包括不同语法单位的混淆。

混淆词性，把副词分为单音节副词、双音节副词、形容词性副词、指称副词、疑问副词、方位副词。其实“形容词性副词”就是形容词，而后三种则分别是代词和处所名词。赛兆祥划分词类的主要标准就是句法位置，如动词性形容词其实是典型的动词，只是因为处于定语的位置就被当作形容词；大部分副词可作谓语，此时变为形容词，如：那件事是这么的。在这里传道是白白的。看书容易。写字难。“呼呼的，哈哈的”是拟声副词，“究竟、到底”做连词均是因句法位置而如此划分。颇有点儿“凡词，依句辨品，离句无品”的意味。

不同语法单位的混淆情况举例如下。

（1）混淆词和词组。如以下短语均看作“词”：张先生、李大哥、包医生；表职业的“掌柜的、看门的、念书的、赶脚的、推车的”。

（2）数量同位语（Quantitative Apposition）把范围副词“都、全、皆、统统、拢总”等看作构成数量同位语的成分，显然不妥，如：风俗各有不同，庙里的神统统是假的。他们大半是江苏人。

（3）把双音节和多音节副词当作从句

（4）把“好比说，好像要走。”当作比较。

（5）补语的分类有交叉。同一类补语内部具有异质性，不同补语间则有交叉。

19 世纪，西方学者做了构建实用汉语语法体系的种种尝试，由于他们借鉴了英语语法的框架，吸收了当时最新的研究理论，把汉语语法研究大大推进了一步。重视语用、实用性强是这些著作的共同特点。赛兆祥的《官话口语》也做出了有益的尝试。《官话口语》前言提到，本书不能算语法书，因为并未讨论文体、语调（tones）、方言差异等语法问题。我们认为这正是《官话口语》的特点所在，当时语法书中讨论文体、语调、方言差异是一种风潮，《官话口语》虽然也有相关描写，但几乎可以忽略，这样其内容更具有同质性，即以口语为基础的语法教材，正如书名副标题所言，为语言学习者而作（For the Use of Learners of the Language）。

四　结语

19 世纪西方人编写的语法书数量众多，此类著作目前进入学界视野的仅是冰山一角，挖掘、整理和研究仍有很大空间，如系统梳理明清西方汉语语法书的董方峰（2011）、叶锋（2014）均未提及《官话口语》。

虽然赛兆祥在前言中声明《官话口语》是原创，但通过比较，我们发现，全书与 19 世纪其他语法书有明显的互文性，如以词类为框架，同时有性、数、格、时、体、式等形态描写，正如董方峰（2014）所言，19 世纪英美传教士汉语研究者更多地以英语作为参照语。《官话口语》受《北方口语语法》影响最深，但其系统更严密，描写更细致，例句丰富，且基本均来自口语，书中不少立足汉语的发现反映了赛兆祥独立的探索和尝试。

参考文献

Absalom Sydenstricker, *An Exposition of the Construction And Idioms of Chinese Sentences: As Found In Colloquial Mandarin*, The American Presbyterian Mission Press, 1889.

Jasper Scudder. Mc Ilvaine, *Grammatical Studies in the Colloquial Language of Northern China-especially Designed for the Use of Missionaries*, The American Presbyterian Mission Press, 1880.

艾约瑟：《汉语官话口语语法》，董方锋、杨洋译，外语教学与研究出版社，2015。

董方峰：《19 世纪英美传教士汉语语法研究》，载张西平、柳若梅编《国际汉语教育史研究》，商务印书馆，2014。

董方峰：《十九世纪英美传教士的汉语语法研究》，外语教学与研究出版社，2011。

黄光域：《基督教传行中国纪年（1807－1949）》，广西师范大学出版社，2017。

李葆嘉：《中国转型语法学：基于欧美模板与汉语类型的沉思》，南京师范大学出版社，2008。

许宝华、杨剑桥等：《大辞海（语言学卷）》，上海辞书出版社，2013。

董方峰：《明清时期西方汉语语法研究的历史》，《外国语文研究》2015 年第 1 期。

孟柱亿：《〈中国北方口语语法研究〉在语法学上的意义》，《汉语学习》2004 年第 6 期。

沈梅丽：《赛珍珠宗教民俗观及其中国小说批评研究》，《江苏大学学报（社会科学版)》2017 年第 4 期。

张微:《禅治文的汉语认识初探》,载张西平、柳若梅编《国际汉语教育史研究》,商务印书馆,2014。

张春蕾:《美国基督教长老会在江苏的传教活动》,《东南文化》2006 年第 5 期。

李秀梅:《马礼逊〈通用汉言之法〉研究》,山东师范大学硕士学位论文,2013。

叶锋:《17-19 世纪欧美汉语语法专著研究》,浙江大学博士学位论文,2014。

岳岚:《晚晴时期西方人所编汉语教材研究》,北京外国语大学博士学位论文,2015。

The Values and Limitations of *An Exposition of the Construction and Idioms of Chinese Sentences*

Guo Lixia

Abstract

"An Exposition of the Construction and Idioms of Chinese Sentences: As Found in Colloquial Mandarin" is an grammar book which was published in 1889. The book was greatly influenced by other grammar books in 19th century, it also reflected the author's opinions on Chinese.

Keywords

Absalom　Sydenstricker　Intertextuality

19世纪中国有关英语的出版物对日本人英语学习的影响：概观与福泽谕吉《增订华英通语》的分析

田野村忠温[*]著　孙　晓 译

摘　要

在19世纪的日本，出版于中国的英语辞典、学习书是有关英语的重要情报源。本文在概观日本人在英语学习时对中国出版物的利用情况的同时，也将考察至今尚未被正确理解的福泽谕吉编译《增订华英通语》的底本及福泽谕吉编辑的内容的问题。

关键词

英语学习　英语辞典　英语学习书　《增订华英通语》　中日语言交流

日本人的英语学习开始于19世纪初。但是，17世纪以来江户幕府推行的闭关锁国政策导致处于英语学习初期的日本既没有英语辞典，也没有相关学习书。最初日本是将出版于荷兰的英语教材作为蓝本，随着英语学习的普及，中国出版的英语辞典、学习书开始被广泛使用。

本文首先概述日本有关英语的初期的著作和出版情况，以及它们和相对应的中国出版物的关系。其次，确定至今未得到正确理解的福泽谕吉编译《增订华英通语》的底本问题，并阐明福泽谕吉编辑的内容。

---

* 田野村忠温，日本大阪大学大学院文学研究科教授。

一　日本人的英语学习史

据笔者看，日本人的英语学习可以分为两个时期。第一时期是 19 世纪上半叶，第二时期是 19 世纪下半叶及以后。

（一）英语学习第一时期——19 世纪上半叶

日本人的英语学习开始于 19 世纪伊始。因外国船只不断来港，出于国防目的，江户幕府向荷兰语翻译们下达了兼修英语的命令。荷兰是锁国时期的日本唯一维持通商关系的西洋国家。

荷兰语翻译们应幕府的要求在短时间内即编著了英语辞典和例句集。最初阶段的著作有以下三部。

吉雄权之助等编译《谙厄利亚言语和解》（1810－1811）；

本木正荣等编译《谙厄利亚兴学小筌》（1811）；

本木正荣等编译《谙厄利亚语林大成》（1814）。

上述各著作的书名中包含的“谙厄利亚”是拉丁语中表示英国的单词 Anglia 的音译，被用于意大利传教士利玛窦（Matteo Ricci）的《坤舆万国全图》（1602）。这一词多见于日本 18 世纪至 19 世纪上半叶的文献，其后随着“英吉利”“イギリス”等源于英语（English）的名称的普及而削减。

当然，起初荷兰语翻译们并没有英语知识储备，他们为什么能够编著英语辞典和学习书呢？实际上这里有个简单的方法。荷兰语翻译们利用面向荷兰人的，即英荷双语对照形式的学习书，将其中的荷兰语部分翻译成日语，用这种方法著成英日双语对照形式的学习书。至于上述三部著作具体是以哪些荷兰的英语学习书为基础编著的，笔者已在其他文献解明（田野村忠温，2017）。

上述著作以后的英语语法书和辞典也是按照这样的方法编著的。其中较为重要的是下列书目。

涩川敬直编译《英文鉴》（1840）；

西成量等编译《エゲレス（英吉利）语辞书和解》（1851 年，未完）。

在英语学习第一时期，只有以荷兰语翻译为主的少数日本人涉足英语学习领域。荷兰语翻译们编著的辞典、例句集、语法书等也未被正式出版，仅限于以手抄本形式流通。

（二）英语学习第二时期——19 世纪下半叶及以后

根据1854 年3 月签署的《日美和亲条约》（《神奈川条约》），日本须向西洋打开国门。同年 8 月、12 月《日英和亲条约》和《日俄和亲条约》也被签署。伴随着开国，日本人的英语学习可以说也进入了新时代，即第二时期，但在当时的日本还没有令人满意的辞典和学习书。

随着时间的推移，下列由英语母语者编著的高质量著作相继出版。

赫本（平文）编《和英语林集成》（初版 1867 年）；

布林克利：《语学独案内》（初版 1875 年）。

美国传教士兼医师赫本（James Curtis Hepburn）的《和英语林集成》作为日英、英日辞典中的畅销书，直到 20 世纪仍在被改订和出版。英国陆军士官布林克利（Francis Brinkley）的《语学独案内》是超过 1000 页的详细的英语学习巨著。

但是，在这样的著作出现前，甚至在其出现后，19 世纪日本有关英语的出版物的主要参照源均是出版于中国的辞典和学习书。

二　以中国出版物为基础的日本的英语辞典、学习书

以中国的出版物为基础编著而成、19 世纪在日本出版的英语辞典、学习书主要有如下几种。在此大致按照出版的时间顺序论述。除此之外，还有部分利用中国的出版物编撰而成的著作，本文不予论述。

（一）以西洋人著作为底本的出版物

以下是较早的出版物。下文均将中国的出版物和以其为底本的日本版成对列举。

底本：罗伯聃《华英通用杂话·上卷》（1843）；

日本版：《汉英通用杂话·上卷》（1860）。

来自苏格兰的英国商人罗伯聃（Robert Thom）在第一次鸦片战争结束后不久的 1843 年出版了《华英通用杂话·上卷》（*Chinese and English Vocabulary*，*Part First*）。此书旨在取代以广东为中心被广泛使用的洋泾浜英语

（Pidgin English），教授正统的英语，内容为词汇集和例句集。对于底本的内容，日本版近乎全盘引用（内田庆市，1997，2001）。顺带一提，因罗伯聃早逝，此书的下卷未能出版面世。

西洋传教士编著的英语辞典同样出现了日本版。

底本：卫三畏编《英华韵府历阶》（1844）；

日本版：柳泽信大校正训点《英华字汇》（1869）。

美国传教士卫三畏（Samuel Wells Williams）所著《英华韵府历阶》（*An English and Chinese Vocabulary*，*In the Court Dialect*）的日本版中，出现了为便于日本读者理解而实施的，对底本中中文注释的变更。以底本中“Bad，歹 *tái*；不好 *pu háu*.”的条目为例，中文的发音书写被删除，对于日语中不被使用的汉字“歹”以及不符合日语语法的“不好”标注了释义和读法，即“アシキ（坏）”“ヨカラ（好）ザル（不）”（见图 1）。

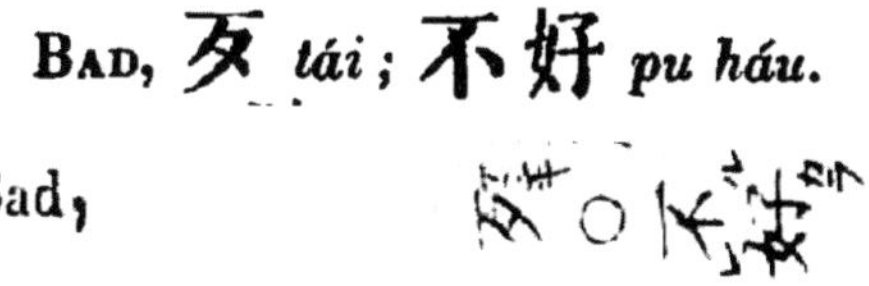

BAD, 歹 *tái*; 不好 *pu háu*.

Bad,

图 1　卫三畏《英华韵府历阶》（上），柳泽信大校正训点《英华字汇》（下）

德国传教士罗存德（Wilhelm Lobscheid）编纂的，由四卷组成的《英华字典》（*English and Chinese Dictionary*，*With the Punti and Mandarin Pronunciation*）的日本版有两个版本。

底本：罗存德编《英华字典》（1866－1869）；

日本版 1：津田仙等译《英华和译字典》（1879）；

日本版 2：井上哲次郎订增《订增英华字典》（1883－1884）。

在津田仙等译《英华和译字典》的条目“Gold”中，底本的中文释义上出现了“キン（金）”“ワウゴン（黄金）”等日语读法，以及“ジュンキン（纯金）”等语义的标注（见图 2）。

井上哲次郎的《订增英华字典》中则未出现类似的补充。

（二）以中国人著作为底本的出版物

邝其照编的英语辞典也有以下日本版本出现。

底本：邝其照编《字典集成》初版《粤东俗字注解》（1868）；

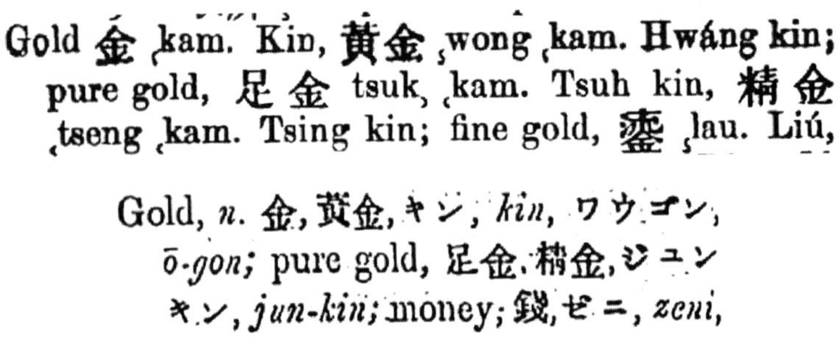

Gold 金 ˏkam. Kin, 黃金 ˏwong ˏkam. Hwáng kin; pure gold, 足金 tsukˎ ˏkam. Tsuh kin, 精金 ˏtseng ˏkam. Tsing kin; fine gold, 鎏 ˏlau. Liú,

Gold, *n.* 金, 黃金, キン, *kin*, ワウゴン, *ō-gon;* pure gold, 足金, 精金, ジュンキン, *jun-kin;* money; 錢, ゼニ, *zeni*,

图 2　罗存德《英华字典》(上), 津田仙等译《英华和译字典》(下)

日本版：柳泽信大编《粤东俗字便蒙解》(1870)。

底本：邝其照编《华英字典》(1879);

日本版：永峰秀树训译《华英字典》(1881)。

底本：邝其照编 *A Dictionary of English Phrases with Illustrative Sentences* (1881);

日本版 1：增田藤之助校订编纂附译《英和双解熟语大字汇》(1899);

日本版 2：由国民英学会出版的底本复刻版 (1901)。

以上日本版在内容的编辑上与卫三畏、罗存德的辞典的日本版大同小异，在此不再举例赘述。邝其照《华英字典》(1879) 是著名的邝其照《字典集成》第二版 (1875 年) 的缩印廉价版，出版于上海 (沈国威，2013；司佳，2013)。

三　福泽谕吉编译《增订华英通语》

上文中与英语相关的著作的日本版的底本均可确认。根据书名、日本版序文、被登载的原书序文、正文内容等，很容易判断其底本。

相反，1860 年福泽谕吉编译出版的《增订华英通语》的底本尚不明确。19 世纪，在中国出版的名为《华英通语》的英语学习书有数版，并且不能排除底本是《华英通语》的未知版本的可能性。除底本问题外，书名《增订华英通语》中"增订"的含义也尚未解明。

以下 (一) 至 (五) 的内容与已发表的日语论文的一部分相同 (田野村忠温，2018)。

（一）《增订华英通语》概要

1860 年福泽谕吉得到了随江户幕府遣美使节团同行的许可，从旧金山的中国商人处得到了英语学习书《华英通语》，回国后将其修订为面向日本人的英语学习书，并于同年以《增订华英通语》为书名出版。《华英通语》的主要内容是汉英双语对照的词汇集和例句集。在这些内容的基础上，《增订华英通语》中加入了片假名注释。

图 3 是《华英通语》的 1855 年版和《增订华英通语》中“眼镜”的词条。

图 3　《华英通语》（上），福泽谕吉编译《增订华英通语》（下）

《华英通语》的各条目均是由汉语“眼镜”、英语“Spectacle”和英语发音的汉字书写“时逼爹斤倪”三个要素构成的。《华英通语》中使用的汉语是广东话。《增订华英通语》中，在汉语单词旁边添加了日语表达“メガネ”和英语发音的假名书写“スペキテクル”，因此各条目由 5 个要素构成。汉语、日语部分和英语部分用竖线隔开等处理，可能是为了防止要素增多导致排版混乱不易读解。

（二）《华英通语》初期的三个版本

截至《增订华英通语》出版的 1860 年，现存可以确认的《华英通语》有表 1 所示的三个版本。

表 1 《华英通语》初期的三个版本的概要

刊行年	书名	封面	序作者	作者	馆藏地
1849 年（道光二十九年）	华英通语	不明（缺页）	郑仁山	郑仁山（推定）	大阪大学附属图书馆
1855 年（咸丰五年）	华英通语	咸丰乙卯 华英通语 协德堂藏板	何紫庭	子卿	东北大学附属图书馆（狩野文库）
1860 年（咸丰十年）	华英通语	咸丰庚申重订 华英通语 恒茂藏板	拙山人	子芳	大阪大学附属图书馆（仅存卷上） 哈佛大学燕京图书馆

根据笔者的推断，1849 年出版的是《华英通语》的最初版本，而且 1860 年及以前出版的《华英通语》只有这三个版本。三个版本的作者均不相同。

为了便于理解，下文将这三个版本分别称为“道光本”、“咸丰五年本”和“咸丰十年本”。

《华英通语》道光本是以罗伯聃《华英通用杂话》上卷为范本，另外并用两本西洋传教士所著的面向西洋人的广东话入门书编撰而成。《华英通语》咸丰五年本以道光本为基础，利用多本西洋人的广东话入门书，大幅改订了内容。咸丰十年本对咸丰五年本进行了微调，两者内容重合度很高（田野村忠温，2018，2019）。

（三）《增订华英通语》的底本

福泽谕吉的《增订华英通语》是以《华英通语》咸丰五年本为底本编著的。可以这样断定是因为两者的内容过于相似，以至于除此之外的可能性微乎其微。即使《增订华英通语》的底本不是咸丰五年本，也一定是一个内容上和咸丰五年本完全或是几乎相同的版本。但我们尚未发现这种版本。

关于《增订华英通语》的底本问题，内田庆市（2001）指出：“从出版年来看，大概可以说这（指《华英通语》咸丰五年本——笔者注）就是底本，抑或说是最接近底本的。”另外，矢放昭文（2015）主张：“可以断定‘福泽购入本’和‘狩野本’（指《华英通语》咸丰五年本——笔者注）极其接近，但从细节看，不能说‘福泽购入本’即为‘狩野本’。”内田庆市回避了断定性的说法，矢放昭文可以说是持否定观点，但由下文中的分析可知，《增订华英通语》的底本确是《华英通语》咸丰五年本。

（四）《增订华英通语》中的“增订”

书名《增订华英通语》中“增订”的具体内容一直以来都不明确。

与《华英通语》咸丰五年本相比，《增订华英通语》中除了添加了日语表达和英语发音的假名书写，被福泽谕吉添加在卷首的凡例、每半页条目数的增加等变化也一目了然。

除此之外福泽谕吉在《增订华英通语》中进行的其他变更，只能通过考察其具体内容才能知晓。在此笔者将阐述从这种角度进行分析后的结果。

关于半页内包含的条目数，《华英通语》从道光本到咸丰十年本基本上是 4 段 ×2 列，即 8 个条目，在《增订华英通语》中则变为 8 段 ×2 列，即 16 个条目。因此咸丰五年本的词汇集和例句集足有 162 页，《增订华英通语》中减少为 97 页。

下文表示资料中位置时，用比如“1a”表示第 1 页右半页，“23b”表示第 23 页左半页。根据具体情况，用“咸 1a”“增 23b”的表示方法区分《华英通语》咸丰五年本和《增订华英通语》。

1. 增补

福泽谕吉进行的“增订”——准确地说，编辑——中，包括增补、删除、订正 3 种要素。

首先，《增订华英通语》中增补的要素只有添加在各条目中的日语和英语发音的假名书写，没有任何《华英通语》咸丰五年本中没有的词语和例句的追加。

内田庆市（2001）、矢放昭文（2015）都认为《华英通语》咸丰五年本和《增订华英通语》中收录的词汇有“出入”，矢放昭文进一步指出：“出入涉及‘绸（细）缎类’‘颜色类’‘茶叶类’等 16 类，特别是‘房室类’，‘福泽本’的收录词汇数多出 16 个。”但实际上福泽谕吉并没有补充词汇。

咸丰五年本和《增订华英通语》中，词语和收录词语的方框之间的关系并非完全一致。也就是说，咸丰五年本中被收录到一个方框中的两个词语，福泽谕吉常常会分为两个方框记录。比如，咸丰五年本中“父母 Parents 父 Father”（13a）在一个方框中，但福泽谕吉把它们分成了“父母 Parents”“父 Father”两个方框。因此，如果在比较词语数量时以方框的数量为准，咸丰五年本和《增订华英通语》两者间自然会出现数量差。

词汇的分类和条目的顺序也完全参照了咸丰五年本。矢放昭文（2004）指出词汇的分类略有不同，但实际上并无变更。矢放昭文应该是根据卷首的目录而不是正文判断的。咸丰五年本的目录中有遗漏的类目，福泽谕吉对其进行了错误的补充（后述），因此只看目录时会发现词汇分类不一致。但是，两书正文中没有出现这种现象。

关于增补可以补充说明的是，并非所有条目上都添加了日语表达。比如，“牛奶饼 Cheese”（31b）、“会（烩）燕窝 Stewed birdnests”（32a）就没有添加日语表达。这种情况多见于表达西洋或中国固有事物的名词中。福泽谕吉在《增订华英通语》卷首的凡例中写道：“对没有日语名称的或虽有类似名称但无法清楚判断是否妥当的事物不注译名。”

近乎所有条目中标注了英语发音的假名书写，没有标注的只有“看银者 Shroff”（6b）等 3 个条目。

2. 删除

截至《华英通语》咸丰五年本词汇集的“三字类”部分，共记载词语达 2517 条，其中 32 条在《增订华英通语》中被删除。

这些省略大致可分为三种。第一种是将部分词类开头的小标题或解说删除。如“地理类”的“地乃圆 The earth is round”（咸 7a），“人伦类”的“五伦 The five relations of mankind, &c.”（咸 13a），“颜色类”的“五色 Five colors”（咸 40a）等 7 例属于这一范畴。

第二种是将重复部分删除。例如，在咸丰五年本中重复出现两次的“艰难 Difficult”（咸 133b、咸 139a）、“做茶 Make tea”（咸 137a、咸 138a），第二次出现被省略。但被删除的只是福泽谕吉偶然发现的重复，咸丰五年本中可被视为重复的词条有 80 组之多，而在《增订华英通语》中被处理的只有 6 处。

笔者将剩余的 19 处统归于第三种，这其中又包含各种不同类型。比如，“茶叶类”中有“大珠 Imperial”和“珠兰 Imperial”2 项（均见于咸 50a），后者被省略。因英语相同，并且实物不详，所以可能福泽谕吉判断只保留一个就足够了。“细锻类”的“四川绸 Sz’ch ‘ün pongee”（咸 32b）的英语拼写中混合着辅助记号很难判读，可能因不易处理而被省略。但是，有很多我们无法推测它们被省略的缘由。比如，“食物类”的“芝麻油 Seasamun（原文如此——笔者注）oil”（咸 63b）、“菓子类”的“杨桃 Carambola”（咸 99b）、“二字类”的“投卖 Auction”（咸 138b）被删除的理由不明。这些词汇看似对日本人的英语学习没有帮助的解释无法成立，因为和《华英通语》的其他版本相同，咸丰五年本的词汇集中收录了极多这样的词语。被省略的词条中一部分可能只是书写遗漏。

收录在“四字类”及其以后的 224 个例句中，有 4 例被删除。首先，有明确删除理由的是：

你重（还）有呢（这）样嘅（的）货吗 Have you more of this article?（咸 164a、咸 166b）

此例在咸丰五年本中重复出现，第二次的出现被删除。

其余 3 例内容如下：

个（那）处打架 There is fighting there（咸 146b）

你在边处（哪里）得钱做 Where do you get for doing this（咸 150a）

部，唔係 Poop noncense（原文如此——笔者注）（咸 153b）

以上 3 例被删除的理由不明。关于第二个例子，有可能是因为中英文翻译不对称而被删除。而第三个可能是因为福泽谕吉判断其内容不必收录到学习书里，或是因为咸丰五年本在引用道光本时拼写错误，导致例句中出现意思不明的“单词”noncense，所以被省略。第一个例子被删除的原因笔者尚无头绪。

3. 订正

《增订华英通语》订正了《华英通语》咸丰五年本中的许多错误。上述对重复出现的词语或例句进行删除也可以说是一种订正，除此之外还有以下类型。

首先，在咸丰五年本中词汇被分为“天文类”“地理类”“职分类”“人伦类”“国宝类”等很多类，但在卷首的目录中本应出现在第四位的“人伦类”被遗漏。福泽谕吉发现了该情况并在《增订华英通语》的目录中追加了“人伦类”。但是，因为添加位置的失误，导致目录呈现“天文类”“地理类”“人伦类”“职分类”“国宝类”这样与正文不符的顺序。这引起了上述的矢放的误解。

更多的是对咸丰五年本中英语拼写错误（或不标准的拼写）的订正。

例如，将“差役 Polisman”（咸15a）改为Policeman（增6a）、“船写字 Pursur”（咸16a）改为Purser（增7a）、“利器匠 Cutter”（咸98b）改为Cutler（增52a）、“安字板 Gally”（咸117b）改为Galley（增63b）、“鬆 Lossen”（咸121a）改为Loosen（增67b）。可以确认的订正接近30处。因为《华英通语》咸丰五年本和《增订华英通语》都是手写版本，所以这个数字会因对一些难辨字的理解的变化而变化。

“回音 A reply answer”（咸133b）这个词条中奇怪的英语表达从道光本一直延续到咸丰五年本，《增订华英通语》将其分为“A reply，answer”（增77a）两个词。

（五）旧错的残存与新错的产生

福泽谕吉在《增订华英通语》中订正了他所发现的《华英通语》咸丰五年本中的英语拼写错误，但仍有一些错误未被订正。这样的订正遗漏有20处以上，现将其中数例列举如下。〔 〕中为正确的写法。在此省略日语注释。

商人 Merchunt〔merchant〕（6a）

大餐房 Dinning room〔dining〕（48a）

火漆 Ceiling wax〔sealing〕（61b）

跌伤了 To be hurted by a fall〔hurt〕（82a）

另外出现了40处以上《华英通语》咸丰五年本中没有的新错误。新错误的数量超过了订正（接近30处）的数量。

仕 Officiels〔officials〕（7a）

老鼠鸡 Ratbit fowl〔rabbit〕（32a）

口 Month〔mouth〕（54b）

我怕佢张银单係假 I am aflaid that the bill is forged.〔afraid〕（85b）

综上所述，《增订华英通语》不过是对《华英通语》咸丰五年本的各个条目加写日语注释的英语学习书。福泽谕吉删除了少数条目并订正了他所发现的错误，那些措施并不算是学习书的基本性质的改变。

（六）《增订华英通语》对此后英语学习书的影响

日本此后出版的其他英语学习书的编辑过程中，仍有对《增订华英通语》的内容的利用。笔者发现了两部。

一部学习书是1872年出版的日英德对译词汇集，即中村顺三郎的《普英通语对译》——书名中的“普”是Prussia的中文音译“普鲁士”的首字简称——就是以《增订华英通语》为基础编著的。通过两书中收录的词语的对应状况以及《普英通语对译》对《增订华英通语》中错误之处的继承可以确认两者的关系。

仕 Officials 坷啡些倪（咸17a）

仕 Officiels 坷啡些倪（增7a）

仕（英）Officiels，（普）Der Official（《普英通语对译》12b）

《增订华英通语》在借用《华英通语》咸丰五年本中的词条“仕 Officials”时，出现了Officiels的拼写错误，《普英通语对译》则是直接引用了这个拼写。而且，《普英通语对译》中英语Official作为德语被引用本身就是错误的。

另一部学习书是1872年出版的松冈章编辑《和英通语》。此书的一部分例句是从《增订华英通语》中摘取的。下列最后的“If they be bad all not by them”这个奇怪的句子的起源，是美国医生、传教士德万（Thomas T. Devan）在1847年出版的粤语入门书 *The Beginner's First Book in the Chinese Language*（*Canton Vernacular*）的例句。

If they are not good, I'll not buy them 货唔（不）好就罢咯（德万107页）

if they are not good all not buy them 货唔好就笼总都唔买咯（道光本131a）

If they be bad all not buy them 若唔好就唔好买（咸163b）

If they be bad all not buy them ワルケレバミナカワヌ（原文如此——笔者注）（增95b）

If they be bad all not by them ワルケレバ皆买（ミナカ）ハヌ（《和英通语》卷之一19a）

德万列举的正确的例句“If they are not good, I'll not buy them”在被从《华英通语》道光本引用到《和英通语》的过程中逐渐变形，错误逐渐增多。

四 日本人在英语学习时对中国出版物的利用

——日本版出版以外的证据

一般来说，除了正式的出版物以外，通过其他资料确认19世纪日本的英语学习状况是困难的，但是有两种资料的留存可以让我们确认日本人在学习英语时对中国出版物的利用。

其中一种是书页空白处有日本学习者标注的中国学习书。

郑仁山《华英通语》道光本（1849）（大阪大学附属图书馆藏）；

唐廷枢《英语集全》（1862）（哈佛大学燕京图书馆藏）。

图 4 的《华英通语》道光本的词条“眼镜 spectacles”中，学习者标注了日语“メガネ（眼镜）”和英语读音的假名书写“スペキテキロス”。在《英语集全》的词条“食指 Forefinger”（为节约篇幅将图逆时针旋转 90 度）中标注了日语“ヒトサシユビ（指人指）”。

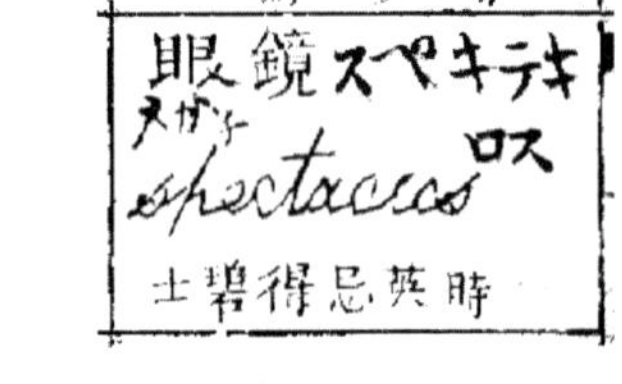

图 4　《华英通语》道光本（上），唐廷枢《英语集全》（下）

另一种是与英语相关的中国出版物手抄本的残存。

马礼逊《英吉利文话之凡例》吉雄权之助手抄本（国立国会图书馆、早稻田大学图书馆藏）；

麦都思 *English and Chinese Dictionary* 中村敬宇手抄本（早稻田大学图书馆藏）。

前者是英国传教士马礼逊（Robert Morrison）在 1823 年出版的英语语法书《英吉利文话之凡例》（*A Grammar of the English Language, For the Use of the Anglo-Chinese College*），后者是英国传教士麦都思（Walter Henry Medhurst）在 1847 年出版的英华辞典 *English and Chinese Dictionary* 的手抄本。但关于《英吉利文话之凡例》手抄者还需进一步确认，因为两所图书馆所藏的手抄本的笔迹不一致。

人们学习英语时使用的学习书或手抄本残存下来应是特殊的事件。可以推测 19 世纪的日本人在英语学习方面对中国的辞典和学习书的利用程度，远高于仅靠现存资料可以确认的程度。

五 结语

本文概述了 19 世纪日本人在英语学习中对中国出版物的利用状况，同时确定了福泽谕吉编译《增订华英通语》的底本和编辑内容。

19 世纪末期以后出版于日本的英语辞典反而影响了中国的英语辞典。对英语的学习和接纳是亚洲近代化中不可或缺的主题。关于 19 世纪至 20 世纪围绕这个主题产生的中日两国间的相互影响，我们的理解尚浅，可以说这是一个残留着许多研究余地的领域。

参考文献

沈国威：《解题：邝其照的〈字典集成〉及其他英语著作》，载内田庆市、沈国威编《邝其照 字典集成：影印与解题（初版・第二版）》，东亚文化交涉学会，2013。

司佳：《邝其照与 1868 年〈字典集成〉初版：兼谈第一本中国人编写的英汉字典及其历史实用价值》，《广东社会科学》2013 年第 1 期。

田野村忠温：《新发现的〈华英通语〉道光版与中国早期英语学习书的谱系》，载沈国威编《近代概念史与词汇史研究论丛》，朱晓平译，南京凤凰出版社，2019。

内田庆市：《清国英语事始》，《关西大学中国文学会纪要》第 18 号，1997。

内田庆市：《近代における东西言语文化接触の研究》，关西大学出版部，2001。

矢放昭文：《〈华英通语〉の价値について》，《东方》第 285 号，东方书店，2004。

矢放昭文：《福泽谕吉と〈增订华英通语〉》，《京都产业大学日本文化研究所纪要》第 20 号，2015。

田野村忠温：《日本最初期英语研究书の依据资料と编集》，《待兼山论丛》第 51 号文化动态论篇，大阪大学大学院文学研究科，2017。

田野村忠温：《新出资料〈华英通语〉道光本と中国初期英语学习书の系谱——附论 福泽谕吉编译〈增订华英通语〉》，《大阪大学大学院文学研究科纪要》第 58 卷，2018。

Influence English-related Publications of the Nineteenth-century China Exerted upon English Study in Japan: An Outline of the Situation and an Analysis of Fukuzawa Yukichi's *Zengding Huaying Tongyu*

Tanomura Tadaharu, Translated by Sun Xiao

Abstract

In the nineteenth-century Japan, English dictionaries and primers published in China were an important source of information about English. This article outlines how Chinese publications were used by the Japanese, and analyzes in particular the source and details of *Zengding Huaying Tongyu* edited and translated by Fukuzawa Yukichi.

Keywords

English learning　English dictionaries　English primers　*Zengding Huaying Tongyu*　Sino-Japan linguistic interaction

《华夷译语－拉氏诺话》初探

李思汉*

摘　要

明朝建立初期，出于外交需求，朝廷设立了作为翻译学校兼中央翻译机构的四夷馆。四夷馆在明清时期编纂了一系列的外文（少数民族语言）－中文对应的词典，将其用作培养外语人才的教科书，学界统称其为《华夷译语》。清乾隆年间由传教士编纂的拉丁语－汉语词典《华夷译语－拉氏诺话》为最早的拉丁语－汉语分类词典，由中文释义、拉丁语释义、注音三部分组成。门类二十，收词语 2071 个。这本词典对于早期语言接触史、词汇史、概念史的研究至关重要。本文主要从微观层面对这本词典进行分析，具体从语义学、句法学、音位学以及语用学这几个角度对《拉氏诺话》进行探讨。

关键词

中拉字典　传教士　早期中外字典

一　《华夷译语》及其研究

元末明初，中国面临内忧外患的处境。国内百废待兴，朝中依旧存在

* 李思汉，日本关西大学东亚文化研究科在读博士生。

很多元朝的残余势力；外部，周边的局势也十分不稳定。为了攘外安内，明初的统治者采取了积极的对外政策。一方面为了了解外部蒙古、女真等族的动向，另一方面为了了解元朝的历史，[①] 明朝廷十分注重外交翻译人才的培养。在这样的大环境下，洪武十五年（1382）洪武帝命火源洁编撰蒙汉词典，于是在洪武二十二年（1389）诞生了第一部《华夷译语》。此后，从永乐年间设立四夷馆直至清朝末期，会同馆和四夷馆（清朝由于忌讳"夷"一字，于是将四夷馆改名为四译馆，但是从功能上来说，四夷馆和清四译馆一致）分别编纂了各个语言的对照词典，学界将这些词典统称为《华夷译语》。

乾隆年间，乾隆帝命传教士魏继晋（Florian Joseph Bahr，1706 – 1771）编纂《华夷译语》的欧洲语言版本。这样便诞生了六部"中文 – 西方欧洲语言"对照的词典。由于其扉页上写着"西洋馆"三个字，后人习惯将这六本统称为西洋馆《华夷译语》。存世 6 种，其中 5 种翻译较为准确，每种有 20 个门类，各收录词汇 2069 个至 2071 个，分别为《弗喇安西雅话》（即法语）《额呼马尼雅话》（即德语）《伊达礼雅话》（即意大利语）《播呼都噶礼雅话》（即葡萄牙语）《拉氏诺话》（即拉丁语）。此外还有 1 种《鞥咭唎国译语》，记录英语，分为 20 个门类，收词 734 个。[②]

由于《华夷译语》数量众多，分类复杂，因此国内外学者基本达成一致，使用日本学者石田干之助（1891 – 1974）的分类方法，将其细分为甲种本、乙种本、丙种本和丁种本四种。

（1）甲种本《华夷译语》指代的是明洪武十五年由火源洁编纂并于洪武二十二年发行的《华夷译语》，只有蒙古译语一本，由于在洪武年间编纂，故称其为洪武本。书由译语（杂字）以及来文两部分组成。[③]

（2）乙种本则是在明永乐年间，设置四夷馆之后，由四夷馆设立的分管进行编纂的。由于在永乐年间编纂，故称其为永乐本。共设十个分管，共出版十种不同的语言的译语，其中包含少数民族语言以及东南亚国家语

① 任萍：《明代四夷馆研究》，北京师范大学出版社，2015，第 163 页。

② 刘红军、孙伯君：《存世"华夷译语"及其研究》，《民族研究》2008 年第 2 期，第 51 页。

③ 乌云高娃：《洪武本〈华夷译语〉鞑靼来文汉字音译规则》，载《西部蒙古论坛》2013 年第 4 期，第 58 – 68 页。

言。不同抄本很多。[①] 书由杂字以及来文两部分组成。

（3）丙种本于明代由会同馆编。故称其为会同本。其语言不仅包含了少数民族语言以及东南亚国家语言，更是加入了朝鲜语、琉球语、日本语等东亚国家的语言。丙种本《华夷译语》只有杂字，没有来文。

（4）德国学者福克斯（Walter Fuchs，1914－1993）发现了并不属于甲、乙、丙种本的《华夷译语》，并将其称为新《华夷译语》。[②] 后人便将这一套由清乾隆十三年四译馆编纂的译语划分为丁种本。[③] 丁种本《华夷译语》除少数民族语言、东南亚以及东亚国家语言，还出现了六套欧洲语言的译语。丁种本均为杂字，没有来文（见表1）。

表1 《华夷译语》分类表

	甲种本	乙种本	丙种本	丁种本
所指	洪武本	永乐本	会同本	四译本
杂字	有	有	有	有
来文	有	有	无	无
语种	只有蒙古语	少数民族语言以及东南亚国家语言	少数民族语言、东南亚国家语言、东亚国家语言	少数民族语言、东南亚国家语言、东亚国家语言、欧洲国家语言

前人对于甲乙丙种本译语的研究成果颇丰，但是对于丁种本，尤其是丁种本西洋馆系列《华夷译语》的研究少之又少。无论是中国学者，还是对《华夷译语》研究贡献极大的日本学者们，都将着眼点放在了中文－少数民族语言的译语或是中文－亚洲语言的译语上面。而对于西洋馆系列的研究则大多数处于简单介绍的阶段。西洋馆译语系列除对英语《鞥咭唎国译语》有相对较多的研究，以及对葡萄牙语《播呼都噶礼雅话》有着零星的研究以外，学界对于其他几本西洋馆译语的研究基本为零。其原因很可能是因为以前六本西洋馆译语抄本只存于故宫当中，对于研究者来说并不便于研究。笔者希望用这篇文章来填补一点拉丁语译语《拉氏诺话》研究

① 冯蒸：《“华夷译语”调查记》，《文物》1981年第2期，第57页

② 乌云高娃：《明四夷馆鞑靼馆及〈华夷译语〉鞑靼“来文”研究》，中国社会科学出版社，2014，第8页。

③ 大友信一、木村晟：《日本館訳語》，东京洛文社，1968，第37页。

的空缺，同时抛砖引玉，让更多的研究者重视起这套已经由紫禁城出版社于2018年4月出版的《华夷译语》西洋馆系列。

二 《拉氏诺话》的基本情况以及中文书名考察

本文主要对西洋馆译语系列当中的《拉氏诺话》进行研究，其基本情况如下：现存的《拉氏诺话》共有五册，线装。封底通为蓝色，五册书名均为“拉氏诺”五字，题写在封底的白色贴页上端。全书按顺序分天文门、地理门、时令门等20门，一共收录了2071个拉-汉对译词汇。其中，各门分类情况依次如下：天文门；地理门；时令门；采色门；身体门；人物门；器用门；宫殿门；饮食门；衣服门；方隅门；经部门；珍宝门；文史门；鸟兽门；数目门；通用门；香药门；花木门；人事门。[①] 在编撰形式上，该词典由拉丁语原词、对译汉词以及用汉字注出的拉丁语发音合构而成。拉丁语词以易于辨认的手写体写出，下面的对译汉字词为楷书。这种分类以及编纂方式和意、德、法、葡等其他西洋馆译语基本相同。乾隆十三年(1748)，乾隆皇帝在学习《西番译语》后，下令按照《西番译语》的编纂方式进行编纂。

《华夷译语》六本西洋馆书籍标题的名字分别为《弗喇安西雅话》《额呼马尼雅话》《伊达礼雅话》《播呼都噶礼雅话》《拉氏诺话》以及《嘆咭唎国译语》。可以看出，编者采用了音译的方式来翻译不同国家的名称，加上“话”一字使其书题成为“×××话”。而在英语的情况下使用的是“译语”一词。西洋馆除英语的五册为传教士所编，[②] 英语是由广东地区的中国人编写而成。鉴于其特殊性，本文不对英语的《嘆咭唎国译语》进行讨论。

接下来笔者将探索西洋馆书题源自何处。

有学者指出，通过分析不难看出，西洋馆译语的题目均来自拉丁语[③](见表2)。

---

① 刘红军、孙伯君：《存世“华夷译语”及其研究》，载《民族研究》2008年第2期，第51页。

② 福克司：《魏继晋司铎首创德华字典》，《中德学志》1940年第2卷第2期。

③ 聂大昕：《乾隆“西洋馆译语”书题语源考》，《文献》2016年第6期，第169页。

表 2

	法语	德语	葡萄牙语	意大利语	拉丁语
额哷马尼雅	Allemagne	Deutschland	Alemanha	Germania	Germania
弗喇安西雅	France	Frankreich	Franca	Francia	Francia
伊达礼雅	Italie	Italien	Italia	Italia	Italia
播哷都噶礼雅	Portugal	Portugal	Portugal	Portogallo	Portugallia
拉氏诺	Latine	Latein	Latino	Latino	Latina

从表 2 来看，法、德、葡、意四馆译语确实是根据拉丁语音译而成。但是只有《拉氏诺话》这本书的书题相对较为特殊。笔者在上文提及过，其余的几本西洋馆译语均采用了“国家名 + ‘话’”的命名方式，但是很显然拉丁并不是一个国家的名称。在拉丁语当中，“拉丁语”一词的拼写为“Latina”，发音为“拉氏娜”。由于最后一个音节与标题的“拉氏诺”不同，所以可以断定《拉氏诺话》当中的“拉氏诺”并不是拉丁语当中的“拉丁语”（Latina）。

有学者认为这是由于屈折语的词尾变化导致，即将《拉氏诺话》视为一部辞典，修饰中性名词“Lexicon”（即拉丁语的“辞典”一词）的“Latina”变成了“Latinum”。由于汉语官话没有鼻化元音韵母，于是将“num”写作“诺”。[①] 然而笔者并不十分赞同此观点。由于《拉氏诺话》采用的是相对严谨的注音系统（笔者会在下文指出）。根据对照，可以得出，如果西文文字为“Latinum”，中文的音译应为“拉氏努穆（穆为小字）”，但事实却非如此。

那么，“拉氏诺”的书题究竟源自何处？笔者猜测，拉丁语第一次出现在中国官方文书上是在康熙二十七年，“康熙二十七年三月十三日理藩援奉旨：朕看所用西洋人真实而悫可信，罗刹着徐日昇去，会喇第诺文字，其文妥当，汝等也行移文，往说罗刹。”[②] 葡萄牙语以及意大利语的拉丁语一词均为“Latino”，可以推断，康熙年间出现的“喇第诺”应是根据意大利语或葡萄牙语“Latino”一词音译的结果。根据西洋馆《华夷译语》当中的

① 聂大昕：《乾隆“西洋馆译语”书题语源考》，《文献》2016 年第 6 期，第 170 页。

② 韩琦、吴旻校注《熙朝崇正集 熙朝定案（外二种）》，中华书局，2006，第 170 页。

音译法，葡萄牙语以及意大利语的“la”音节译作“拉”，“di”和“ti”均译为“氐”，“no”译为“诺”。“Latino”与“拉氐诺”完美对应了起来。既然在康熙年间，已经将拉丁语称为“喇第诺文字”了，那么在乾隆年间开始编纂的西洋馆系列的《华夷译语》，标题很可能是延续了康熙年间的发音，但是采取了一套不同的音译方法。

综上所述，我们可以认为，西洋馆译语《拉氐诺话》的题目是从“Latino”音译而成。由于拉丁语是明清时期来华传教士的通用语言，可以推测“Latino”一词很有可能来自意大利或者葡萄牙的来华传教士。所以《华夷译语》当中的题目“拉氐诺”并不是来自拉丁语，而很可能是由意大利语或葡萄牙语翻译而成。

三　从语言学的角度对《拉氐诺话》进行分析

《华夷译语》最早不是作为词典，而是作为朝廷用来培养翻译外交人才的教科书来编纂的。作为明代四夷馆的主要教材以及清代四译馆的教材，《华夷译语》无疑发挥着重要作用。无论是教科书编写的优质与否或是教师的优良，都会直接影响学生学习效果的好坏。本节对《拉氐诺话》进行分析，探讨它作为教科书存在哪些优点以及不足，研究它究竟能否教会一个以中文为母语的人掌握拉丁语。

首先，学界一般将语言知识分为四个领域，分别为语义学、句法学、音位学以及语用学。① 四个领域分别对应着语言相关的不同知识：语义学知识处理语言词汇以及句子的含义；句法学知识负责语法，即如何组合词以及句子；音位学知识关注语言的发音系统，分析此种语言如何发音；语用知识学则与语言使用的社会规则、社会知识相关。换句话说，想学习并掌握一门语言，这四个方面的知识必不可少。然而很明显，《华夷译语》西洋馆系列作为语言的教科书，并没有完全顾及以上这四个方面。也就是说，通过学习《华夷译语》西洋馆系列并不能够掌握其对应的语言。接下来，笔者将对西洋馆系列当中涉及的语义学、句法学、音位学以及语用学的知识情况进行分析。由于《拉氐诺话》本身只有杂字，而没有来文部分，也

① D. W. Carroll, *Psychology of Language*, 4th Edition, Thomson Learning, 2004, p. 4

就是说，这本书的内容只有文字的对照以及外文的注音。所以无奈笔者只能将分析侧重点放在音位学以及语义学上。

（一）音位学：注音体系分析

《拉氏诺话》采用从第一本《华夷译语》开始沿用下来的注音方式：利用汉字注外语的音。可以看到，这种注音方法由三部分组成，第一部分为汉字，在图一的汉字为“斗”，即北斗七星的意思；第二部分为拉丁语的翻译，图中为“ursa minor”，为小熊星座；第三部分便是汉字注音的部分了。可以看出，这里的汉字注音将单词分解成音节，然后每个音节对应了一个汉字。

图 1

本文对《华夷译语－拉氏诺话》所有出现过的注音进行了总结。对其进行分析后，归纳出以下特点。

1. 相对严谨的注音体系

首先，全本《拉氏诺话》遵循着相对严谨的注音体系，也就是说，一个拉丁语的音节将对应一个汉字，而这种对应关系在整本书中是大致相对固定的。

大致固定，而不是完全固定，也就是说，在书中，出现了很多次一个音节对应两种甚至两种以上注音的情况。比如“an”这个音节，书中有将其注音为“安”的情况，也有将其注音为“昂”的情况。而这种一个音节对应两种或者以上的情况，很少发生在经常出现的音节上。比如以“b”为辅音，“aiueo”为元音的音节，在书中出现了多次，而这多次中并没有出现一音节多注音的情况；相比经常出现的音节，出现次数少的音节，一音节多注音状况出现的频率相对来说会多一些。作者推测，本书的编者一开始的确想让整本词典的音译系统遵照十分严谨的注音体系，一个音节对应一个注音，但是由于不同的音节众多，编者之间缺乏有效的信息交换以及沟通，导致编者在对待很少出现的音节时，并不能够确定这个音节是否已经有固定的发音了。

另外，书中也出现了多个音节对应同一种注音（同一个汉字）的情况。出现这种情况十分正常。本身用中文标注拉丁语发音这件事就是一种无奈妥协的做法。所以中文注音和拉丁语本身音节的读音之间就有着一定的区别。在很多情况下，尽管拉丁语是不同的发音，但是并不能够找到两个不同的汉字分别进行注音，于是两个音节就对应上了同一个汉字。详细的例子笔者将在下文列举。

2. 元音和辅音

大多数语言的音素都可以分成两部分，即元音和辅音，拉丁语亦然。总的来说，元音是指发音时不受发音器官阻碍发出的声音，而辅音则是指代在发音时受到发音器官阻碍而发出的声音。

拉丁语中，元音可分成两类，一类为单元音（vowels），另一类则为双元音（diphthongs），无论是单元音还是双元音，由于在拉丁语的发音当中，都为一个音节，所以在《拉氏诺话》当中，编者寻找了与这个元音发音相近的汉字对其进行注音。拉丁语的单元音包含一般语言常见的五个元音，即 a、i、u、e、o，加上一个在其他语言当中并不常见的 y。然而，拉丁语区别于其他语言的地方是，六个元音均有长短音之分。在元音上面标记横线则为长音，没有任何标记则为短音。在《拉氏诺话》的发音中，并不区分长音以及短音。所有的单元音均采用短音的标记方法。关于双元音，拉丁语中存在 ae、oe、ei、au、eu、ui 六种。在《拉氏诺话》中，编者将 ae 两个字母缩到一起，其发音注音与单元音的 e 基本相同。然后便是 au 和 eu，由于 au 在拉丁语中的发音与汉语拼音的 ao 很像，eu 的发音与 ou 很像，所以在《拉氏诺话》中，将 au 的发音标注为“傲”，eu 的发音标注为“欧”。剩下的双元音多采用分开注音的方法，即 ui 的注音为 u 的注音加上 i 的注音。

拉丁语的辅音共有24种，从《拉氏诺话》看，辅音的发音可分为两大类：第一种是辅音加元音的组合；另外一种则是单个的辅音。对于第一种情况由于本身从拉丁语的读音上来讲，这种组合能够成为一个音节，《拉氏诺话》便用一个与这个音节发音相近的中文汉字为这个音节注音。其书写方式与元音的注音相同。在第二种情况下，即单独出现辅音时，由于单独出现的辅音就能作为一个音节，所以编者找到了一个与这个音节发音相近的中文汉字进行注音。单个辅音的发音一般来说是单纯舌头的发音，而不会带来声带的震动，字典的编者在这种情况下，将与这个音节发音相似的汉字用小字标记了出来，从而使学习者能够分辨出单个辅音和辅音元音的组合的不同发音。

3. 清辅音和浊辅音

在不同的语言中，人们称发音时声带震动的辅音为浊辅音，声带不震动的辅音为清辅音。在拉丁语中，字母b与p的发音以及字母d与t的发音都是不一样的：前者为浊音，后者为清音。即在发b以及d音时声带振动，而在发p与t时则不震动。然而在中文中，并没有采用清浊音，而是用另一种方式区别这两种发音——送气音以及不送气音。在汉语拼音当中，b、p、d、t均为清音，其区别在于送气与不送气。b、d为不送气；p、t为送气。这样的区别使得编者并不能够使用中文注音区别拉丁语的清音和浊音。毕竟“夏虫不可语冰”，所以，《拉氏诺话》采用了一种破罐子破摔的方法，即完全不理会清音浊音，一律按照清音进行标注。从整理出来的发音列表中可以看出，b列的注音与p列完全一致；d列的注音与t列完全一致（见表3）。

表3

	b	d	p	t
a	巴	达	巴	达
e	伯	德	伯	德
i	毕	氐	毕	氐
o	博	多	博	多
u	补	都	补	都

4. 元音之后的“n”

在拉丁语中，元音之后，n 的发音为/n/。这样的发音与汉语中的前鼻音发音十分相像，于是编者便采用了使用汉语前鼻音读音的汉字对 n 进行注音。如表 3 所示，这样的注音方式很清晰明了地对字母组合进行了注释。但是，这样的注音方式却有着自己的缺陷。由于很多时候，并不能够找出和元音加 n 这样组合发音相似的中文，所以编者用了两种方式为元音与 n 的组合进行注音。在第一种情况下，编者能够找到和元音与 n 组合发音相近的中文，便用其进行注音，例如：“ven”（见图二）在拉丁语的发音与中文“文”相对接近，于是编者便将“ven”这个音节注音为“文”，再比如“fun”（见图三）这个音节在拉丁语当中与中文“冯”的发音相似，于是编者便将“fun”注为“冯”，以此类推。但是，正如前文所说，并不一定都能够找到对应的中文，所以在第二种情况下，编者采用了另一种方法，即将音节分成两部分，一部分为 n 前面，一部分为 n。n 前面部分按照之前所说的注音规则进行注音，然后将 n 注为“安”，随后将两个汉字缩成一个字便完成了注音。比如，“ten”注音为“te”的“德”以及“n”的“安”，缩合后变成了如图所示的“德安”。

图 2

图 3

5. 不够准确的音节划分

在《拉氏诺话》中，出现了很多次音节划分不准确的情况。一般来说，拉丁语的音节均采用辅音加元音组合的形式，但有时会出现连续元音或者辅音的情况，这种情况下便需要根据经验划分音节。在对《拉氏诺话》进行分析的过程中，笔者多次发现编者出现了划分音节错误的情况。如“obviamire”一词，理论上来说，“o”为一个元音音节，“b”为一个辅音音节，“vi”为一个辅音加元音的音节，“a”为一个元音音节，“mi”为一个辅音加元音的音节，“re”为一个辅音加元音的音节。编者不仅完全没有对“b”这个音节进行注音，还将“mi”这个音节分成了两个音节。利用中文对拉丁语进行注音就会使发音信息传递的时候发生很大的偏差，也就是说，通过中文注音并不能够很好地念出拉丁语的正确读音，而这样错误的音节划分会导致注音更加不准确。

6. 利用拉丁语为中文注音

在《拉氏诺话》中出现了极少数的利用拉丁语为中文注音的情况。出现这种情况的原因大概是这个词语本身来源于中文，翻译成拉丁语则采用了最简单的音译方式。比如“人参”一词，拉丁语的翻译为“gin xen”，按照这本词典的发音规则来说，应该将其发音标注为“因克参”，然而有趣的是，编者直接将其读音标注为了“人参”。也就是说，本身“gin xen”一词便是拉丁语“人参”一词的音译，再回译的过程当中，编者没有选择“因克参”，而是使用了原本的“人参”的发音，颇有一种从中文来的单词，读音要回归到中文去的意味。

temperatum

温和

葉哩伯德

斯 穆

图 4

gin xen

图 5

7. 明显的注音错误

在《拉氏诺话》中，编者在编写的过程中犯了一些在今天看来很明显的错误，原因可能是因缺乏认真的校对所致。注音错误的情况一般来说是很容易发现的。举例来说，第一册当中“温和”一词的拉丁语为“temperarum”（见图4），注音为“德穆伯哩叶斯”，很明显前半部分“tempe”的注音没有问题，但是后面的“rarum”部分应为“喇噜穆”，这样的错误在整本词典当中还有几处。这种错误很明显是笔误，或者与其他的某些单词看混了。

通过对上述特点的分析，我们可以归纳出以下三点结论。

首先，《拉氏诺话》采用的是一种创新的给欧洲语言注音的方式。《华夷译语》的西洋馆系列延续了整个系列最早使用的注音方法，即利用汉字给外文注音。从明初开始，四夷馆将这种注音方式应用于少数民族语言的词典，随后应用到了亚洲语言的字典中，直到乾隆年间，编纂西洋馆系列的时候又将这种方式应用于欧洲语言。这是一种很好的尝试，能够让知晓中文发音的国人尝试发出欧洲语言单词的音。

其次，《拉氏诺话》采用的创新型欧洲语言注音的方式存在系统因素上的不足。由于两种语言（中文以及某种欧洲语言）音节发音相差甚远，所以这种注音方式并不是一种十分科学的、有效的教科书的注音方式。我们从之前的特点分析当中可以看出，编者确实花费了一番心思来整理、构思并且决定注音方式，但这种系统本身的缺陷导致了无论注音方式如何巧妙，利用中文汉字的发音，永远也无法将拉丁语的发音完全标注出来，当然反之亦然。

最后，这种注音方式还存在非系统因素上的缺陷。《拉氏诺话》共五册，收录的单词超过2000个，不同的发音以及对应的汉字更是有数百个之多。清朝乾隆年间，在人力、物力及技术均受限的情况下，出现了一些注音的错误以及汉字注音系统不够严谨等一系列的问题。

《拉氏诺话》对拉丁语进行了注音，旨在让读者通过这样的方式学习拉丁语。尽管如上所说，这部书籍的注音系统存在着诸多缺陷，但从其是否存在音位学的知识以及是否能够帮助人们学习拉丁语的发音角度来看，答案无疑是肯定的。也就是说，通过学习《拉氏诺话》，尽管最终的效果不尽如人意，但学生确实能够掌握拉丁语的发音。

（二）语义学：与释义相关的研究

无论是作为教科书还是词典来说，《拉氏诺话》都存在着释义系统。这样的释义系统是从甲种本《华夷译语》传承下来的。它具有以下三种特点。

第一，这是一套“中外词汇对照集”，而不是“外中词汇对照集”。西洋馆系列采用的都是“从中文翻译成外文”的释义系统。由于乾隆皇帝在学习《西番译语》的时候认为其编纂精细、分门别类，于是命人以《西番译语》为底本修纂以前编过的《华夷译语》，并以西番译语为底本编纂新的华夷译语。[①] 这样的编纂使得西洋馆六部译语的释义均是从中文翻译到外文。也就是说，这并不是一系列的“外－中”词典，而是“中－外”词典。这样编纂带来的弊端便是，所有的词汇以及释义都是以中文为视角出发的。尽管中外语言进行了交流，但是作为西洋馆系列的《华夷译语》没有从外语中学习吸收到任何东西。举例来说，西洋馆系列中有关于报时相关词汇的翻译，西洋馆的中文部分均采用中国传统的“子丑寅卯”时辰的报时方式，而非小时制。然后将时辰报时的方式十分生硬地翻译成了外文。这样的编纂方式使得清政府不仅拒绝了国外的词汇，还将国外的各种文化以及技术挡在了门外。

第二，一词对一词的释义系统。在《华夷译语》的编纂过程中，从甲种本开始，始终没有人意识到这样的问题，即两种语言的词汇很多情况下是不能够一一对等的。一种语言的一个词汇对应另一种语言的很多词汇是十分常见的事情。如果将这种对应关系限定在一对一当中，势必会引起歧义或者解释不清的情况。

第三，西洋馆系列整体存在对应语言系统过于局限的情况。人类的语言系统一般可分为屈折语、黏着语以及孤立语三种。一般来说，我们将中文看作孤立语，日语韩语等看作黏着语，并将大多数欧洲语言视为屈折语。一旦语言发生屈折，那么除了需要学习单词本身的含义之外，还需要学习其变位变格等。而在孤立语当中则不需要学习这样的规则（这样的规则可以称其为词法）。也就是说，在《拉氏诺话》中，尽管我们能够将每一个拉

---

① “乾隆十五年七月”，载《大清高宗纯（乾隆）皇帝实录（八）》，华文书局，1969，第5562页。

丁语词与中文对应起来，但是由于缺少词法的相关知识，《拉氏诺话》提供的信息并不能够让我们了解拉丁语词组的准确含义。

综上所述，《拉氏诺话》采用了一套尽管有些问题但是依旧能够使用的释义系统。但是由于缺乏对屈折语的认识，不论是作为教科书还是词典，《拉氏诺话》都不能给予读者足够的信息清楚一个词的意思。

（三）句法学以及语用学

通过上述分析我们可以看出，《拉氏诺话》完全没有涉及任何有关句法学以及语用学方面的知识。在甲种本以及乙种本的《华夷译语》中，除了中外文对照的词汇（我们称其为“杂字”），还有中外文对照的文章（也就是所谓的“来文”），但是在丙种本以及丁种本的《华夷译语》中，取消了这些文章，使得其完全没有涉及任何有关句法学以及语用学的知识。

四　结论

由德国传教士魏继晋带领编纂的五本西洋馆《华夷译语》作为政府为培养翻译外交人才的教材，无疑对整个中外交流史有着重要的意义。通过上述对于《华夷译语－拉氏诺话》微观层面的分析，我们可以看出，《拉氏诺话》作为一本教科书，在音位学方面做得相对来说比较出色，确实能够教会以中文为母语的人掌握拉丁语的发音；在语义学方面，尽管《拉氏诺话》想要传授翻译的能力，但由于乾隆帝缺乏对于屈折语的认识，延续了《华夷译语》系列的编纂方式，从而使得这本教科书只有词义，而缺乏词法相关的内容；关于句法学以及语用学，只有“杂字”的《拉氏诺话》不涉及任何与句法以及语用相关的内容。所以总体而言，如果《拉氏诺话》以“教会别人拉丁语”为目标的话，其记载并且教授的知识体系是有很大缺失的，这样的缺失使得学习者构建的语言体系不够完整，从而无法真正学会并掌握这门语言。

当然，本文的研究尚存在很多可以改进或者可以继续深入的地方。首先，本文只对《拉氏诺话》的微观层面进行了分析，这样的分析对于这样一系列的词典来说很显然是不够的。因此有必要横向、纵向拓展关于西洋馆的研究。横向来说，除了拉丁语的《拉氏诺话》以外，还有四本魏继晋带领编纂的词典。此外，《鞥咭唎国译语》是一本编者不详，并且无论注音还是选词都和剩下几本西洋馆译语大相径庭，横向来说，如果将其融会贯通，就能够解决单纯研究一本译语解决不了的问题。纵向来说，西洋馆译语的五册书并不是中国历史上第一套中外词典，因此，我们可以研究前后的中外词典发展，对明末至清末中外词典的注音方式、词汇选择以及语法讲解进行系统分析。

A Research on《华夷译语 - 拉氏诺话》

Li Sihan

Abstract

At the beginning of the founding of the Ming Dynasty, due to the demand for diplomacy, the imperial court set up a translation school and translation agency which is called "四夷馆". From the Ming Dynasty to the Qing Dynasty, "四夷馆" complied a series of foreign language (minority languages) - Chinese dictionaries titled as "华夷译语". The Latin-Chinese dictionary compiled in the Qing Dynasty during the Emperor Qianlong period, titled "华夷译语 - 拉氏诺话", has 2071 words classified as 20 categories, which is the earliest Latin-Chinese dictionary. It is important for the study of the history of early language contact. This article analyzes this dictionary from the microscopic level and also from the perspectives of semantics, syntax, phonology and pragmatics. It analyzes "拉氏诺话" to judge whether its content can be used as a textbook and teach a person Latin.

Keywords

Chinese-Latin dictionary　Missionary　Dictionaries in Early Stage

图书在版编目（CIP）数据

亚洲与世界. 第2辑 / 李雪涛，(日) 沈国威主编. -- 北京：社会科学文献出版社，2019.11
ISBN 978-7-5201-5296-9

Ⅰ. ①亚… Ⅱ. ①李… ②沈… Ⅲ. ①亚洲-研究
Ⅳ. ①D73

中国版本图书馆CIP数据核字（2019）第159249号

亚洲与世界（第2辑）

主　　编 / 李雪涛　[日] 沈国威

出 版 人 / 谢寿光
责任编辑 / 史晓琳
文稿编辑 / 赵　冉

出　　版 / 社会科学文献出版社·国际出版分社（010）59367142
地址：北京市北三环中路甲29号院华龙大厦　邮编：100029
网址：www.ssap.com.cn
发　　行 / 市场营销中心（010）59367081　59367083
印　　装 / 三河市尚艺印装有限公司

规　　格 / 开　本：787mm × 1092mm　1/16
印　张：22.25　字　数：360千字
版　　次 / 2019年11月第1版　2019年11月第1次印刷
书　　号 / ISBN 978-7-5201-5296-9
定　　价 / 98.00元

本书如有印装质量问题，请与读者服务中心（010-59367028）联系